Effective Databases for Text & Document Management

Shirley A. Becker
Northern Arizona University, USA

IRM Press
Publisher of innovative scholarly and professional information technology titles in the cyberage
Hershey • London • Melbourne • Singapore • Beijing

Acquisitions Editor:	Mehdi Khosrow-Pour
Senior Managing Editor:	Jan Travers
Managing Editor:	Amanda Appicello
Development Editor:	Michele Rossi
Copy Editor:	Maria Boyer
Typesetter:	Jennifer Wetzel
Cover Design:	Kory Gongloff
Printed at:	Integrated Book Technology

Published in the United States of America by
IRM Press (an imprint of Idea Group Inc.)
1331 E. Chocolate Avenue, Suite 200
Hershey PA 17033-1117
Tel: 717-533-8845
Fax: 717-533-8661
E-mail: cust@idea-group.com
Web site: http://www.irm-press.com

and in the United Kingdom by
IRM Press (an imprint of Idea Group Inc.)
3 Henrietta Street
Covent Garden
London WC2E 8LU
Tel: 44 20 7240 0856
Fax: 44 20 7379 3313
Web site: http://www.eurospan.co.uk

Library of Congress Cataloging-in-Publication Data

Becker, Shirley A., 1956-
Effective databases for text & document management / Shirley A. Becker.
p. cm.
Includes bibliographical references and index.
ISBN 1-931777-47-0 (softcover) -- ISBN 1-931777-63-2 (e-book)
1. Business--Databases. 2. Database management. I. Title: Effective databases for text and document management. II. Title.
HD30.2.B44 2003
005.74--dc21
2002156233

British Cataloguing in Publication Data
A Cataloguing in Publication record for this book is available from the British Library.

Effective Databases for Text & Document Management

Table of Contents

Preface

The focus of this book is effective databases for text and document management inclusive of new and enhanced techniques, methods, theories and practices. The research contained in these chapters is of particular significance to researchers and practitioners alike because of the rapid pace at which the Internet and related technologies are changing our world. Already there is a vast amount of data stored in local databases and Web pages (HTML, DHTML, XML and other markup language documents). In order to take advantage of this wealth of knowledge, we need to develop effective ways of extracting, retrieving and managing the data. In addition, advances in both database and Web technologies require innovative ways of dealing with data in terms of syntactic and semantic representation, integrity, consistency, performance and security.

One of the objectives of this book is to disseminate research that is based on existing Web and database technologies for improved information extraction and retrieval capabilities. Another important objective is the compilation of international efforts in database systems, and text and document management in order to share the innovation and research advances being done at a global level.

The book is organized into four sections, each of which contains chapters that focus on similar research in the database and Web technology areas. In the section entitled, *Information Extraction and Retrieval in Web-Based Systems*, Web and database theories, methods and technologies are shown to be efficient at extracting and retrieving information from Web-based documents. In the first chapter, "System of Information Retrieval in XML Documents," Saliha Smadhi introduces a process for retrieving relevant information from XML documents. Smadhi's approach supports keyword-based searching, and ranks the retrieval of information based on the similarity with the user's query. In "Information Extraction from Free-Text Business Documents," Witold Abramowicz and Jakub Piskorski investigate the applicability of information extraction techniques to free-text documents typically retrieved from Web-based systems. They also demonstrate the indexing potential of lightweight linguistic text processing techniques in order to process large amounts of textual data.

In the next chapter, "Interactive Indexing of Documents with a Multilingual Thesaurus," Ulrich Schiel and Ianna M.S.F. de Sousa present a method for semi-automatic indexing of electronic documents and construction of a multilingual thesaurus. This method can be used for query formulation and information retrieval. Then in the next chapter, "Managing Document Taxonomies in Relational Databases," Ido Millet addresses the challenge of applying relational technologies in managing taxonomies used to classify documents, knowledge and websites into topic hierarchies. Millet explains how denormalization of the data model facilitates data retrieval from these topic hierarchies. Millet also describes the use of database triggers to solving data maintenance difficulties once the data model has been denormalized.

Yangjun Chen and Gerald Huck, in "Building Signature-Trees on Path Signatures in Document Databases," introduce PDOM (persistent DOM) to accommodate documents as permanent object sets. They propose a new indexing technique in combination with signature-trees to accelerate the evaluation of path-oriented queries against document object sets and to expedite scanning of signatures stored in a physical file. In the chapter, "Keyword-Based Queries of Web Databases," Altigran S. da Silva, Pável Calado, Rodrigo C. Vieira, Alberto H.F. Laender and Berthier A. Ribeiro-Neto describe the use of keyword-based querying as a suitable alternative to the use of Web interfaces based on multiple forms. They show how to rank the possible large number of answers returned by a query according to relevant criteria and typically done by Web search engines. Virpi Lyytikäinen, Pasi Tiitinen and Airi Salminen, in "Unifying Access to Heterogeneous Document Databases Through Contextual Metadata," introduce a method for collecting contextual metadata and representing metadata to users via graphical models. The authors demonstrate their proposed solution by a case study whereby information is retrieved from European, distributed database systems.

In the next section entitled, *Data Management and Web Technologies*, research efforts in data management and Web technologies are discussed. In the first chapter, "Database Management Issues in the Web Environment," J.F. Aldana Montes, A.C. Gómez Lora, N. Moreno Vergara and M.M. Roldán García address relevant issues in Web technology, including semi-structured data and XML, data integrity, query optimization issues and data integration issues. In the next chapter, "Applying JAVA-Triggers for X-Link Management in the Industrial Framework," Abraham Alvarez and Y. Amghar provide a generic relationship validation mechanism by combining XLL (X-link and X-pointer) specification for integrity management and Java-triggers as an alert mechanism.

The third section is entitled, *Advances in Database and Supporting Technologies*. This section encompasses research in relational and object databases, and it also presents ongoing research in related technologies. In this section's first chapter, "Metrics for Data Warehouse Quality," Manuel Serrano, Coral Calero and Mario Piattini propose a set of metrics that has been formally and empirically validated for assessing the quality of data warehouses. The overall objective of their research is to provide a practical means of assessing alternative data warehouse designs. R. Chbeir, Y. Amghar and A. Flory identify the importance of new management methods in image retrieval in their chapter, "Novel Indexing Method of Relations Between Salient Objects." The authors propose a novel method for identifying and indexing several types of relations between salient objects. Spatial relations are used to show how the authors' method can provide high expressive power to relations when compared to traditional methods.

In the next chapter, "A Taxonomy for Object-Relational Queries," David Taniar, Johanna Wenny Rahayu and Prakash Gaurav Srivastava classify object-relational queries into REF, aggregate and inheritance queries. The authors have done this in order to provide an understanding of the full capability of object-relational query language in terms of query processing and optimization. Aphrodite Tsalgatidou and Mara Nikolaidou describe a criteria set for selecting appropriate Business Process Modeling Tools

(BPMTs) and Workflow Management Systems (WFMSs) in "Re-Engineering and Automation of Business Processes: Criteria for Selecting Supporting Tools." This criteria set provides management and engineering support for selecting a toolset that would allow them to successfully manage the business process transformation. In the last chapter of this section, "Active Rules and Active Databases: Concepts and Applications," Juan M. Ale and Mauricio Minuto Espil analyze concepts related to active rules and active databases. In particular, they focus on database triggers using the SQL-1999 standard committee's point of view. They also discuss the interaction between active rules and declarative database constraints from both static and dynamic perspectives.

The final section of the book is entitled, *Advances in Relational Database Theory, Methods and Practices*. This section includes research efforts focused on advancements in relational database theory, methods and practices. In the chapter, "On the Computation of Recursion in Relational Databases," Yangjun Chen presents an encoding method to support the efficient computation of recursion. A linear time algorithm has also been devised to identify a sequence of reachable trees covering all the edges of a directed acyclic graph. Together, the encoding method and algorithm allow for the computation of recursion. The author proposes that this is especially suitable for a relational database environment. Robert A. Schultz, in the chapter "Understanding Functional Dependency," examines whether functional dependency in a database system can be considered solely on an extensional basis in terms of patterns of data repetition. He illustrates the mix of both intentional and extensional elements of functional dependency, as found in popular textbook definitions.

In the next chapter, "Dealing with Relationship Cardinality Constraints in Relational Database Design," Dolores Cuadra Fernández, Paloma Martínez Fernández and Elena Castro Galán propose to clarify the meaning of the features of conceptual data models. They describe the disagreements between main conceptual models, the confusion in the use of their constructs and open problems associated with these models. The authors provide solutions in the clarification of the relationship construct and to extend the cardinality constraint concept in ternary relationships. In the final chapter, "Repairing and Querying Inconsistent Databases," Gianluigi Greco, Sergio Greco and Ester Zumpano discuss the integration of knowledge from multiple data sources and its importance in constructing integrated systems. The authors illustrate techniques for repairing and querying databases that are inconsistent in terms of data integrity constraints.

In summary, this book offers a breadth of knowledge in database and Web technologies, primarily as they relate to the extraction retrieval, and management of text documents. The authors have provided insight into theory, methods, technologies and practices that are sure to be of great value to both researchers and practitioners in terms of effective databases for text and document management.

Acknowledgment

The editor would like to acknowledge the help of all persons involved in the collation and review process of this book. The authors' contributions are acknowledged in terms of providing insightful and timely research. Also, many of the authors served as referees for chapters written by other authors. Thanks to all of you who have provided constructive and comprehensive reviews. A note of thanks to Mehdi Khosrow-Pour who saw a need for this book, and to the staff at Idea Group Publishing for their guidance and professional support.

Shirley A. Becker
Northern Arizona University, USA
February 2003

Section I

Information Extraction and Retrieval in Web-Based Systems

Chapter I

System of Information Retrieval in XML Documents

Saliha Smadhi
Université de Pau, France

ABSTRACT

This chapter introduces the process to retrieve units (or subdocuments) of relevant information from XML documents. For this, we use the Extensible Markup Language (XML) which is considered as a new standard for data representation and exchange on the Web. XML opens opportunities to develop a new generation of Information Retrieval System (IRS) to improve the interrogation process of document bases on the Web.

Our work focuses instead on end-users who do not have expertise in the domain (like a majority of the end-users). This approach supports keyword-based searching like classical IRS and integrates structured searching with the search attributes notion. It is based on an indexing method of document tree leafs which authorize a content-oriented retrieval. The retrieval subdocuments are ranked according to their similarity with the user's query. We use a similarity measure which is a compromise between two measures: exhaustiveness and specificity.

INTRODUCTION

The World Wide Web (WWW) contains large amounts of information available at websites, but it is difficult and complex to retrieve pertinent information. Indeed, a large part of this information is often stored as HyperText Markup Language (HTML) pages that are only viewed through a Web browser.

This research is developed in the context of the MEDX project (Lo, 2001) of our team. We use XML as a common structure for storing, indexing and querying a collection of XML documents.

Our aim is to propose the suited solutions which allow the end-users not specialized in the domain to search and extract portions of XML documents (called units or subdocuments) which satisfy their queries. The extraction of documents portion can be realized by using XML query languages (XQL, XML-QL) (Robie, 1999; Deutsch, 1999).

An important aspect of our approach concerns the indexation which is realized on leaf elements of the document tree and not on the whole document.

Keywords are extracted from a domain thesaurus. A thesaurus is a set of descriptors (or concepts) connected by hierarchical relations, equivalence relations or association relations. Indexing process results are stored in a resources global catalog that is exploited by the search processor.

This chapter is organized as follows. The next section discusses the problem of relevant information retrieval in the context of XML documents. We then present the model of XML documents indexing, followed by the similarity measure adopted and the retrieval strategy of relevant parts of documents. The chapter goes on to discuss related work, before its conclusion. An implementation of SIRX prototype is currently underway in Python language on Linux Server.

INFORMATION RETRIEVAL AND XML DOCUMENTS

The classical retrieval information involves two principal issues, the representation of documents and queries and the construction of a ranking function of documents.

Among Information Retrieval (IR) models, the most-used models are the Boolean Model, Vector Space Model and Probabilist Model. In the Vector Space Model, documents and queries are represented as vectors in the space of index terms. During the retrieval process, the query is also represented as a list of terms or a term vector. This query vector is matched against all document vectors, and a similarity measure between a document and a query is calculated. Documents are ranked according to their values of similarity measure with a query.

XML is a subset of the standard SGML. It has a richer structure that is composed mainly of an elements tree that forms the content. XML can represent more useful information on data than HTML. An XML document contains only data as opposed to an HTML file, which tries to mix data and presentation and usually ignores structure. It preserves the structure of the data that it represents, whereas HTML flattens it out. This meta markup language defines its own system of tags representing the structure of a document explicitly. HTML presents information and XML describes information.

A well-formed XML document doesn't impose any restrictions on the tags or attribute names. But a document can be accompanied by a Document Type Definition (DTD), which is essentially a grammar for restricting the tags and structure of a document. An XML document satisfying a DTD is considered a valid document.

The Document Object Model (DOM) is simply a set of plans or guidelines that enables the user to reconstruct a document right down to the smallest detail.

The structure of a document can be transformed with XSLT (1999) and its contents displayed by using the eXtensible Style Language (XSL) language or a programming language (Python, Java, etc.). XSL is a declarative language in which the model refers the data by using patterns. It is limited when one wants to retrieve data with specific criteria, as one can realize that with the query language XQL (or OQL) for relational databases (or object). This extension is proposed by three languages coming from the database community: XML-QL (Florescu, 2000), Lorel (Abiteboul, 1997) and XQL (Robie, 1999) from the Web community.

Requirements for a System of Relevant Information Retrieval for XML Documents

We propose an approach for information retrieval with relevance ranking for XML documents of which the basic functional requirements are:

a) to support keyword-based searching and structured searching (by proposing a set of search attributes) by end-users who have no expertise in the domain and of that the structure is then unknown (like a majority of the end-users);
b) to retrieve relevant parts of documents (called subdocuments) ranked by their relevancy with the query; and
c) to navigate in the whole document.

In order to satisfy the essential requirements of this approach, we have opted to:

a) use a domain thesaurus;
b) define an efficient model of documents indexing that extends the classic "inverted index" technology by indexing document structure as well as content;
c) integrate search attributes that concern a finite number of sub-structure types, which we like to make searchable;
d) propose an information retrieval engine with ranking of relevant document parts.

Architectural Overview of SIRX

We present an overview of the **S**ystem of **I**nformation **R**etrieval in **X**ML documents (SIRX) showing its mains components (see Figure 1).

The main architectural components of the system are the following:

1) *User Interface:* This is used to facilitate the interaction between the user and the application. It allows the user to specify his query. It also displays retrieved documents or parts of documents ranked by relevance score. It does not suppose an expertise or a domain knowledge of the end-user.
2) *Search Processor:* This allows retrieval of contents directly from the Resources Global Catalog on using the various index and keywords expressed in an input query.

Figure 1. The General Architecture of SIRX

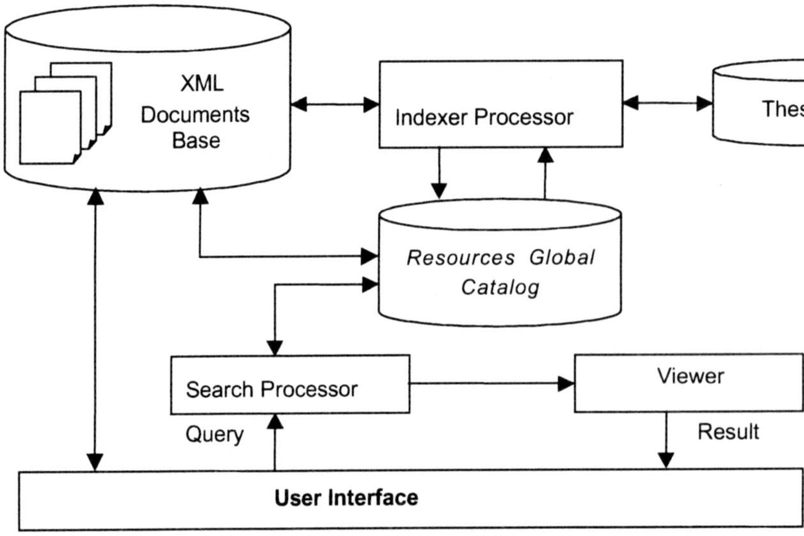

3) *XML Documents Base:* This stores XML documents well-formed in their original formats.
4) *Thesaurus:* The domain thesaurus contains the set of descriptors (keywords) which allow the user to index documents of this domain.
5) *Indexer Processor:* For every XML document, the indexer processor creates indexes by using the thesaurus and the XML documents base. These indexes allow the user to build the Resources Global Catalog.
6) *Resources Global Catalog:* This is an indexing structure that the search processor uses to find the relevant document parts. It is exploited mainly by the search processor.
7) *Viewer:* The viewer displays retrieved document parts. The results are recombined (XML + XSL) to show the document to the user in an appropriate manner (into HTML).

THE MODEL OF XML DOCUMENTS INDEXING

In our approach that is based on Vector Space Model, we propose to index the leafs of the document tree (Shin, 1998) and the keywords that correspond to the descriptor terms extracted from the domain thesaurus (Lo, 2000). Indexing process results are structured by using the XML language in meta-data collection which is stored in the *Resources Global Catalog* (see Figure 2). This catalog is the core of the SIRX system. It encapsulates all semantic content of the XML document's base and thesaurus.

Elementary Units and Indexing

In classic information retrieval, the documents are considered as atomic units. The keyword search is based on classic index structures that are inverted files. A classic inverted file contains <keyword, document> pairs, meaning that the word can be found in the document. This classical approach allows the user to retrieve the whole document. It is not necessary to forget that documents can often be quite long and in many cases only a small part of documents may be relevant to the user's query. It is necessary to be able to retrieve only the part of document that may be relevant to the end-user's query.

To accomplish this objective, we extend the classic inverted file by making the unit structure explicit. The indexing processor extracts terms from the thesaurus and calculates their frequencies in each element at the text level.

Every elementary unit is identified in a unique way by an *access-path* showing his position in the document. The form of this index is <keyword, unit, frequency> where:

1) keyword is a term appearing in the content of element or values of an attribute of this document;
2) unit specifies the access path to element content that contains keyword; the access path is described by using XPath (1999) compliance syntax;
3) frequency is the frequency of the keyword in the specified unit.

This indexation method allows a direct access to any elementary unit which appears in the result of the query and regroups results of every document by using XSLT.

Search Attributes

Methods of classical information retrieval propose a function of search from signaletic metadata (author, title, date, etc.) that concerns mostly characteristics related to a whole document. To be able to realize searches on sub-structures of a document, we propose to integrate a search based on the document structure from a finite number of element types, which we like to make searchable from their semantic content. These specific elements are called *search attributes*. They are indexed like keywords in the Resources Global Catalog. Every search attribute has the following form: <identifier, unit>, where identifier is the name (or tag) of the search attribute under which it will appear to the user, and unit indicates the access path to a elementary unit (type 1) or an another node (type 2) of document that will carry this structural search based on its content. Search attribute names are available at the level of the user's interface.

In the following example, the tag of elementary unit is 'title,' and 'author' is the name of an attribute of the tag 'book.'

```
<info idinfo="title" path="//title"/>
<info idinfo="author" path="//book/@author"/>
```

The query result depends on type of search attribute.

If the indexed search attribute is an elementary unit, then the returned result is the node that is the father of this unit. If the indexed search attribute is a node different from elementary unit, then the returned result is this node.

Query Examples

Query 1: title = 'dataweb'. This query returns the following result: all the names of documents of which value of <title> contains 'dataweb' text.

Query 2: author = 'smadhi'. This query returns the following result: all the sub-structures (at first level) which have for name 'book' and for that the attribute 'author' contains 'smadhi' text.

Resources Global Catalog

The Resources Global Catalog is defined as a generalized index that allows the user to maintain for SIRX, to efficiently support keyword searching and sub-structure searching. It is used by the search processor use to find the relevant documents (or parts of documents).

It is represented by an XML document which describes every XML document that is indexed by the indexing processor. This catalog is described in XML according the following DTD:

Figure 2. The Catalog DTD

```
<!ELEMENT catalog(doc*)>
<!ELEMENT doc(address, search-attributes, keywords)>
<!ATTLIST doc iddoc ID #REQUIRED>
<!ELEMENT search-attributes(info*)>
<!ELEMENT info (#PCDATA)>
<!ATTLIST info idinfo ID #REQUIRED)
<!ATTLIST info path CDATA #REQUIRED>
<!ELEMENT address(#PCDTA)>
<!ELEMENT keywords(key*)>
<!ELEMENT key (#PCDATA)>
<!ATTLIST key idkey ID #REQUIRED>
<!ATTLIST key path CDATA #REQUIRED>
<!ATTLIST key freq CDATA #REQUIRED>
```

The following example illustrates the structure of this catalog:

Figure 3. An Example of Resources Global Catalog

```
<catalog>
<doc iddoc="d1" >
   <address>c:/SRIX/mcseai.xml</address>
   <search-attributes>
         <info idinfo="title" path="//title"/>
         <info idinfo="author" path="//book/@author"/>
   </search-attributes>
   <keywords>
         <key idkey ="k1" path="//dataweb/integration" freq=2>xml </key>
         <key idkey ="k2" path="// mapping/@base" freq=1>xml </key>
```

```
        ...
    </keywords>
</doc>
<doc iddoc="d2" >
    <address>c:/SRIX/cari2000.xml</address>
    <search-attributes>
        <info idinfo="title" path="//title"/>
        <info idinfo="author" path="//book/@author"/>
    </search-attributes>
    <keywords>
        <key idkey ="k25" path="//architecture/integration" freq=2>web </
        key>
        <key idkey ="k26" path="// architecture/integration" freq=2>dataweb
        </key>
        ...
    </keywords>
</doc>
....
</catalog>
```

Keyword Weights

In the Vector Space Model, documents and queries are represented as vector weighted terms (the word term refers to keyword) (Salton, 1988; Yuwono, 1996). In our approach each indexed elementary unit j of document i is represented by a vector as follows:

$$U^i_j = (w^i_{j1}, w^i_{j2},..., w^i_{jk},...,w^i_{jp}),\ k = 1, 2, ..., p$$

- *nu*: number of elementary units *j* of document *i*
- *p:* number of indexing keywords
- w^i_{jk}: weight of the *k*th term in the *j*th elementary unit of the *i*th document

We use the classical *tf.idf* weighting scheme (Salton, 1988) to calculate w^i_{jk}.

$$w^i_{jk} = tf^i_{jk} \times idf_k$$

- tf^i_{jk}: the frequency of the *k*th term in the *j*th elementary unit of the *i*th document
- idf_k: the inverse document frequency of the index term *tk*. It is computed as a function of the elementary unit frequency by the following formula:

$$idf_k = log(tnu/nu_k)$$

- *tnu*: the total number of elementary units in the document base
- nu_k: the number of elementary units which the *k*th term occurs at least once

RELEVANT INFORMATION RETRIEVAL

SIRX supports two ways to retrieve parts of documents:

a) *Querying by Search Attributes:* Authorizes a search based on a document structure from a list of search attributes proposed to a user. It allows one to retrieve documents or parts of documents according the type search attributes. This aspect is not detailed in this chapter.

b) *Querying by Content with Keywords:* Allows retrieval of documents or parts of documents.

In this section we describe the search process of relevant information retrieval that involves two issues: generating query vector, and computing the similarity between vector query and each elementary unit vector.

The adopted model of data rests mainly on the use of the catalog in memory central for an exploitation, during the process of interrogation by a set of end-users.

Query Processing

A user's query is a list of one or more keywords which belong to the thesaurus. When the user inputs a query, the system generates a query vector by using the same indexing method as that of the element unit vector. A query vector Q is as follows:

$$Q = (q_1, q_2, \ldots, q_k, \ldots, q_m) \text{ with } m \leq p$$

Query terms q_k $(j=1 \ldots m)$ are weighted by the *idf* value where *idf* is measured by $log(tnu/nu_k)$.

Retrieval and Ranking of Relevant XML Information Units

The search process returns the relevant elementary units of an XML document. These information units are ranked according to their similarity coefficients measuring the relevance of elementary units of an XML document to a user's query.

In the Vector Space Model, this similarity is measured by cosine of the angle between the elementary unit vector and query vector. On considering the two vectors U_i and Q in the Euclidean space with scalar product noted $<,>$ and norm noted $||.||$, the similarity is (Smadhi, 2001):

$$Sim(U_i, Q) = \frac{\sum_{j=1}^{m} q_j w_{ij}}{\sqrt{\sum_{j=1}^{m} q_j^2} \sqrt{\sum_{j=1}^{m} w_{ij}^2}}$$

This measure like others (Salton, 1988; Wang, 1992) is based on the following hypothesis: the more a document looks like the query, the more it is susceptible to be relevant for the user. We question this hypothesis because the query and the document do not play a symmetric role in the search for information (Simonnot & Smail, 1996; Fourel, 1998). It is necessary to note that the user expresses in his query only characteristics of the document which interests him at the given moment. It is necessary to take into account two important criteria: the exhaustiveness of the query in the document and the specificity of the document with regard to the query (Nie, 1988).

Now, we show how to spread this measure of similarity to take into account these two criteria.

A measure is based on the exhaustiveness if it estimates the degree of inclusion of the query Q in the unit U_i. Conversely, a measure based on the specificity measures the degree of inclusion of U_i elementary unit in the query Q.

We propose the two following measures:

a) The exhaustiveness measure noted mexh is:

$$mexh(U_i, Q) = \frac{\cos(U_i, Q)\|U_i\|}{\|Q\|}$$

b) The specificity measure noted mspec is:

$$mspec(U_i, Q) = \frac{\cos(U_i, Q)\|Q\|}{\|U_i\|}$$

These two measures have intuitively a comprehensible geometrical interpretation because mexh(Ui,Q) represents the norm of the vector projection Ui on the vector Q. In the same way, mspec(Ui,Q) represents the norm of vector projection Q on the Ui vector. The similarity measure became:

$$Sim(U_i, Q) = \sqrt{mspec(U_i, Q)mexh(U_i, Q))}$$

Experiments Results

The reference collection that we built is not very important. This collection has 200 XML documents which correspond to articles extracted from proceedings of conferences. First estimates seem to us very interesting: the measure of similarity that we proposed allowed us to improve about 20% the pertinence of restored subdocuments. These tests are realized on a Linux Server using a Dell computer with an 800Mhz Intel processor with 512 MB RAM.

RELATED WORK AND CONCLUSION

Many works are done to propose methods of information retrieval in XML documents. Among various approaches (Luk, 2000), the database-oriented approach and information retrieval-oriented approach seem the most used.

In the database-oriented approach, some query languages — such as XIRQ (Fuhr, 2000), XQL and XML-QL — are proposed, but these languages are not suitable for end-users in spite of the integration of a keyword search into an XML query language (Florescu, 2000). Xset (Zhao, 2000) supposes to have knowledge about document structure. If XRS (Shin, 1998) proposes an interesting indexing method at the leaf elements, it still may present an inconvenience with the use of DTD.

Our approach proposes, like XRS, an indexing at the leaf elements, and it extends the inverted index with XML path specifications. It also takes into account the structure of the XML document. Moreover we introduce a particular measure of similarity which is a compromise between two measures: exhaustiveness and specificity.

This new approach allows users to retrieve parts of XML documents with relevance ranking.

REFERENCES

Abiteboul, S., Quass, D., McHugh, D., Widom, J. and Wiener, J. (1997). The Lorel query language for semi-structured data. *Journal of Digital Libraries,* 68-88.

Deutsch, A., Fernandez, M.F., Florescu, D. and Levy, A. (1999). A query language for XML. *WWW8/Computer Networks*, 31, 1155-1169.

Florescu, D., Manolescu, I. and Kossman, D. (2000). Integrating search into XML query processing. *Proceedings of the Ninth International WWW Conference.*

Fuhr, N. and Grossjohann, K. (2000). XIRQ: An extension of XQL for information retrieval. *Proceedings of the ACM SIGIR 2000 Workshop on XML and Information Retrieval.*

Govert, N., Lalmas, M. and Fuhr, N. (1999). A probabilistic description-oriented approach for categorising Web documents. *Proceedings of the Ninth International Conference on Information and Knowledge Management* (pp. 475-782) New York: ACM.

Hayashi, Y., Tomita, J. and Kikui, G. (2000). Searching text-rich XML documents with relevance ranking. *Proceedings of the ACM SIGIR 2000 Workshop on XML and Information Retrieval.*

Lo, M. and Hocine, A. (2000). Modeling of Dataweb: An approach based on the integration of semantics of data and XML. *Proceedings of the Fifth African Conference on the Search in Computing Sciences,* Antananarivo, Madagascar.

Lo, M., Hocine, A. and Rafinat, P. (2001). A designing model of XML-Dataweb. *Proceedings of International Conference on Object Oriented Information Systems (OOIS'2001)* (pp. 143-153) Calgary, Alberta, Canada.

Luk, R., Chan, A., Dillon, T. and Leong, H.V. (2000). A survey of search engines for XML documents. *Proceedings of the ACM SIGIR 2000 Workshop on XML and Information Retrieval.*

Nie, J. (1988). An outline of a general model for information retrieval systems. *Proceedings of the ACM SIGIR International Conference on Research and Development in Information Retrieval* (pp. 495-506).

Robie, J. (1999). *The Design of XQL, 1999.* Available online at: http://www.texcel.no/whitepapers/xql-design.html.

Salton, G. and Bukley, D. (1988). Term weighting approaches in automatic text retrieval. *Information Processing and Management,* 24(5), 513-523.

Shin, D., Chang, H. and Jin, H. (1998). Bus: An effective indexing and retrieval scheme in structured documents. *Proceedings of Digital Libraries '98* (pp. 235-243).

Simonnot, B. and Smail, M. (1996). Modèle flexible pour la recherche interactive de documents multimedias. *Proceedings of Inforsid'96* (pp. 165-178) Bordeaux.

Smadhi, S. (2001). Search and ranking of relevant information in XML documents. *Proceedings of IIWAS 2001* (pp. 485-488) Linz, Austria.

Wang, Z.W., Wong, S.K. and Yao, Y.Y. (1992). An analysis of Vector Space Models based on computational geometry. *Proceedings of the AMC SIGIR International Conference on Research and Development in Information Retrieval* (pp. 152-160) Copenhagen, Denmark.

Xpath. (1999). Available online at: http://www.w3.org/TR/1999/REC-xpath-19991116.

XSLT. (1999). Available online at: http://www.w3.org/TR/1999/REC-xslt-19991116.

Yuwono, B. and Lee, D.L. (1996). WISE: A World Wide Web Resource Database System. *IEEE TKDE*, 8(4), 548-554.

Zhao, B.Y. and Joseph, A. (2000). *Xset: A Lightweight XML Search Engine for Internet Applications.* Available online at: http://www.cs.berkeley.edu/ravenben/xset/html/xset-saint.pdf.

Chapter II

Information Extraction from Free-Text Business Documents

Witold Abramowicz
The Poznan University of Economics, Poland

Jakub Piskorski
German Research Center for Artificial Intelligence in Saarbruecken, Germany

ABSTRACT

The objective of this chapter is an investigation of the applicability of information extraction techniques in real-world business applications dealing with textual data since business relevant data is mainly transmitted through free-text documents. In particular, we give an overview of the information extraction task, designing information extraction systems and some examples of existing information extraction systems applied in the financial, insurance and legal domains. Furthermore, we demonstrate the enormous indexing potential of lightweight linguistic text processing techniques applied in information extraction systems and other closely related fields of information technology which concern processing vast amounts of textual data.

INTRODUCTION

Nowadays, knowledge relevant to business of any kind is mainly transmitted through free-text documents: the World Wide Web, newswire feeds, corporate reports, government documents, litigation records, etc. One of the most difficult issues concerning applying search technology for retrieving relevant information from textual data collections is the process of converting such data into a shape for searching. Information retrieval (IR) systems using conventional indexing techniques applied even to a homogenous collection of text documents fall far from obtaining optimal recall and precision simultaneously. Since structured data is obviously easier to search, an ever-growing need for effective and intelligent techniques for analyzing free-text documents and building expressive representation of their content in the form of structured data can be observed.

Recent trends in information technology such as Information Extraction (IE) provide dramatic improvements in converting the overflow of raw textual information into valuable and structured data, which could be further used as input for data mining engines for discovering more complex patterns in textual data collections. The task of IE is to identify a predefined set of concepts in a specific domain, ignoring other irrelevant information, where the domain consists of a corpus of texts together with a clearly specified information need. Due to the specific phenomena and complexity of natural language, this is a non-trivial task. However, recent advances in Natural Language Processing (NLP) concerning new robust, efficient, high coverage shallow processing techniques for analyzing free text have contributed to the size in the deployment of IE techniques in business information systems.

INFORMATION EXTRACTION

Information Extraction Task

The task of IE is to identify instances of a particular pre-specified class of events or relationships and entities in natural language texts, and the extraction of the relevant arguments of the events or relationships (SAIC, 1998). The information to be extracted is pre-specified in user-defined structures called templates (e.g., company information, meetings of important people), each consisting of a number of slots, which must be instantiated by an IE system as it processes the text. The slots are usually filled with: some strings from the text, one of a number of pre-defined values or a reference to other already generated template. One way of thinking about an IE system is in terms of database construction, since an IE system creates a structured representation of selected information drawn from the analyzed text.

In recent years IE technology has progressed quite rapidly, from small-scale systems applicable within very limited domains to useful systems which can perform information extraction from a very broad range of texts. IE technology is now coming to the market and is of great significance to finance companies, banks, publishers and governments. For instance, a financial organization would want to know facts about foundations of international joint-ventures happening in a given time span. The process of extracting such information involves locating the names of companies and finding linguistic relations between them and other relevant entities (e.g., locations and temporal expressions). However, in this particular scenario an IE system requires some specific domain knowledge (understanding the fact that ventures generally involve at least two partners and result in the formation of a new company) in order to merge partial information into an adequate template structure. Generally, IE systems rely to some degree on domain knowledge. Further information such as appointment of key personnel or announcement of new investment plans could also be reduced to instantiated templates.

Designing IE Systems

There are two basic approaches to designing IE systems: the Knowledge Engineering Approach and the Learning Approach (Appelt & Israel, 1999). In the knowledge engineering approach, the development of rules for marking and extracting sought-after information is done by a human expert through inspection of the test corpus and his or her own intuition. In the learning approach the rules are learned from an annotated corpus and interaction with the user. Generally, higher performance can be achieved by handcrafted systems, particularly when training data is sparse. However, in a particular scenario automatically trained components of an IE system might show better performance than their handcrafted counterparts. Approaches to building hybrid systems based on both approaches are currently being investigated. IE systems built for different tasks often differ from each other in many ways. Nevertheless, there are core components shared by nearly every IE system, disregarding the underlying design approach.

The coarse-grained architecture of a typical IE system is presented in Figure 1. It consists of two main components: text processor and template generation module. The task of the text processor is performing general linguistic analysis in order to extract as much linguistic structure as possible. Due to the problem of ambiguity pervading all levels of natural language processing, this is a non-trivial task. Instead of computing all possible interpretations and grammatical relations in natural language text (so-called *deep text processing* — DTP), there is an increased tendency towards applying only partial analysis (so-called *shallow text processing* — STP), which is considerably less time consuming and could be seen as a trade-off between pattern matching and fully fledged linguistic analysis (Piskorski & Skut, 2000). There is no standardized definition of the term shallow text processing.

Shallow text processing can be characterized as a process of computing text analysis which is less complete than the output of deep text processing systems. It is usually restricted to identifying non-recursive structures or structures with limited amount of structural recursion, which can be identified with high degree of certainty. In shallow text analysis, language regularities which cause problems are not handled and, instead of computing all possible readings, only underspecified structures are computed. The use of STP instead of DTP may be advantageous since it might be sufficient for the

Figure 1. A Coarse-Grained Architecture of an Information Extraction System

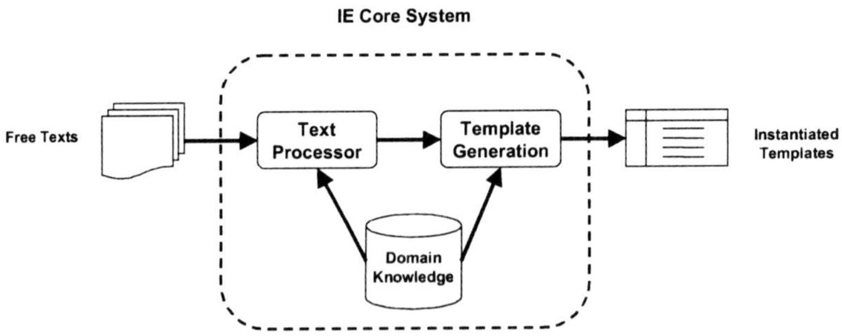

extraction and assembly of the relevant information and it requires less knowledge engineering, which means a faster development cycle and fewer development expenses. Most of the STP systems follow the finite-state approach, which guarantees time and space efficiency.

The scope of information computed by the text processor may vary depending on the requirements of a particular application. Usually, linguistic analysis performed by the text processor of an IE system includes following steps:

- Segmentation of text into a sequence of sentences, each of which is a sequence of lexical items representing words together with their lexical attributes
- Recognition of small-scale structures (e.g., abbreviations, core nominal phrases, verb clusters and named entities)
- Parsing, which takes as input a sequence of lexical items and small-scale structures and computes the structure of the sentence, the so-called parse tree

Depending on the application scenario, it might be desirable for the text processor to perform additional tasks such as: part-of-speech disambiguation, word sense tagging, anaphora resolution or semantic interpretation (e.g., translating the parse tree or parse fragments into a semantic structure or logical form). A benefit of the IE task orientation is that it helps to focus on linguistic phenomena that are most prevalent in a particular domain or particular extraction task.

The template generation module merges the linguistic structures computed by the text processor and using domain knowledge (e.g., domain-specific extraction patterns and inference rules) derives domain-specific relations in the form of instantiated templates. In practice, the boundary between text processor and template generation component may be blurred.

The input and output of an IE system can be defined precisely, which facilitates the evaluation of different systems and approaches. For the evaluation of IE systems, the precision, recall and f-measures were adopted from the IR research community (e.g., the recall of an IE system is the ratio between the number of correctly filled slots and the total number of slots expected to be filled).

Information Extraction vs. Information Retrieval

IE systems are obviously more difficult and knowledge intensive to build and they are more computationally intensive than IR systems. Generally, IE systems achieve higher precision than IR systems. However, IE and IR techniques can be seen as complementary and can potentially be combined in various ways. For instance, IR could be embedded within IE for pre-processing a huge document collection into a manageable subset to which IE techniques could be applied. On the other side, IE can be used as a subcomponent of an IR system to identify terms for intelligent document indexing (e.g., conceptual indices). Such combinations clearly represent significant improvement in the retrieval of accurate and prompt business information. For example, Mihalcea and Moldovan (2001) introduced an approach for document indexing using named entities, which proved to reduce the number of retrieved documents by a factor of two, while still retrieving relevant documents.

Message Understanding Conferences

The rapid development of the field of IE has been essentially influenced by the Message Understanding Conferences (MUCs). These conferences were conducted under the auspices of several United States government agencies with the intention of coordinating multiple research groups and government agencies seeking to improve IE and IR technologies (Grishman & Sundheim, 1996). The MUCs defined several generic types of IE tasks. These were intended to be prototypes of IE tasks that arise in real-world applications, and they illustrate the main functional capabilities of current IE systems. The IE tasks defined in MUC competitions focused on extracting information from newswire articles (e.g., concerning terrorist events, international joint venture foundations and management succession). Altogether seven MUC competitions took place (1987-1998), where the participants were given the same training data for the adaptation of their systems to a given scenario. Analogously, the evaluation was performed using the same annotated test data. The generic IE tasks for MUC-7 (1998) were defined as follows:

- Named Entity Recognition (NE) requires the identification and classification of named entities such as organizations, persons, locations, product names and temporal expressions.
- Template Element Task (TE) requires the filling of small-scale templates for specified classes of entities in the texts, such as organizations, persons, certain artifacts with slots such as name variants, title, description as supplied in the text.
- Template Relation Task (TR) requires filling a two-slot template representing a binary relation with pointers to template elements standing in the relation, which were previously identified in the TE task (e.g., an employee relation between a person and a company).
- Co-Reference Resolution (CO) requires the identification of expressions in the text that refer to the same object, set or activity (e.g., variant forms of name expressions, definite noun phrases and their antecedents).
- Scenario Template (ST) requires filling a template structure with extracted information involving several relations or events of interest, for instance, identification of partners, products, profits and capitalization of joint ventures.

State-of-the-art results for IE tasks for English reported in MUC-7 are presented in Figure 2.

IE SYSTEMS IN THE BUSINESS DOMAIN

Early IE Systems

The earliest IE systems were deployed as commercial products already in the late eighties. One of the first attempts to apply IE in the financial field using templates was the ATRANS system (Lytinen & Gershman, 1986), based on simple language processing techniques and script-frames approach for extracting information from telex messages regarding money transfers between banks. JASPER (Andersen, Hayes, Heuttner, Schmandt, Nirenburg & Weinstein, 1992) is an IE system that extracts information from

Figure 2. State-of-the-Art Results Reported in MUC-7

MEASURE\TASK	NE	CO	RE	TR	ST
RECALL	92	56	86	67	42
PRECISION	95	69	87	86	65

reports on corporate earnings from small sentence fragments using robust NLP methods. SCISOR (Jacobs & Rau, 1990) is an integrated system incorporating IE for extraction of facts related to the company and financial information. These early IE systems had a major shortcoming, namely they were not easily adaptable to new scenarios. On the other side, they demonstrated that relatively simple NLP techniques are sufficient for solving IE tasks narrow in scope and utility.

LOLITA

The LOLITA System (Costantino, Morgan, Collingham & Garigliano, 1997), developed at the University of Durham, was the first general purpose IE system with fine-grained classification of predefined templates relevant to the financial domain. Further, it provides a user-friendly interface for defining new templates. LOLITA is based on deep natural language understanding and uses semantic networks. Different applications were built around its core. Among others, LOLITA was used for extracting information from financial news articles which represent an extremely wide domain, including different kinds of news (e.g., financial, economical, political, etc.). The templates have been defined according to the "financial activities" approach and can be used by the financial operators to support their decision-making process and to analyze the effect of news on price behavior. A financial activity is one potentially able to influence the decisions of the players in the market (brokers, investors, analysts, etc.). The system uses three main groups of templates for financial activities: *company-related activities* — related to the life of the company (e.g., ownership, shares, mergers, privatization, takeovers), *company restructuring activities* — related to changes in the productive structure of companies (e.g., new product, joint venture, staff change) and *general macroeconomics activities* — including general macroeconomics news that can affect the prices of the shares quoted in the stock exchange (e.g., interest rate movements, inflation, trade deficit).

In the "takeover template" task, as defined in MUC-6, the system achieved precision of 63% and recall of 43%. However, since the system is based on DTP techniques, the performance in terms of speed can be, in particular situations, penalized in comparison to systems based on STP methods. The output of LOLITA was fed to the financial expert system (Costantino, 1999) to process an incoming stream of news from online news providers, companies and other structured numerical market data to produce investment suggestions.

MITA

IE technology has been successfully used recently in the insurance domain. MITA (Metalife's Intelligent Text Analyzer) was developed in order to improve the insurance underwriting process (Glasgow, Mandell, Binney, Ghemri & Fisher, 1998). Metalife's life insurance applications contain free-form textual fields (an average of 2.3 textual fields per application) such as: *physician reason field* — describing a reason a proposed insured last visited a personal physician, *family history field* — describing insured's family medical history and major treatments and *exams field* — which describes any major medical event within the last five years. In order to identify any concepts from such textual fields that might have underwriting significance, the system applies STP techniques and returns a categorization of these concepts for risk assessment by subsequent domain-specific analyzers. For instance, MITA extracts a three-slot template from the family history field, consisting of the concept slot which describes a particular type of information that can be found, value slot for storing the actual word associated with a particular instance of the concept and the class slot representing the semantic class that the value denotes.

The MITA system has been tested in a production environment and 89% of the information in the textual field was successfully analyzed. Further, a blind testing was undertaken to determine whether the output of MITA is sufficient to make underwriting decisions equivalent to those produced by an underwriter with access to the full text. Results showed that only up to 7% of the extractions resulted in different underwriting conclusions.

History Assistant

Jackson, Al-Kofahi, Kreilick and Grom (1998) present History Assistant — an information extraction and retrieval system for the juridical domain. It extracts rulings from electronically imported court opinions and retrieves relevant prior cases, and cases affected from a citator database, and links them to the current case. The role of a citator database enriched with such linking information is to track historical relations among cases. Online citators are of great interest to the legal profession because they provide a way of testing whether a case is still good law.

History Assistant is based on DTP and uses context-free grammars for computing all possible parses of the sentence. The problem of identifying the prior case is a non-trivial task since citations for prior cases are usually not explicitly visible. History Assistant applies IE for producing structured information blocks, which are used for automatically generating SQL queries to search prior and affected cases in the citator database. Since information obtained by the IE module might be incomplete, additional domain-specific knowledge (e.g., court hierarchy) is used in cases when extracted information does not contain enough data to form a good query. The automatically generated SQL query returns a list of cases, which are then scored using additional criteria. The system achieved a recall of 93.3% in the prior case retrieval task (i.e., in 631 out of the 673 cases, the system found the prior case as a result of an automatically generated query).

Trends

The most recent approaches to IE concentrated on constructing general purpose, highly modular, robust, efficient and domain-adaptive IE systems. FASTUS (Hobbs, Appelt, Bear, Israel, Kameyama, Stickel & Tyson, 1997), built in the Artificial Intelligence Center of SRI International, is a very fast and robust general purpose IE system which deploys lightweight linguistic techniques. It is conceptually very simple, since it works essentially as a set of cascaded nondeterministic finite-state transducers. FASTUS was one of the best scoring systems in the MUCs and was used by a commercial client for discovering an ontology underlying complex Congressional bills, for ensuring the consistency of laws with the regulations that implement them.

Humphreys, Gaizauskas, Azzam, Huyck, Mitchell, Cunningham and Wilks (1998) describe LaSIE-II, a highly flexible and modular IE system, which was an attempt to find a pragmatic middle way in the shallow versus deep analysis debate which characterized the last several MUCs. The result is an eclectic mixture of techniques ranging from finite-state recognition of domain-specific lexical patterns to using restricted context-free grammars for partial parsing. Its highly modular architecture enabled one to gain deeper insight into the strengths and weaknesses of the particular subcomponents and their interaction.

Similarly to LaSIE-II, the two top requirements on the design of the IE2 system (Aone, Halverson, Hampton, Ramos-Santacruz & Hampton, 1999), developed at SRA International Inc., were modularity and flexibility. SGML was used to spell out system interface requirements between the sub-modules, which allow an easy replacement of any sub-module in the workflow. The IE2 system achieved the highest score in TE task (recall: 86%, precision 87%), TR task (recall: 67%, precision: 86%) and ST task (recall: 42%, precision: 65%) in the MUC-7 competition. REES (presented in Aone & Santacruz, 2000) was the first attempt to constructing a large-scale event and relation extraction system based on STP methods. It can extract more than 100 types of relations and events related to the area of business, finance and politics, which represents much wider coverage than is typical of IE systems. For 26 types of events related to finance, it achieved an F-measure of 70%.

BEYOND INFORMATION EXTRACTION

The last decade has witnessed great advances and interest in the area of information extraction using simple shallow processing methods. In the very recent period, new trends in information processing, from texts based on lightweight linguistic analysis closely related to IE, have emerged.

Textual Question Answering

Textual Question Answering (Q/A) aims at identifying the answer of a question in large collections of online documents, where the questions are formulated in natural language and the answers are presented in the form of highlighted pieces of text containing the desired information. The current Q/A approaches integrate existing IE and IR technologies. Knowledge extracted from documents may be modeled as a set of entities extracted from the text and relations between them and further used for concept-oriented indexing. Srihari and Li (1999) presented Textract — a Q/A system based on relatively simple IE techniques using NLP methods. This system extracts open-ended domain-independent general-event templates expressing the information like WHO did WHAT (to WHOM) WHEN and WHERE (in predicate-argument structure). Such information may refer to argument structures centering around the verb notions and associated information of location and time. The results are stored in a database and used as a basis for question answering, summarization and intelligent browsing. Textract and other similar systems based on lightweight NLP techniques (Harabagiu, Pasca & Maiorano, 2000) achieved surprisingly good results in the competition of answering fact-based questions in Text Retrieval Conference (TREC) (Voorhess, 1999).

Text Classification

The task of *Text Classification* (TC) is assigning one or more pre-defined categories from a closed set of such categories to each document in a collection. Traditional approaches in the area of TC use word-based techniques for fulfilling this task. Riloff and Lorenzen (1998) presented AutoSlog-TS, an unsupervised system that generates domain-specific extraction patterns, which was used for the automatic construction of a high-precision text categorization system. Autoslog-TS retrieves extraction patterns (with a single slot) representing local linguistic expressions that are slightly more sophisticated than keywords. Such patterns are not simply extracting adjacent words since extracting information depends on identifying local syntactic constructs (verb and its arguments). AutoSlog-TS takes as input only a collection of pre-classified texts associated with a given domain and uses simple STP techniques and simple statistical methods for automatic generation of extraction patterns for text classification. This new approach of integrating STP techniques in TC proved to outperform classification using word-based approaches. Further, similar unsupervised approaches (Yangarber, Grishman, Tapanainen & Huttunen, 2000) using light linguistic analysis were presented for the acquisition of lexico-syntactic patterns (syntactic normalization: transformation of clauses into common predicate-argument structure), and extracting scenario-specific terms and relations between them (Finkelstein-Landau & Morin, 1999), which shows an enormous potential of shallow processing techniques in the field of text mining.

Text Mining

Text mining (TM) combines the disciplines of data mining, information extraction, information retrieval, text categorization, probabilistic modeling, linear algebra, machine learning and computational linguistics to discover valid, implicit, previously unknown and comprehensible knowledge from unstructured textual data. Obviously, there is an overlap between text mining and information extraction, but in text mining the knowledge to be extracted is not necessarily known in advance. Rajman (1997) presents two examples of information that can be automatically extracted from text collections using simple shallow processing methods: probabilistic associations of keywords and prototypical document instances. Association extraction from the keyword sets allows the user to satisfy information needs expressed by queries like "find all associations between a set of companies including Siemens and Microsoft and any person." Prototypical document instances may be used as representative of classes of repetitive document structures in the collection of texts and constitute good candidates for a partial synthesis of the information content hidden in a textual base. Text mining contributes to the discovery of information for business and also to the future of information services by mining large collections of text (Abramowicz & Zurada, 2001). It will become a central technology to many businesses branches, since companies and enterprises "don't know what they don't know" (Tkach, 1999).

Figure 3. Application Potential of Shallow Text Processing

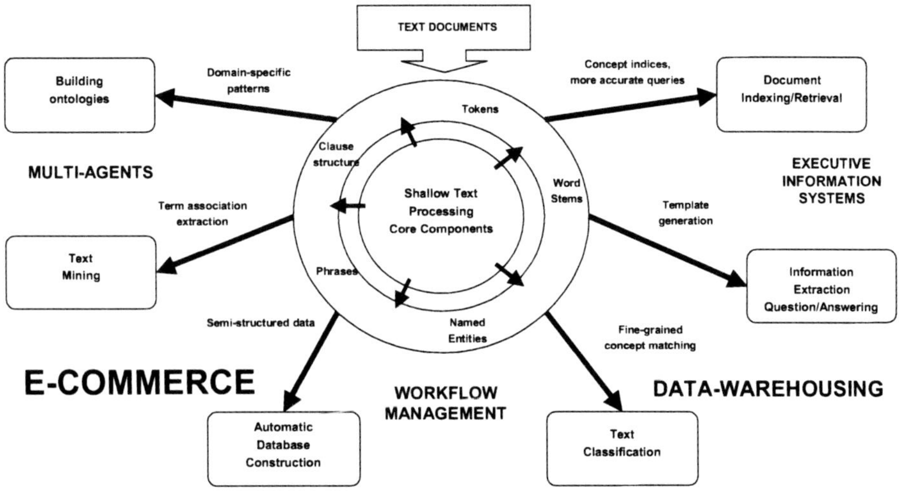

SUMMARY

We have learned that IE technology based on lightweight linguistic analysis has been successfully used in various business applications dealing with processing huge collections of free-text documents. The diagram in Figure 3 reflects the enormous application potential of STP in various fields of information technology discussed in this chapter. STP can be considered as an automated generalized indexing procedure. The degree and amount of structured data an STP component is able to extract plays a crucial role for subsequent high-level processing of extracted data. In this way, STP offers distinct possibilities for increased productivity in workflow management (Abramowicz & Szymanski, 2002), e-commerce and data warehousing (Abramowicz, Kalczynski & Wecel, 2002). Potentially, solving a wide range of business tasks can be substantially improved by using information extraction. Therefore, an increased commercial exploitation of IE technology could be observed (e.g., Cymfony's InfoXtract — IE engine, http:\\www.cymfony.com).

The question of developing a text processing technology base that applies to many problems is still a major challenge of the current research. In particular, future research in this area will focus on multilinguality, cross-document event tracking, automated learning methods to acquire background knowledge, portability, greater ease of use and stronger integration of semantics.

REFERENCES

Abramowicz, W. & Szymanski, J. (2002). Workflow technology supporting information filtering from the Internet. *Proceedings of IRMA 2002,* Seattle, WA, USA.

Abramowicz, W. & Zurada, J. (2001). *Knowledge Discovery for Business Information Systems.* Boston, MA: Kluwer Academic Publishers.

Abramowicz, W., Kalczynski, P. & Wecel, K. (2002). *Filtering the Web to Feed Data Warehouses*. London: Springer.

Andersen, P.M., Hayes, P.J., Heuttner, A.K., Schmandt, L.M., Nirenburg, I.B. & Weinstein, S.P. (1992). Automatic extraction of facts from press releases to generate news stories. *Proceedings of the 3rd Conference on Applied Natural Language Processing,* Trento, Italy, 170-177.

Aone, C. & Ramos-Santacruz, M. (2000). RESS: A large-scale relation and event extraction system. *Proceedings of ANLP 2000,* Seattle, WA, USA.

Aone, C., Halverson, L., Hampton, T., Ramos-Santacruz, M. & Hampton, T. (1999). *SRA: Description of the IE2 System Used for MUC-7.* Morgan Kaufmann.

Appelt, D. & Israel, D. (1999). An introduction to information extraction technology. Tutorial prepared for the *IJCAI 1999 Conference.*

Chinchor, N.A. (1998). Overview of MUC7/MET-2. *Proceedings of the Seventh Message Understanding Conference (MUC7).*

Costantino, M. (1999). IE-Expert: Integrating natural language processing and expert system techniques for real-time equity derivatives trading. *Journal of Computational Intelligence in Finance,* 7(2), 34-52.

Costantino, M., Morgan, R.G., Collingham R.J. & Garigliano, R. (1997). Natural language processing and information extraction: Qualitative analysis of financial news articles. *Proceedings of the Conference on Computational Intelligence for Financial Engineering 1997,* New York.

Finkelstein-Landau, M. & Morin, E. (1999). Extracting semantic relationships between terms: Supervised vs. unsupervised methods. *Proceedings of International Workshop on Ontological Engineering on the Global Information Infrastructure,* Dagstuhl Castle, Germany, May, 71-80.

Glasgow, B., Mandell, A., Binney, D., Ghemri, L. & Fisher, D. (1998). MITA: An information-extraction approach to the analysis of free-form text in life insurance applications. *AI Magazine,* 19(1), 59-71.

Grishman, R. & Sundheim, B. (1996). Message Understanding Conference–6: A brief history. *Proceedings of the 16th International Conference on Computational Linguistics (COLING),* Kopenhagen, Denmark, 466-471.

Harabagiu, S., Pasca, M. & Maiorano, S. (2000). Experiments with open-domain textual question answering. *Proceedings of the COLING-2000 Conference.*

Hobbs, J., Appelt, D., Bear, J., Israel, D., Kameyama, M., Stickel, M. & Tyson, M. (1997). FASTUS—A cascaded finite-state transducer for extracting information from natural language text. Chapter 13 in Roche, E. & Schabes, Y. (1997). *Finite-State Language Processing.* Cambridge, MA: MIT Press.

Humphreys, K., Gaizauskas, R., Azzam, S., Huyck, C., Mitchell, B., Cunningham, H. & Wilks, Y. (1998). University of Sheffield: Description of the LaSIE-II system as used for MUC-7. *Proceedings of the Seventh Message Understanding Conference (MUC-7).*

Jackson, P., Al-Kofahi, K., Kreilick, C. & Grom, B. (1998). Information extraction from case law and retrieval of prior cases by partial parsing and query generation. *Proceedings of the ACM 7th International Conference on Information and Knowledge Management,* Washington, DC, USA, 60-67.

Jacobs, P. & Rau, L. (1990). SCISOR: Extracting information from online news. *Communications of the ACM,* 33(11), 88-97.

Lytinen, S. & Gershman, A. (1986). ATRANS: Automatic processing of money transfer messages. *Proceedings of the 5th National Conference of the American Association for Artificial Intelligence.* IEEE Computer Society Press (1993), 93-99.

Mihalcea, R. & Moldovan, D. (2001). Document indexing using named entities. *Studies in Informatics and Control Journal,* 10(1).

Piskorski, J. & Skut, W. (2000). Intelligent information extraction. *Proceedings of Business Information Systems 2000,* Poznan, Poland.

Rajman, M. (1997). Text mining, knowledge extraction from unstructured textual data. *Proceedings of EUROSTAT Conference,* Frankfurt, Germany.

Riloff, E. & Lorenzen, J. (1998). Extraction-based text categorization: Generating domain-specific role relationships automatically. In Strzalkowski, T. (Ed.), *Natural Language Information Retrieval.* Kluwer Academic Publishers.

SAIC. (1998). *Seventh Message Understanding Conference (MUC-7).* Available online at: http://www.muc.saic.com.

Srihari, R. & Li, W. (1999). Information extraction-supported question answering. *Proceedings of the Eighth Text Retrieval Conference (TREC-8).*

Tkach, D. (1999). The pillars of knowledge management. *Knowledge Management,* 2(3), 47.

Voorhess, E. & Tice, D. (1999). *The TREC-8 Question Answering Track Evaluation.* Gaithersburg, MD: National Institute of Standards and Technology.

Yangarber, R., Grishman, R., Tapanainen, P. & Huttunen, S. (2000). Unsupervised discovery of scenario-level patterns for information extraction. *Proceedings of the Conference on Applied Natural Language Processing ANLP-NAACL 2000,* Seattle, WA, USA, May.

Chapter III

Interactive Indexing of Documents with a Multilingual Thesaurus

Ulrich Schiel
Universidade Federal de Campina Grande, Brazil

Ianna M.S.F. de Sousa
Universidade Federal de Campina Grande, Brazil

ABSTRACT

With the growing significance of digital libraries and the Internet, more and more electronic texts become accessible to a wide and geographically disperse public. This requires adequate tools to facilitate indexing, storage and retrieval of documents written in different languages. We present a method for semi-automatic indexing of electronic documents and construction of a multilingual thesaurus, which can be used for query formulation and information retrieval. We use special dictionaries and user interaction in order to solve ambiguities and find adequate canonical terms in the language and an adequate abstract language-independent term. The abstract thesaurus is updated incrementally by new indexed documents and is used to search for documents using adequate terms.

INTRODUCTION

The growing relevance of digital libraries is generally recognized (Haddouti, 1997). A digital library typically contains hundreds or thousands of documents. It is also recognized that, even though English is the dominant language, documents in other languages are of great significance and, moreover, users want to retrieve documents in several languages associated to a topic, stated in their own language (Haddouti, 1997; Go02). This is especially true in regions such as the European Community or Asia. Therefore a multilingual environment is needed to attend user requests to digital libraries.

The multilingual communication between users and the library can be realized in two ways:

- The user query is translated to the several languages of existing documents and submitted to the library.
- The documents are indexed and the extracted terms are converted to a language-neutral thesaurus (called multilingual thesaurus). The same occurs with the query, and the correspondence between query terms and documents is obtained via the neutral thesaurus.

The first solution is the most widely used in the Cross-Language Information Retrieval (CLIR) community (Go02; Ogden & Davis, 2000; Oard, 1999). It applies also to other information retrieval environments, such as the World Wide Web. For digital libraries, with thousands of documents, indexing of incoming documents and a good association structure between index terms and documents can become crucial for efficient document retrieval.

In order to get an extensive and precise retrieval of textual information, a correct and consistent analysis of incoming documents is necessary. The most broadly used technique for this analysis is indexing. An index file becomes an intermediate representation between a query and the document base.

One of the most popular structures for complex indexes is a semantic net of lexical terms of a language, called thesaurus. The nodes are single or composed terms, and the links are pre-defined semantic relationships between these terms, such as synonyms, hyponyms and metonyms.

Despite that the importance of multilingual thesauri has been recognized (Go02), nearly all research effort in Cross-Lingual Information Retrieval has been done on the query side and not on the indexing of incoming documents (Ogden & Davis, 2000; Oard, 1999; Haddouti, 1997).

Indexing in a multilingual environment can be divided in three steps:

1. language-dependent canonical term extraction (including stop-word elimination, stemming, word-sense disambiguation);
2. language-neutral term finding; and
3. update of the term-document association lattice.

Bruandet (1989) has developed an automatic indexing technique for electronic documents, which was extended by Gammoudi (1993) to optimal thesaurus generation for a given set of documents. The nodes of the thesaurus are bipartite rectangles where the left side contains a set of terms and the right side the set of documents indexed by the terms. Higher rectangles in the thesaurus contain broader term sets and fewer documents. One extension to this technique is the algorithm of Pinto (1997), which permits an incremental addition of index terms of new incoming documents, updating the thesaurus.

We show in this chapter how this extended version of Gammoudi's technique can be used in an environment with multilingual documents and queries whose language need not be the same as that of the searched documents. The main idea is to use monolingual dictionaries in order to, with the user's help, eliminate ambiguities, and associate to each unambiguous term an abstract, language-independent term. The terms of a query are also converted to abstract terms in order to find the corresponding documents.

Next we introduce the mathematical background needed to understand the technique, whereas the following section introduces our multilingual rectangular thesaurus. Then, the chapter shows the procedure of term extraction from documents, finding the abstract concept and the term-document association and inclusion of the new rectangle in the existing rectangular thesaurus. We then show the query and retrieval environment and, finally, discuss some related work and conclude the chapter.

RECTANGULAR THESAURUS: BASIC CONCEPTS

The main structure used for the indexing of documents is the *binary relation*. A binary relation can be decomposed in a minimal set of optimal rectangles by the method of *Rectangular Decomposition of a Binary Relation* (Gammoudi, 1993; Belkhiter, Bourhfir, Gammoudi, Jaoua, Le Thanh & Reguig, 1994). The extraction of rectangles from a finite binary relation has been extensively studied in the context of Lattice Theory and has proven to be very useful in many computer science applications.

A rectangle of a binary relation R is a pair of sets (A, B) such that $A \times B \subseteq R$. More precisely:

Definition 1: Rectangle

Let R be a binary relation defined from E to F. A rectangle of R is a pair of sets (A,B) such that $A \subseteq E$, $B \subseteq F$ and $A \times B \subseteq R$. A is the domain of the rectangle where B is the co-domain.

A rectangle (A,B) of a relation R is **maximal** if, for each rectangle (A',B'):

$$A \times B \subseteq A' \times B' \subseteq R \rightarrow A = A' \text{ e } B = B'.$$

A binary relation can always be represented by sets of rectangles, but this representation is not unique. In order to gain storage space, the following coefficient is important for the selection of an optimal set of rectangles representing the relation.

Definition 2: Gain in Storage Space

The **gain** in storage space of a rectangle $RE=(A,B)$ is given by:

$$g(RE)= [Card(A) \times Card(B)] - [Card(A) + Card(B)]$$

where Card(A) is the cardinality of the set A.

The gain becomes significant if Card(A) > 2 and Card(B) > 2, then g(RE) > 0 and grows with Card(A) and Card(B). On the other hand, there is no gain (g(GE)<0) if Card(A) = 1 or Card(B) = 1. The notion of gain is very important because it allows us to save memory space, in particular when we need to store a large volume of terms.

Definition 3: Optimal Rectangle

A maximal rectangle containing an element (x, y) of a relation R is called **optimal** if it produces a maximal gain with respect to other maximal rectangles containing (x, y).

Figure 1(a) presents an example of a relation R, and Figures 1(b), 1(c) and 1(d) represent three maximal rectangles containing the element (y,3). The corresponding gains are 1, 0 e -1. Therefore, the optimal rectangle containing (y,3) of R is the rectangle of Figure 1(b).

Definition 4: Rectangular Graph

Let "≤≤ " be a relation defined over a set of rectangles of a binary relation *R*, as follows:

$\forall\ (A_1,B_1)$ *e* (A_2, B_2) *two rectangles of R:*
$(A_1,B_1) \leq\leq (A_2, B_2) \Leftrightarrow A_1 \subseteq A_2$ *and* $B_2 \subseteq B_1$

We call *(R, ≤≤)* a **Rectangular Graph**.
Note that "≤≤" defines a partial order over the set of rectangles.

Definition 5: Lattice

A partially ordered set *(R, <)* is called a **lattice** if each subset $X \subseteq R$ has a minimal upper bound and a maximal lower bound.

Proposition 1:

Let $R \subseteq E \times G$ be a binary relation. The set of optimal rectangles of *R*, ordered by "≤≤" *(R, ≤≤)*, is a lattice with a lower bound *(∅, G)* and an upper bound *(E, ∅)*.

Semantic Relations. Semantic relations are the basis for the transformation of a rectangular graph in a rectangular thesaurus. They connect the nodes of a rectangular

Figure 1. Finding the Optimal Rectangle

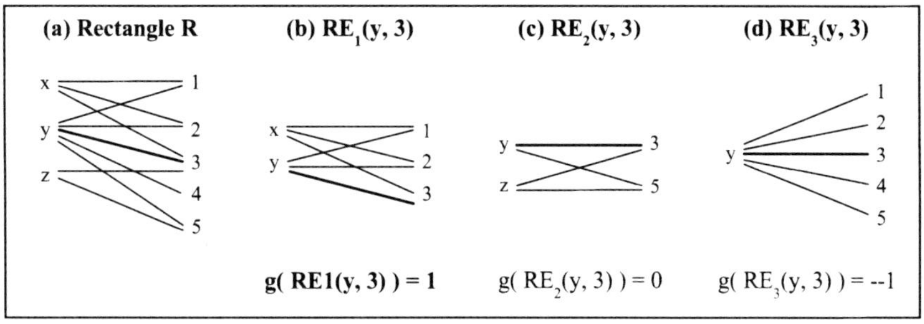

thesaurus in order to find more generic, more specific or other related rectangles. There are three kinds of semantic relations in a rectangular thesaurus: hierarchical relations (generic and specific), equivalence relations (synonyms and pseudo-synonyms) and neighborhood relations.

The hierarchical relations are based on the following definition:

Definition 6: Hierarchic Relation

Let $RE_i = (A_i, B_i)$ and $Re = (A_j, B_j)$ be two optimal rectangles of a relation R. RE_i is a **generic** of RE_j if:

$$(A_i, B_i) \leq\leq (A_j, B_j)$$

If the domains are terms and the co-domains are document identifiers, then A_i indexes more documents than A_j. The rectangles of interest in this chapter will all be of this format, i.e., relating terms to documents. Each term in a rectangle is the representative of an equivalence relation of synonyms. The (representative) terms in the rectangle are called pseudo-synonyms. Note that two terms are pseudo-synonyms if they index the same set of documents.

Non-hierarchic relations between rectangles occur when two rectangles have some information in common, but none of them is a generic of the other (Gammoudi, 1993).

Definition 8: Non-Hierarchic Relation

Let $RE_i = (A_i, B_i)$ and $RE_j = (A_j, B_j)$ be two optimal rectangles of R. RE_i is a **neighbor** RE_j if and only if the following conditions hold:

$$A_i \cap A_j \neq \emptyset \text{ or } B_i \cap B_j \neq \emptyset \text{ and}$$
$$(A_i, B_i) \not\leq\leq (A_j, B_j) \text{ and } (A_j, B_j) \not\leq\leq (A_i, B_i)$$

Figure 2 shows two neighbor rectangles.

The central structure, associating index terms to documents of a digital library, is a language-independent thesaurus of bipartite rectangles, containing the relation between sets of index terms and of sets of documents. Each term in a rectangle is the representative of an equivalence relation of synonyms. The terms in the rectangle are called pseudo-synonyms. Note that two terms are pseudo-synonyms if they index the same set of documents.

For a lattice of rectangles with the hierarchic relation $(A_1, B_1) \leq\leq (A_2, B_2)$, defined above, we consider a simplified representation, in order to save space. We eliminate the

Figure 2. Neighbor Rectangles

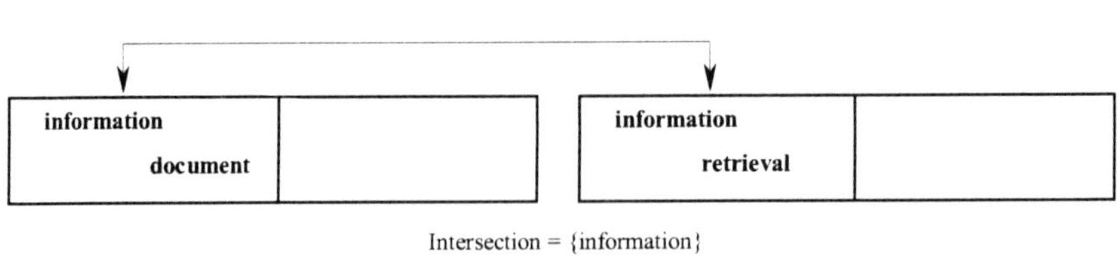

Figure 3. Example Lattice of Rectangles — Full and Simplified Version

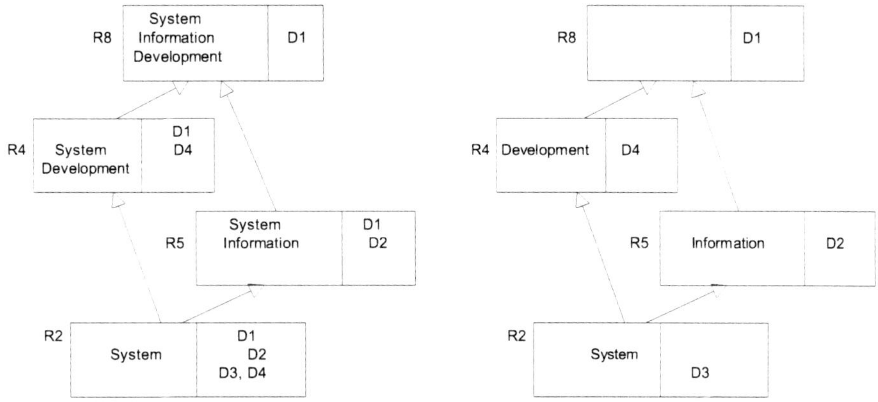

repetition of terms in the hierarchy. If $(A_1, B_1) \leq\leq (A_2, B_2)$, the rectangle (A_2, B_2) is represented by $(A_2\text{-}A_1 , B_1\text{-}B_2)$, without loss of information content.

Figure 3 illustrates a lattice of four rectangles, disrespecting language independence at this moment, in its full and its simplified versions.

Figure 4 shows a relation between synonyms and pseudo-synonyms. The terms *Information, Retrieval* and *Document* are pseudo-synonyms representing: *fact* and *data, search* and *query,* and *report, formulary* and *article,* respectively.

Finally we define a **Rectangular Thesaurus** as a graph where the nodes are optimal rectangles and the edges are the semantic relations defined above. With the hierarchic relation <<, the graph forms a lattice.

MULTILINGUAL RECTANGULAR THESAURUS

The idea of creating a language-independent conceptual thesaurus has been defined by Sosoaga (1991). The textual structure of specific languages is mapped to a conceptual thesaurus (see Figure 5).

One problem of this mapping is the elimination of multiple senses of terms. For instance, the term 'word' has 10 distinct meanings in the WordNet (Princeton University, n.d.) system. In general, each meaning occurs in a different context of using the word.

Figure 4. Example of Synonyms and Pseudo-Synonyms

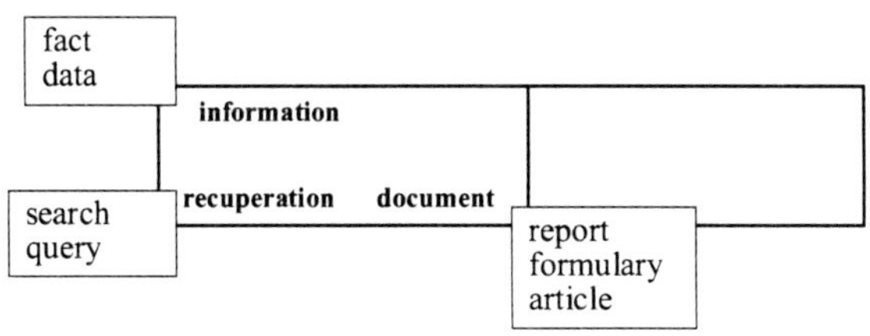

Figure 5. Multilingual Thesaurus

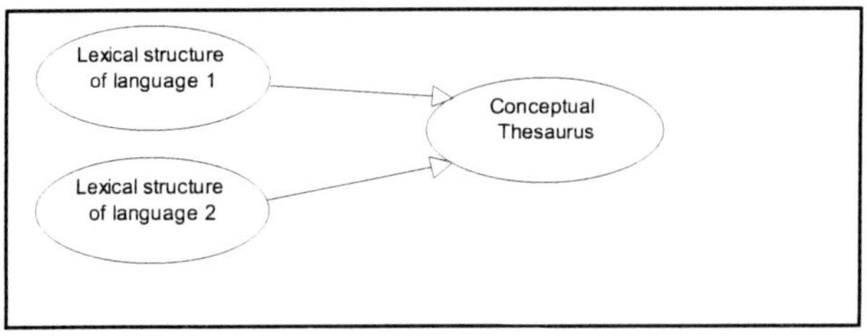

We extend the definition of multilingual thesaurus of Sosoaga to include a notion of contexts that permits the elimination of ambiguities.

A **multilingual thesaurus** is a classification system defined as:

$$MTh = (V, n, r; L_1, \ldots, L_n, C_1, \ldots, C_m, t_1, \ldots, t_{n*m})$$

composed of a unique set of abstract concepts (V), a set of lexicons $\{L_1, \ldots, L_n\}$, a set of contexts $\{C_1, \ldots, C_k\}$ a set of functions t_k: $L_i \times C_j \rightarrow V$ which associates to each term of the lexicon in a given context a unique abstract term. The hierarchic and non-hierarchic relationships are given by n (narrower term) and r (related term). Therefore, both n and r are subsets of $V \times V$.

A **rectangular multilingual thesaurus** is a rectangular thesaurus as defined in the previous section, where the terms at the left part of each rectangle are elements of the abstract concepts (V) of a multilingual thesaurus, and the right side are identifiers of documents.

Note that the way to obtain the rectangular multilingual thesaurus of a set of documents is: (1) indexing each document, (2) defining the correct meaning of each term and (3) finding the abstract concept applying the corresponding function *t*.

In order to construct rectangles with representative terms, we can decompose each function *t* in two parts, t_0 and t_1, with $t(x, c) = t_1(t_0(x, c))$. The function t_0 is responsible for the selection of the canonical representative for the synonyms in a given context, and t_1 is an injective function that determines the abstract term associated to the original term in a given language.

CONSTRUCTION AND MAINTENANCE OF A RECTANGULAR MULTILINGUAL THESAURUS

In a digital library each incoming document (which can be a full document, an abstract or an index card) must be indexed and integrated in the library. Instead of indexing documents one by one, we can consider many incoming documents to be inserted in the library.

Figure 6: Semi-Automatic Indexing

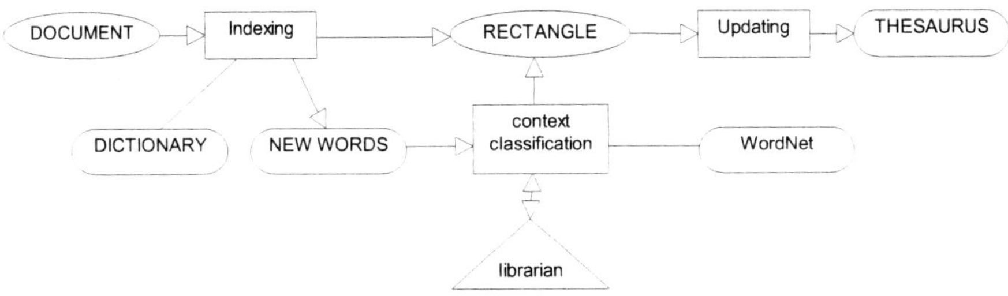

The construction of a Rectangular Multilingual Thesaurus is completed in three steps:

1. term extraction from one or more documents and determination of the abstract concept, using a monolingual dictionary (semi-automatic indexing);
2. generation of one or more optimal rectangles;
3. optimal insertion of the new rectangles in the existing abstract thesaurus.

Figure 6 shows the main modules of the system called SIM-System for Indexing of Multilingual Documents.

Indexing, Disambiguation and Abstraction

The construction of a rectangular thesaurus referencing a set of electronic documents in natural language begins with relevant term extraction contained in the document. Our semi-automatic method allows the user to eliminate ambiguities interactively. In the current version of the system, the format of an incoming document can be pure text (txt), Microsoft Word documents (doc) or html. Other formats must be converted to pure text.

The first step consists of words selection, stopword elimination and, for significant words, finding of the abstract term. As shown in Figure 7, two dictionaries are used for this step. First, the dictionary of term variations contains all lexical variations of words in a language and determines its normal form. Compound words, such as 'Data Base' or 'Operating System' must be considered as single terms, since in other languages they are written as single words (e.g., 'Datenbank' and 'Betriebssystem' in German) and should be associated to a single abstract term code. These are identified by a look-ahead step when the dictionary identifies a candidate compound word.

Having found the normal form of a term, the main dictionary is then used to find the abstract language-independent term, depending on the context.

In the main dictionary, the column "Representative" and the list of "Related Terms" will be used in the construction of the thesaurus in a given language for query formulation (see "Information Retrieval" section).

Updating the Rectangular Thesaurus

Each rectangle obtained in the previous step relates a set of terms to a set of documents. If we are processing a single document, one rectangle is generated with the

Figure 7. Dictionaries

Term	Compound Term	
Data	1	
Base		
Database		

Term	Category	Context	Concept	Represent.	Related
Data Base	noun	C. Science	10125	Database	
Data	noun	C.Science	10230	Information	
Data	noun	Ling.		Data	0
Date	noun	History		Age	
					0
					0

significant terms indexing that document. We must now insert the new rectangles in the existing abstract rectangular thesaurus.

Figure 8 shows the rectangular thesaurus for a document base, where the abstract terms of the domains of the rectangles has been exchanged by its representatives in English. Since it is in the simplified form, term redundancy has been eliminated.

Note that in a rectangular thesaurus, we can identify several cardinality levels, due to the cardinality of the rectangle domain. This level goes from 0 to n, where n is the total number terms of the thesaurus. Each new rectangle must be placed in the corresponding level. In the example, the second level has cardinality 5 and the third level has cardinality 12, since seven terms have been added to the level below.

The following algorithm, from Pinto (1997), provides the insertion of a new rectangle in an existing rectangular thesaurus. We consider the thesaurus in its original definition, without simplification. The simplification is straightforward.

Figure 8: Document Thesaurus

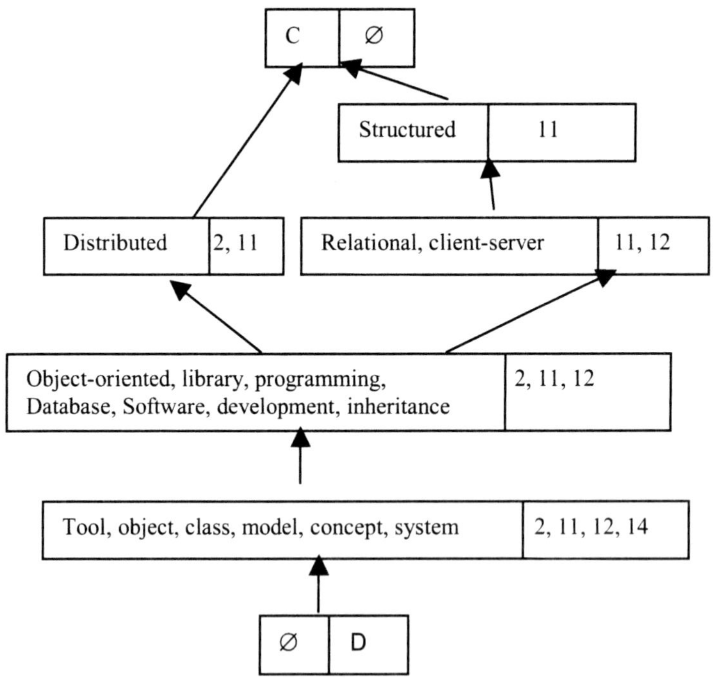

1. Check if the cardinality level of the new rectangle exists in the thesaurus
- *1.1. If it does not exist, create the new level for the rectangle*
- *1.2. else*
  - *1.2.1. If the domain of the new rectangle coincides with an existing rectangle, then add the new document to the co-domain of the existing rectangle else insert the new rectangle in the level*

2. If a new rectangle has been created, establish the hierarchic connections, searching for the higher level rectangles containing the new terms

3. New terms not occurring in the supremum, are inserted there

4. If the descendants of the new rectangle are empty, connect it to the infimum

INFORMATION RETRIEVAL

The purpose of an information retrieval system is to return to the user a set of documents that match the keywords expressed in a query. In our system we present an interface, using the user's preferred language, representing the thesaurus of concepts occurring in the document database. This thesaurus includes synonyms, related terms and hierarchic relations. Using pre-existing terms obtained from the documents in the library helps users to formulate a query in an adequate terminology, reducing significantly natural language interpretation problems.

The dictionary-like form of the interface guarantees fast access to the documents searched for. As it was reported by LYCOS, typical user queries are only two or three words long. Figure 9 shows the prototype's interface (Sodré, 1998) with terms defined in Portuguese.

In a rectangular thesaurus, the retrieval process consists of finding a rectangle $R_i = C_i \times D_i$, such that C_i is a minimal domain containing the set of terms from the query Q. If $C_i \neq Q$ the user can receive feedback from the system concerning other terms which

Figure 9. Query Interface

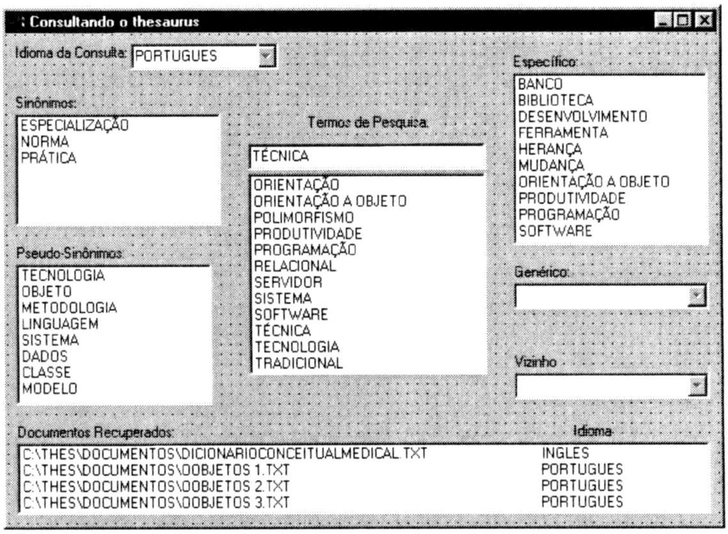

index the retrieved documents. This fact is identified as a Galois connection in Gammoudi (1993). Note that we can obtain several rectangles matching the query. On the other hand, the user can eliminate some terms from the query in order to obtain more documents.

As can be seen in the figure, the prototype allows one to choose a language and, as he/she is selecting the terms, the system lists the corresponding documents.

The prototype has been implemented in the Delphi Programming Environment and, in its first release, recognizes Word (.doc), html and text (.txt) documents.

RELATED WORK

The model HiMeD (Ribeiro-Neto, Laender & Lima, 2001; Lima, Laender & Ribeiro-Neto, 1998) deals with the indexing and retrieval of documents. It is specialized on medical documents and the indexing step is completely automatic. Since the domain is restricted, the occurrence of polysemic terms is not as frequent as for general digital libraries. As with language-neutral ontology of medical terms, they use the medical vocabulary MeSH (NLM, 2000) combined with a generic dictionary.

Gilarranz, Gonzalo and Verdejo (1997) proposed an approach of indexing documents using the information stored in the EuroWordNet database. From this database they take the language-neutral InterLingual Index. For the association of queries to documents, they use the well-known vectorial approach.

The MULINEX project (Erbach, Newmann & Uszkoreit, 1997) is a European Union effort to develop tools to allow cross-language text retrieval for the WWW, concept-based indexing, navigation tools and facilities for multilingual WWW sites. The project considers several alternatives for document treatment, such as translation of the documents, translation of index terms and queries, relevance feedback with translation.

CONCLUSION

Most work on thesaurus construction uses automatic indexing of a given set of documents (Bruandet, 1989; Gammoudi, 1993) and, in the case of a multilingual framework, uses machine translation techniques applied on the query (Yang, Carbonell, Brown & Frederking, 1998). In Pinto (1997) an incremental version of the approach on automatic generation of rectangular thesauri has been developed. The main contribution of this chapter is to integrate the incremental approach with a dictionary-based multilingual indexing and information retrieval, including an interactive ambiguity resolution. This approach eliminates problems of automatic indexing, linguistic variations of a single concept and restrictions of monolingual systems. Furthermore the problem of terms composed of more than one word has been solved with a look-ahead algorithm for candidate words found in the dictionary.

It is clear that the interaction with the user is very time consuming. But, it seems to be a good trade-off between the precision of manual thesaurus construction and the efficiency of automatic systems. With an 'apply to all' option, one can avoid repetition of the same conflict resolution.

Lexical databases, such as WordNet and the forthcoming EuroWordNet, can be useful to offer a semantic richer query interface using the hierarchic relations between terms. These hierarchies must also be included in the abstract conceptual thesaurus.

REFERENCES

Belkhiter, N., Bourhfir, C., Gammoudi, M.M., Jaoua, A., Le Thanh, N. & Reguig, M. (1994). Décomposition rectangulaire optimale d'une relation binaire: Aplication aux bases de données documentaires. *INFOR*, 32(1), 33-54.

Bruandet, M.-F. (1989). Outline of a knowledge-base model for an intelligent information retrieval system. *Information Processing & Management*, 25(1), 89-115.

Erbach, G., Neumann, G. & Uszkoreit, H. (1997). MULINEX multilingual indexing, navigation and editing extensions for the World Wide Web. *Proceedings of the Third DELOS Workshop—Cross-Language Information Retrieval and Proceedings*, Zurich, Switzerland.

Gammoudi, M.M. (1993). *Méthode de Décomposition Rectangulaire d'une Relation Binaire: Une Base Formelle et Uniforme pour la Génération Automatique des Thesaurus et la Recherche Documentaire*. Thése de Doctorat, Université de Nice - Sophia Antipolis Ecole Doctorale des Sciences pour L'Ingenieur.

Gilarranz, J., Gonzalo, J. & Verdejo, F. (1997). An approach to conceptual text retrieval using the EuroWordNet Multilingual Semantic Database. *Working Notes of the AAAI Symposium on Cross Language Text and Speech Retrieval.*

Haddouti, H. (1997). Survey: Multilingual text retrieval and access. *Working Notes of the AAAI Symposium on Cross Language Text and Speech Retrieval.*

Lima, L.R.S., Laender, A.F. & Ribeiro-Neto, B. (1998). A hierarchical approach to the automatic categorization of medical documents. *Proceedings of the 7th International Conference on Information Knowledge Management*, 132-138.

NLM. (2000). *Tree Structures & Alphabetic List—12th Edition.* National Library of Medicine.

Oard, D. (1999). Global access to multilingual information. *Keynote Address at the Fourth International Workshop on Information Retrieval with Asian Languages-IRAL99*, Taipei, Taiwan.

Ogden, W. & Davis, M. (2000). Improving cross-language text retrieval with human interaction. *Proceedings of the 33rd Hawaii International Conference on System Sciences*, Maui, Hawaii, USA.

Pinto, W.S. (1997). *Sistema de Recuperação de Informação com Navegação Através de Pseudo Thesaurus.* Master's Thesis, Universidade Federal do Maranhão.

Princeton University. (n.d.). *WordNet—A Lexical Database for the English Language.* Available online at: http://www.cogsci.princeton.edu/~wn/.

Ribeiro-Neto, B., Laender, A.F. & Lima, R.S. (2001). An experimental study in automatically categorizing medical documents. *Journal of the American Society for Information Science and Technology*, 391-401.

Sodré, I.M. (1998). *SISMULT—Sistema de Indexação Semiautomática Multilingüe.* Master's Thesis, Universidade Federal da Paraíba/COPIN, Campina Grande.

Sosoaga, C.L. (1991). Multilingual access to documentary databases. In Lichnerowicz, A. (Ed.), *Proceedings of the Conference on Intelligent Text and Image Handling (RIAO91)*, Amsterdam, April, 774-778.

Yang, Y., Carbonell, J., Brown, R. & Frederking, R. (1998). Translingual information retrieval: Learning from bilingual corpora. *Artificial Intelligence*, 103, 323-345.

Chapter IV

Managing Document Taxonomies in Relational Databases

Ido Millet
Penn State Erie, USA

ABSTRACT

This chapter addresses the challenge of applying relational database technologies to manage taxonomies, which are commonly used to classify documents, knowledge and websites into a hierarchy of topics. It first describes how denormalizing the data model can facilitate data retrieval from such topic hierarchies. It then shows how the typical data maintenance difficulties associated with denormalized data models can be solved using database triggers.

INTRODUCTION

The need to maintain classification and retrieval mechanisms that rely on concept hierarchies is as old as language itself. Familiar examples include the Dewey decimal classification system used in libraries and the system for classifying life forms developed in the 1700s by Carolus Linnaeus. A more recent example is Yahoo's subject taxonomy.

Information technology has led to an explosive growth in digital documents, records, multi-media files and websites. To facilitate end-user access to these resources, topic hierarchies are frequently maintained to allow intuitive navigation and searching for resources related to specific categories. This chapter deals with the challenges of using relational database technology to maintain and facilitate queries against such topic hierarchies.

In a chapter written for another book (Millet, 2001), I discuss the generic issue of managing hierarchies in relational databases. This chapter focuses on applying these techniques to the specific needs of managing document, website and knowledge management taxonomies. For example, this domain is complicated by the typical need to classify a single document or website under multiple topics.

Relational databases and the current SQL standard are poorly suited to retrieval of hierarchical data. After demonstrating the problem, this chapter describes how two approaches to data denormalization can facilitate hierarchical data retrieval. Both approaches solve the problem of data retrieval, but as expected, come at the cost of difficult and potentially inconsistent data updates. This chapter then describes how we can address these update-related shortcomings via database triggers. Using a combination of denormalized data structure and triggers, we can have the best of both worlds: easy data retrieval and simple, consistent data updates.

THE CHALLENGE

To demonstrate the data retrieval difficulties associated with topic hierarchies, consider a document database where each document is classified into a hierarchy of topics shown in Figure 1.

First, let us discuss how the topic hierarchy itself is stored in a relational database. Since each subtopic has at most one parent topic, we can implement this hierarchy via a recursive relationship. This means that each topic record maintains a foreign key pointing to the topic record above it. Figure 2 shows a data model for this situation. Note that the classify table allows us to assign a single document to multiple topics.

To demonstrate the difficulty of hierarchical data retrieval against the normalized data model in Figure 2, consider the following requests:

- Show a list of all Topics (at all levels) under Topic 1
- Show a list of all Documents (at all levels) under Topic 1
- Show how many Documents (at all levels) are classified under each Topic at Level 1 of the hierarchy

Figure 1. A Topic Hierarchy

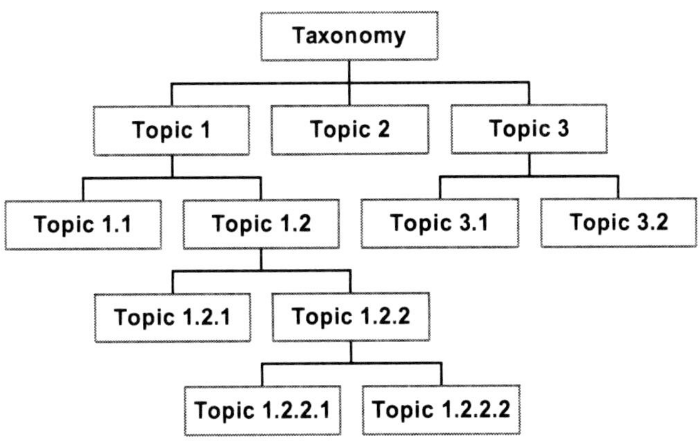

Figure 2. A Normalized Data Model with a Topic Hierarchy

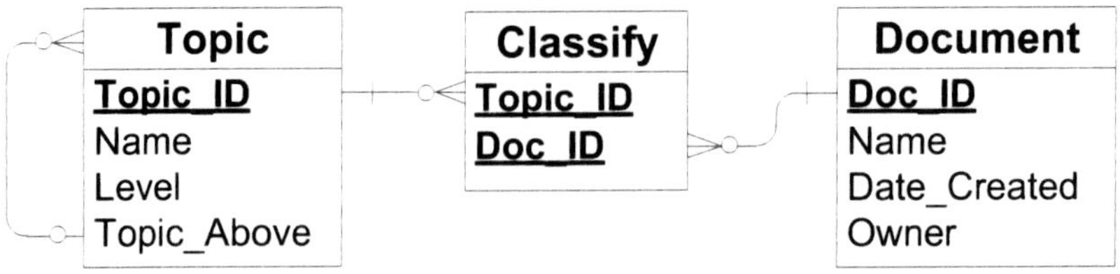

Using SQL, we can easily join each topic to all the documents associated with it via the classify records. However, we cannot easily identify the documents indirectly associated with a topic via its subtopics (at all levels). This is because for each topic we know only its immediate parent topic. This difficulty in locating parent or child nodes at any given level is at the heart of the problem.

SQL-BASED SOLUTIONS

While hierarchies pose a significant challenge, complex SQL can solve surprisingly tough problems. For example, the SQL statement in Listing 1 will return all topics under (and including) Topic 1.

Listing 1. Hierarchy Retrieval with UNION Statements

```
SELECT topic_id, name FROM TOPIC WHERE topic_id = 1
UNION ALL
SELECT topic_id, name FROM TOPIC WHERE topic_above = 1
UNION ALL
SELECT topic_id, name FROM TOPIC WHERE topic_above IN
  (SELECT topic_id FROM TOPIC WHERE topic_above = 1)
UNION ALL
SELECT topic_id, name FROM TOPIC WHERE topic_above IN
  (SELECT topic_id FROM TOPIC WHERE topic_above IN
    (SELECT topic_id FROM TOPIC WHERE topic_above = 1)) ;
```

The result set, shown in Table 1, can then be established as a view and joined with the classify and document tables to answer more complex queries. The main limitation of this approach is the complexity of the required SQL statement, the dependence on a known top node and the need to extend the statement to the maximum number of possible levels in the hierarchy.

The SQL:1999 standard (ANSI/ISO/IEC 9075-2-1999) removes the need to know how many levels the hierarchy may have by supporting recursive queries. For example, the request to show how many documents belong to each main topic, including all subtopics below it, can be handled using the SQL:1999 query shown in Listing 2.

This query starts by creating a table expression (TOPIC_PATHS) populated with all main topic records as parents of themselves and appends (UNION) records for all paths of length one from these nodes to the topics directly below them. The RECURSIVE

Table 1. Result Set Produced by the UNION Statement

Topic	Topic_Below
1	Topic 1
1.1	Topic 1.1
1.2	Topic 1.2
1.1.1	Topic 1.1.1
1.1.2	Topic 1.1.2
1.2.1	Topic 1.2.1
1.2.2	Topic 1.2.2
1.2.2.1	Topic 1.2.2.1
1.2.2.2	Topic 1.2.2.2

option continues the process to build all indirect paths from each topic to all its descendants.

Listing 2. Recursive Hierarchy Retrieval Using SQL:1999

```
WITH RECURSIVE TOPIC_PATHS (topic_above, topic_below, level) AS
(SELECT topic_id, topic_id, level FROM TOPIC
UNION ALL
SELECT TOPIC_PATHS.topic_above, TOPIC.topic_id, TOPIC_PATHS.level
FROM TOPIC_PATHS, TOPIC
WHERE TOPIC_PATHS.topic_below = TOPIC.topic_above)
SELECT TOPIC_PATHS.topic_above, DistinctCount (CLASSIFY.Doc_ID)
FROM TOPIC_PATHS, CLASSIFY
WHERE TOPIC_PATHS.topic_below = CLASSIFY.Topic_ID AND
TOPIC_PATHS.level = 1
GROUP BY TOPIC_PATHS.topic_above;
```

The query then joins the end points (Topic_Below) of all paths in the TOPIC_PATHS result set to the documents assigned to these topics. By limiting the start points of these paths to main topics (topics at Level 1) and grouping the end result by those topics, we get the requested information.

It is important to note that since each document may be assigned to multiple topics, we must guard against counting the same document multiple times. For example, if one of the documents has been assigned to both Topic 1.1 and Topic 1.2.2, we probably want to include it only once in the total count of documents classified under Topic 1. This is achieved by using *DistinctCount*(Classify.Doc_ID) rather than *Count*(Classify.Doc_ID).

Again, relying on such complex SQL is beyond the reach of many IT professionals and most end-user reporting tools. This issue can be addressed by implementing the complex portion of these SQL statements as database views. However, another limitation that cannot be addressed via views is that running such queries or views can be too slow in reporting applications with large hierarchies and frequent queries.

Celko (2000) reports on a technique leading to significant improvements in query speeds by storing the hierarchy data not as parent-child relationships but as "nested sets" using a somewhat complex numbering scheme. However, this chapter focuses on another approach that can achieve very significant query performance gains while maintaining intuitive data storage and SQL syntax.

The following section describes two data denormalization approaches that can support high performance data retrieval against topic hierarchies with simple and intuitive SQL queries. The first approach relies on a Path Table capturing all ancestor-descendant relations in the topic hierarchy. The second approach relies on maintaining the complete ancestry information in columns within each topic record. Though they simplify and accelerate data retrieval, both approaches carry the burden of redundant data and potential update anomalies. These limitations are addressed later in the chapter.

THE PATH TABLE APPROACH

The Path Table approach uses a "navigation bridge table" (Kimball et al., 1998) with records enumerating all paths starting from each node to all nodes in the branch above it, including itself. As demonstrated by Table 2, Topic 1.1.1 would require four records in the Path Table reflecting the paths up to itself, Topic 1.1, Topic 1 and Topic 0 (the top node of the hierarchy). These are just four of the 37 records required to capture all paths for the sample hierarchy in Figure 1.

To demonstrate how the Path Table can simplify data retrieval, consider the same challenge of showing how many documents belong to each main topic, including all subtopics below it. By joining the tables as shown in Figure 3, we can easily select all documents that belong under each Level-1 topic. Since the Path Table includes a zero-length path between each topic and itself, documents that belong directly to Level-1 topics would be included in the result set.

The relatively simple SQL statement in Listing 3 will return the requested information. Other requests for information can use the same approach or variations such as connecting to the Topic table via the Topic_ID column in the Path Table or adding path length and terminal node information to the Path Table (Kimbal et al., 1998).

Table 2. A Path Table for the Sample Hierarchy

Topic_ID	Topic_Above
1.1.1	1.1.1
1.1.1	1.1
1.1.1	1
1.1.1	0

Figure 3. A Path Table Connects Each Classification with all its Parents

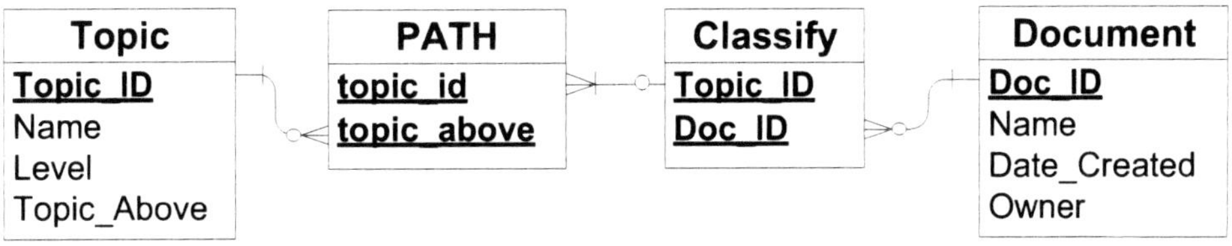

Listing 3. Retrieval via a Path Table

```
SELECT TOPIC.name, DistinctCount(CLASSIFY.Doc_ID)
FROM (TOPIC INNER JOIN PATH ON TOPIC.topic_id = PATH.topic_above)
   INNER JOIN CLASSIFY ON PATH.topic_id = CLASSIFY.topic_id
WHERE TOPIC.level = 1
GROUP BY TOPIC.name ;
```

One limitation of the Path Table approach is that the number of records in the Path Table can grow quite large for deep hierarchies. The following section describes another approach that avoids that problem.

THE DENORMALIZED TOPIC TABLE APPROACH

The denormalized topic table approach maintains information about all higher-level topics within each topic record. As demonstrated by Figure 4, if we assume that our topic hierarchy will not exceed six levels, then we need six more columns to maintain this information. Each node will be indicated as its own parent at its own level. For example, Topic 1.1.1 in Figure 1 would have '0' (the topic_id for the top node in the hierarchy) as

Figure 4. Using a Denormalized Topic Table

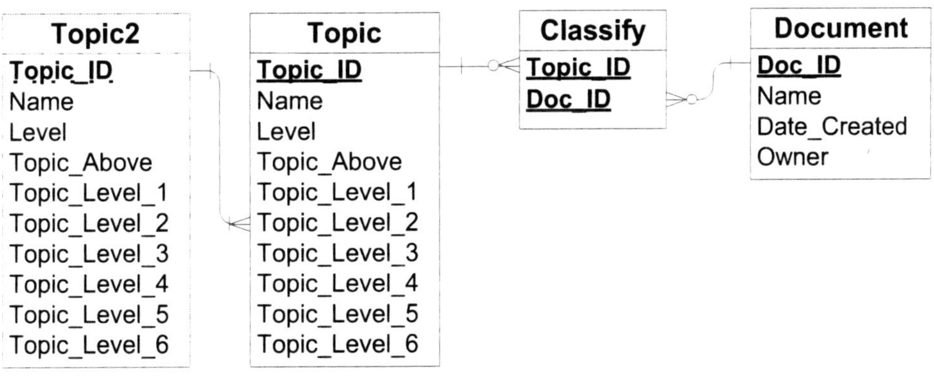

its Topic_Level_1, '1' as its Topic_Level_2, '1.1' as its Topic_Level_2, '1.1.1' (itself) as its Topic_Level_4, and null values for Topic_Level_5 and Topic_Level_6.

To demonstrate how the denormalized topic table can simplify data retrieval, consider again the challenge of showing how many documents belong to each main topic, including all subtopics below it. By joining the tables as shown in Figure 4, we can easily select and group all topics according to Topic_Level_2. Documents classified directly under that topic would be included in the result set because each topic is its own parent at its own level. Listing 4 shows that using this approach, a simple SQL statement can generate the requested information.

Listing 4. Retrieval via a Denormalized Topic Table

```
SELECT TOPIC2.Name, DistinctCount(CLASSIFY.Doc_ID)
FROM (TOPIC2 INNER JOIN TOPIC ON TOPIC2.topic_id =
    TOPIC.Topic_Level_2)
INNER JOIN CLASSIFY ON PATH.Topic_Level_2 = CLASSIFY.topic_id
GROUP BY topic.Topic_Level_2;
```

Note that in order to return the topic name, we resorted to adding an aliased (Topic2) copy of the topic table to the SQL statement.

COMPARING THE TWO APPROACHES

As demonstrated above, both the Path Table and the Denormalized Topic Table approaches facilitate data retrieval against topic hierarchies. However, both approaches achieve this at the cost of maintaining redundant data. The redundancy is caused by storing explicit path information from each node to all its ancestor nodes instead of just to its direct parent. While the Path approach is more flexible, the Denormalized Topic Table approach is simpler and easier to maintain.

The Path Table approach is more flexible since it does not impose a limit on the number of levels in the hierarchy. In contrast, the Denormalized Topic Table approach limits the number of levels in the hierarchy to the number of Topic_Level_N columns. However, in most application areas one can guard against exceeding the number of levels limitation by assigning several Topic_Level_N columns beyond the maximum expected for the application. For example, if our current taxonomy has five levels, we can design the topic table with eight Topic_Level_N columns. The chances of exceeding this safety margin are slim.

While the Path Table is more flexible, it requires slightly more complex SQL due to the addition of one more physical table and its associated joins. Another disadvantage of this approach is that for deep hierarchies, the size of the Path Table can grow quite large, degrading query performance.

The most important criterion for comparing the two approaches is probably the ease of maintaining the redundant data required by both methods. The following section discusses this issue.

MAINTENANCE OF DENORMALIZED HIERARCHY DATA

Asking users to maintain the redundant information required by either approach can be a career-limiting move. Users would resist the additional burden, and the chance of incomplete or inconsistent updates would pose significant data quality risk. This section suggests methods that can simplify and automate the maintenance of redundant hierarchy data. The proposed approach and the sample SQL code provide a concrete example of an "incremental evaluation system" for handling recursive SQL queries as advanced by previous literature (Libkin & Wong, 1997; Dong et al., 1999).

A key observation is that the redundant information maintained for each topic is a simple extension of the redundant information already maintained for its parent topic. Consider a situation where Topic 1.2.2.2 in Figure 5 is moved from under Topic 1.2.2 to under Topic 3.2. Let us review the procedural logic required for updating the records in the Path Table.

We can start by deleting all path records where Topic 1.2.2.2 is a subtopic (1.2.2.2→1.2.2, 1.2.2.2→1.2, 1.2.2.2→1, 1.2.2.2→0), except the path record of the topic to itself (1.2.2.2→1.2.2.2). We can then reconstruct the path records going up from Topic 1.2.2.2 by copying all path records going up from the new parent topic (3.2→3.2, 3.2→3, 3.2→0), and inserting those records to the Path Table after replacing the Topic_Below column in these records with the Topic_ID of the newly attached topic (1.2.2.2). After this procedure, Topic 1.2.2.2 would have the following path records (1.2.2.2 →1.2.2.2, 1.2.2.2 →3.2, 1.2.2.2 →3, 1.2.2.2→0), reflecting the correct state of the updated hierarchy, as shown in Figure 5.

While the shortcomings of "intelligent" primary keys are well known, we must recognize that topic taxonomies (such as the Dewey decimal classification system used in libraries) frequently use "intelligent" primary keys reflecting the position of each topic within the taxonomy. In cases where Topic_ID is indeed an "intelligent" rather than a "surrogate" key, we would obviously need to change the Topic_ID to reflect changes in location of topic nodes. In our example, we would neeed to change the primary key from

Figure 5. Moving Topic 10 from Parent 6 to Parent 4

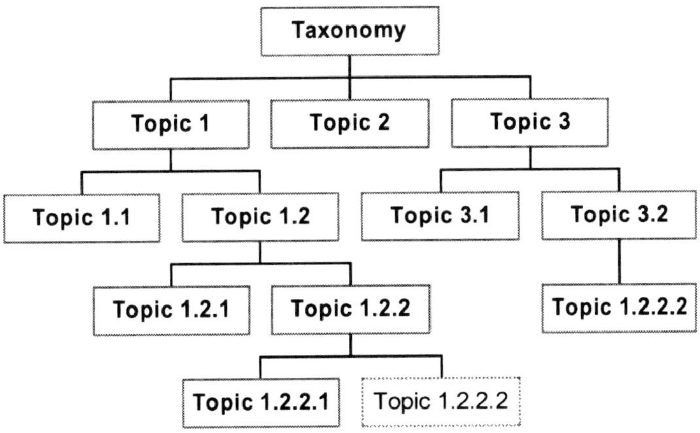

1.2.2.2 to 3.2.1. Using referential integrity to cascade such primary key updates to the foreign keys in the Path Table would take care of propagating such a change to all affected records.

Similar and even simpler logic applies to the same situation when using a denormalized topic table. In that case, the Topic_Level_N columns from the new parent node are first copied to the updated topic record (Topic 1.2.2.2). We then simply add the topic as its own parent at its own level. Because the denormalized topic table allows for simpler maintenance logic, the remainder of this chapter uses that approach as the assumed data structure.

Using this update logic, users would update the structure of the hierarchy by specifying only the Topic_Above information for each node. The level of the topic can always be established and updated automatically as the level of the parent node plus one. When inserting or updating a topic record to have a null Topic_Above, we can establish the node level as 1. In such cases the node is at the top of the hierarchy and is its own parent at Level 1. All other Topic_Level_N columns for such a top node would be automatically set to null.

The main remaining challenge is to handle situations where a whole branch (a topic with subtopics) is moved in the hierarchy. Consider, for example, moving Topic 1.2.2 in Figure 5 from under Topic 1.2 to under Topic 1.1. The procedural logic above would update the redundant data for Topic 1.2.2, but we now need to update the information for all its descendants. The most elegant solution is to recursively extend the procedural logic by applying it to all descendant nodes, as if their Topic_Above column was updated as well.

There is one more threat to our hierarchy data integrity that must be addressed by our procedural logic. When the user specifies Topic_Above information, we must guard against loops and self-references. In other words, the Topic_Above node cannot be a descendant of the current topic nor can it be the topic node itself. For example, given the hierarchy in Figure 5, the user should be blocked from changing the Topic Above of node 1.2 to 1.2.1 or 1.2. This test can be implemented by checking that none of the Topic_Level_N columns of the Topic_Above node is the current topic.

APPLYING THE PROCEDURE THROUGH FRONT-END LOGIC

This procedural logic can be implemented as a front-end function that gets called in application screens each time a user changes the Topic_Above column. The function accepts as arguments a Topic_ID and its new Topic_Above. After completing the logic for that topic, the function would use embedded SQL to identify the descendants of the topic and call itself recursively against all these descendants.

One limitation of using such front-end logic to maintain the redundant hierarchy data is that it would require multiple communications between the client and the server. A much more important limitation is that we are dependent on uniform and full compliance by all client applications. The integrity of the hierarchy data can be compromised if some screens or client applications neglect to call or implement the front-end logic appropriately.

APPLYING THE PROCEDURE THROUGH DATABASE TRIGGERS

Moving the procedural logic from front-end functions to back-end triggers removes the threat of multiple points of failure and achieves better performance. We need to implement an Update and Insert triggers on the Topic_Above column of the topic table. Assuming referential integrity takes care of blocking attempts to delete a topic record if a Topic_Above foreign key is pointing to it from another topic record, we do not need a Delete trigger.

Appendix A and Appendix B provide commented implementations of the Update and Insert triggers. These particular versions are designed for the Sybase *Adaptive Server Anywhere* DBMS. Since triggers are not supported uniformly by all DBMSs, the implementations may differ across DBMSs.

An example of DBMS-specific consideration in the implementation of these triggers is the issue of calling the trigger recursively by re-setting the Topic_Above code of the descendant nodes. *Adaptive Server Anywhere* would not fire an "After Update" trigger if the value in the column has not changed. Hence the "Before Update" declaration of the update trigger.

CONCLUSION

This chapter reviewed the data retrieval and data maintenance problems posed by topic hierarchies such as the ones used to classify and search for documents, websites and knowledge areas. Beyond the generic issues imposed by any hierarchy domains, there are two special needs imposed by such taxonomies. First, the need to support classifying the same document or website under multiple topic nodes leads to different SQL, but more importantly requires care in avoiding biased aggregate results due to double counting. Since topic taxonomies frequently utilize intelligent rather than surrogate primary keys, updates to the location of topic nodes require updates to the primary keys as well.

In most situations a good solution to fast and simple data retrieval against topic hierarchies is to maintain redundant information. The approach of denormalizing the topic table may be preferred over maintaining a separate Path Table because the Path Table can grow too large and requires more complex data maintenance logic.

The limitation of denormalized and redundant hierarchy information is that updates to the hierarchy require special processing logic in order to avoid update anomalies. This chapter describes techniques for selectively refreshing the hierarchy data by exploiting the redundant information already maintained for the specified parent topic as topic records are inserted or updated. The process can then be extended recursively for lower level nodes.

If the necessary trigger options are available for the DBMS in use, it is recommended that the processing logic for maintaining the redundant hierarchy information be implemented as triggers. This removes the burden of hierarchy maintenance from client applications. It also ensures that client applications cannot circumvent the hierarchy maintenance logic.

REFERENCES

ANSI/ISO/IEC 9075-2-1999. *ANSI's Electronic Standards Store.* Available online at: http://webstore.ansi.org.

Celko, J. (2000). Joe *Celko's SQL for Smarties: Advanced SQL Programming.* San Francisco, CA: Morgan Kaufmann.

Dong, G., Libkin, L., Su, J. & Wong, L. (1999). Maintaining the transitive closure of graphs in SQL. *International Journal of Information Technology,* 5, 46-78.

Kimball, R., Reeves, L., Ross, M. & Thornthwaite, W. (1998). *The Data Warehouse Lifecycle Toolkit: Expert Methods for Designing, Developing, and Deploying Data Warehouses.* New York: Wiley Computer Publishing.

Libkin, L. & Wong, L. (1997). Incremental recomputation of recursive queries with nested sets and aggregate functions. *Database Programming Languages.* Springer, 222-238.

Millet, I. (2001). Accommodating hierarchies in relational databases. In Becker, S. (Ed.), *Developing Complex Database Systems: Practices, Techniques, and Technologies.* Hershey, PA: Idea Group Publishing.

APPENDIX A

Update Trigger for Topic Hierarchy Maintenance

This trigger completely takes over the task of maintaining:

1. topic_level:
   - If topic_above is Null then topic_level = 1
   - Otherwise, topic_level = topic_level of parent + 1
2. Topic_Level_n:
   - If topic_above is Null then Topic_Level_1 is the topic itself and Parents_Level_n at all levels below are Null
   - Otherwise, the Parents at all levels are the parents of the topic above and the topic is its own parent at its own level.

This trigger fires just before the Topic_Above column in the topic table gets updated.

In order to cascade the updates down the hierarchy branch, this trigger also updates (resets) the Topic_Above of all the topic's children to their old values. This causes the trigger to fire in those children, and thus a recursive cascade of the update logic ripples down the hierarchy.

```
CREATE trigger Topic_Hierarchy before UPDATE of TOPIC_ABOVE order 3
on "DBA".TOPIC
referencing old as old_topic new as new_topic
for each row

BEGIN
    declare v_parent_level integer;
    declare v_p1 integer;
    declare v_p2 integer;
    declare v_p3 integer;
    declare v_p4 integer;
    declare v_p5 integer;
    declare v_p6 integer;
    declare err_illegal_parent exception for sqlstate value '99999';
    declare err_parent_is_child exception for sqlstate value '99998';

    // check that this is not a top node
    IF(new_topic.topic_above is not null) THEN

        BEGIN

        SELECT topic.topic_level, Topic_Level_1, Topic_Level_2,
            Topic_Level_3, Topic_Level_4, Topic_Level_5, Topic_Level_6 INTO
            v_parent_level, v_p1, v_p2, v_p3, v_p4, v_p5, v_p6 FROM "dba".topic
            WHERE topic.Topic_ID = new_topic.topic_above;
```

```
IF new_topic.Topic_ID = v_p1
    or new_topic.Topic_ID = v_p2
    or new_topic.Topic_ID = v_p3
    or new_topic.Topic_ID = v_p4
    or new_topic.Topic_ID = v_p5
    or new_topic.Topic_ID = v_p6 THEN
    // call the exception handling specified in the EXCEPTION block
    signal err_parent_is_child
END IF;

IF v_parent_level > 5 THEN
    // call the exception handling specified in the EXCEPTION block
    signal err_illegal_parent
END IF;

UPDATE "dba".topic SET
    topic.topic_level = v_parent_level + 1,
    topic.Topic_Level_1 = v_p1,
    topic.Topic_Level_2 = v_p2,
    topic.Topic_Level_3 = v_p3,
    topic.Topic_Level_4 = v_p4,
    topic.Topic_Level_5 = v_p5,
    topic.Topic_Level_6 = v_p6
    WHERE topic.Topic_ID = new_topic.Topic_ID;

    // We must use UPDATE rather than just set the values in new_topic
    // because this is BEFORE update and we need the recursive
    // children to have access to the updated property.

    CASE v_parent_level
    when 1 THEN
     UPDATE "dba".topic SET topic.Topic_Level_2 = new_topic.Topic_ID
       WHERE Topic_ID = old_topic.Topic_ID

    when 2 THEN
     UPDATE "dba".topic SET topic.Topic_Level_3 = new_topic.Topic_ID
       WHERE Topic_ID = old_topic.Topic_ID

    when 3 THEN
     UPDATE "dba".topic SET topic.Topic_Level_4 = new_topic.Topic_ID
       WHERE Topic_ID = old_topic.Topic_ID

    when 4 THEN
     UPDATE "dba".topic SET topic.Topic_Level_5 = new_topic.Topic_ID
       WHERE Topic_ID = old_topic.Topic_ID
```

```
        when 5 THEN
         UPDATE "dba".topic SET topic.Topic_Level_6 = new_topic.Topic_ID
           WHERE Topic_ID = old_topic.Topic_ID

        else
         signal err_illegal_parent
        ENDCASE;

        // Refresh topic_above of all children to cause recursion
            UPDATE "dba".topic SET
        topic.topic_above = new_topic.Topic_ID
        WHERE topic.topic_above = new_topic.Topic_ID;

    EXCEPTION
    When err_illegal_parent
        THEN
        message 'Parent Level Is Too Low (below 5)';
        // signal to the outside world to abort
        signal err_illegal_parent

    when err_parent_is_child
        THEN
        message 'This topic cannot be a child of its own child!';
        // signal to the outside world to abort
        signal err_parent_is_child

        when others THEN
        // for other exceptions not explicitly handled in the Exception block,
        // simply pass them up to the procedure that caused the Trigger
        resignal
        END
    ENDIF;
// NULL PARENT (top node handling)
IF (new_topic.topic_above is null) THEN
// For top node, set level to 1, parent at level 1 to itself and others to Null
    UPDATE "dba".topic SET
        topic.topic_level = 1,
        topic.Topic_Level_1 = new_topic.Topic_ID,
        topic.Topic_Level_2 = null,
        topic.Topic_Level_3 = null,
        topic.Topic_Level_4 = null,
        topic.Topic_Level_5 = null,
        topic.Topic_Level_6 = null
    WHERE topic.Topic_ID = new_topic.Topic_ID;
```

```
    // Refresh topic_above of all children to cause recursion.
    UPDATE "dba".topic SET
        topic.topic_above = new_topic.Topic_ID
        WHERE topic.topic_above = new_topic.Topic_ID ;
    END IF;
END
```

APPENDIX B

Insert Trigger for Topic Hierarchy Maintenance

This trigger is very similar to the Update trigger, except that there is no need for recursive calls since a newly inserted topic doesn't have descendant nodes. The other change is that instead of attempting to UPDATE the denormalized information, we just SET new values in the columns of the record that is about to be inserted.

```
Create trigger Insert_Into_Hierarchy before insert order 4 on "DBA".TOPIC
referencing new as new_topic
for each row
begin
    declare v_parent_level integer;
    declare v_p1 integer;
    declare v_p2 integer;
    declare v_p3 integer;
    declare v_p4 integer;
    declare v_p5 integer;
    declare v_p6 integer;
    declare err_illegal_parent exception for sqlstate value '99999';
    declare err_parent_is_child exception for sqlstate value '99998';

// Topic is not a Top Node
    if(new_topic.topic_above is not null) then
begin
        select topic.topic_level,Topic_Level_1,Topic_Level_2,
        Topic_Level_3,Topic_Level_4,Topic_Level_5,Topic_Level_6 into
        v_parent_level, v_p1,v_p2,v_p3,v_p4,v_p5,v_p6 from "dba".topic
        where topic.Topic_ID=new_topic.topic_above;

    IF new_topic.Topic_ID=v_p1
    or new_topic.Topic_ID=v_p2
    or new_topic.Topic_ID=v_p3
    or new_topic.Topic_ID=v_p4
    or new_topic.Topic_ID=v_p5
    or new_topic.Topic_ID=v_p6 then
```

```
    // call the exception handling specified in the EXCEPTION block
    signal err_parent_is_child
end if;

IF v_parent_level>5 then
    // call the exception handling specified in the EXCEPTION block
    signal err_illegal_parent
end if;

    set new_topic.topic_level=v_parent_level+1;
    set new_topic.Topic_Level_1=v_p1;
    set new_topic.Topic_Level_2=v_p2;
    set new_topic.Topic_Level_3=v_p3;
    set new_topic.Topic_Level_4=v_p4;
    set new_topic.Topic_Level_5=v_p5;
    set new_topic.Topic_Level_6=v_p6;

    case v_parent_level
    when 1 then set new_topic.Topic_Level_2=new_topic.Topic_ID
    when 2 then set new_topic.Topic_Level_3=new_topic.Topic_ID
    when 3 then set new_topic.Topic_Level_4=new_topic.Topic_ID
    when 4 then set new_topic.Topic_Level_5=new_topic.Topic_ID
    when 5 then set new_topic.Topic_Level_6=new_topic.Topic_ID
    else signal err_illegal_parent
    end case

exception
    when err_illegal_parent
    then
        message 'Parent Level Is Too Low (below 5)';
        signal err_illegal_parent

    when err_parent_is_child
    then
        message 'This topic cannot be a child of its own child!';
        signal err_parent_is_child

    when others then
        resignal
  end
end if;

IF(new_topic.topic_above is null) then
    // this is a top node: set Level to 1, parent at level 1 to itself and others to Null.
    set new_topic.topic_level=1;
    set new_topic.Topic_Level_1=new_topic.Topic_ID;
    set new_topic.Topic_Level_2=null;
```

```
    set new_topic.Topic_Level_3=null;
    set new_topic.Topic_Level_4=null;
    set new_topic.Topic_Level_5=null;
    set new_topic.Topic_Level_6=null
  end if

END
```

Chapter V

Building Signature-Trees on Path Signatures in Document Databases

Yangjun Chen*
University of Winnipeg, Canada

Gerald Huck
IPSI Institute, Germany

ABSTRACT

Java is a prevailing implementation platform for XML-based systems. Several high-quality in-memory implementations for the standardized XML-DOM API are available. However, persistency support has not been addressed. In this chapter, we discuss this problem and introduce PDOM (persistent DOM) to accommodate documents as permanent object sets. In addition, we propose a new indexing technique: path signatures to speed up the evaluation of path-oriented queries against document object sets, which is further enhanced by combining the technique of signature-trees with it to expedite scanning of signatures stored in a physical file.

INTRODUCTION

With the rapid advance of the Internet, management of structured documents such as XML documents has become more and more important (Suciu & Vossen, 2000; World Wide Web, 1998a; Marchiori, 1998). As a subset of SGML, XML is recommended by the W3C (World Wide Web Consortium) as a document description metalanguage to

* *The author is supported by NSERC 239074-01 (242523) (Natural Science and Engineering Council of Canada)*

exchange and manipulate data and documents on the WWW. It has been used to code various types of data in a wide range of application domains, including a Chemical Markup Language for exchanging data about molecules and the Open Financial Exchange for swapping financial data between banks, and between banks and customers (Bosak, 1997). Also, a growing number of legacy systems are adapted to output data in the form of XML documents.

In this chapter, we introduce a storage method for documents called *PDOM* (persistent DOM), implemented as a lightweight, transparent persistency memory layer, which does not require the burdensome design of a fixed schema. In addition, we propose a new indexing technique: *path signatures* to speed up the evaluation of path-oriented queries against document object sets, which are organized into a tree structure called *a signature-tree*. In this way, the scanning of a signature file is reduced to a binary tree search, which can be performed efficiently. To show the advantage of our method, the time complexity of searching a signature-tree is analyzed and the permanent storage of signature-trees is discussed in great detail.

BACKGROUND

The Document Object Model (DOM) is a platform- and language-neutral interface for XML. It provides a standard set of objects for representing XML data: a standard model of how these objects can be combined and a standard interface for accessing and manipulating them (Pixley 2000). There are half a dozen DOM implementations available for Java from several vendors such as IBM, Sun Microsystems and Oracle, but all these implementations are designed to work in main memory only. In recent years, efforts have been made to find an effective way to generate XML structures that are able to describe XML semantics in underlying relational databases (Chen & Huck, 2001; Florescu & Kossmann, 1999; Shanmugasundaram et al., 1999; Shanmugasundaram & Shekita, 2000; Yosjikawa et al., 2001). However, due to the substantial difference between the nested element structures of XML and the flat relational data, much redundancy is introduced, i.e., the XML data is either flattened into tuples containing many redundant elements, or has many disconnected elements. Therefore, it is significant to explore a way to accommodate XML documents, which is different from the relational theory. In addition, a variety of XML query languages have been proposed to provide a clue to manipulate XML documents (Abiteboul et al., 1996; Chamberlin et al., 2001; Christophides et al., 2000; Deutsch et al., 1989; Robie et al., 1998; Robie, Chamberlin & Florescu, 2000). Although the languages differ according to expressiveness, underlying formalism and data model, they share a common feature: *path-oriented queries*. Thus, finding efficient methods to do path matching is very important to evaluation of queries against huge volumes of XML documents.

SYSTEM ARCHITECTURE

The system architecture can be pictorially depicted as shown in Figure 1, which consists of three layers: persistent object manager, standard DOM API and specific PDOM API, and application support.

1. *Persistent Object Manager* — The PDOM mediates between in-memory DOM object hierarchies and their physical representation in binary random access files. The central component is the persistent object manager. It controls the life cycle of objects, serializes multi-threaded method invocations and synchronizes objects with their file representation. In addition, it contains two sub-components: a cache to improve performance and a commit control to mark recovery points in case of system crashes. These two components can be controlled by users through tuning parameters.
2. *Standard DOM API and Specific PDOM API* — The standard DOM API methods for object hierarchy manipulation are transparently mapped to physical file operations (read, write and update). The system aims at hiding the storage layer from an application programmer's view to the greatest possible extent. Thus, for most applications, it is sufficient to use only standard DOM methods. The only exception is document creation, which is deliberately left application-specific by the W3C DOM standard. The specific PDOM API allows an application to be aware of the PDOM to tune system parameters for the persistent object manager as well as its subsystems: cache and commit control. The specific API is mainly for the fine-grained control of the PDOM, not intended for the casual programmers. Rather, it is the place to experiment with ideas and proof concepts.
3. *Application Support* — This layer is composed of a set of functions which can be called by an application to read, write, update or retrieve a document. In addition, for a programmer with deep knowledge on PDOM, some functions are available to create a document, to commit an update operation and to compact a PDOM file, in which documents are stored as object hierarchies.

In the database (or PDOM pool), the DOM object hierarchies are stored as binary files while the index structures/path signatures are organized as a pat-tree.

Figure 1. Logical Architecture of the System

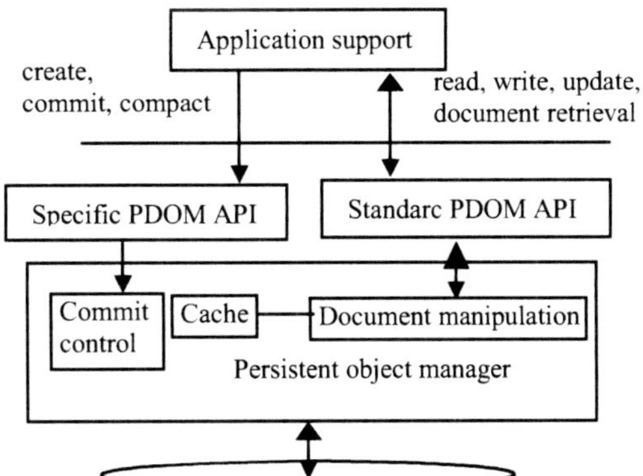

Figure 2. Binary File for Documents

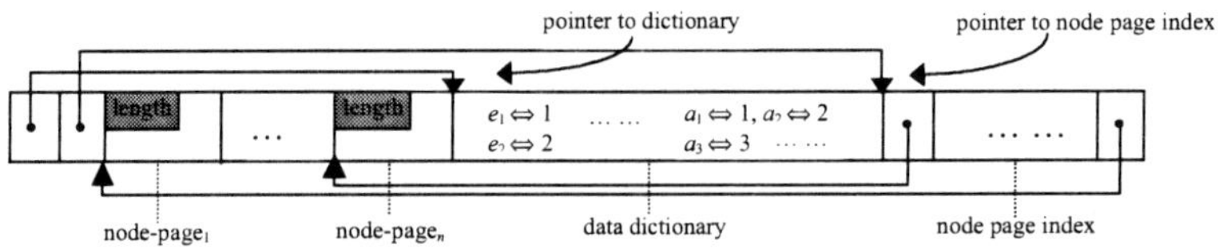

STORAGE OF DOCUMENTS AS BINARY FILES

The format of the PDOM binary files used to accommodate the object hierarchies is depicted in Figure 2.

It is organized in node pages, each containing 128 serialized DOM objects. In PDOM, each object (node) corresponds to a document identifier, an element name, an element value, a "Comment" or a "Processing Instruction." The attributes of an element are stored with the corresponding element name. These object (node) types are equivalent to the node types in XSL (World Wide Web Consortium, 1998b) data model. Thus, a page does not have a fixed length in bytes, but a fixed number of objects it holds. At the beginning of the file, there are two pointers. The first points to a dictionary containing two mappings, by which each element name e_i and attribute a_j are mapped to a different number, respectively; the numerical values are used for compact storage. The second points to the node page index (NPI). The NPI holds an array of pointers to the start of each node page.

Each object is serialized as follows:

1. A *typeflag* indicating the DOM-type: document identifier, element name, element value, "Comment" or "Processing Instruction."
2. The *object content* may be an integer representing an element name, a PCDATA (more or less comparable to a string) or a string (WTF-8 encoded) representing a "Comment" or a "Processing Instruction."
3. A *parent-element identifier* (if available).
4. A *set of attribute-value pairs*, where each attribute name is represented by an integer, which can be used to find the corresponding attribute name in the associated data dictionary. The attribute value is a WTF-8 encoded string.
5. The *number of sub-elements of an element and its sub-element identifiers.*

This serialization approach is self-describing, i.e., depending on the type flag, the serialization structure and the length of the remaining segments can be determined. The mapping between object identifiers in memory (OID) and their physical file location is given by the following equation:

$$OID = PI * 128 + i,$$

where PI is the index of the containing node page in the NPI and i is the object index within that page. Obviously, this address does not refer directly to any byte offset in the file

Figure 3. A Simple Document and its Storage

(a)

```
<letter filecode="9302">
    <date>January 27, 1993</date>
    <greeting>&salute; Jean Luc,</greeting>
    <body>
        <para>How are you doing?</para>
        <para>Isn't it
            <emph>about time</emph>
            you visit?
        </para>
    </body>
    <closing>See you soon,</closing>
    <sig>Genise</sig>
</letter>
```

(b)

byte number		
0:	500	pointer to the data dictionary
4:	565	pointer to the node page index
8:	0	first page number
9:	0	node type "document"
10:	1	number of children
11:	1	integer representing the child's id
12:	2	node type "element name"
13:	0	integer representing "letter"
14:	0	parent ID of this node
15:	1	number of attributes
16:	0	integer representing "filecode"
17:	"9302"	attribute value
22:	5	number of children
23:	2	ID of a child ("date" element)
...	...	...
		the following is the data dictionary
500:	7	number of element names
501:	letter	an element name "letter"
508:	date	an element name "date"
...	...	...
557	1	number of attribute names
...	...	...
565	8	

or page (which may change over time). Because of this, it can be used as unique, immutable object identifier within a single document. In the case of multiple documents, we associate each OID with a docID, to which it belongs. Example 1 helps for illustration.

Example 1

In Figure 3(a), we show a simple XML document. It will be stored in a binary file as shown in Figure 3(b).

From Figure 3(b), we can see that the first four bytes are used to store a pointer to the dictionary, in which an element name or an attribute name is mapped to an integer. (For example, the element name "letter" is mapped to "0," "date" is mapped to "1" and so on.) The second four bytes are a pointer to the node page index, which contains only one entry (four bytes) for this example, pointing to the beginning of the unique node page stored in this file. In this node page, each object (node) begins at a byte which shows the object type. In our implementation, five object types are considered. They are "document," "text" (used for an element value), "3," "4," respectively. The physical identifier of an object is implicitly implemented as the sequence number of the object appearing within a node page. For example, the physical identifier of the object with the type "document" is "0," the physical identifier of the object for "letter" is "1" and so on. The logic object identifier is calculated using the above simple equation when a node page is loaded into the main memory. Finally, we pay attention to the data dictionary structure. In the first line of the data dictionary, the number of the element names is stored, followed by the sequence of element names. Then, each element name is considered to be mapped implicitly to its sequence number in which it appears. The same method applies to the mapping for attribute names.

Beside the binary files for storing documents, another main data structure of the PDOM is the file for path signatures used to optimize the query evaluation. To speed up the scanning of the signatures, we organize them into a pat-tree, which reduces the time complexity by an order of magnitude or more. We discuss this technique in the next section in detail.

PATH-ORIENTED LANGUAGE AND PATH SIGNATURES

Now we discuss our indexing technique. To this end, we first outline the path-oriented query language in the following section, which is necessary for the subsequent discussion. Then, we will describe the concept of path signatures, discuss the combination of path signatures and pat-trees, as well as the corresponding algorithm implementation in great detail.

Path-Oriented Language

Several path-oriented languages such as XQL (Robie et al., 1998) and XML-QL (Deutsch et al., 1998) have been proposed to manipulate tree-like structures as well as attributes and cross-references of XML documents. XQL is a natural extension to the XSL pattern syntax, providing a concise, understandable notation for pointing to specific elements and for searching nodes with particular characteristics. On the other hand, XML-QL has operations specific to data manipulation such as joins and supports transformations of XML data. XML-QL offers tree-browsing and tree-transformation operators to extract parts of documents to build new documents. XQL separates transformation operation from the query language. To make a transformation, an XQL query is performed first, then the results of the XQL query are fed into XSL (World Wide Web Consortium, 1998b) to conduct transformation.

An XQL query is represented by a line command which connects element types using path operators (‘/’ or ‘//’). ‘/’ is the child operator which selects from immediate child nodes. ‘//’ is the descendant operator which selects from arbitrary descendant nodes. In addition, the symbol ‘@’ precedes attribute names. By using these notations, all paths of tree representation can be expressed by element types, attributes, ‘/’ and ‘@’. Exactly, a simple path can be described by the following Backus-Naur Form:

<simplepath>::=<PathOP><SimplePathUnit>|<PathOp><SimplePathUnit>‘@’<AttName>
<PathOp> ::= ‘/’ | ‘//’
<SimplePathUnit>::=<ElementType> | <ElementType><PathOp><SimplePathUnit>

The following is a simple path-oriented query:

/letter//body [para $contains$’visit’],

where /letter//body is a path and [para $contains$’visited’] is a predicate, enquiring whether element “para” contains a word ‘visited.’

Signature and Path Signature

To speed up the evaluation of the path-oriented queries, we store all the different paths in a separate file and associate each path with a set of pointers to the positions of

Figure 4. Illustration for Path File

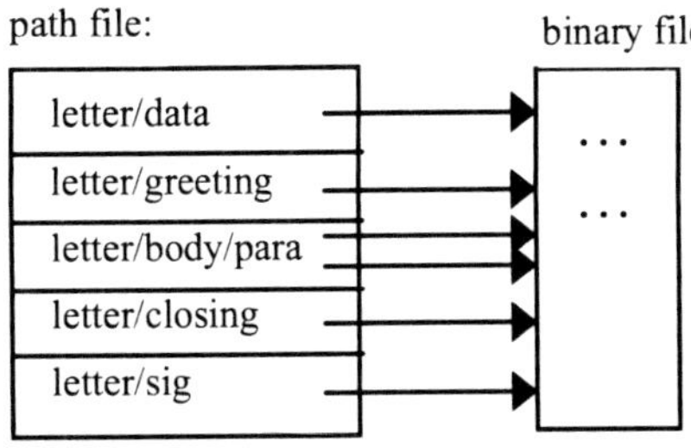

the binary file for the documents, where the element value can be reached along the path (see Figure 4 for illustration).

This method can be improved greatly by associating each path with a so-called path signature used to locate a path quickly. In addition, all the path signatures can be organized into a pat-tree, leading to a further improvement of performance.

Signature files are based on the inexact filter. They provide a quick test, which discards many of the nonqualifying values. But the qualifying values definitely pass the test, although some values which actually do not satisfy the search requirement may also pass it accidentally. Such values are called "false hits" or "false drops." The signature of a value is a hash-coded bit string of length *k* with *m* bit set to one, stored in the "signature file" (Faloutsos, 1985, 1992). The signature of an element containing some values is formed by superimposing the signatures of these values. The following figure depicts the signature generation and comparison process of an element containing three values, say "SGML," "database" and "information."

When a query arrives, the element signatures (stored in a signature file) are scanned and many nonqualifying elements are discarded. The rest are either checked (so that the "false drops" are discarded) or they are returned to the user as they are. Concretely, a query specifying certain values to be searched for will be transformed into a query signature s_q in the same way as for the elements stored in the database. The query signature is then compared to every element signature in the signature file. Three possible outcomes of the comparison are exemplified in Figure 3:

1. the element matches the query; that is, for every bit set to 1 in s_q, the corresponding bit in the element signature s is also set (i.e., $s \wedge s_q = s_q$) and the element really contains the query word;

Figure 5. Signature Generation and Comparison

text: ... SGML ... databases ... information ...

representative word signature:		queries:	query signatures:	matchin results:
SGML	010 000 100 110	SGML	010 000 100 110	match with OS
database	100 010 010 100	XML	011 000 100 100	no match with OS
information	∨ 010 100 011 000	informatik	110 100 100 000	false drop
object signature (OS)	110 110 111 110			

2. the element doesn't match the query (i.e., $s \wedge s_q \neq s_q$); and
3. the signature comparison indicates a match but the element in fact does not match the search criteria (false drop). In order to eliminate false drops, the elements must be examined after the element signature signifies a successful match.

The purpose of using a signature file is to screen out most of the nonqualifying elements. A signature failing to match the query signature guarantees that the corresponding element can be ignored. Therefore, unnecessary element accesses are prevented. Signature files have a much lower storage overhead and a simple file structure than inverted indexes.

The above filtering idea can be used to support the path-oriented queries by establishing path signatures in a similar way. First, we define the concept of tag trees.

Definition 1 (*tag trees*): Let d denote a document. A tag tree for d, denoted T_d, is a tree, where there is a node for each tag appearing in d and an edge ($node_a$, $node_b$) if $node_b$ represents a direct sub-element of $node_a$.

Based on the concept of tag trees, we can define path signatures as follows.

Definition 2 (*path signature*): Let $root \rightarrow n_1 \rightarrow \ldots \rightarrow n_m$ be a path in a tag tree. Let s_{root}, s_i ($i = 1, \ldots, m$) be the signatures for $root$ and n_i ($i = 1, \ldots, m$), respectively.

The path signature of n_m is defined to be $Ps_m = s_{root} \vee s_1 \vee \ldots \vee s_m$.

Example 1

Consider the tree for the document shown in Figure 3(a). Removing all the leave nodes from it (a leaf always represents the text of an element), we will obtain the tag tree for the document shown in Figure 3(a). If the signatures assigned to 'letter,' 'body' and 'pare' are s_{letter} = 011 001 000 101, s_{body} = 001 000 101 110 and s_{para} = 010 001 011 100, respectively, then the path signature for 'para' is $Ps_{para} = s_{letter} \vee s_{body} \vee s_{para}$ = 011001111111.

According to the concept of the path signatures, we can evaluate a path-oriented query as follows:

1. Assign each element name appearing in the path of the query a signature using the same hash function as for those stored in the path signature file.
2. Superimpose all these signatures to form a path signature of the query.
3. Scan the path signature file to find the matching signatures.
4. For each matching signature, check the associated path. If the path really matches, the corresponding page of the binary file will be accessed to check whether the query predicate is satisfied.

Compared to the path file, the path signature file has the following advantages:

i) If the paths (instead of the path signatures) are stored in a separate file, the path matching is more time-consuming than the path signatures. In the worst-case, O(n) time is required for a path matching, where n represents the length of the path (or the number of element names involved in a path). Assume that the average length of element names is w and each letter is stored as a bit string of length l. The time complexity of a path matching is then $O(w \cdot l \cdot n)$. But for a path signature matching, only O(F) time is required, where F is the length of a path signature. In the terms of Christodoulakis and Faloutsos (1984), F is on the order of O($m \cdot n / ln2$), where m represents the number of 1s in a path signature (bit string). (Here, we regard each path as a "block" (Christodoulakis & Faloutsos, 1984), which is a set of words whose signatures will be superimposed together. Thus, the size of a block is the length of a path.) In general, $w \cdot l \geq m/ln2$. Therefore, some time can be saved using the path signatures instead of the paths themselves.

ii) We can organize all the path signatures into a pat-tree. In this way, the scanning of the path signatures can be expedited tremendously.

SIGNATURE-TREES ON PATH SIGNATURES

If a path signature file is large, the amount of time elapsed for scanning it becomes significant. Especially, the binary searching technique cannot be used to speed-up the searching of such a file since path signatures work only as an inexact filter. As a counter example, consider the following simple binary tree, which is constructed for a path signature file containing only three signatures (see Figure 6).

Assume that s = 000010010100 is a signature to be searched. Since $s_1 > s$, the search will go left to s_2. But s_2 does not match s. Then, the binary search will return a 'nil' to indicate that s cannot be found. However, in terms of the definition of the inexact matching, s_3 matches s. For this reason, we try another tree structure, the so-called *signature* index over path signatures, and change its search strategy in such a way that the behavior of signatures can be modeled. In the following, we first describe how to build a signature-tree. Then, we discuss how to establish an index for path signatures using signature-trees. Finally, we discuss how to search a signature-tree.

Definition of Signature-Trees

A signature-tree works for a signature file is just like a *trie* (Knuth, 1973; Morrison, 1968) for a text. But in a signature-tree, each path is a signature identifier which is not a continuous piece of bits, which is quite different from a trie in which each path corresponds to a continuous piece of bits.

Consider a signature s_i of length m. We denote it as $s_i = s_i[1]\, s_i[2] \ldots s_i[m]$, where each $s_i[j] \in \{0, 1\}$ ($j = 1, \ldots, m$). We also use $s_i(j_1, \ldots, j_h)$ to denote a sequence of pairs w.r.t. s_i: $(j_1, s_i[j_1])(j_2, s_i[j_2]) \ldots (j_h, s_i[j_h])$, where $1 \leq j_k \leq m$ for $k \in \{1, \ldots, h\}$.

Definition 3 (*signature identifier*): Let $S = s_1.s_2 \ldots .s_n$ denote a signature file. Consider s_i ($1 \leq i \leq n$). If there exists a sequence: $j_1, \ldots, j_h$ such that for any $k \neq i$ ($1 \leq k \leq n$) we

Figure 6. A Counter Example

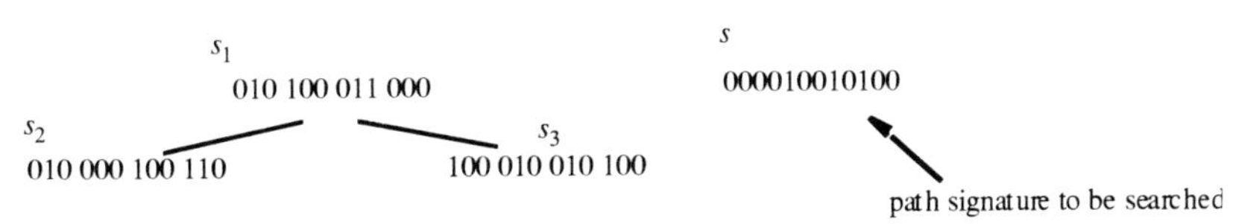

have $s_i(j_1, ..., j_h) \neq s_k(j_1, ..., j_h)$, then we say $s_i(j_1, ..., j_h)$ identifies the signature s_i or say $s_i(j_1, ..., j_h)$ is an identifier of s_i w.r.t. S.

For example, in Figure 6(a), $s_6(1, 7, 4, 5) = (1, 0)(7, 1)(4, 1)(5, 1)$ is an identifier of s_6 since for any $i \neq 6$ we have $s_i(1, 7, 4, 5) \neq s_6(1, 7, 4, 5)$. (For instance, $s_1(1, 7, 4, 5) = (1, 0)(7, 0)(4, 0)(5, 0) \neq s_6(1, 7, 4, 5)$, $s_2(1, 7, 4, 5) = (1, 1)(7, 0)(4, 0)(5, 1) \neq s_6(1, 7, 4, 5)$ and so on. Similarly, $s_1(1, 7) = (1, 0)(7, 0)$ is an identifier for s_1 since for any $i \neq 1$ we have $s_i(1, 7) \neq s_1(1, 7)$.)

In the following, we'll see that in a signature-tree each path corresponds to a signature identifier.

Definition 4 (*signature-tree*): A signature-tree for a signature file $S = s_1.s_2 \ldots .s_n$, where $s_i \neq s_j$ for $i \neq j$ and $|s_k| = m$ for $k = 1, ..., n$, is a binary tree T such that:

1. For each internal node of T, the left edge leaving it is always labeled with 0 and the right edge is always labeled with 1.
2. T has n leaves labeled 1, 2, ..., n, used as pointers to n different positions of s_1, s_2 ... and s_n in S.
3. Each internal node is associated with a number which tells how many bits to skip when searching.
4. Let $i_1, ..., i_h$ be the numbers associated with the nodes on a path from the root to a leaf labeled i (then, this leaf node is a pointer to the ith signature in S). Let $p_1, ..., p_h$ be the sequence of labels of edges on this path. Then, $(j_1, p_1) \ldots (j_h, p_h)$ makes up a signature identifier for s_i, $s_i(j_1, ..., j_h)$.

Example 2

In Figure 7(b), we show a signature-tree for the signature file shown in Figure 6(a). In this signature-tree, each edge is labeled with 0 or 1 and each leaf node is a pointer to a signature in the signature file. In addition, each internal node is marked with an integer (which is not necessarily positive) used to calculate how many bits to skip when searching. Consider the path going through the nodes marked 1, 7 and 4. If this path is searched for locating some signature s, then three bits of s: $s[1]$, $s[7]$ and $s[4]$ will be checked at that moment. If $s[4] = 1$, the search will go to the right child of the node marked "4." This child node is marked with 5 and then the 5th bit of s: $s[5]$ will be checked.

Figure 7. A Path Signature File and its Signature Tree

(a)

s_1.	011 001 000 101
s_2.	111 011 001 111
s_3.	111 101 010 111
s_4.	011 001 101 111
s_5.	011 101 110 101
s_6.	011 111 110 101
s_7.	011 001 111 111
s_8.	111 011 111 111

(b)

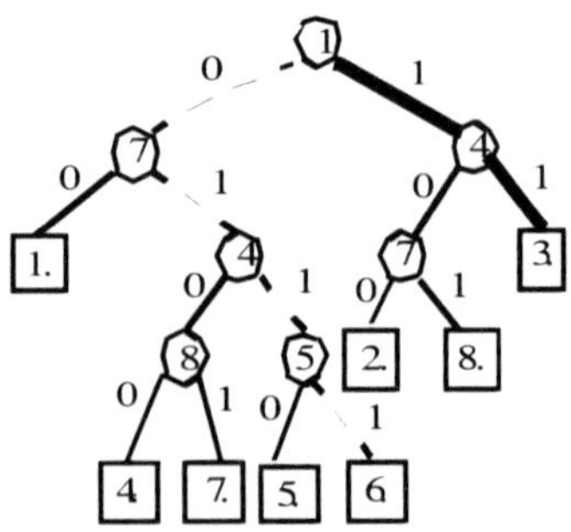

See the path consisting of the dashed edges in Figure 7(b), which corresponds to the identifier of s_6: $s_6(1, 7, 4, 5) = (1, 0)(7, 1)(4, 1)(5, 1)$. Similarly, the identifier of s_3 is $s_3(1, 4) = (1, 1)(4, 1)$ (see the path consisting of thick edges).

In the next subsection, we discuss how to construct a signature-tree for a signature file.

Construction of Signature-Trees

Below we give an algorithm to construct a signature-tree for a signature file, which needs only $O(N)$ time, where N represents the number of signatures in the signature file.

At the very beginning, the tree contains an initial node: a node containing a pointer to the first signature.

Then, we take the next signature to be inserted into the tree. Let s be the next signature we wish to enter. We traverse the tree from the root. Let v be the node encountered and assume that v is an internal node with $sk(v) = i$. Then, $s[i]$ will be checked. If $s[i] = 0$, we go left. Otherwise, we go right. If v is a leaf node, we compare s with the signature s_0 pointed by v. s cannot be the same as v since in S there is no signature which is identical to anyone else. But several bits of s can be determined, which agree with s_0. Assume that the first k bits of s agree with s_0; but s differs from s_0 in the $(k + 1)$th position, where s has the digit b and s_0 has $1 - b$. We construct a new node u with $sk(u) = k + 1$ and replace v with u. (Note that v will not be removed. By "replace," we mean that the position of v in the tree is occupied by u. v will become one of u's children.) If $b = 1$, we make v and the pointer to s be the left and right children of u, respectively. If $b = 0$, we make v and the pointer to s be respectively the right and left children of u.

The following is the formal description of the algorithm.

```
Algorithm sig-tree-generation(file)
begin
   construct a root node r with sk(r) = 1; /*where r corresponds to the first signature
                                            s_1 in the signature file*/
   for j = 2 to n do
       call insert(s_j);
end

Procedure insert(s)
begin
   stack ← root;
   while stack not empty do
       {v ← pop(stack);
        if v is not a leaf then
          {i ← sk(v);
            if s[i] = 1 then {let a be the right child of v; push(stack, a);}
            else {let a be the left child of v; push(stack, a);}
          }
        else     (*v is a leaf.*)
            {compare s with the signature s_0 pointed by p(v);
            assume that the first k bit of s agree with s_0;
```

```
10        but s differs from s_0 in the (k + 1)th position;
11        w ← v; replace v with a new node u with sk(u) = k + 1;
12        if s[k + 1] = 1 then
            make s and w be respectively the right and left
            children of u
13        else make s and w be the right and left children of u, respectively;}
14 }
end
```

In the procedure *insert*, *stack* is a stack structure used to control the tree traversal. We trace the above algorithm against the signature file shown in Figure 8.

In the following, we prove the correctness of the algorithm *sig-tree-generation*. To this end, it should be specified that each path from the root to a leaf node in a signature-tree corresponds to a signature identifier. We have the following proposition:

Proposition 1: Let T be a signature tree for a signature file S. Let $P = v_1.e_1 \ldots v_{g-1}.e_{g-1}.v_g$ be a path in T from the root to a leaf node for some signature s in S, *i.e.*, $p(v_g) = s$. Denote $j_i = sk(v_i)$ ($i = 1, \ldots, g - 1$). Then, $s(j_1, j_2, \ldots, j_{g-1}) = (j_1, b(e_1)) \ldots (j_{g-1}, b(e_{g-1}))$ constitutes an identifier for s.

Proof. Let $S = s_1.s_2 \ldots .s_n$ be a signature file and T a signature tree for it. Let $P = v_1e_1 \ldots v_{g-1}e_{g-1}v_g$ be a path from the root to a leaf node for s_i in T. Assume that there exists another signature s_t such that $s_t(j_1, j_2, \ldots, j_{g-1}) = s_i(j_1, j_2, \ldots, j_{g-1})$, where $j_i = sk(v_i)$ ($i = 1, \ldots, g - 1$). Without loss of generality, assume that $t > i$. Then, at the moment when s_t is inserted into T, two new nodes v and v' will be inserted as shown in Figure 9(a) or (b) (see lines 10-15 of the procedure *insert*). Here, v' is a pointer to s_t and v is associated with a number indicating the position where $p(v_t)$ and $p(v')$ differs.

It shows that the path for s_i should be $v_1.e_1 \ldots v_{g-1}.e.ve'.v_g$ or $v_1.e_1 \ldots v_{g-1}.e.ve''.v_g$, which contradicts the assumption. Therefore, there is not any other signature s_t with $s_t(j_1, j_2, \ldots, j_{n-1}) = (j_1, b(e_1)) \ldots (j_{n-1}, b(e_{n-1}))$. So $s_i(j_1, j_2, \ldots, j_{n-1})$ is an identifier of s_i.

The analysis of the time complexity of the algorithm is relatively simple. From the procedure *insert*, we see that there is only one loop to insert all signatures of a signature

Figure 8. Sample Trace of Signature Tree Generation

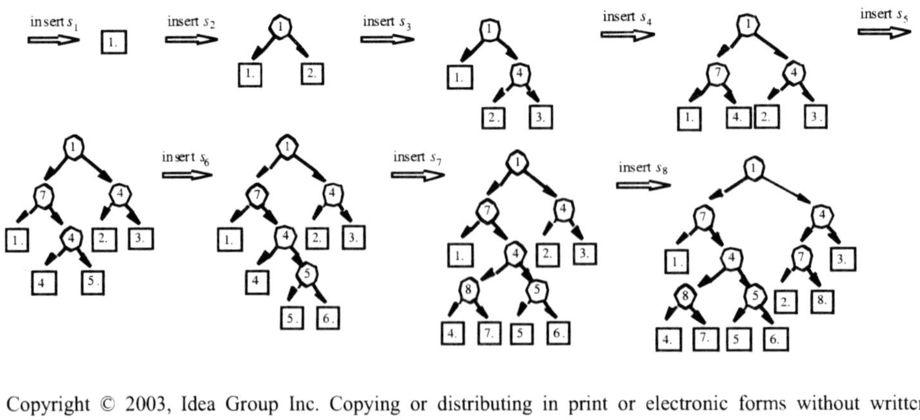

Figure 9. Inserting a Node 'v' into 'T'

file into a tree. At each step within the loop, only one path is searched, which needs at most O(m) time. (m represents the length of a signature.) Thus, we have the following proposition:

Proposition 2: The time complexity of the algorithm *sig-tree-generation* is bounded by O(N), where N represents the number of signatures in a signature file.
Proof. See the above analysis.

Searching of Signature-Trees

Now we discuss how to search a signature-tree to model the behavior of a signature file as a filter. Let s_q be a query signature. The i-th position of s_q is denoted as $s_q(i)$. During the traversal of a signature-tree, the inexact matching is defined as follows:

i) Let v be the node encountered and $s_q(i)$ be the position to be checked.
ii) If $s_q(i) = 1$, we move to the right child of v.
iii) If $s_q(i) = 0$, both the right and left child of v will be visited.

In fact, this definition corresponds to the signature matching criterion.

To implement this inexact matching strategy, we search the signature-tree in a depth-first manner and maintain a stack structure $stack_p$ to control the tree traversal.

Algorithm Signature-Tree-Search

input: a query signature s_q;
output: set of signatures which survive the checking;

1. $S \leftarrow \varnothing$.
2. Push the root of the signature-tree into $stack_p$.
3. If $stack_p$ is not empty, $v \leftarrow$ pop($stack_p$); else return(S).
4. If v is not a leaf node, $i \leftarrow sk(v)$.
5. If $s_q(i) = 0$, push c_r and c_l into $stack_p$; (where c_r and c_l are v's right and left child, respectively) otherwise, push only c_r into $stack_p$.
6. Compare s_q with the signature pointed by $p(v)$. /*$p(v)$ - pointer to the block signature*/
   If s_q matches, $S \leftarrow S \cup \{p(v)\}$.
7. Go to (3).

Figure 10. Signature Tree Search

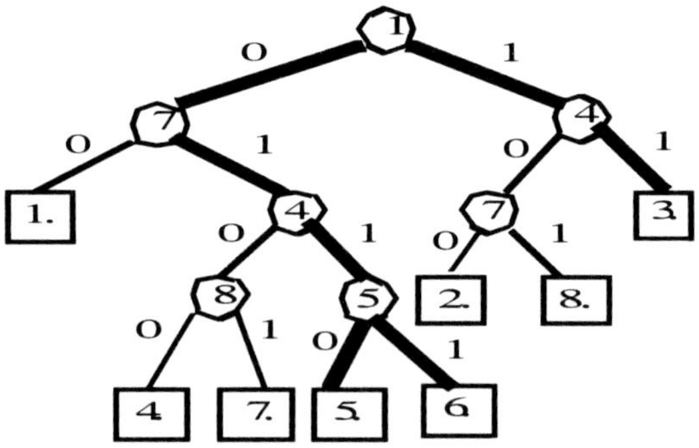

The following example helps to illustrate the main idea of the algorithm.

Example 3

Consider the signature file and the signature-tree shown in Figure 7(a) once again.

Assume s_q = 000 100 100 000. Then, only part of the signature-tree (marked with thick edges in Figure 10) will be searched. On reaching a leaf node, the signature pointed by the leaf node will be checked against s_q. Obviously, this process is much more efficient than a sequential searching since only three signatures need to be checked while a signature file scanning will check eight signatures. For a balanced signature-tree, the height of the tree is bounded by $O(\log_2 N)$, where N is the number of the leaf nodes. Then, the cost of searching a balanced signature-tree will be $O(\lambda \cdot \log_2 N)$ on average, where λ represents the number of paths traversed, which is equal to the number of signatures checked. Let t represent the number of bits which are set in s_q and checked during the search. Then, $\lambda = O(N/2^t)$. It is because each bit set to 1 will prohibit half of a subtree from being visited if it is checked during the search. Compared to the time complexity of the signature file scanning $O(N)$, it is a major benefit. We will discuss this issue in the next section in more detail.

Time Complexity

In this section, we compare the costs of signature file scanning and signature-tree searching. First, we show that a signature-tree is balanced on the average. Based on this, we analyze the cost of a signature-tree search.

Analysis of Signature-Trees

Let T_n be a family of signature-trees built from n signatures. Each signature is considered as a random bit string containing 0s and 1s. We assume that the probability of appearances of 0 and 1 in a string is equal to p and $q = 1 - p$, respectively. The occurrence of these two values in a bit string is independent of each other.

To study the average length of paths from the root to a leaf, we check the *external path length* L_n - the sum of the lengths of all paths from the root to all leaf nodes of a signature-tree in T_n. Note that in a signature-tree, the n signatures are split randomly into the left subtree and the right subtree of the root. Let X denote the number of signatures in the left subtree. Then, for $X = k$, we have the following recurrence:

$$L_n = \begin{cases} n + L_k + L_{n-k}, & \text{for } k \neq 0, n \\ \text{undefined}, & \text{for } k = 0, k = n \end{cases}$$

where L_k and L_{n-k} represent the external path length in the left and right subtrees of the root, respectively. Note that a signature-tree is never degenerate (i.e., $k = 0$ or $k = n$). So one-way branching on internal nodes never happens. The above formula is a little bit different from the formula established for the external path length of a binary tree:

$$B_n = n + B_k + B_{n-k}, \qquad \text{for all } k = 0, 1, 2, \ldots, n,$$

where B_k represents the sum of the lengths of all paths from the root to all leaf nodes of a binary tree having k leaf nodes.

According to Knuth (1973), the expectation of B_n is:

$$EB_0 = EB_1 = 0,$$

$$EB_n = \sum_{k=0}^{n} \binom{n}{k} p^k q^{n-k} (B_k + B_{n-k}), \qquad n > 1.$$

When $p = q = 0.5$, we have:

$$EB_n = \sum_{k=2}^{n} (-1)^k \binom{n}{k} \frac{k}{1 - 2^{1-k}}.$$

For large n the following holds:

$$EB_n = n\log_2 n + n\left[\frac{\gamma}{L} + \frac{1}{2} + \delta_1(\log_2 n)\right] - \frac{1}{2}L + \delta_2(\log_2 n),$$

where $L = \log_e 2$, $\gamma = 0.577\ldots$ is the *Euler* constant, $\delta_1(x)$ and $\delta_2(x)$ are two periodic functions with small amplitude and mean zero (see Knuth, 1973, for a detailed discussion).

In a similar way to Knuth (1973), we can obtain the following formulae:

$$EL_0 = EL_1 = 0,$$

$$EL_n = n(1 - p^n - q^n) + \sum_{k=0}^{n} \binom{n}{k} p^k q^{n-k} (B_k + B_{n-k}), \qquad n > 1.$$

When $p = q = 0.5$, we have:

$$EL_n = \sum_{k=2}^{n} (-1)^k \binom{n}{k} \frac{k2^{1-k}}{1-2^{1-k}} = EB_n - n + d_{n,1},$$

where $\delta_{n,1}$ represents the *Kronecker delta function* (Riordan, 1968) which is 1 if $n = 1$, 0 otherwise.

From the above analysis, we can see that for large n we have the following:

$$EL_n = O(n\log_2 n).$$

This shows that the average value of the external path length is asymptotically equal to $n\log_2 n$, which implies that a signature-tree is normally balanced.

Time for Searching a Signature-Tree

As shown in Example 4, using a balanced signature-tree, the cost of scanning a signature file can be reduced from $O(N)$ to $O(N/2^t)$, where t represents the number of some bits which are set in s_q and occasionally checked during the search. If $t = 1$, only half of the signatures will be checked. If $t = 2$, one-quarter of the signatures will be checked, and so on.

For a balanced signature-tree, the average height of the tree is $O(\log_2 N)$. During a search, if half of the s_q's bits checked are set to 1. Then, $t = O(\log_2 N)/2$. Accordingly, the cost of a signature file scanning can be reduced to $O(N/2^{(\log N)/2})$. If one-third of the s_q's bits checked are set to 1, the cost of a signature file scanning can be reduced to $O(N/2^{(\log N)/3})$.

Table 1 shows the calculation of this cost for different signature file sizes.

Figure 11 is the pictorial illustration of Table 1.

This shows that the searching of signature-trees outperforms the searching of signature files significantly.

SIGNATURE-TREE MAINTANENCE

In this section, we address how to maintain a signature-tree. First, we discuss the case that a signature-tree can entirely fit in main memory. Then, we discuss the case that a signature-tree cannot entirely fit in main memory.

Table 1. Cost Calculation

N	2000	4000	6000	8000	10000	12000
$N/2^{(\log N)/2}$	44.68	63.36	77.76	89.44	100.00	109.56
$N/2^{(\log N)/3}$	159.36	251.92	330.10	399.98	463.90	524.13

Figure 11. Time Complexity of Signature File Scanning and Signature Tree Searching

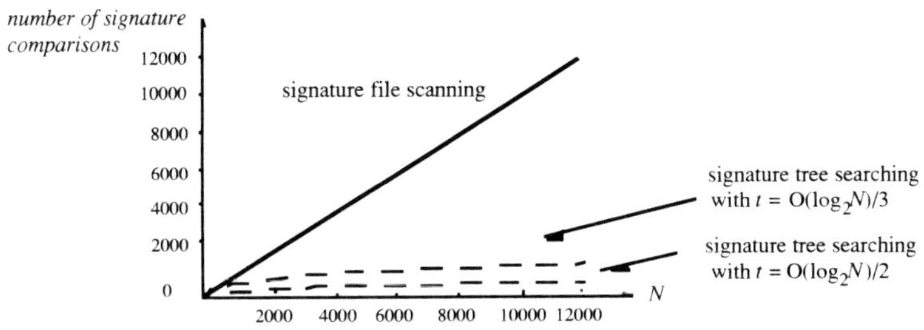

Maintenance of Internal Signature-Trees

An internal signature-tree refers to a tree that can fit entirely in main memory. In this case, insertion and deletion of a signature into a tree can be done quite easily as discussed below.

When a signature *s* is added to a signature file, the corresponding signature-tree can be changed by simply running the algorithm *insert*() once with *s* as the input. When a signature is removed from the signature file, we need to reconstruct the corresponding signature-tree as follows:

i) Let *z*, *u*, *v* and *w* be the nodes as shown in Figure 12(a) and assume that the *v* is a pointer to the signature to be removed.

ii) Remove *u* and *v*. Set the left pointer of *z* to *w*. (If *u* is the right child of *z*, set the right pointer of *z* to *w*.)

The resulting signature-tree is as shown in Figure 12(b).

From the above analysis, we see that the maintenance of an internal signature-tree is an easy task.

Maintenance of External Signature-Trees

In a database, files are normally very large. Therefore, we have to consider the situation where a signature-tree cannot fit entirely in main memory. We call such a tree an external signature-tree (or an external structure for the signature-tree). In this case, a signature-tree is stored in a series of pages organized into a tree structure as shown in Figure 13, in which each node corresponds to a page containing a binary tree.

Figure 12. Illustration for Deletion of a Signature

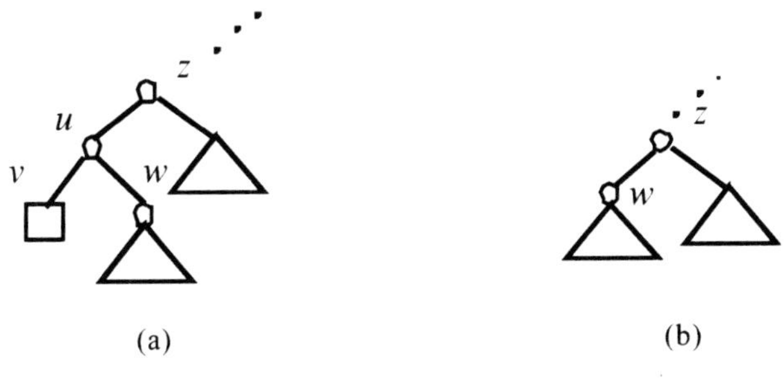

Figure 13. A Sample External Signature Tree

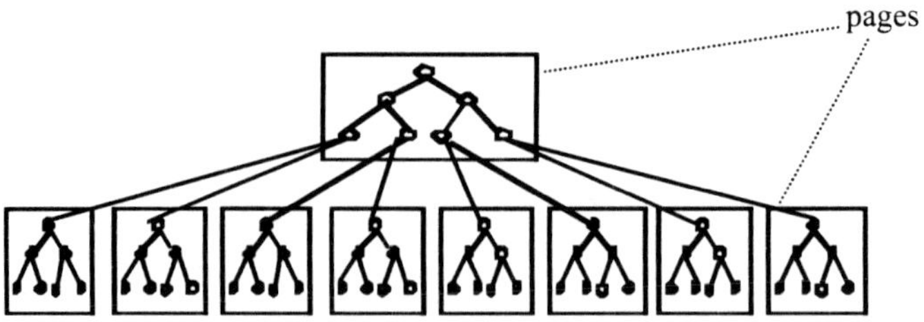

Formally, an external structure *ET* for a signature-tree *T* is defined as follows. (To avoid any confusion, we will, in the following, refer to the nodes in *ET* as the page nodes while the nodes in *T* as the binary nodes or simply the nodes.)

1. Each internal page node *n* of *ET* is of the form: $b_n(r_n, a_{n1}, ...,)$, where b_n represents a subtree of *T*, r_n is its root and $a_{n1}, ...,$ are its leaf nodes. Each internal node *u* of b_n is of the form: $<v(u), l(u), r(u)>$, where $v(u)$, $l(u)$ and $r(u)$ are the value, left link and right link of *u*, respectively. Each leaf node of b_n is of the form: $<v(), lp(), rp()>$, where $v()$ represents the value of , and $lp()$ and $rp()$ are two pointers to two pages containing the left and right subtrees of, respectively.
2. Let *m* be a child page node of *n*. Then, *m* is of the form: $b_m(r_m, a_{m1}, ...,)$, where b_m represents a binary tree, r_m is its root and $a_{m1}, ...,$ are its leaf nodes. If *m* is an internal page node, $a_{m1}, ...,$ will have the same structure as $a_{n1}, ...,$ described in (1). If *m* is a leaf node, each $= p(s)$, the position of some signature *s* in the signature file.
3. The size $|b|$ of the binary tree *b* (the number of nodes in *b*) within an internal page node of *ET* satisfies:

   $$|b| \le 2^k,$$

   where *k* is an integer.
4. The root page of *ET* contains at least a binary node and the left and right links associated with it.

If $2^k\text{-}1 \le |b| \le 2^k$ holds for each node in *ET*, it is said to be balanced; otherwise, it is unbalanced. However, according to the earlier analysis, an external signature-tree is normally balanced, i.e., $2^k\text{-}1 \le |b| \le 2^k$ holds for almost every page node in *ET*.

As with a B$^+$-tree, insertion and deletion of page nodes begin always from a leaf node. To maintain the tree balance, internal page nodes may split or merge during the process. In the following, we discuss these issues in great detail.

Insertion of Binary Nodes

Let *s* be a signature newly inserted into a signature file *S*. Accordingly, a node a_s will be inserted into the signature-tree *T* for *S* as a leaf node. In effect, it will be inserted into a leaf page node *m* of the external structure *ET* of *T*. It can be done by taking the binary tree within that page into main memory and then inserting the node into the tree. If for the binary tree *b* in *m* we have $|b| > 2^k$, the following node-splitting will be conducted.

1. Let $b_m(r_m, a_{m1}, ...,)$ be the binary tree within m. Let r_{m1} and r_{m2} be the left and right child node of r_m, respectively. Assume that $b_{m1}(r_{m1}, a_{m1}, ...,)$ $(i_j < i_m)$ is the subtree rooted at r_{m1} and $b_{m2}(r_{m1}, , ...,)$ is rooted at r_{m2}. We allocate a new page m' and put $b_{m2}(r_{m1}, , ...,)$ into m'. Afterwards, promote r_m into the parent page node n of m and remove $b_{m2}(r_{m1}, , ...,)$ from m.
2. If the size of the binary tree within n becomes larger than 2^k, split n as above. The node-splitting repeats along the path bottom-up until no splitting is needed.

Deletion of Binary Nodes

When a node is removed from a signature-tree, it is always removed from the leaf level as discussed in the above subsection. *Let a* be a leaf node to be removed from a signature-tree *T*. In effect, it will be removed from a leaf page node *m* of the external structure *ET* for *T*. Let *b* be the binary tree within *m*. If the size of *b* becomes smaller than 2^k-1, we may merge it with its left or right sibling as follows.

1. Let m' be the left (right) sibling of m. Let $b_m(r_m, a_{m1}, ...,)$ and $b_{m'}(r_{m'}, a_{m'1}, ...,)$ be two binary trees in m and m', respectively. If the size of $b_{m'}$ is smaller than 2^k-1, move $b_{m'}$ into m and afterwards eliminate m'. Let n be the parent page node of m and r be the parent node of r_m and $r_{m'}$. Move r into m and afterwards remove r from n.
2. If the size of the binary tree within n becomes smaller than 2^k-1, merge it with its left or right sibling if possible. This process repeats along the path bottom-up until the root of *ET* is reached or no merging operation can be done.

Note that it is not possible to redistribute the binary trees of *m* and any of its left and right siblings due to the properties of a signature-tree, which may leave an external signature-tree unbalanced. According to our analysis, however, it is not a normal case.

Finally, we point out that for an application where the signature files are not frequently changed, the internal page nodes of an *ET* can be implemented as a heap structure. In this way, a lot of space can be saved.

CONCLUSION

In this chapter, a document management system is introduced. First, the system architecture and the document storage strategy have been discussed. Then, a new indexing technique, *path signature,* has been proposed to speed up the evaluation of the path-oriented queries. On the one hand, path signatures can be used as a filter to get away non-relevant elements. On the other hand, the technique of signature-trees can be utilized to establish index over them, which make us find relevant signatures quickly. As shown in the analysis of time complexity, high performance can be achieved using this technique.

REFERENCES

Abiteboul, S., Quass, D., McHugh, J., Widom, J. & Wiener, J. (1996). The Lorel Query Language for semi-structured data. *Journal of Digital Libraries,* 1(1).

Bosak, J. (1997, March). Java, and the future of the Web. Available online at: http://sunsite.unc.edu/pub/sun-info/standards/xml/why/xmlapps.html.
Chamberlin, D., Clark, J., Florescu, D., Robie, J., Simeon, J. & Stefanescu, M. (2001). *Xquery 1.0: An XML Query Language*. Technical Report, World Wide Web Consortium, Working Draft 07.
Chen, Y. & Huck, G. (2001). On the evaluation of path-oriented queries in document databases. *Lecture Notes in Computer Science,* 2113, 953-962.
Christodoulakis, S. & Faloutsos, C. (1984). Design consideration for a message file server. *IEEE Transactions on Software Engineering,* 10(2), 201-210.
Christophides, V., Cluet, S. & Simeon, J. (2000). On wrapping query languages and efficient XML integration. *Proceedings of the ACM SIGMOD Conference on Management of Data,* 141-152.
Deutsch, A., Fernandez, Florescu, D., Levy, A. & Suciu, D. (1988, August). *XML-QL: A Query Language for XML*. Available online at: http://www.w3.org/TR/NOTE-xml-ql/.
Faloutsos, C. (1985). Access methods for text. *ACM Computing Surveys*, 17(1), 49-74.
Faloutsos, C. (1992). Signature files. In Frakes, W.B. & Baeza-Yates, R. (Eds.), *Information Retrieval: Data Structures & Algorithms*. Englewood Cliffs, NJ: Prentice Hall, 44-65.
Florescu, D. & Kossman, D. (1999). Storing and querying XML data using an RDBMS. *IEEE Data Engineering Bulletin,* 22(3).
Huck, G., Macherius, I. & Fankhauser, P. (1999). PDOM: Lightweight persistency support for the Document Object Model. *Proceedings of the OOPSLA '99 Workshop: Java and Databases: Persistence Options,* November.
Knuth, D.E. (1973). *The Art of Computer Programming: Sorting and Searching*. London: Addison-Wesley.
Marchiori, M. (1998). *The Query Languages Workshop (QL '98)*. Available online at: http://www.w3.org/TandS/QL/QL98.
Morrison, D.R. (1968). PATRICIA—Practical Algorithm To Retrieve Information Coded in Alphanumeric. *Journal of Association for Computing Machinery*, 15(4), 514-534.
Pixley, T. (2000). *Document Object Model (DOM) Level 2 Events Specification Version 1.0.* W3C Recommendation.
Riordan, J. (1968). *Combinatorial Identities.* New York: John Wiley & Sons.
Robie, J., Chamberlin, D. & Florescu, D. (2000). Quilt: An XML query language for heterogeneous data sources. *Proceedings of the International Workshop on the Web and Databases.*
Robie, J., Lapp, J. & Schach, D. (1998). XML Query Language (XQL). *Proceedings of W3C QL '98—The Query Languages Workshop.*
Shanmugasundaram, J., Shekita, R., Carey, M.J., Lindsay, B.G., Pirahesh, H. & Reinwald, B. (2000). Efficiently publishing relational data as XML documents. *Proceedings of the International Conference on Very Large Data Bases (VLDB '00),* 65-76.
Shanmugasundaram, J., Tufte, K., Zhang. C., He,. D.J., DeWitt, J. & Naughton, J.F. (1999). Relational databases for querying XML documents: Limitations and opportunities. *Proceedings of the International Conference on Very Large Data Bases (VLDB '99),* 302-314.

Suciu, D. & Vossen, G. (2000). *Proceedings of the Third International Workshop on the Web and Databases (WebDB 2000)*, LNCS. Springer-Verlag.

World Wide Web Consortium. (1998a, February). *Extensible Markup Language (XML) 1.0.* Available online at: http//www.w3.org/TR/ 1998/REC-xml/19980210.

World Wide Web Consortium. (1998b, December). *Extensible Style Language (XML) Working Draft.* Available online at: http/ /www.w3.org/TR/1998/WD-xsl-19981216.

World Wide Web Consortium. (1998c). *Document Object Model (DOM) Level 1.* Available online at: http://www.w3.org/TR/ REC-DOM-Level-1/.

Yoshikawa, M., Amagasa, T., Shimura, T. & Uemura, S. (2001). Xrel: A path-based approach to storage and retrieval of XML documents using relational databases. *ACM Transactions on Internet Technology,* 1(1).

Chapter VI

Keyword-Based Queries Over Web Databases

Altigran S. da Silva
Universidade Federal do Amazonas, Brazil

Pável Calado
Universidade Federal de Minas Gerais, Brazil

Rodrigo C. Vieira
Universidade Federal de Minas Gerais, Brazil

Alberto H.F. Laender
Universidade Federal de Minas Gerais, Brazil

Bertheir A. Ribeiro-Neto
Universidade Federal de Minas Gerais, Brazil

ABSTRACT

In this chapter, we propose an approach to using keywords (as in a Web search engine) for querying databases over the Web. The approach is based on a Bayesian network model and provides a suitable alternative to the use of interfaces based on multiple forms with several fields. Two major steps are involved when querying a Web database using this approach. First, structured (database-like) queries are derived from a query composed only of the keywords specified by the user. Next, the structured queries are submitted to a Web database, and the retrieved results are presented to the user as ranked answers. To demonstrate the feasibility of the approach, a simple prototype Web search system based on the approach is presented. Experimental results obtained with this system indicate that the approach allows for accurately structuring the user queries and retrieving appropriate answers with minimum intervention from the user.

INTRODUCTION

Online information services, such as online stores and digital libraries, have become widespread on the Web nowadays. Such services allow a great number of users to access a large volume of data stored in local databases, also called *Web databases*. Web users, however, are usually non-specialized and their interests vary greatly. Thus, two important problems are posed to designers of interfaces for Web databases: simplicity and uniformity. Interfaces for accessing Web databases are expected to be simple, since they are intended for laymen users. In addition, if an online service is to provide access to different types of information (i.e., many distinct databases), its interface should be as uniform as possible. Otherwise, users will be required to learn how to use a different interface for each distinct database.

The most common solution for implementing online services that access Web databases is the use of customized forms, navigation menus and similar browsing mechanisms. Although useful in some cases, this approach has some important shortcomings. Websites that provide access to multiple databases, such as Amazon.com (http://www.amazon.com), MySimon (http://www.mysimon.com) or Travelocity (http://www.travelocity.com), include dozens of different forms, one for each type of product, where each form might be composed of a large number of fields. From the point of view of a Web user, this type of interface might seem rather complex. From the point of view of a Web developer, it increases the development time and maintenance costs.

Another common inconvenience of query interfaces for Web databases is the fact that the answer set is frequently too large. In a traditional database system, appropriate tools and query languages are available to restrict the search results. In a Web search engine, document ranking (Baeza-Yates & Ribeiro-Neto, 1999) is used to deal with this problem. In Web database interfaces, however, such a method is usually not available.

In this chapter, we describe the use of keyword-based querying (as in a Web search engine) with Web databases and argue that this approach provides a suitable alternative to the use of interfaces based on multiple forms with several fields. Additionally, we show how to use a relevance criteria to rank a possibly large set of answers retrieved by a keyword-based query, as done in Web search engines.

Our approach uses a Bayesian network (Ribeiro-Neto & Muntz, 1996) to model and derive structured (database-like) queries from a query composed only of the keywords specified by the user. The structured queries are then submitted to a Web database and the retrieved results are presented to the user as ranked answers. This means that the user needs just to fill in a single search box to formulate a query. Our approach is thus able to provide online services with: (1) an interface that is simple and intuitive to Web users, and (2) the possibility of querying several heterogeneous databases using a single interface.

To demonstrate the feasibility of our approach, a simple prototype Web search system was implemented. Results obtained using this prototype on databases of three distinct domains (Calado, Silva, Vieira, Laender & Ribeiro-Neto, 2002) indicate that our approach allows accurately structuring the user queries and retrieving appropriate answers with minimum intervention from the user.

The remainder of this chapter is organized as follows. First, we briefly review the traditional paradigm employed for querying Web databases. We then discuss the use of keywords for formulating queries, and the following section presents our framework for allowing keyword-based queries over Web databases. Finally, we present our conclusions and discuss future work.

TRADITIONAL QUERY PARADIGMS FOR WEB DATABASES

One of the important benefits introduced by the Web was the possibility of making data of general interest, stored in local databases, universally available in a uniform manner. Before the Web, specific interfaces and data access protocols had to be used. In some cases, standard data access protocols (e.g., ODBC) were (and continue to be) used. However, such protocols have limited applications. For instance, they require the use of software layers not always available to the casual user. Thus, the Web (and its HTTP protocol) has emerged as a practical and flexible way of sharing database contents.

The access to Web databases is usually done through mechanisms that allow a Web server to contact a DBMS, submit queries to it, receive the results and further process them to fulfill a user request. Figure 1 illustrates the execution of a query submitted to a database over the Web. In this figure, we distinguish two major steps. In Step 1, the Web server receives a query from a client (usually a browser) and, in Step 2 the Web server interacts with the DBMS (in practice, these two steps can be further divided into smaller ones but for our explanatory purposes here, they suffice).

There are several options for implementing the interaction between the Web server and the DBMS (Step 2). However, since discussing these options is out of the scope of this chapter, we refer the interested user to more appropriate references on this topic such as Ehmayer, Kappel and Reich (1997) and Labrinidis and Roussopoulos (2000).

For processing Step 1, the Web server receives a query encoded according to some standard as input. This query is produced by the Web client as the result of an interaction with a user. By far, the most common solution for implementing Step 1 is by means of customized HTML forms, navigation menus and similar browsing mechanisms. By navigating through menus, the users implicitly select one among several "template"

Figure 1. Execution of a Query Submitted to a Database over the Web

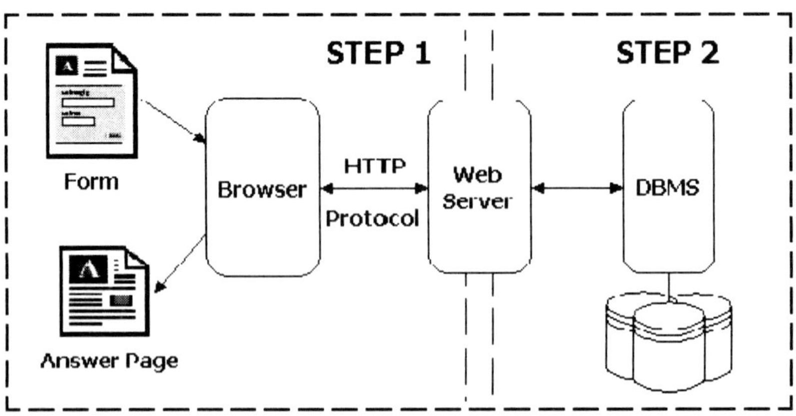

Figure 2. Examples of Typical Forms for Querying Web Databases

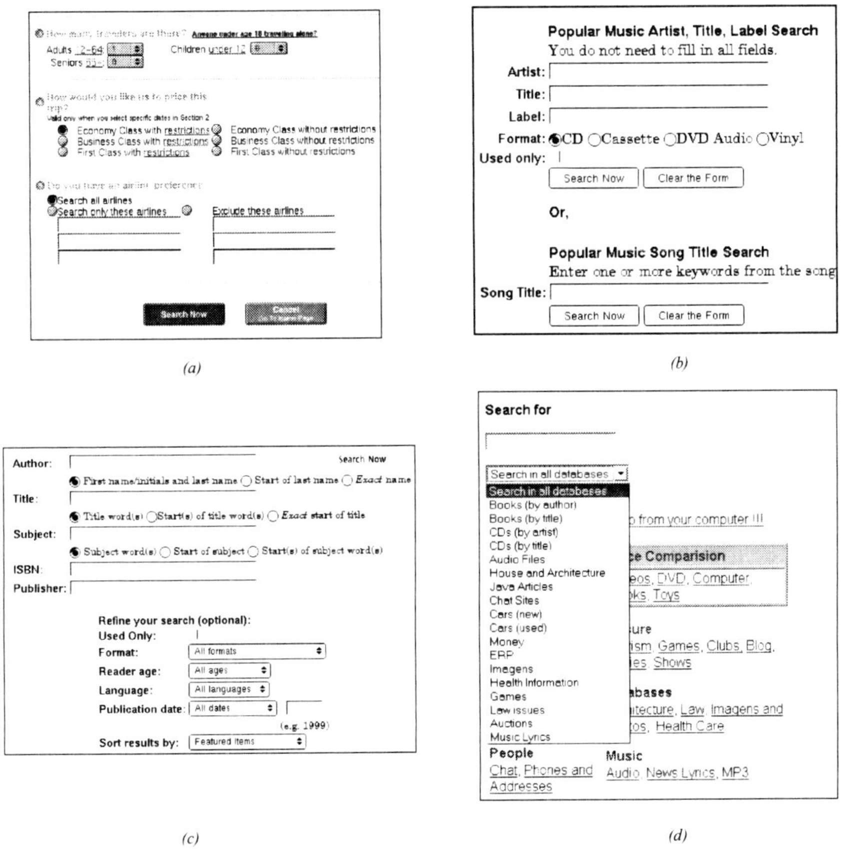

queries encoded in the HTML pages (or similar documents). By filling in form fields, the users supply the arguments needed for the query parameters.

Figure 2(a) illustrates a typical form for querying Web databases. It contains several fields, but just a few need be actually filled in to produce a valid query. For instance, at the bottom of the form there is no obligation of filling in any of the airline fields.

In Figure 2(b), we show another typical type of form, in this case for searching music products on the Amazon.com website. Notice that there are also several distinct types of fields to be filled (text box, check box, check buttons, etc.). Further, there is one such form for each product type by Amazon.com (e.g., books, movies, etc.). For instance, Figure 2(c) shows the advanced search form for books. Having a multitude of distinct forms represents a problem not only for the users, who have to deal with the peculiarities of each of them, but also for the developers, who have to design and implement a specific type of form for each product type.

A third example of a form for querying Web databases is presented in Figure 2(d). This form features a single field, where a user can provide a value for a single-parameter query. In cases like this, the actual parameter also has to be selected using a menu that appears as a companion to the single field. Thus, a user can only search for a book by its title or by the name of its author, but not by both. Similarly, the value provided in the single field can be used exclusively as the title of a CD, a name of an artist and so on.

From these example cases, we can say that, despite its apparent simplicity, the solution of using multi-field forms for building queries to Web databases has important shortcomings, particularly for websites that provide access to multiple databases.

KEYWORD-BASED QUERIES

The use of keywords for query formulation is a quite common resource in information retrieval systems, like Web search engines (Ribeiro-Neto & Muntz, 1996; Silva, Ribeiro-Neto, Calado, Moura & Ziviani, 2000). In the context of structured and Web databases, however, only more recently have some proposals for the use of keyword-based queries appeared (Agrawal, Chaudhuri & Das, 2002; Dar, Entin, Geva & Palmon, 1998; Florescu, Kossmann & Manolescu, 2000; Ma, 2002).

Agrawal et al. (2002) introduce a system that allows querying databases through keywords. Their work, however, focuses on relational databases and does not provide any ranking for the *approximate* answers. The DataSpot system, described in Dar et al. (1998), proposes the use of "plain language" queries and navigations to explore a *hyperbase*, built for publishing contents of a database on the Web. The work described in Florescu, Kossmann and Manolescu (2000) proposes the extension of XML-QL, a well-known query language for XML, with keyword-based searching capabilities. Our solution is distinct since it adopts a much simpler query language. Although this can make our approach less expressive, it also makes it more accessible to regular Web users. In addition, we propose to rank the answers, since spurious data will necessarily be present. In Ma (2002), a strategy is proposed that allows users to search a set of databases and determine the ones that might contain the data of interest. Different from what we propose, this strategy is based on controlled vocabularies, which are used to match the provided keywords with human-provided characterizations of the databases.

The vector space model has been widely used as a solution to the problem of ranking query results in text databases (Baeza-Yates & Ribeiro-Neto, 1999). In Cohen (1999), for instance, the vector model is used to determine the similarity between objects in a database composed of relations whose attribute values are free text. For ranking structured objects returned as answers to queries over a database, the work described in Chaudhuri and Gravano (1999) combines application-oriented scoring functions. To exemplify, in a query over a real-state database, scoring functions that evaluate the values of the attributes *price* and *numberofbedrooms* may be used for determining the ranking of the answers. An extension of such an idea is proposed in Bruno, Gravano and Marian (2002) for the case of Web-accessible databases. In this case, the scoring functions may be based on evidence coming from distinct Web databases. For instance, while one of these Web databases supplies values for evaluating the *rating* attribute, another database may supply values for evaluating the *price* attribute. For determining the final ranking, the evaluations of the individual attributes are combined.

In Golman, Shivakumar, Venkatasubramanian and Garcia-Molina (1998), object ranking is based on a measure of the proximity between the objects (seen as nodes) in the database (seen as a graph). In a movie database, for instance, the movies somehow related to "Cage" and "Travolta" can be retrieved by ranking the *movie* nodes (objects) that present the smallest distance from the *actor* or *director* nodes (objects) whose values contain the strings "Cage" or "Travolta." This approach led to a search system similar to ours in functionality, since it also allows keyword-based queries, but one that is based on a rather distinct approach.

A FRAMEWORK FOR QUERYING WEB DATABASES USING KEYWORDS

We now present an overview of our approach to query Web databases by using simple keyword-based queries. To simplify the discussion, we start with some basic definitions.

In our work, query structuring and the ranking of query results are performed using vectorial techniques modeled in a Bayesian belief network, similar to the one described in Ribeiro-Neto and Muntz (1996). Bayesian networks were first used to model information retrieval problems by Turtle and Croft (1991), and as demonstrated in Ribeiro-Neto, Silva and Muntz (2000), they can be used to represent any of the classic models in information retrieval. Bayesian network models are especially useful when we need to determine the relevance of the answers in view of much independent evidence (Baeza-Yates & Ribeiro-Neto, 1999). In our case, Bayesian networks are used to compute: (a) the likeliness that a structured query assembled by the system represents the user information need and (b) the relevance of the retrieved answers with regard to the user information need.

Definitions

Consider a database D accessible through a Web query interface (for instance, an HTML form). We define this database as a collection of *objects*:

$$D = \{o_1, o_2, \ldots, o_n\}, n \geq 1.$$

Each object o_i is a set of *attribute-value* pairs:

$$o_i = \{\langle A_1, v_{1i}\rangle, \cdots, \langle A_{k_i}, v_{k_i i}\rangle\}, k_i \geq 1$$

where each A_j is an attribute and each v_{ji} is a value belonging to the domain of A_j. We note that the attributes do not need, necessarily, to be the same for all objects.

For some attributes, instead of a single value, we may have a list of values. For instance, in an object representing a movie, the attribute *actor* might be a list of names. To represent this, we allow a same attribute to appear several times. Thus, if the attribute A_j of an object o_i has n different values, we can represent object o_i as:

$$o_i = \{\cdots, \langle A_j, v_1\rangle, \langle A_j, v_2\rangle, \cdots \langle A_j, v_n\rangle, \cdots\}.$$

We define a *database schema* S_D as the set of all attributes that compose any of the stored objects. Thus, the schema of a database D is defined as:

$$S_D = \{A_j \mid A_j \text{ is an attribute of some object } o_i \in D\}.$$

We define an *unstructured query* U as a set of keywords (or *terms*) t_k, as follows:

$$U = \{t_1, t_2, \cdots, t_k\}.$$

A *structured query* Q is defined as a set of ordered pairs:

$$Q = \{\langle A_1, v_{1q}\rangle, \cdots, \langle A_m, v_{mq}\rangle\} m \geq 1$$

where each A_j is an attribute and each v_{jq} is a value belonging to the domain of A_j.

This simplified definition of a database allows us to ignore the details of how its structure is represented. Also, we can regard the database simply as a data repository available through some high-level user interface, ignoring whether it is composed of a single relational table, of a set of relational tables, of a set of XML documents or any other.

Throughout the text, we informally use the term *application domain* of a database to refer to the common knowledge semantic domain associated with the objects in the database. For instance, a database with the application domain Book stores objects with information on books. The database to be queried by the user is called the *target database*. As an example, consider a database D with the application domain Book. An object o_i in D could be:

$$o_i = \{\langle \text{Title}, \text{"I, Robot"}\rangle, \langle \text{Author}, \text{"Isaac Asimov"}\rangle\}$$

An example of an unstructured query is:

$$K = \{\text{"Asimov"}, \text{"robot"}\}$$

An example of a corresponding structured query is:

$$Q = \{\langle \text{Author}, \text{"Isaac Asimov"}\rangle\}$$

Overview

Querying Web databases using keyword-based queries involves four main steps: (1) specifying an unstructured query as input, (2) building a set of candidate structured queries associated with the unstructured query given as input, (3) selecting one or more candidate structured queries as the "best" ones and (4) processing the results of these selected queries. Figure 3 illustrates the architecture of a search system using this approach.

Figure 3. Search System Architecture for Querying Web Databases Using Unstructured Queries

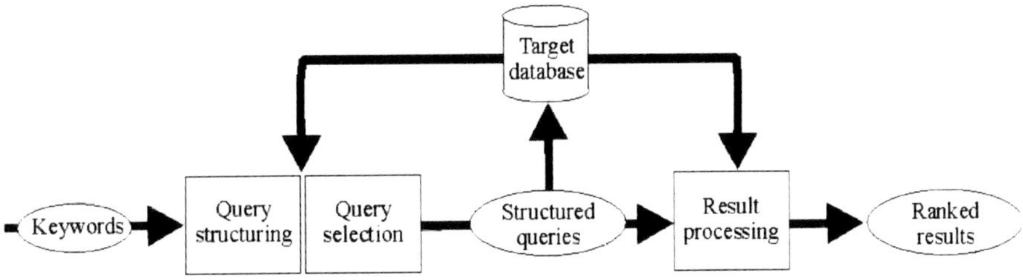

Step 1 consists simply of receiving the unstructured query from the user as a set of keywords. This can be easily accomplished using a simple search box interface, as shown in Figure 4, in which the queries are specified as sets of keywords.

In Step 2, for a given unstructured query $K = \{t_1, t_2, \ldots t_n\}$, we need to determine a set P_k of candidate structured queries. Let D be a database with a schema S_D. A simple way to determine P_k is to build all possible combinations of all query terms $t_i \in K$ and all attributes $A_j \in S_D$. Clearly, in the worst case, this operation would be of combinatorial complexity. In practice, however, it is possible to discard many combinations of terms and attributes (i.e., many attribute value pairs) in advance. For instance, if there are little or no occurrences of the word "Hamlet" in the *Author* attribute, we can discard all possible queries that make such an assignment.

Once we have determined a set $P_k = \{Q_1, \ldots, Q_n\}$ of candidate structured queries, we proceed to Step 3 that consists of selecting which queries are most likely to match the user information need. For instance, the unstructured query K = {*"asimov", "robot"*} might lead to the structured query Q_1 = {<Author, *"Asimov"*>,<Title, *"robot"*>}. More precisely, the query structuring process consists of determining the database attributes which are most likely to correspond to each term in K. In Figure 4 some structured queries for the keyword-based query "little prince" are shown. The best candidate structured query is the one that maximizes the likelihood that its component attribute-value pairs correspond to the user query intention. To determine such best candidate query, we need to rank the candidate (structured) queries with regard to the input query, as we later discuss.

In Step 4, we take the top-ranked candidate structured queries in P_K and process them. For instance, we can pick the best ranked query and process it without user interference. Alternatively, we can present the top-ranked queries to the user and let him choose one of them for processing. In both cases, a structured query Q is submitted to the target database D and a set of objects RD_Q is retrieved. The objects are then ranked according to the probability of satisfying the user information need, as we later discuss. Figure 5 illustrates ranked results produced by the unstructured query *"Little Prince."*

Ranking the retrieved objects is especially important when the query can be sent to more than one target database and the results merged together. For instance, in an application domain like *Computer Science Bibliography*, the same unstructured query can be used to search the ACM and IEEE digital libraries. Notice that this is accomplished without the need to define a unifying common database schema.

Figure 4. Candidate-Structured Queries for the Keyword-Based Query "Little Prince"

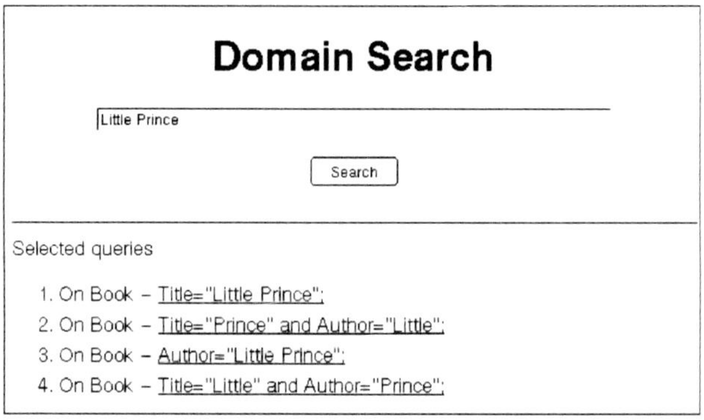

To rank the candidate queries in Step 3 (from set P_k) and the retrieved objects in Step 4 (from set RD_Q), we adopt the framework of Bayesian belief networks (Pearl, 1988). The following section gives a brief introduction to the use of Bayesian networks in information retrieval problems. We then present a Bayesian network model for ranking candidate queries, followed by a Bayesian network model for ranking the retrieved objects.

Bayesian Networks

Bayesian networks were introduced in the context of information retrieval by Turtle and Croft (1991). Later, Ribeiro-Neto and Muntz (1996) refined this model and used it to combine information from past queries. Both versions take an epistemological view (as opposed to a frequentist view) of the information retrieval problem, interpreting probabilities as degrees of belief devoid of experimentation. For this reason, they are also called *belief networks*.

Figure 5. Results for the Keyword-Based Query "Little Prince"

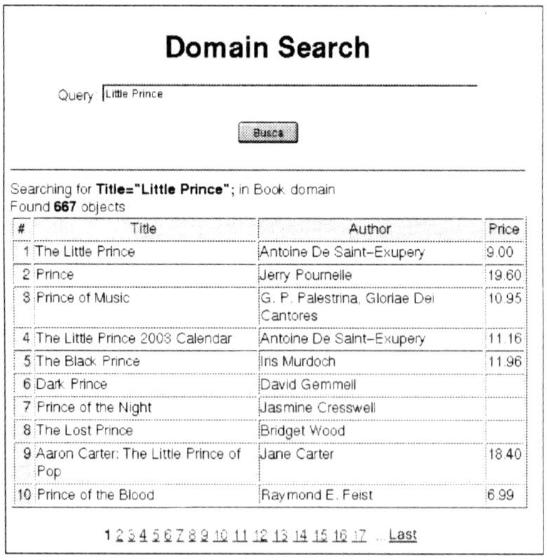

Figure 6. Belief Network for a Query Composed of the Keywords K_1 and K_2

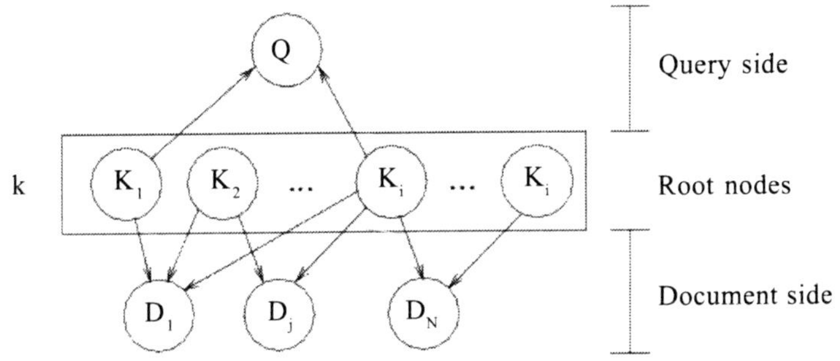

Bayesian networks provide a graphical formalism for explicitly representing independencies among the variables of a joint probability distribution. The probability distribution is represented through a directed acyclic graph, whose nodes represent the random variables of the distribution. Thus, two random variables, X and Y, are represented in a Bayesian network as two nodes in a directed graph. An edge directed from Y to X represents the influence of the node Y, the *parent* node, on the node X, the *child* node. The intensity of the influence of the variable Y on the variable X is quantified by the conditional probability $P(x|y)$, for every possible set of values (x,y).

According to the model proposed by Ribeiro-Neto and Muntz (1996), queries, documents and keywords are seen as events. These events are not independent, since, for instance, the occurrence of a term will influence the occurrence of a document. Using a Bayesian network, we can model these events and their interdependencies. Considering the fact that both documents and queries are composed of keywords, we can model the document retrieval problem using the network in Figure 6.

In this network, each node D_j models a document, the node Q models the user query, and the K_i nodes model the terms in the collection. The vector **k** is used to refer to any of the possible states of the K_i root nodes.

The similarity between a document D_j and the query Q can be interpreted as the probability of document D_j occurring given that query Q has occurred. Thus, using Bayes' law and the rule of total probabilities, we compute the similarity $P(d_j|q)$ as:

$$P(d_j \mid q) = \eta \sum_{k} P(d_j \mid k) P(q \mid k) P(k)$$

where $\eta = 1/P(q)$ is a normalizing constant. This is the generic expression for the ranking of a document D_j with regard to a query Q, in the belief network model. To represent any traditional information retrieval model using the network in Figure 6, we need only to define the probabilities $P(d_j|k)$, $P(q|k)$ and $P(k)$ appropriately.

Using a similar approach, we can build Bayesian network models that allow us to both select the structured query most likely to correspond to the users' needs and to rank the final query results. In the following sections we present these two models.

Figure 7. Bayesian Network Model for Query Structuring

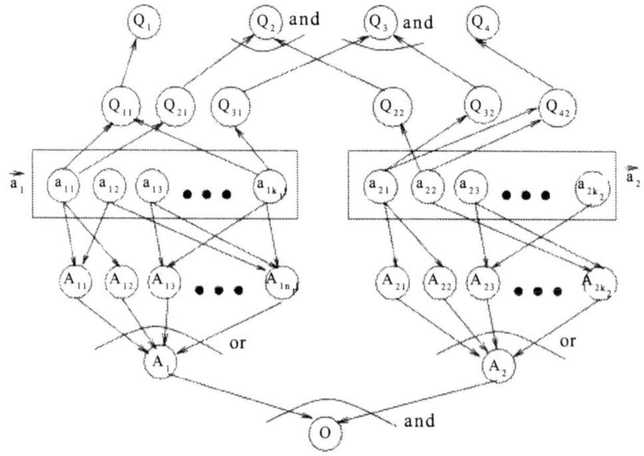

Finding the Best Queries

The query structuring process associates structure to a given query *K*, consisting only of keywords. Several structured queries are generated for a same unstructured query. For this reason, we need a consistent way of ranking the queries according to their similarity to the database, in other words, their similarity to the application domain in question. The ranking of structured queries is accomplished through the use of the Bayesian network model shown in Figure 7. Although the network can be easily expanded to model any database schema, for simplicity, here we show only two attributes, A_1 and A_2.

The network consists of a set of nodes, each representing a piece of information from the problem to be solved. To each node in the network is associated a binary random variable. This variable takes the value 1 to indicate that the corresponding information will be accounted for in the ranking computation. In this case, we say that the information was *observed.*

To simplify the notation, we define T_i as the set of all terms in the database that compose the values in the domain of attribute A_i. In this case, each value is considered as a string and the terms are the words in the string. In the network of Figure 7, the database is represented by the node *O*. Each node A_i represents an attribute in the database. Each node a_{ij} represents a term in T_i. Each node Q_i represents a structured query to be ranked. Each node Q_{ij} represents the portion of the structured query Q_i that corresponds to the attribute A_j. Vectors $\vec{a}_1$ and $\vec{a}_2$ represent a possible state of the variables associated to the nodes a_{1i} and a_{2i}, respectively.

This network can be used to model, for instance, a database on books, with attributes A_1 = Title and A_2 = Author. In this case, node A_{11} represents the title of a stored book, like "I, Robot," where the term "I" is represented by node a_{11} and the term "Robot" is represented by node a_{12}. In a similar fashion, node Q_2 represents the structured query Q2 = {<Title, "I, Robot">, <Author, "Asimov">}, where Q_{21} is the part referring to the Title attribute, Q_{22} the part referring to the Author attribute. Node a_{22} is the term "Asimov."

The similarity of a structured query Q_i with the database O can be seen as the probability of observing Q_i, given that the database O was observed, $P(Q_i|O)$. Examining the network in Figure 7, we can derive the following equation:

$$P(Q_i \mid O) = \alpha \times \sum_{\vec{a}_1,\vec{a}_2} P(Q_i \mid \vec{a}_1,\vec{a}_2) \times P(O \mid \vec{a}_1,\vec{a}_2) \times P(\vec{a}_1,\vec{a}_2)$$

$$= \alpha \times \sum_{\vec{a}_1,\vec{a}_2} P(Q_{i1} \mid \vec{a}_1) \times P(Q_{i2} \mid \vec{a}_2) \times$$

$$P(A_1 \mid \vec{a}_1) \times P(A_2 \mid \vec{a}_2) \times P(\vec{a}_1) \times P(\vec{a}_2)$$

where α is a normalizing constant (see Pearl, 1988, and Ribeiro-Neto & Muntz, 1996, for details).

The following equation is the general equation for ranking a structured query. The conditional probabilities can now be defined according to the values stored in the database. We start with the probability of observing the part of the query Q_i assigned to an attribute A_j, given that a set of terms (indicated by a_j) was observed:

$$P(Q_{ij} \mid \vec{a}_j) = \begin{cases} 1 & \text{if } \forall k, g_k(\vec{a}_j) = 1 \text{ iff } t_{jk} \text{ ocurs in } Q_{ij} \\ 0 & \text{otherwise} \end{cases}$$

where $g_k(\vec{a}_j)$ gives the value of the k-th variable of the vector $\vec{a}_j$ and t_{jk} is the k-th term in T_j. This equation guarantees that the only states considered are those in which the only active terms are those that compose the query Q_i.

The probability of observing the attribute A_i, given the terms indicated by $\vec{a}_i$, is defined as a disjunction of all probabilities for each possible value of A_i, i.e.:

$$P(A_i \mid \vec{a}_i) = 1 - \prod_{1 \le j \le n_i} (1 - P(A_{ij} \mid \vec{a}_i))$$

where n_i is the number of values in the database for attribute A_i. If we consider that $P(A_{ij}|\vec{a}_j)$ measures the similarity between the value A_{ij} and the terms indicated by $\vec{a}_i$, then the equation above tells us that, if the terms in $\vec{a}_i$ fit exactly one of the values A_{ij}, the final probability is 1. If not, the final probability will accumulate all the partial similarities between the terms in $\vec{a}_i$ and the values A_{ij}.

To define the probability of observing a value A_{ij} given a set of terms indicated by $\vec{a}_i$, $P(A_{ij}|\vec{a}_i)$, we use the cosine measure, as defined for the vector space model in information retrieval systems (Salton & McGill, 1983). The value A_{ij} for attribute A_i is seen as a vector of $|T_i|$ terms. To each term t_k in A_{ij}, we assign a weight w_{ik} that reflects the importance of the term t_k for attribute A_i, in the database, i.e.:

$$w_{ik} = \begin{cases} \dfrac{\log(1+f_{ki})}{\log(1+n_i)} & \text{if } t_k \text{ occurs in } A_{ij} \\ 0 & \text{otherwise} \end{cases}$$

where f_{ki} is the number of occurrences of term t_k in the values of the attribute A_i, and n_i is the total number of values for attribute A_i, in the database. Notice that we do not consider the traditional *idf* normalization (Salton & McGill, 1983), since this would penalize the most frequent terms, which are the most important ones in our approach.

The probability of observing A_{ij} is, therefore, defined as the cosine of the angle between vector A_{ij} and vector $\vec{a}_i$, i.e.:

$$P(A_{ij} \mid \vec{a}_i) = \cos(A_{ij}, \vec{a}_i) = \frac{\sum_{t_k \in T_i} w_{ik} \times g_k(\vec{a}_i)}{\sqrt{\sum_{t_k \in T_i} w_{ik}^2}}.$$

Finally, since we have no *a priori* preference for any set of terms, the following equation defines the probability of vector $\vec{a}_i$ as a constant:

$$P(\vec{a}_i) = \frac{1}{2^{|T_i|}}.$$

In sum, the probability $P(Q_i|O)$ is the conjunction of the similarities between the attribute values in the database and the values assigned to the respective attributes in the structured query. This is translated by the equation:

$$P(Q_i \mid O) = \eta \times \left[1 - \prod_{1 \le j \le n_1} (1 - \cos(A_{1j}, \vec{a}_1))\right] \times \left[1 - \prod_{1 \le j \le n_2} (1 - \cos(A_{2j}, \vec{a}_2))\right]$$

where $\vec{a}_1$ and $\vec{a}_2$ are the states where only the query terms referring to attributes A_1 and A_2, respectively, are active; n_1 and n_2 are the total number of values for attributes A_1 and A_2 in the database; and η accounts for the constants α and $P(\vec{a}_i)$.

We can now rank all the structured queries by computing $P(Q_i|O)$ for each of them. The user can then select one query for processing among the top-ranked ones, or the system can simply process the highest ranked query.

Finding the Best Answers

Once a structured query is selected, it is submitted to the target database. The set of objects retrieved can then be ranked according to the probability of satisfying the user

Figure 8. Bayesian Network Model for Result Ranking

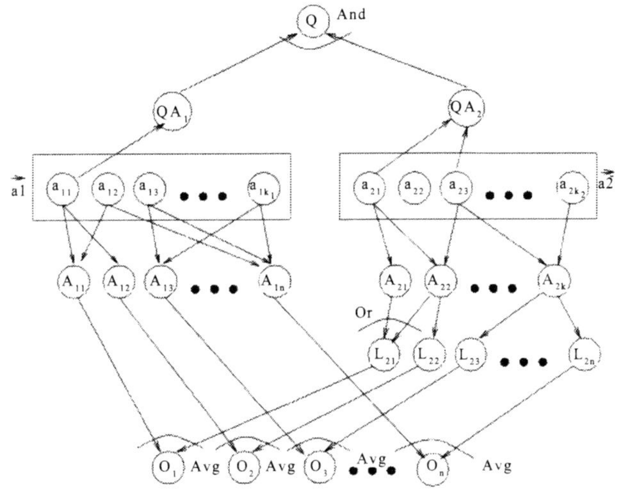

information need. To this effect, the structured query and the retrieved objects are modeled using the Bayesian network model shown in Figure 8. Again, although the network can be easily expanded to model any database schema, here we show only two attributes, A_1 and A_2. To simplify the notation, we define T_i as the set of all terms that compose the values in the domain of the attribute A_i.

When ranking the returned objects, special attention needs to be paid to value lists, i.e., attribute values that form a list. To exemplify how this type of attribute is treated, in the network we represent attribute A_2 as a value list attribute.

In the network in Figure 8, node Q represents the structured query, submitted for processing. Each node QA_i represents the part of the structured query Q relative to the attribute A_i. Each node a_{ij} represents a term in T_i. Each node A_{ij} represents the value of the attribute A_i in object O_j. Since attribute A_2 is a list attribute, we add one more level to the network. Each node L_{2j} represents the list of values assigned to the attribute A_2 in object O_j. Finally, each node O_j represents a returned object. As before, with each node in the network is associated a random variable that takes the value 1 to indicate that information regarding the respective node was observed. Vectors $\vec{a}_1$ and $\vec{a}_2$ represent a possible state of the variables associated with nodes a_{1i} and a_{2i}, respectively.

An object O_j is ranked according to the probability of satisfying the structured query Q, i.e., the probability of observing O_j, given that Q was observed, $P(O_j|Q)$. Examining the network in Figure 8, we have that:

$$P(O_j \mid Q) = \beta \times \sum_{\vec{a}_1,\vec{a}_2} P(Q \mid \vec{a}_1,\vec{a}_2) \times P(O_j \mid \vec{a}_1,\vec{a}_2) \times P(\vec{a}_1,\vec{a}_2)$$

$$= \beta \times \sum_{\vec{a}_1,\vec{a}_2} P(QA_1 \mid \vec{a}_1) \times P(QA_2 \mid \vec{a}_2) \times$$

$$\frac{P(A_{1j} \mid \vec{a}_1) + P(L_{2j} \mid \vec{a}_2)}{2} \times P(\vec{a}_1) \times P(\vec{a}_2)$$

where β is a normalizing constant. The average between $P(A_{1j} | \vec{a}_1)$ and $P(L_{2j} | \vec{a}_1)$ allows us to accumulate the evidence associated with each attribute value for the final probability.

We define a list as a disjunction of its values. Therefore, the probability for the list attribute is given by:

$$P(L_{2j} \mid \vec{a}_2) = 1 - \prod_{\forall k \in v} (1 - P(A_{2k} \mid \vec{a}_2)$$

where v is the set of indexes for the values in the list represented by L_{2j}. This equation determines that, for a value list to be observed, it is enough that one of its values is observed.

The following equations offer the general formula to rank a returned object. The conditional probabilities can now be defined. We start by the probability of observing the part of Q relative to an attribute A_i, given that a set of terms, indicated by $\vec{a}_i$ was observed:

$$P(QA_i \mid \vec{a}_i) = \begin{cases} 1 & \text{if } \forall k, g_k(\vec{a}_i) = 1 \text{ iff } t_{ik} \text{ ocurs in } QA_i \\ 0 & \text{otherwise} \end{cases}$$

where $g_k(\vec{a}_i)$ indicates the value of the k-th variable of the vector $\vec{a}_i$, and t_{ik} is the k-th term in T_i. This equation guarantees that only the states where the only active terms are those of the query Q will be taken into consideration.

As for query structuring, the probability of observing the value A_{ij}, given that the terms indicated by $\vec{a}_i$ were observed, $P(A_{ij} | \vec{a}_i)$, is defined using the cosine measure. The value A_{ij} of the object O_j (the value associated with the attribute A_i) is seen as a vector of $|T_i|$ terms. This time, however, we are simply interested in determining whether each term t_k occurs, or not, in the value A_{ij}. Therefore, we define the term weight w_{ik} simply as:

$$w_{ij} = \begin{cases} 1 & \text{if } t_k \text{ occurs in } A_{ij} \\ 0 & \textit{otherwise} \end{cases}$$

The probability of A_{ij} is defined as:

$$P(A_{ij} \mid \vec{a}_i) = \cos(A_{ij}, \vec{a}_i) = \frac{\sum_{t_k \in T_i} w_{ik} \times g_k(\vec{a}_i)}{\sqrt{\sum_{t_k \in T_i} w_{ik}^2}}$$

Since we have no preference for any particular set of terms, Equation 7 defines the probability associated with the vector $\vec{a}_i$ as a constant:

$$P(\vec{a}_i) = \frac{1}{2^{|T_i|}}$$

In summary, the probability $P(O_j|Q)$ is the average of the similarities between the attribute values in object O_j and the values for the respective attributes in the structured query, i.e.:

$$P(O_j \mid Q) = \eta \times \frac{1}{2}\left[\cos(A_{1j}, \vec{a}_1) + \left[1 - \prod_{\forall k \in v}(1 - \cos(A_{2k}, \vec{a}_2))\right]\right]$$

where $\vec{a}_i$ is the state where the only active terms are those in the query part referring to the attribute A_i, η summarizes the constants β and $P(\vec{a}_i)$, and v is the set of indexes for the values in the list for attribute A_2.

Once we compute the values of $P(O_j|Q)$ for all the returned objects, they can be presented to the user as a ranked list.

Querying Remote Web Databases

In our discussion, we have assumed that the database we intend to query is fully available to the query structuring system. However, and especially on the Web, this is not often the case. Instead, many Web systems (for instance, meta-search engines) perform queries over remote, independent databases that provide access only through a simple form interface. In such cases, alternative sources of information must be used for the query structuring process.

Figure 9. Search System Architecture Using a Sample Database for Query Structuring

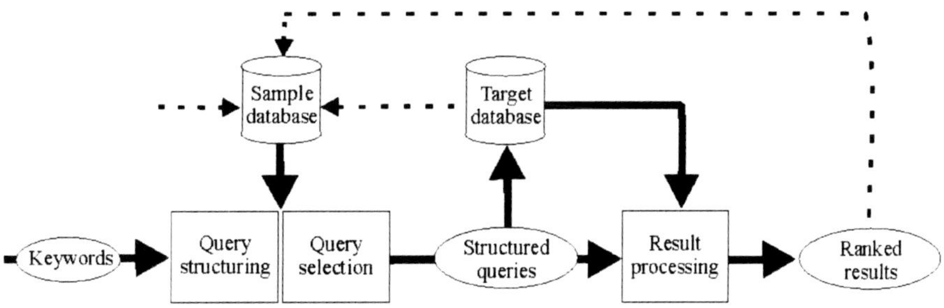

Figure 9 shows the architecture of a search system for querying remote databases. In this case, we use a local *sample database*, containing information on the values of the objects in the remote target database. The querying process is the same as described earlier, but the candidate structured queries are built based on data stored in the sample database, instead of the target database.

The sample database does not necessarily need to be structured. It can consist simply of lists of values for each attribute in the target database schema. These lists, however, must be representative enough to provide valid information on the distribution of values for the attributes in the target database. Thus, some care must be taken when building the sample database.

There are three main, non-exclusive approaches to this problem: (1) to take a random sample from the target database; (2) to build the sample database incrementally, using query results; and (3) to use an external source of information.

The first solution consists of simply extracting several random objects stored in the target database and using them as the data in the sample database. Although this approach is a good starting point to build a sample database, it presents some disadvantages. First, to guarantee that the sample will be representative, the number of objects to retrieve might depend on the domain of the target database and must be determined experimentally. Also, randomly extracting objects from a remote Web database may be a difficult task, depending on how the database is made available on the Web.

The second solution can be used to complement the first one. In this solution, every time a user queries the system, the returned results are taken and stored in the sample database. This will keep the sample database up to date with user trends and guarantee that the most popular queries will always be well represented. As a disadvantage, some rare queries may have poorer results, since we are not certain to keep a representative set of objects for the whole target database.

Finally, in some cases, external sources of information are available for the domain of the target database. For instance, if we are querying a database with the application domain *Movies*, an independent database on movies may be used as the sample database.

By using any combination of these approaches, we are able to remotely query several different databases, keeping only a smaller, local sample database for query structuring.

CONCLUSIONS AND FUTURE WORK

In this chapter, we have discussed a novel approach to querying Web databases using unstructured queries, i.e., queries composed of keywords only. The approach is based on a Bayesian network model, which combines evidence from object attributes to provide structure to the keyword-based user query given as input. Once a corresponding structured query is determined, it is submitted to one or more databases. Since the retrieved list of results can be quite extensive, we also propose a Bayesian network model to rank the results according to their probability of satisfying the user information need.

Our query structuring and result ranking models provide a framework for querying Web databases that: (1) allows the formulation of queries using a very simple interface (one single text search box); (2) allows the use of a single interface to query any number of different databases; and (3) provides the results as a ranked set, where the objects most likely to answer the user's query are shown first. These qualities make our proposal ideal for querying Web databases such as the ones available from online stores or digital libraries.

To verify our approach, we implemented a prototype Web search system that allows querying several distinct databases using the same interface. Experimental results using databases on three different domains have been reported in Calado et al. (2002). These results show that, for each unstructured query given as input, our system was able to rank the most appropriate candidate structured query among the top three, from 77% to 95% of the time. Further, when the user selected one of these three top queries for processing, the retrieved answers were ranked and presented average precision figures ranging from 60% to about 100%.

In the future, additions to the query language, such as numeric operators or allowing the user to restrict certain terms to certain attributes, may increase its expressiveness without greatly increasing its complexity. These extensions, of course, will imply some changes on the proposed Bayesian network models. Also, although we have not discussed the issue in this chapter, we believe that our approach is very adequate for building query interfaces for devices in which display space is limited, such as Personal Digital Assistants (PDAs), palmtops and cellular phones. Indeed, we plan to explore this idea in the near future.

ACKNOWLEDGMENTS

This work was partially supported by Project SIAM (MCT/CNPq/Pronex grant 76.97.1016.00), the MCT/FCT scholarship SFRH/BD/4662/2001, the CNPq grant 304890/02-5 and research funding from the Brazilian National Program in Informatics (Decree-law 3800/01).

REFERENCES

Agrawal, S., Chaudhuri, S. & Das, G. (2002). DBXplorer: A system for keyword-based search over relational databases. *Proceedings of the 18th International Conference on Data Engineering,* San Jose, CA, USA, February.

Baeza-Yates, R. & Ribeiro-Neto, B. (1999). *Modern Information Retrieval.* New York: Addison Wesley.

Bruno, N., Gravano, L. & Marian, A. (2002). Evaluating top-k queries over Web-accessible databases. *Proceedings of the 18th International Conference on Data Engineering,* San Jose, CA, USA, February.

Calado, P., Silva, A.S., Vieira, R.C., Laender, A.H.F. & Ribeiro-Neto, B.A. (2002). Searching Web databases by structuring keyword-based queries. *Proceedings of the 11th International Conference on Information and Knowledge Management,* McLean, VA, USA, November, 26-33.

Chaudhuri, S. & Gravano, L. (1999). Evaluating top-k selection queries. *Proceedings of the 25th International Conference on Very Large Data Bases,* Edinburgh, Scotland, UK, September, 397-410.

Cohen, W.W. (1999). Reasoning about textual similarity in a Web-based information access system. *Autonomous Agents and Multi-Agent Systems,* 2(1), 65-86.

Dar, S., Entin, G., Geva, S. & Palmon, E. (1998). DTL's DataSpot: Database exploration using plain language. *Proceedings of the 24th International Conference on Very Large Data Bases,* New York, New York, USA, August, 645-649.

Ehmayer, G., Kappel, G. & Reich, S. (1997). Connecting databases to the Web: A taxonomy of gateways. *Proceedings of the 8th International Conference on Database and Expert Systems Applications,* Toulouse, France, September, 1-15.

Florescu, D., Kossmann, D. & Manolescu, I. (2000). Integrating keyword search into XML query processing. *WWW9/Computer Networks,* 33(1-6), 119-135.

Goldman, R., Shivakumar, N., Venkatasubramanian, S. & Garcia-Molina, H. (1998). Proximity search in databases. *Proceedings of the 24th International Conference on Very Large Data Bases,* New York, USA, August, 26-37.

Labrinidis, A. & Roussopoulos, N. (2000). Generating dynamic content at database-backed Web servers: cgi-bin vs. mod perl. *SIGMOD Record,* 29(1), 26-31.

Ma, W. (2002). A database selection expert system based on reference librarians' database selection strategy: A usability and empirical evaluation. *Journal of the American Society for Information Science and Technology,* 53(7), 567-580.

Pearl, J. (1988). *Probabilistic Reasoning in Intelligent Systems: Networks of Plausible Inference.* San Francisco, CA: Morgan Kaufmann.

Ribeiro-Neto, B. & Muntz, R. (1996). A belief network model for IR. *Proceedings of the 19th Annual International ACM SIGIR Conference on Research and Development in Information Retrieval,* Zurich, Switzerland, August, 253-260.

Ribeiro-Neto, B., Silva, I. & Muntz, R. (2000). Bayesian network models for IR. In Crestani, F. & Pasi, G. (Eds.), *Soft Computing in Information Retrieval: Techniques and Applications.* Berlin: Springer Verlag, 259-291.

Salton, G. & McGill, M.J. (1983). *Introduction to Modern Information Retrieval.* New York: McGraw-Hill.

Silva, I., Ribeiro-Neto, B., Calado, P., Moura, E. & Ziviani, N. (2000). Link-based and content-based evidential information in a belief network model. *Proceedings of the 23rd Annual International ACM SIGIR Conference on Research and Development in Information Retrieval,* Athens, Greece, July, 96-103.

Turtle, H. & Croft, W.B. (1991). Evaluation of an inference network-based retrieval model. *ACM Transactions on Information Systems,* 9(3), 187-222.

Chapter VII

Unifying Access to Heterogeneous Document Databases Through Contextual Metadata

Virpi Lyytikäinen
University of Jyväskylä, Finland

Pasi Tiitinen
University of Jyväskylä, Finland

Airi Salminen
University of Jyväskylä, Finland

ABSTRACT

Document databases available on the Internet carry massive information resources. To a person needing a piece of information on a specific domain, finding the piece, however, is often quite problematic even though there were a representative collection of databases available on the domain. The languages used in the content, the names of document types, their structures, the ways documents are organized and their retrieval techniques often vary in the databases. The databases containing legal information on the Internet offer a typical example. For finding relevant documents and for being able to interpret the content of the documents correctly, the user may need information about the context where the documents have been created. In this chapter we introduce a method for collecting contextual metadata and for representing the metadata to the users by graphical models. The solution is demonstrated by a case of retrieving information from distributed European legal databases.

INTRODUCTION

Document databases available on the Internet carry massive information resources. To a person needing a piece of information on a specific domain, finding the piece is often quite problematic even though there were a representative collection of databases available on the domain. The databases containing legal information on the Internet offer a typical example. Recent trend towards electronic government (e-government) has tremendously increased the amount of public information available to citizens and organizations on the Internet. In Europe, due to the development towards European integration, this information is increasingly needed also regarding foreign European legal systems and the European Union itself. The legal databases are, however, organized in different ways, their content is written in different languages and their retrieval techniques vary. Differences in legal systems aggravate the problems of information retrieval. Similarly, on the intranets and extranets of organizations, information resources are often scattered in heterogeneous repositories. In paper machine manufacturing, for example, the amount of cooperating organizations and documents involved is always immense, and the information related to the manufacturing process is more and more stored on documents available via intranets and extranets.

Document retrieval tools always utilize metadata in information access. The *metadata* is data about the documents in the repository. It can be, for example, data about their content, about the way they are organized or about their structure. It can also be data about the context where the documents have been created. Especially in cases where the language of the content, the ways documents are organized, as well as their structures, vary in the databases of the repository, the role of *contextual metadata* becomes important both for finding relevant documents and for being able to interpret the content of the documents correctly. In this chapter, we introduce a method for collecting contextual metadata and for representing the metadata to the users by graphical models. The solution is demonstrated by a case of retrieving information from distributed European legal databases.

The rest of the chapter is organized as follows. The next section describes legal information in Europe as a case and demonstrates the challenges related to information retrieval in the case. A method for collecting contextual metadata is then introduced, and we show a way to visualize the contextual metadata in a user interface. An interface for finding legal information from European legal databases is described as an example. Finally, we discuss future directions related to the metadata support in information access.

EUROPEAN LEGAL INFORMATION AS A CASE

The legal domain in Europe offers an interesting and important example of distributed, heterogeneous information resources. The case was studied in a project called EULEGIS (European User Views to Legislative Information in Structured Form) belonging to the Telematics Application Programme of the European Commission. The main practical intent of the project was to offer single-point Web access to European legal information created in different legal systems and at different levels — European Union, a country, a region or a municipality — through a unified interface.

Documents created in the legislative processes in different European countries contain information important to all people and organizations in Europe. Some decades ago, people rarely needed other legal information except information created in their own country and own local area. Nowadays legal information from foreign countries and from the European Commission is often required in the activities of European people and organizations. The retrieval of European legal information, however, causes problems even for experts of legal matters. The problems are mainly related to three different areas: differences of the legal systems in different countries, heterogeneity of the databases and heterogeneity of the users of the information (Lyytikäinen, Tiitinen & Salminen, 2000).

Legal Systems in Europe

In all European countries, the legal rules are created in processes that are quite different in detail, although they bear resemblance to each other. When the legislation and the role of the courts are examined in different countries, two main traditions can be distinguished: a common law and a civil law (see, e.g., Gallagher, Laver & Mair, 1995). Within Europe, the United Kingdom and Ireland have a common law tradition. Most European countries belong to the civil law tradition, where the role of case law has much less significance.

Another major difference in the producing of legal rules in different countries is in the role of regions. In some countries (e.g., Germany, Austria and Belgium), legislative power has been decentralized so that several power centers have their own legal systems. On the other hand, there are countries, such as Finland, which only have minor legislative power at a regional level. A certain amount of regulative power has often also been left with, e.g., provinces or municipalities.

The various types of legal documents and their significance vary in different countries. However, three major groups of legal documents can be identified: normative documents including acts and decrees, preparatory works and court judgments. The types of documents, their structures and the languages used in them are, however, different. Even if the same language were used in two countries, the terminology can vary considerably.

Legal Databases in Europe

The number of legal information providers on the Internet has been growing rapidly. The dissemination of normative and preparative documents on the Internet free-of-charge has become policy in many countries (e.g., in Finland, http://www.finlex.fi; Sweden, http://www.riksdagen.se/debatt/; or Norway, http://www.lovdata.no). In addition, many fee-based services offer national legal information. Legal information concerning the European Union is also available at many websites, for example, CELEX (http:/europa.eu.int/celex).

Legal websites in Europe usually contain documents from one country or region only. Some databases specialize in one or more subject areas or contain only selected types of legal rules. Also, temporal coverage may vary among databases; some contain only recently published rules, while others may include legal norms dating back to the 18th century.

A website can offer several ways of accessing the legal information it contains. Legal rules may be accessed by date of publication, type of document, the organization which originated the document or subject. However, subject classification methods differ between websites. In addition, the functionality and presentation offered to the users of these databases vary, and even the most frequently used functions may have been implemented in different ways. Moreover, different fonts, colors and layout make the casual use of multiple databases problematic.

Users of European Legal Information

All people need legal information, but there are several particular user groups to whom foreign and EU legal information seems to be especially important. A problem in designing retrieval capabilities is that the experience and expertise of the users varies widely. In-depth interviews arranged in Finland revealed that several groups of people regarded the accessibility of foreign legal information and EU legal information as important (Tiitinen, Lyytikäinen, Päivärinta & Salminen, 2000). Examples of these groups are people involved in national legislative processes, working in international and large companies, law firms, small and medium sized companies doing business with foreign partners, law institutions and the mass media, as well as researchers and public administrators in general. The groups include both those highly expert in legal information retrieval as well as laymen. Legal information is also becoming increasingly important for ordinary citizens who may, e.g., be changing their country of residence or buying property or goods from another EU state.

In spite of the differences in the interviewed user groups, in several of them similar needs were identified. The differences in various legal systems of Europe were mentioned as a major problem by the interviewed people. These differences often hindered both the search and the use of foreign legal information. Even where the access to the relevant documents had been gained, the utilization of the documents was difficult without sufficient knowledge of the particular legal system. This was a common problem especially for information specialists working in libraries and other public services whose clients regularly ask about legal situations in various European countries.

A METHOD FOR COLLECTING CONTEXTUAL METADATA

The contextual metadata should contain information concerning the processes where documents are created, about organizations involved and about document types produced. The models created by information systems analysis methods provide information about processes, organizations and information units in the systems (see, for example, Yourdon, 1989; UML-1.4, 2001). A special methodology has been tailored for analyzing and describing document management environments. The methodology was initiated in a project called RASKE. The method development in the project was tied to the document standardization in the Finnish Parliament and ministries. (The name RASKE comes from the Finnish words Rakenteisten AsiakirjaStandardien KEhittäminen, meaning development of standards for structured documents.) The RASKE methods are based on a simple model of document management environments and include methods for data gathering, modeling and user needs analysis (Salminen, 2000; Salminen, Lyytikäinen & Tiitinen, 2000; Salminen et al., 2001). The methods offer tools for gathering and representing contextual metadata about documents.

Electronic Document Management Environments

Representing contextual metadata to the end-users of a heterogeneous document repository in a uniform way requires a uniform understanding of electronic document management (EDM) environments and their components. Figure 1 shows the RASKE model for an EDM environment. An EDM environment is modeled by the central notions of Information Control Nets (ICNs): *activities* and *resources* (Ellis, 1979). Information in an EDM environment is produced and used in activities. The resources are information repositories where information produced can be stored, or from where information can be taken. The resources are divided into three types: documents, systems and actors. *Documents* consist of the recorded data intended for human perception. A document can be identified and handled as a unit in the activities, and it is intended to be understood as information pertaining to a topic. *Systems* consist of devices, software and data used to support the performance of activities. *Actors* are people and organizations performing activities and using documents as well as systems in the activities.

Document Analysis

Document analysis in the RASKE methodology is a process for collecting information about activities, actors and documents in an EDM environment. Some information about systems may be collected, but the primary focus is on the other three components of the EDM environment. Figure 2 shows the phases of a document analysis.

The analysis starts with *specifying the domain* to be analyzed. The domain is an activity like "Creation of the Legal Sources in European Union" or "Paper Machine Manufacturing." The phase includes the identification of the major organizational actors of the activity. After the specification of the domain, three phases are started in parallel: process modeling, document modeling and role modeling. *Process modeling* is used as a means to identify smaller activities and their interrelationships within the domain, the organizations responsible for those activities and the documents created or used. *Document modeling* covers the description of document types, their lifecycles, contents and relationships to each other. In *role modeling,* the key users of documents are

Figure 1. Electronic Document Management Environment

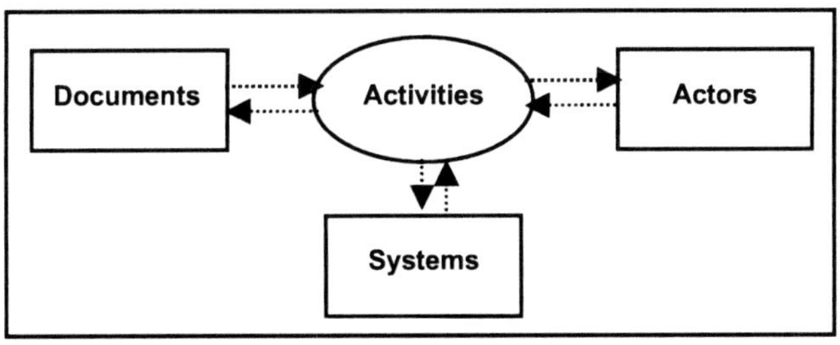

Figure 2. Phases of Document Analysis

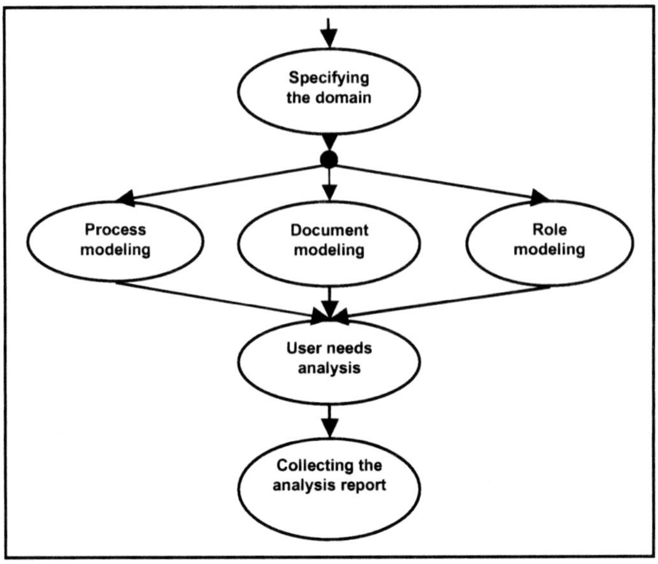

identified and their document management activities are described. *User needs analysis* studies the problems in current document management and the needs for the future as identified by document users. *Collecting the analysis report* takes place at the end of the analysis. The report is collected on the basis of the descriptions and models produced in the earlier phases. The analysis method is described in detail in the literature (Salminen, Lehtovaara & Kauppinen, 1996; Salminen, Kauppinen & Lehtovaara, 1997; Salminen, 2000; Salminen, Lyytikäinen & Tiitinen, 2000; Tiitinen, Lyytikäinen, Päivärinta & Salminen, 2000).

Modeling Techniques in Document Analysis

The modeling techniques of document analysis are intended for describing documents, activities where documents are created and manipulated, and actors in the activities. The most important origins of the techniques chosen are in the object-based modeling methodology of Shlaer and Mellor (1992), in Information Control Nets (Ellis, 1979), and in the document structure specification methods of SGML standard and elm graphs (Goldfarb, 1990; Maler & Andaloussi, 1996). The domain is described by an *organizational framework model* using the ICN notations. Quite the same result could be achieved by using notations from data flow diagrams of structured analysis and design (Yourdon, 1989). In the process modeling phase, *document output models* and *document input models* are used to show the activities and actors of the processes together with the document types produced in the activities and the document types used in the activities, respectively. During the document modeling phase, the relationships of different document types with each other are described by a *document-relationship diagram* corresponding to the information structure diagram of OOA, or the entity-relationship diagram. The hierarchic structure of document types is described by elm graphs (Maler & Andaloussi, 1996) and SGML or XML DTDs or schemas (Goldfarb, 1990; Bray, Paoli & Sperberg-McQueen, 1998). The dynamic behavior of each document type is described by *state transition diagrams* originating from OOA modeling methodology. The role modeling phase includes the identification of different uses of documents by actors. The role is an abstraction of the document management needs, tasks and responsibilities of a group of people. A textual description of each of the roles is written and the relationships between the roles and document types are described in tables.

VISUALIZATION OF THE CONTEXTUAL METADATA

To support the users in coping with the challenges in retrieving information from a complex domain, as for example the legal domain in Europe, we suggest different models created during the document analysis to be used as visualizations of information.

Information Visualization

Information visualization aims at transforming data, information and knowledge into visual form to exploit humans' natural visual capabilities (Gershon, Eick & Card, 1998). Visualization of organizational structures, processes, and the information created and used in them is common in many areas. *Graphical models* are familiar tools, for example in software engineering (e.g., UML; Booch, Rumbaugh & Jacobson, 1999) and in business process redesign (Abeysinghe & Phalp, 1997), where the visualizations are used by the experts who are doing the design work. In office information systems, workflow management systems (Ellis, 1983) and computer-supported cooperative work systems (Sarin, Abbott & McCarthy, 1991), graphical models are used in the user interfaces, which in turn are used in everyday work tasks. Such has also been the case in the visualization of organizational processes and roles for use, e.g., in organizational learning (Käkölä, 1995) and for the management of multiple roles and related documents in the workplace (Plaisant & Shneiderman, 1995). Dourish, Bentley, Jones and MacLean (1999) have discussed the visualization of the history of one document instance within the workflow description. In addition, visualizations have been used to illustrate social networks, especially in military environments (Dekker, 2001).

The visualizations we propose in this chapter add a new perspective for the above-mentioned uses of visual presentations. Our solution for visualizing contextual metadata by graphical models is indented to be used as a retrieval interface for distributed document repositories. The visualized metadata is designed to help the users of the document repositories in coping with the complex environment.

Three Views to Information

We have used three different models to represent three different views to information (Lyytikäinen, Tiitinen, Salminen, Mercier & Vidick, 2000): the *actor view* describes the most significant actors in the domain, the *information source view* shows the different kinds of documents and their relationships, and the *process view* describes activities related to the information production process. In order to enable querying the document databases, links from each element of the view to the query form of the database can be defined. Also, additional information concerning the element visualized in the views is offered to the users.

The views have been implemented in the prototype version in the demonstrator built during the EULEGIS project. The feedback from the users has been encouraging. The views have been seen as a good tool to become acquainted with a previously unfamiliar legal system and to limit the scope of a query statement. In the following, the actor view, information source view and process view will be discussed in more detail.

Actor View

The actor view describes the most significant actors that create information in a given domain. The actors are shown in graphical form, and their roles are concisely described. The graphical model is the same that in the document analysis was called organizational framework model. Figure 3 shows an example of the actor view, where producers of the legal sources in Finland are described. The circle in the middle of the actor view graph represents the domain whose information is created by these actors. The actors in turn are depicted by rectangles connected by arrows to the domain circle. Actors can be put into subgroups, which are shown graphically by nested rectangles.

The actors belonging to an actor group may be part of a larger organization (e.g., Parliament) or may otherwise have similar roles in the creation of the information in question (e.g., different courts). The broken arrows are labeled by identifiers with phrases in the bottom part briefly describing the tasks of the actors or actor groups of the graph.

Figure 3. Actor View of Finnish Legal System

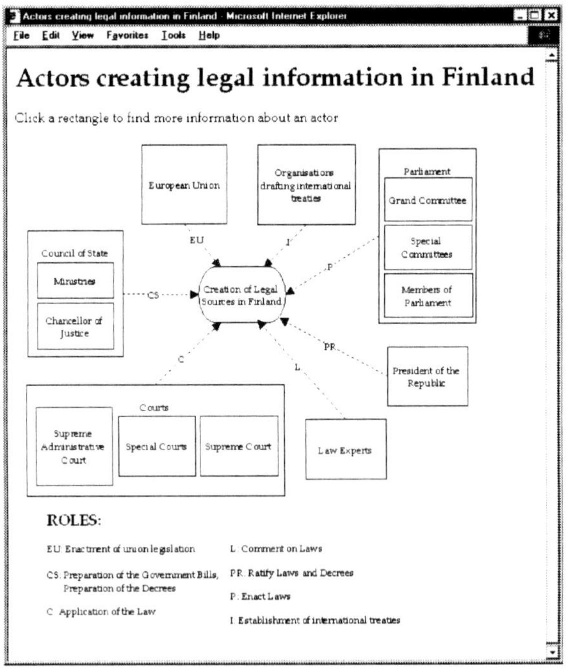

Figure 4. Information about Supreme Court

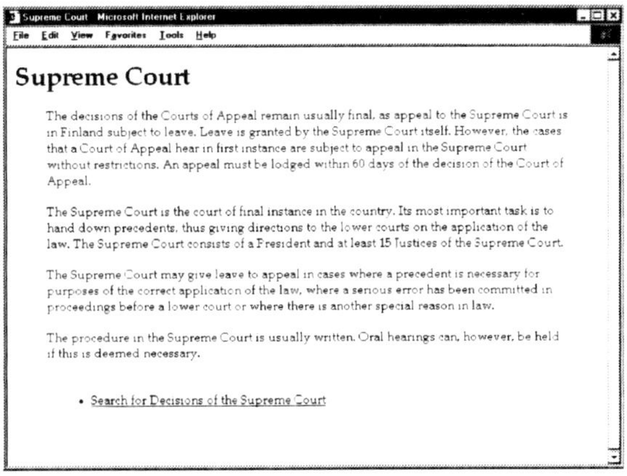

By clicking the name of an actor, the user can obtain more information about the role of that actor. From this additional information, a link leads to a search form by which the user can search for the documents that originate from the selected actor (Figure 4).

Information Source View

The information source view shows the most significant documents in a given domain and their relationships to each other. The graphical representation shows the document types, document type groups and hierarchy connectors. The representation is a modified form of a document-relationship diagram used in the document modeling phase of the document analysis.

Figure 5 describes the legal information sources of the Finnish legal system as an example. National legal documents are categorized into five categories that exist in almost every country: preparatory works, normative documents, court judgments, legal literature and miscellaneous parliamentary documents, including, for example, parliamentary questions and minutes of plenary sessions. The hierarchical relations of the constitution, act, decree and administrative act are represented by their vertical relation to each other and by the line connecting them. As a reminder to the user, the significance of the related international legal documents is emphasized by referring to them in a separate box above the national legal documents.

As in the actor view, additional information about the document types can be offered to users. From the information page related to a document type a hypertext link leads to a search form allowing the user to target to the selected document type.

Process View

The process view gives a graphical overview of the most significant activities related to the creation of information sources in a given domain. It contains information about the order of activities, the actors responsible for performing the activities and the documents created by those activities. The process view is described by the document output model provided by the RASKE analysis. As an example of the process view, the Finnish national legal system is presented in Figure 6.

Figure 5. Legal Information Source View of Finland

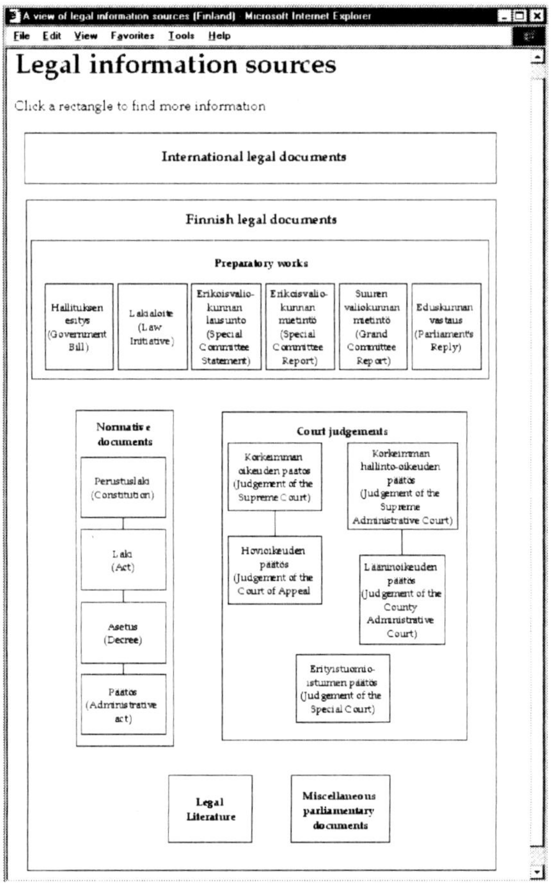

The main activities of the modeled process are depicted by circles. Each circle shows both the name(s) of the activity and the actor(s) performing that activity. The actors in the view should be the same as those presented in the actor view. The order of activities is expressed by unbroken arrows. The direction of the arrow refers to the order in which the activities start. Thus, several activities can actually be performed in parallel. A black dot preceding two or more activities indicates that the activities may start at the same time or in any order. Alternative control flows are indicated by a hollow dot.

As with the other views, additional information can be linked to the components of the process view. When the user clicks an activity symbol in the graph, more information about that activity will appear. That information will provide a link to a search form by which the documents created by that activity can be queried.

Specification of the Views by XML

For the dynamic generation of graphical views, the data pertaining to those views has to be formally defined. For this purpose we used Extensible Markup Language

Figure 6. Process View of the Finnish National Legal System

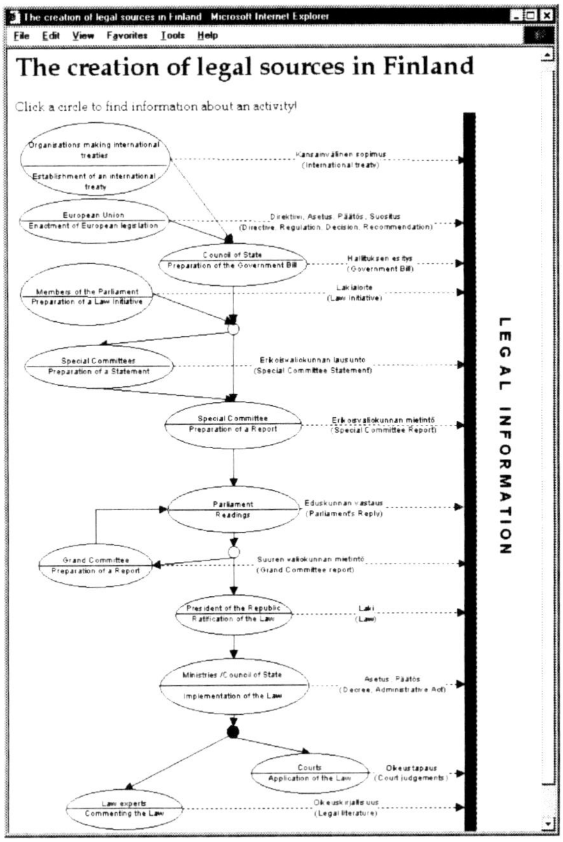

(XML), which has been developed especially for specifying document standards for use in Web information systems (Bray, Paoli & Sperberg-McQueen, 1998). We have designed an XML document type definition by which a domain and the different views can be described. The document type definition for defining the data is presented in Figure 7 in a graphical form created by Near & Far Designer 3.0.

With this DTD all three separate views — actor view, information source view and process view — can be described. In the DTD, the data sources, documents, actors and processes of a certain domain are defined together with their relationships to each other. The DTD is also designed in a way that enables the models to be described in many languages.

The first element in the DTD describes the domain in general terms. The domain has some *goal* (e.g., creation of the legal sources in Finland), and it covers some *area* (e.g., Finland). Both area and goal can be described in several languages. With the *info* element more detailed textual description about the domain can be inserted.

The document repositories of the domain are defined as query interfaces (*qis*). Each query interface needs to have at least a *name* and some identification, which is defined

Figure 7. Graphical Representation of the XML DTD for Describing Metadata for Inter-Organizational Domain

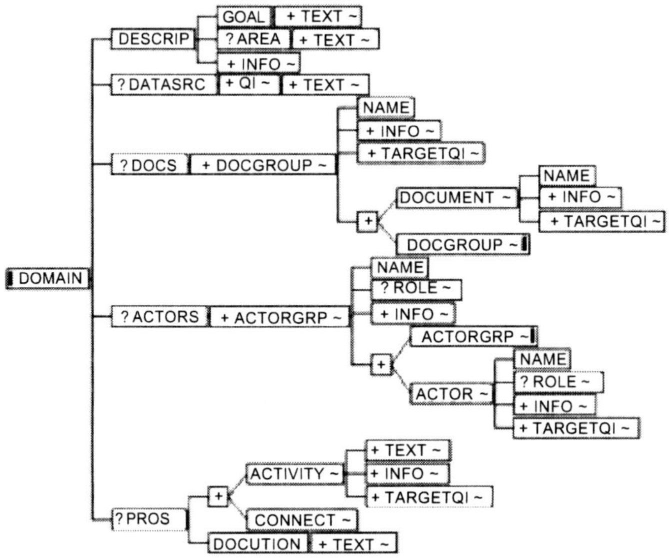

as an attribute. *Docs*, *actors* and *pros* elements are each used to describe the corresponding views. The *targetqi* element is used to link query interfaces of original repositories to elements in the view description.

An advantage of the XML solution is in its capability to express multiple models in multiple languages. Since slightly different versions of models are needed, conversion from one basic model is useful. XML files are also easy to transfer in the network environment since XML solutions are system and vendor independent. This also enables long-term archiving of the data.

FUTURE DIRECTIONS

In the global and organizational networks, documents are increasingly created in complex inter-organizational processes. At the same time, the improved authoring and communication technology increases document production. In Europe, the expansion of the European Union within the past years and in the future is creating a situation where organizations and citizens all over the Europe have a need for legal information not only concerning their own country, but also related to foreign countries and European Union in general. The similar trend can also be seen in the business world where corporations operate in global markets and information related to a business process is produced in different countries.

To assure the accessibility of information created in complicated processes, different kinds of new techniques and support for information retrieval is needed. The contextual metadata approach discussed in this chapter is intended to help information access and understanding, but in building services for uniform access from heterogeneous document databases of the Web, other kinds of metadata support are needed as well. The notion of metadata has a prominent role in the future extension of the current Web to Semantic Web (Berners-Lee, Hendler & Lassila, 2001). Especially metadata about the meaning of Web content and metadata improving the trustworthiness of the content as well as trustworthiness of services is essential in the Semantic Web technologies. The contextual metadata is one technique to add meaning to the content. Another approach for adding meaning is to associate ontologies with text content. The techniques and methods for building and sharing ontologies are an active area of the current Semantic Web research (see, for example, Fensel et al., 2000).

The metadata of the Semantic Web is intended both for people and software. Therefore the metadata has to be presented in a formal, standardized form. XML, suggested also for the contextual metadata earlier in this chapter, forms the basis for the metadata presentation formats. Access to rich metadata in Web services creates new challenges to the design and evaluation of user interfaces. In some cases, like in the case of the contextual metadata, graphical presentations offer a way to show the metadata. Usability studies are needed to evaluate alternative solutions.

Semantic metadata is intended to solve problems related to the explosive growth of Web content. An increase in the metadata resources, however, brings new problems in metadata management. For example, the metadata resources have to be transmitted between collaborative partners, updated occasionally and combined. At the time when all components of organizational networks are reshaping all the time, maintaining the currency and accuracy of metadata resources is a challenge. Where graphical representations are used to show metadata for users, the representations should be automatically generated from a form which is easy to maintain in a metadata database. The XML format of metadata resources supports, for example, the resource exchange and reuse of resources. The common syntax, however, is only the first step towards effective metadata management. Adoption of the Semantic Web technologies on a domain first requires development and agreement of metadata schemes for the specific domain, and then continuing further development of the schemes. Methods for the development are an important area for future research.

CONCLUSION

For the information needed by people, more and more is available in Web repositories. The lack of knowledge about the repositories, differences in the organization of the repositories and in their user interfaces, and the lack of knowledge about the context where the information is created hinder the use of the repositories. In the chapter, we suggested collecting metadata concerning the context of the documents in the repositories. Graphical information models were used to visualize document types, their relationships to each other, actors and activities in the documentation creation process. In order to formally define the models, an XML schema was designed. The graphical interface has been tested in the EULEGIS project. The test users regarded the interface as a valuable tool for retrieving information from foreign legal systems. More systematic user testing is an important area of future research.

REFERENCES

Abeysinghe, G. & Phalp, K. (1997). Combining process modelling methods. *Information and Software Technology 39*, 107-124.

Berners-Lee, T., Hendler, J. & Lassila, O. (2001). The Semantic Web. *The Scientific American (May 2001)*. Retrieved October 17, 2002, from the World Wide Web: http://www.sciam.com/article.cfm?articleID=00048144-10D2-1C70-84A9809EC588EF21&catID=2.

Booch, G., Rumbaugh, J. & Jacobson, I. (1999). *The Unified Modeling Language User Guide*. Reading, MA: Addison-Wesley.

Bray, T., Paoli, J. & Sperberg-McQueen, C.M. (Eds.). (1998). *Extensible Markup Language (XML) 1.0. (Second Edition)*. W3C Recommendation 6-October-2000. Retrieved October 17, 2002, from the World Wide Web: http://www.w3.org/TR/REC-xml.

Dekker, A. (2001). Visualisation of social networks using CAVALIER. *Australian Symposium on Information Visualisation*, 9, 49-55. Sydney, Australia: Australian Computer Society, Inc.

Dourish, P., Bentley, R., Jones, R. & MacLean, A. (1999). Getting some perspective: Using process descriptions to index document history. *Proceedings of the International ACM SIGGROUP Conference on Supporting Group Work*. New York: ACM Press, 375-384.

Ellis, C.A. (1979). Information control nets: A mathematical model of office information flow. *Proceedings of the Conference on Simulation, Measurement and Modeling of Computer Systems, ACM SIGMETRICS Performance Evaluation Review*, 8(3), 225-238.

Ellis, C.A. (1983). Formal and informal models of office activity. In Mason, R.E.A. (Ed.), *Proceedings of the IFIP 9th World Computer Congress*, Paris, France, September 19-23. North-Holland: Elsevier Science Publishers B.V., 11-22.

Fensel, D., Horrocks, I., van Harmelen, F., Decker, S., Erdmann, M. & Klein, M. (2000). OIL in a nutshell. *Knowledge Acquisition, Modeling, and Management, Proceedings of the European Knowledge Acquisition Conference (EKAW-2000)*, Juan-les-Pins, France, October 2-6. *Lecture Notes in Artificial Intelligence 1937*. Springer-Verlag, 1-16.

Gallagher, M., Laver, M. & Mair, P. (1995). *Representative Government in Modern Europe*. New York: McGraw-Hill.

Gershon, N., Eick, S.G. & Card, S. (1998). Information visualization. *Interactions, 5*(2), 9-15.

Goldfarb, C.F. (1990). *The SGML Handbook*. Oxford: Oxford University Press.

Käkölä, T. (1995). Fostering organizational learning with embedded application systems: The XTEND2 prototype. *Proceedings of the 28th Annual Hawaii International Conference on System Sciences*. Los Alamitos, CA: IEEE Computer Society Press, 199-208.

Lyytikäinen, V., Tiitinen, P. & Salminen, A. (2000). Challenges for European legal information retrieval. In Galindo, F. & Quirchmayer, G. (Eds.), *Proceedings of the IFIP 8.5 Working Conference on Advances in Electronic Government*. Zaragoza: Seminario de Informática y Derecho, Universidad de Zaragoza, 121-132.

Lyytikäinen, V., Tiitinen, P., Salminen, A., Mercier, L. & Vidick, J.-L. (2000). Visualizing legal systems for information retrieval. In Khosrow-Pour, M. (Ed.), *Challenges of Information Technology Management in the 21st Century, Proceedings of 2000 Information Resources Management Association International Conference.* Hershey, PA: Idea Group Publishing, 245-249.

Maler, E. & El Andaloussi, J. (1996). *Developing SGML DTDs. From Text to Model to Markup.* Upper Saddle River, NJ: Prentice Hall.

Plaisant, C. & Shneiderman, B. (1995). Organization overviews and role management: Inspiration for future desktop environments. *IEEE Proceedings of the 4th Workshop on Enabling Technologies: Infrastructure for Collaborative Enterprises,* 14-22.

Salminen, A. (2000). Methodology for document analysis. In Kent, A. (Ed.), *Encyclopedia of Library and Information Science,* 67(Supplement 30), 299-320. New York: Marcel Dekker, Inc.

Salminen, A., Kauppinen, K. & Lehtovaara, M. (1997). Towards a methodology for document analysis. *Journal of the American Society for Information Science, 48*(7), 644-655.

Salminen, A., Lehtovaara, M. & Kauppinen, K. (1996). Standardization of digital legislative documents, a case study. In Lynn, M.S. (Ed.), *Proceedings of the 29th Annual Hawaii International Conference on System Sciences.* Los Alamitos, CA: IEEE Computer Society Press, 72-81.

Salminen, A., Lyytikäinen, V. & Tiitinen, P. (2000). Putting documents into their work context in document analysis. *Information Processing & Management, 36*(4), 623-641.

Salminen, A., Lyytikäinen, V., Tiitinen, P. & Mustajärvi, O. (2001). Experiences of SGML standardization: The case of the Finnish legislative documents. In Sprague, J.R.H. (Ed.), *Proceedings of the 34th Hawaii International Conference on Systems Sciences* (file etegv01.pdf at CD-ROM). Los Alamitos, CA: IEEE Computer Society Press.

Sarin, S.K., Abbott, K.R. & McCarthy, D.R. (1991). A process model and system for supporting collaborative work. *Conference on Organizational Computing Systems, SIGOIS Bulletin, 12*(2,3), 213-224.

Shlaer, S. & Mellor, S.J. (1992). *Object Lifecycles: Modeling the World in States.* Englewood Cliffs, NJ: Yourdon Press.

Tiitinen, P., Lyytikäinen, V., Päivärinta, T. & Salminen, A. (2000). User needs for electronic document management in public administration: A study of two cases. In Hansen, H.R., Bichler, M. & Mahler, H. (Eds.), *Proceedings of the 8th European Conference on Information Systems, Volume 2.* Wien: Wirtschaftsuniversität Wien, 1144-1151.

UML-1.4. (2001, September). *OMG Unified Modeling Language Specification. Version 1.4.* Retrieved October 17, 2002, from the World Wide Web: http://cgi.omg.org/docs/formal/01-09-67.pdf.

Yourdon, E. (1989). *Modern Structured Analysis.* Englewood Cliffs, NJ: Prentice-Hall.

Section II

Data Management and Web Technologies

Chapter VIII

Database Management Issues in the Web Environment

J.F. Aldana Montes
Universidad de Málaga, Spain

A.C. Gómez Lora
Universidad de Málaga, Spain

N. Moreno Vergara
Universidad de Málaga, Spain

M.M. Roldán García
Universidad de Málaga, Spain

ABSTRACT

The focus of this chapter is on the progressive adaptation of database techniques to Web usage in a way quite similar to the evolution from integrated file management systems to database management systems. We review related and open issues, such as the semi-structured data and XML, integrity problem, query optimization problem, and integration issues in both the Web and Semantic Web environments. The representation of meta-information along with data opens up a new way to automatically process Web information due to the use of explicit semantic information. We hope that researchers will take into account traditional database techniques and how they can assist new Web technologies. In this sense, the amalgamation of Web and database technology appears to be very promising.

INTRODUCTION

The focus of this chapter is on introducing a new paradigm: the Web as the database, i.e., the progressive adaptation of database techniques to Web usage. We consider that this will be done in a way quite similar to the evolution from integrated file management systems to database management systems. In any case, this is a much more difficult goal and quite a lot of work is still to be done.

The database community has been seriously disturbed with the Web technologies expansion. Particularly, two reports have produced a special commotion in database field. The first one, the Asilomar report (Bernstein et al., 1998), postulates the new directives in databases tendencies, previewing the Web impact in this field. The second one, Breaking out of the Box (Silberschatz & Zdonik, 1996), proposes how the database community must transfer its technology to be introduced into Web technology. In this sense, we have broken out of the database box into its autonomous functional components, and we are using these to reach a solution for the problem of heterogeneous data sources integration.

It is within this context that we are going to study the different issues of data management in the Web. This chapter reviews related and open issues, such as the semi-structured data and XML, integrity problem, query optimization problem, and integration issues in both the Web and Semantic Web environments. Finally, we will briefly discuss how traditional database technologies can be used to solve these open points. The special features of the Web environment make techniques for querying or maintaining the Web different from those for traditional databases.

Thinking about the Web as a huge, highly distributed database, we may consider different dimensions to conceptually describe it. Tamer Özsu and Valduriez (1999) define a classification of database systems with respect to: (1) their distribution, (2) the autonomy of local systems and (3) the heterogeneity of database systems. The autonomy concept is considered as the distribution of control, not of data. This indicates the degree to which individual DBMSs can operate independently. Whereas autonomy refers to the distribution of control, the distribution dimension deals with the physical distribution of data over multiple sites. With respect to heterogeneity, this can range from hardware heterogeneity, differences in networking protocols, variations in DBMSs, etc., to the data model or the policy for managing integrity on the database.

Figure 1. Extending the Cube

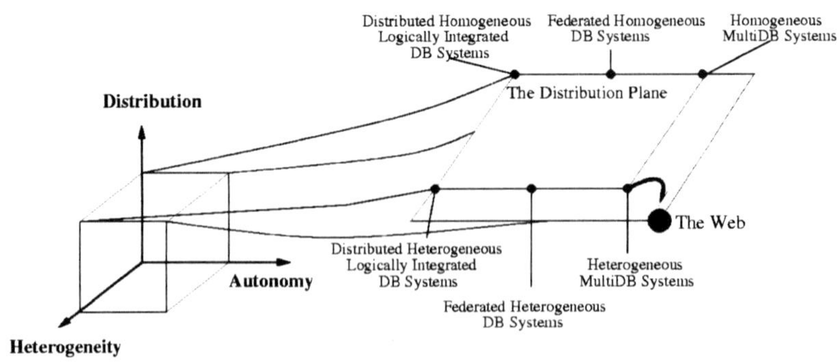

Obviously, the Web is in the distribution plane, and, as shown in Figure 1, we think that "it falls out" of the cube because it presents the highest degree of distribution, heterogeneity and autonomy. Therefore, traditional distributed database techniques must be further extended to deal with this new environment.

The distribution paradigm in databases is well known in both the research and industry communities. Nowadays, many commercial databases support certain degrees of parallelism and distribution in both data and control. Nevertheless, almost all of them are based on the relational model. The relational model manages structured information in a formal data model using a simple and well-defined algebra. However, even in this well-known model, the distribution paradigm has no trivial solution.

But the Web environment is not equivalent to a traditional distributed environment for a relational database. One of these differences is the problem of managing semi-structured information in such an environment, which is significantly more complex.

At first glance, the Web is a huge repository of information without any structure whatsoever. Nowadays, this is changing quickly. The consolidation of the Extensible Markup Language (XML, 2002), as a new standard adopted by the World Wide Web Consortium (W3C), has made the publication of electronic data easier. With a simple syntax for data, XML is, at the same time, human and machine understandable. XML has important advantages over HTML (HyperText Markup Language). While HTML is a data visualization language for the Web (even though this was not its initial intended purpose), with XML, data structure and rendering are orthogonal. We can represent meta-information about data through user-defined tags. No rendering information is included in an XML document. In spite of the main feature of XML being a data exchange format, in this chapter we will see that it is much more.

It is generally accepted that XML and its associated recommendations will be the future model for Web query processing. However, XML introduces new additional problems to the paradigm of semi-structured information management in the Web environment.

The representation of meta-information along with data opens up a new way to automatically process Web information because of the use of explicit semantic information. In this sense, the amalgamation of Web and database technology appears to be very promising.

In any case, a lot of work must still be carried out in the database community to resolve all the issues related to such a distributed and heterogeneous database, which is what the Web actually is.

SEMI-STRUCTURED DATA AND XML

With respect to the information available on the Web, we can distinguish between data which is completely unstructured (for instance, images, sounds and raw text), and highly structured data, such us data from a traditional database systems (relational, object-oriented or object-relational).

However, we can also find many documents on the Web that fall in between these two extremes. Such data have become relevant during the last few years and have been named semi-structured data. A good introduction to this topic is found in Buneman (1997). In semi-structured data, the information normally associated with a schema is contained within the data (self-describing data). In some cases there is no separate schema, whereas in others it exists but only places loose constraints on the data.

Therefore, semi-structured data is characterized by the lack of any fixed and rigid schema, although typically the data has some implicit structure. The most immediate example of data that cannot be constrained by a schema is the Web itself.

Semi-structured data may be irregular and incomplete and does not necessarily conform to a unique schema. As with structured data, it is often desirable to maintain a history of changes to data, and to run queries over both the data and the changes. Representing and querying changes in semi-structured data is more difficult than in structured data due to the irregularity and lack of schema. In Chawathe, Abiteboul and Widom (1998), a model for representing changes in semi-structured data and a language for querying these changes is presented.

Several languages, such as Lorel (Abiteboul, Quass, McHugh, Widom & Wiener, 1997) and UnQL (Fernández, 1996), support querying semi-structured data. Others, for example WebSQL (Mihaila, 1996) and WebLog (Lakshmanan, Sadri & Subramanian, 1996), query websites. All these languages model data as labeled graphs and use regular path expressions to express queries that traverse arbitrary paths in the graphs. As the data model is an edge-labeled directed graph, a path expression is a sequence of edge labels $l_1, l_2, \ldots l_n$. Abiteboul, Buneman and Suciu (2000) consider a path expression as a simple query whose result, for a given data graph, is a set of nodes. In general, the result

Figure 2. Data Model in LORE

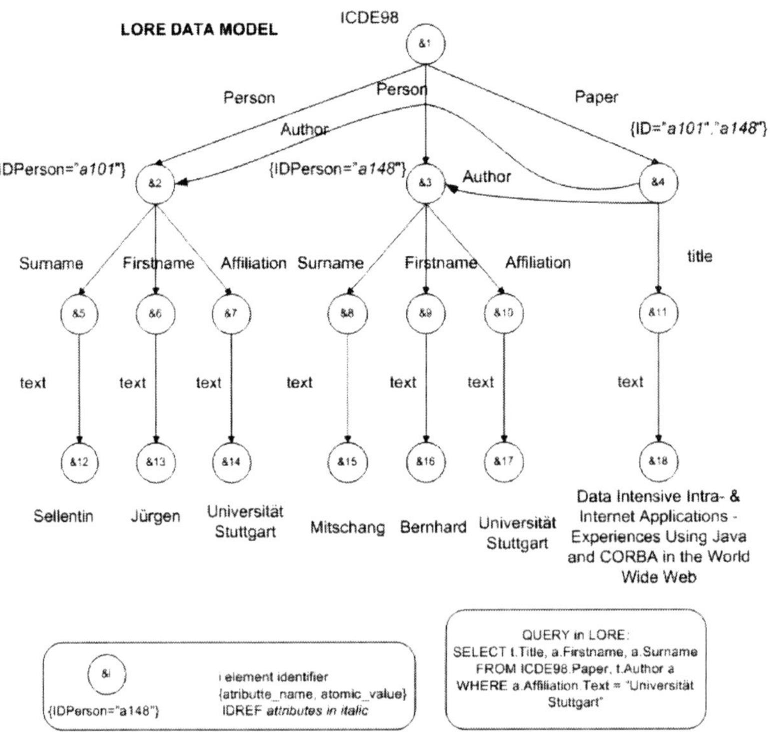

Figure 3. Data Model in XML

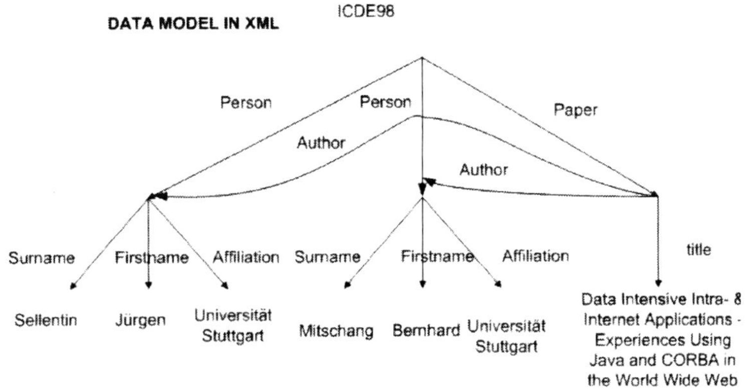

of the path expression $l_1l_2 \ldots l_n$ on a data graph is the set of nodes v_n such that there exist edges (r,l_1,v_1), (v_1,l_2,v_2),..., (v_{n-1},l_n,v_n), where r is the root. Thus, path expressions result in sets of nodes and not in pieces of semi-structured data. In Fernández and Suciu (1998), two optimization techniques for queries with regular path expressions are described, both of them relying on graph schemas which specify partial knowledge of a graph's structure.

All semi-structured data models have converged around a graph-based data representation that combines both data and structure into one simple data format. Some works (Nestorov, Abiteboul & Motwani, 1998) on typing semi-structured data have been proposed based on labeled and directed graphs as a general form of semi-structured data. eXtensible Markup Language (XML) (XML, 2002) has this kind of representation based on labeled and directed graphs. Although minor differences exist between them, the semi-structured data model is based on unordered collections, whereas XML is ordered. The close similarity of both models (Figures 2 and 3) made systems like LORE (Goldman, McHugh & Widom, 1999), initially built for a semi-structured model, migrate from semi-structured data to XML data.

XML was designed specifically to describe content, rather than presentation. XML is a textual representation of data that allows users to define new tags to indicate structure. In Figure 4, we can see that the textual structure enclosed by <Publication>...</Publication> is used to describe a publication tuple (the prefix of the tag names is relative to the namespace where the elements are going to be defined). An XML document does not provide any instructions on how it is to be displayed, and you can include such information in a separate stylesheet. With the use of XSL stylesheets (XSL, 1999), it is possible to translate XML data to HTML for visualization purposes by standard browsers.

XML-Related Technology

A Document Type Definition (DTD) is a context-free grammar, which defines the structure for an XML document type. DTDs are part of the XML standard. A DTD can also serve as the "schema" for the data represented by an XML document. Unfortunately this is not as close as we would like to a database schema language, because it lacks

Figure 4. Example of XML Document Representing a Publication Page

```
<?xml version="1.0" encoding="ISO-8859-1" standalone="no"?>
<?xml-stylesheet type="text/xsl" href="../../XSL-Stylesheets/Publication.xsl"?>
<pri:Publication xmlns:pri="http://www.lcc.uma.es"
xmlns:xsi="http://www.w3.org/1999/XMLSchema-instance">
    <pri:Title Url="http://128.253.154.5/Proyecto/XML-Docs/Publications/
    icde98.xml">Data Intensive Intra- & Internet Applications - Experiences
Using Java and CORBA in the World Wide Web</pri:Title>
    <pri:Author xsi:type="pri:Author_Type">
        <pri:Name>Jürgen Sellentin</pri:Name>
        <pri:Identificator>JSELL1</pri:Identificator>
    </pri:Author>
    <pri:Author xsi:type="pri:Author_Type">
        <pri:Name>Bernhard Mitschang</pri:Name>
        <pri:Identificator>BMIT1</pri:Identificator>
    </pri:Author>
    <pri:PublicationYear>1998</pri:Year>
    <pri:Scope>International</pri:Scope>
    <pri:Congress>
        <pri:CongressName>
    International Conference on Data Engineering
        </pri:CongressName>
        <pri:StartPage>302</pri:StartPage>
        <pri:EndPage>311</pri:EndPage>
        <pri:Isbn>0-8186-8289-2</pri:Isbn>
        <pri:PublicationPlace>Orlando, Florida, USA</pri:PublicationPlace>
    </pri:Congress>
</pri:Publication>
```

semantics. Other limitations we find are that a DTD imposes order and lacks the notion of atomic types. That is, we cannot express that a 'weight' element has to be a non-negative integer, and moreover, we cannot express a range for constraining the weight between 0 and a maximum value. These and other limitations make DTDs inadequate from a database viewpoint. Therefore, new XML-based standards for representing structural and semantic information about the data have arisen. One of these proposals is the Resource Description Framework (RDF, 1999) and the RDF Schema (2000).

RDF is a foundation for processing metadata, providing a simple data model and a standardized syntax for metadata. Basically, it provides the language for writing down factual statements. Its intended applications are mainly: 1) providing better search engine capabilities for resource discovery; 2) cataloging for describing the content and content relationships available at a particular website; and 3) allowing intelligent software agents to share and exchange knowledge (Abiteboul et al., 2000). RDF consists of a data model (an edge-labeled graph with nodes called resources and edge labels called properties) and a syntax for representing this model in XML.

On top of RDF, the simple schema language RDFS, Resource Description Framework Schema (RDF Schema, 2000), has been defined offering a specific vocabulary to model class and property hierarchies and other basic schema primitives that can be referred to from RDF models. The RDF Schema provides an instrument to define vocabulary, structure and integrity constraints for expressing metadata about Web resources. Once again, the main problem with RDF is its lack of a standard semantics and, therefore, this semantics must be defined in each of its instances. An RDF Schema instance allows for the standardization of the metadata defined over Web resources, and the specification of predicates and integrity constraints on these resources. In knowledge engineering terminology, a RDF Schema defines a simple ontology that particular RDF documents may be checked against to determine its consistency. In addition, the RDF Schema is a type system for RDF since it provides a mechanism to define classes of resources and property types which restrict the domain and range of a property.

The RDF and RDF Schema specifications use XML as an interchange format to exchange RDF and RDF Schema triples (Bowers & Delcambre, 2000).

As mentioned above, some schema languages for describing XML data structures and constraints have been proposed. XML DTD is the *de facto* standard XML schema language but has limited capabilities compared to other schema languages, including its successor XML-Schema (2001). Its main building block consists of an element and an attribute, and it uses hierarchical element structures. Other schema languages have been proposed, such as Schematron, DSD, SOX, XDR, among others. A comparative analysis of the more representative XML schema languages is found in Lee and Chu (2000). In this chapter, the focus will be on XML-Schema because it is an ongoing effort by the W3C for replacing DTD with a more expressive language.

XML-Schema is written in XML enabling the use of XML tools. It presents a rich set of data types, capabilities for declaring user-defined datatypes, mechanisms such as inheritance and so on. In fact, XML schemas are object oriented.

Although XML-Schema identifies many commonly recurring schema constraints and incorporates them into the language specification, it will be interesting to see how constraint support will evolve in XML-Schema in the future.

THE INTEGRITY PROBLEM OF THE WEB

A part of the semantics of a database is expressed as integrity constraints. Constraints are properties that the data of a database are required to satisfy and they are expected to be satisfied after each transaction performed on the database. The verification of constraints in a database is often quite expensive in terms of time as well as being complex. Some important factors related to this issue include the structure of the underlying database upon which the constraints are imposed, the nature of the imposed constraints and the method adopted for their evaluation. We are going to consider *Domain Restriction* and *Structural Restrictions* and their representation in a Web data model.

From a database perspective, XML-Schema (2001) provides a new technological standard which enables us to represent data semantics like a database does. We can find a discussion about schema languages in Lee and Chu (2000).

Domain Restrictions

A domain restriction defines the set of values that an attribute may have. For example, the following declaration in XML-Schema defines a type expressed with a regular expression indicating the template to follow for correct e-mail addresses:

```
<xsd:simpleType name="E-mail_Type">
   <xsd:restriction base="typ:string">
      <xsd:pattern value="([A-Z]|[a-z]|\.|\d|_)*@([A-Z]|[a-z]|\.|\d|_)*"/>
   </xsd:restriction>
</xsd:simpleType>
```

XML-Schema provides enhanced data types and user-defined data types. New data types can be created from base data types specifying values for one or more facets for the base data type. Moreover, on XML-Schema we can define subclasses and superclasses of types.

We can restrict some of the elements of a more general type, making them only accept a more restricted range of values, or a minor number of instances. If we have defined the following data type:

```
<complexType name="Publication">
        <sequence>
          <element name="Title" type="string" minOccurs="1"
maxOccurs="1"/>
          <element name="Author" type="string" minOccurs="1"
maxOccurs="unbounded"/>
          <element name="PublicationYear" type="year" minOccurs="1"
maxOccurs="1"/>
        </sequence>
   </complexType>
```

Then, we can derive for extension a type for a Publication, such as:

```
<complex Typename = "Proceedings" base="Publication"
derivedBy="extension">
    <sequence>
        <element name="ISBN" type="string" minOccurs="1" maxOccurs="1"/>
        <element name="Publisher" type="string" minOccurs="1"
maxOccurs="1"/>
        <element name="PlaceMeeting" type="string" minOccurs="1"
maxOccurs="1"/>
        <element name="DateMeeting" type="date" minOccurs="1"
```

```
maxOccurs="1"/>
    </sequence>
</complexType>
```

Or we can derive for restriction a type for a Publication:

```
<complexType name= "SingleAuthor" base="Publication"
derivedBy="restriction">
    <sequence>
        <element name="Title" type="string" minOccurs="1"
maxOccurs="unbounded"/>
        <element name="Author" type="string" minOccurs="1"
maxOccurs="1"/>
        <element name="PublicationYear" type="year" minOccurs="1"
maxOccurs="1"/>
    </sequence>
</complexType>
```

Sometimes we want to create a data type and disable any kind of derivation from it. For example, we can specify that Publication cannot be extended or restricted:

```
<complexType name="Publication" final="#all" ...>
```

Or we can disable the restriction of the type Publication:

```
<complexType name="Publication" final="restriction" ...>
```

Similarly, we can disable the extension:

```
<complexType name="Publication" final="extension" ...>
```

Structural Restrictions and Relationships

With respect to structural restrictions, in this schema language we can represent:

1) *Uniqueness for attribute:* XML-Schema supports this feature using <Unique>, where the scope and target object of the uniqueness are specified by <Selector> and <Field> constructs, respectively. Furthermore, XML-Schema specifies uniqueness not only for attributes but also for arbitrary elements or even composite objects.
2) *Key for attribute:* In databases, being a key requires being unique as well as not being null. A similar concept is defined in XML-Schema.
3) *Foreign key for attribute:* Foreign key states: a) who is a referencing key using <Keyref>; and b) who is being referenced by the referencing key using constructs <Refer> and <PointsTo>, respectively.

```
<key name="dNumKey">
        <selector>departments/department</selector>
```

```
        <field>@number</field>
</key>
<keyref refer="dNumKey">
        <selector>subject/department</selector>
        <field>@number</field>
</keyref>
```

The *key/keyref* mechanism complements the *id/idref* of one of the previous versions of XML-Schema and solves its associated problems. It also allows us to define complex types as keys, generating new, interesting, practical problems.

QUERY OPTIMIZATION ON THE WEB

The processing of XML documents is computationally more expensive than the processing of relations. More generally, the computational management of semi-structured data is more complex and expensive than the management of structured data. This means that semi-structured data management requires more and better optimization techniques than relational database management systems do. XML optimization techniques are still quasi-unexplored, since query language and algebra specification are not definitive and stable. However, there is much work in specific areas and many optimization techniques developed under different paradigms that could be adapted to XML.

Optimization on regular path queries (Grahne & Thomo, 2000, 2001) and indexing techniques over semi-structured information (McHugh & Widom, 1999) have already been studied. However, other relevant aspects, such as composition reordering and restriction propagations, still have not been analyzed under the XML data model, although they can be performed in this new model with relatively low effort. These techniques are well known and used in relational data models. More complex and sophisticated techniques, magic rewriting for example (Bancilhon, Maier, Sagiv & Ullman, 1986), which have demonstrated goods results, have yet to be tested in the XML context.

Some algorithms will require less effort; others will require more complex and refined translation. Thus, semantic query optimization via residue computation (Chakravarthy, Grant & Minker, 1990) could be complex in XML, because it would require a complete redesign of the original technique. However, if we introduce domain restrictions in the query graph, Predicate Move Around (Levy, Mumick & Sagiv, 1994), which could be easily adapted to XML, would yield a similar optimization level.

One of the most important studies on XML and semi-structured data optimization (McHugh & Widom, 1999) has been developed for the LOREL system (Abiteboul, Quass, McHugh, Widom & Wiener, 1997). It defines several index structures over XML data and schema, yielding efficient data management. In the physical query plan, LORE not only supports the traditional value index, but also label, edge and path indexes.

Domain and Column Constraint Propagation techniques have the same basis as selection propagation techniques; they are based on query algebra laws. Traditional selection propagation methods are based on the axioms and properties of the query algebra, especially on those defining the commutation of selection with the rest of the operators. They use these algebra equivalences as rewriting rules, but each algorithm determines how these must be applied (when, where and how many times). Some good examples for relational algebra can be found in traditional database literature (Ullman,

Figure 5a. Monad Laws

for v in e1 do e2	=	e2{v := e1}
for v in e do v	=	E
for v2 in (for v1 in e1 do e2) do e3	=	for v1 in e1 do (for v2 in e2 do e3)

1989; Abiteboul, Hull & Vianu, 1995). Predicate Move Around (Levy et al., 1994) is an extension of the selection propagation algorithm that brings in better results and, furthermore, those constraints that could be expressed as selections in the query could be used in the optimization process.

Constraint propagation must follow the laws defined in XML algebra. The initial draft proposed three basic groups of rules (Figures 5a, 5b and 5c) than can be used for query optimization, including constraints propagation. In current drafts (XQuery Formal Semantics, 2002), these groups are not explicitly defined.

As mentioned, constraint propagation and selection propagation are similar in the relational algebra context. In XML algebra, selection is not defined explicitly, but we can use the WHEN algebra element to define it, which is semantically defined as a particular case of the IF-THEN-ELSE structure. This construction is more generic than selection because it implements both filters and complex compositions. WHEN or IF-THEN-ELSE structures act like filters and can implement any derived condition from known constraints, at least in the simplest algorithms.

Example

Let's see a single example of constraint propagation in XML, assuming the following schema:

```
<xsd:simpleType name="distance" type="xs:integer" minIncluded="0"/>
<xsd:simpleType name="autonomy" type="xs:integer" minIncluded="0"
maxIncluded="900"/>

<xsd:element name="car">
    <xsd:complexType>
        <xsd:sequence>
```

Figure 5b. Equivalence Between Projection and Iteration

```
e/a → For v1 in e do
          for v2 in nodes(v1) do
            match v2
              case v3 : a[AnyComplexType] do v3
              else ()
```

Figure 5c. Optimization Laws

for v in ( ) do e	→	( )
for v in (e1, e2) do e3	→	(for v in e1 do e3), (for v in e2 do e3)
for v in e1 do e2	→	E2{e1/ v}, if e1 : u
for v in e do v	→	E
e1 : {t1}, e2 : {t2}, v1 free in e2	→	for v2 in e2 do for v1 in e1 do e3
for v1 in e1 do for v2 in e2 do e3		
E[if e1 then e2 else e3]	→	if e1 then E[e2] else E[e3]
E[let v = e1 do e2]	→	let v = e1 do E[e2]
E[for v in e1 do e2]	→	for v in e1 do E[e2]
E[match e1	→	match e1
case v : t do e2		case v : t do E[e2]
...		...
case v : t do en-1		case v : t do E[en-1]
else E[en]		else E[en]

```
                <xsd:element name=“model” type=“xs:string” use=“required”/>
                <xsd:element name=“kilometers” type=“xs:autonomy”
use=“required”/>
            </xsd:sequence>
        </xsd:complexType>
</xsd:element>
<xsd:element name=“road”
        <xsd:complexType>
            <xsd:sequence>
                <xsd:element name=“sourcecity” type=“xs:string” use=“required”/>
                <xsd:element name=“targetcity” type=“xs:string” use=“required”/>
                <xsd:element name=“kilometers” type=“xs:distance”
use=“required”/>
            </xsd:sequence>
        </xsd:complexType>
</xsd:element>
```

In the following, the W3C query algebra (XQuery Formal Semantics, 2002) is used. This algebra is based on the *for* iteration operator, as SQL is based on the select statement.

And now, for the query:

```
for $r in base/road
    where $r/sourcecity = "Madrid" return
        for $c in base/car
            where $c/model = "mondeo" return
                where $c/kilometres/data() <= $r/kilometres/data() return
                    possibleroad[ $r/targetcity, $r/kilometres ]
```

with the derived type:

```
<xsd:element name="possibleroad"
    <xsd:complexType>
        <xsd:sequence>
            <xsd:element name="targetcity" type="xs:string" use="required"/>
            <xsd:element name="kilometers" type="xs:distance"
use="required"/>
        </xsd:sequence>
    </xsd:complexType>
</xsd:element>
```

An adapted version of the Predicate Move Around technique (Levy et al., 1994) propagates the constraint "*car/kilometres < 900*." We indicate this constraint propagation using C comments (/*…*/).

```
for $r in base/road
    where $r/sourcecity = "Madrid" return
        for $c in base/car /* base/car/kilometres < 900 */
            where $c/model = "mondeo" return
                where $c/kilometres/data() <= $r/kilometres/data() return
                    possibleroad[ $r/targetcity, $r/kilometres ]
```

→

```
for $r in base/road
    where $r/sourcecity = "Madrid" return
        for $c /* $c/kilometres < 900 */ in base/car
            where $c/model = "mondeo" return
                where $c/kilometres/data() <= $r/kilometres/data() return
                    possibleroad[ $r/targetcity, $r/kilometres ]
```

→

```
for $r in base/road
    where $r/sourcecity = "Madrid" return
        for $c in base/car
            where $c/model = "mondeo" /* $c/kilometres < 900 */ return
                where $c/kilometres/data() <= $r/kilometres/data() return
                    possibleroad[ $r/targetcity, $r/kilometres ]
```

→

```
for $r in base/road
    where $r/sourcecity = "Madrid" return
        for $c in base/car
```

```
                where $c/model = "mondeo" return
                    where $c/kilometres/data()/* $c/kilometres < 900 */ <= $r/
kilometres/data() return
                        possibleroad[ $r/targetcity, $r/kilometres ]
→
for $r in base/road
    where $r/sourcecity = "Madrid" return
        for $c in base/car
            where $c/model = "mondeo" return
                where $c/kilometres/data() <= $r/kilometres/data() /* $r/
kilometres < 900 */ return
                    possibleroad[ $r/targetcity, $r/kilometres ]
```

Here, the restriction can take two ways: upwards (towards the inner do) and downwards (towards the outer for).

```
for $r in base/road
    where $r/sourcecity = "Madrid" /* $r/kilometres < 900 */ return
        for $c in base/car
            where $c/model = "mondeo" return
                where $c/kilometres/data() <= $r/kilometres/data() return
                    possibleroad[ $r/targetcity, $r/kilometres ] /* $r/kilometres
< 900 */
```

Finally, no more propagation can be done.

```
for $r in base/road
    where $r/sourcecity = "Madrid" and $r/kilometres < 900 return
        for $c in base/car
            where $c/model = "mondeo" return
                    where $c/kilometres/data() <= $r/kilometres/data()return
                        possibleroad[ $r/targetcity, $r/kilometres ]
```

We can observe that not only the query is more efficient, but the query derived type is now:

```
<xsd:element name="possibleroad"
    <xsd:complexType>
        <xsd:sequence>
            <xsd:element name="targetcity" type="xs:string" use="required"/>
            <xsd:element name="kilometers" type="xs:distance"
use="required" maxExcluded="900"/>
        </xsd:sequence>
    </xsd:complexType>
</xsd:element>
```

The propagation can be viewed graphically in Figure 6.

Figure 6. Constraint Propagation

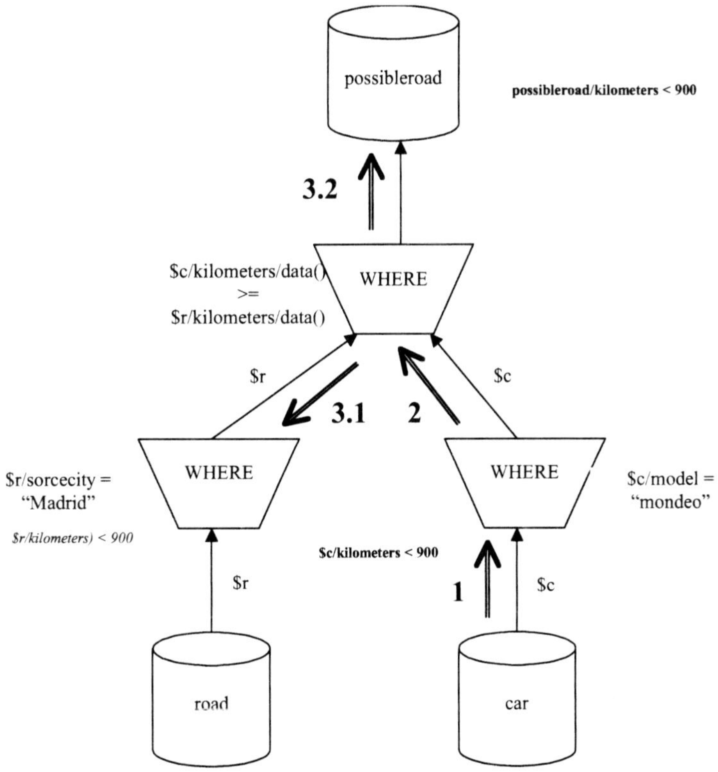

From the XML perspective, constraint propagation cannot be used exclusively for query optimization, but it can and must be used during new type derivation or inference (Fan, Kuper & Siméon, 2001). This is generically called subtyping. One of the main characteristics of XML is that it allows new type extensions and restrictions through inheritance. When a new type is defined or derived from an existing one, it not only inherits its members, but also a new set of associated constraints. Some of these new restrictions will be explicitly defined, but others will be inherited from the base type. The computation of this new set of constraints is fundamental in object-oriented systems, and very important in preventing integrity constraints violations in our schema. There are two basic ways to implement and validate a particular object of a known type: on the one hand, verifying each of the defined constraints for the object type and all its ancestors; and, on the other hand, deriving and making explicit all the constraints that must be validated during type definition, allowing us to verify each object exclusively using the set of constraints previously computed. From an optimization point of view, the second choice is better, because it can detect inconsistencies at type definition time, and not at query time.

Constraint derivation in subtyping is useful with domain and column constraints, but it is also useful with entity and referential constraints (Fan et al., 2001). The existence of physical index associated with keys and references in order to accelerate relationship composition is common.

INTEGRATION ISSUES ON THE WEB

The Web can be seen not only as a set of HTML pages but also as a set of heterogeneous and distributed data sources. Heterogeneity in formats and storage media, diversity and dispersion in data makes it difficult to use this plethora of interrelated information. The integration of these information sources, in order to achieve an unified access with independency of possible internal changes in their organization, is a clear and important technological issue. Therefore, an integration system must address the problems of information heterogeneity and query solving, for different platforms, syntactic heterogeneity (e.g., file formats), structural aspects (e.g., schema definitions) and semantic differences (e.g., concepts and relationships among entities).

Wrappers were the first building block in Web integration. They act as interfaces to each data source, providing (semi) structure to non-structured sources or mapping the original data source structure to a common one. Unfortunately, it is very difficult to switch unstructured data into a specific schema. Issues related to wrappers design and implementation can be found in Roth and Schwarz (1997) and Sahuguet and Azavant (1999).

Ashish and Knoblock (1997) present an approach for semi-automatically generating wrappers through a wrapper-generation toolkit. The key idea is to exploit the formatting information in pages from the source to hypothesize the underlying structure of a page. From this structure, the system generates a wrapper that facilitates querying a source and possibly integrating it with other sources.

The knowledge about evaluating a query over multiple wrappers is encapsulated by mediators. The wrapper-mediator approach provides an interface to a group of (semi-) structured data sources, combining their local schemas in a global one and integrating the information of local sources. So the views of the data that mediators offer are coherent, performing semantic reconciliation of the common data model representations carried out by the wrappers. One of the main problems in data integration is related to the maintaining of the integrity constraints. As this problem is not yet solved, mediators need to deal with the problem of evaluating consistent queries over possible inconsistent sources with respect to the common schema constraints.

Some good examples of the wrapper-mediator systems are AMOS (Fahl, Risch & Sköld, 1993), TSIMMIS (García-Molina et al., 1995), DISCO (Tomasic, Raschid & Valduriez, 1995), GARLIC (Roth et al., 1996; Haas, Kossmann, Wimmers & Yang, 1997; Haas et al., 1999). Recently, many of these approaches have moved toward XML standard, like AMOS and TSIMMIS. On the other hand, MIX (Baru et al., 1999) (the successor to the TSIMMIS project) and MOCHA (Rodríguez-Martínez & Roussopoulos, 2000) projects are initially XML based.

The next level of abstraction on Web integration corresponds to ontology-based systems. Its main advantage over the mediators is their capacity of managing *a priori* unknown schemas. This is achieved by means of a mechanism that allows contents and query capabilities of the data source to be described declaratively. From the data perspective, ontologies enrich the semantics of the schema, resolving synonymy and polysemy problems (Heflin, 2001).

The reader can find an excellent review in ontology engineering in Corcho, Fernández-López and Gómez-Pérez (2001). Well-known environments for building ontologies are WebODE (Arpirez, Corcho, Fernández-López & Gómez-Pérez, 2001) and WebOnto (Domínguez, 1998). The first one provides an API for ontology access (based on Prolog) and import/export utilities from/to diverse markup and ontology languages. WebOnto is a powerful collaborative environment focused on the ontology creation and navigation.

From the integration point of view, many studies have been and still are being developed using ontologies. We note two main projects: Ariadne (Arens, Knoblock & Shen, 1996; Baris, Knoblock, Chen, Minton, Philpot & Shahabi, 2000) and OBSERVER (Mena, Illarramendi, Kashyap & Sheth, 2000). Ariadne aims at the development of technologies and tools for rapidly constructing intelligent agents to extract, query and integrate data from Web sources. OBSERVER uses different ontologies to represent information data sources. The user explicitly selects the ontology that will be used for query evaluation. The existence of mapping among ontologies allows the user to change the ontology initially selected.

INTEGRATION ISSUES IN THE SEMANTIC WEB

In a keynote session at XML 2000, the Director of the World Wide Web Consortium, Tim Berners-Lee (2000), outlined his vision for the Semantic Web: "...in the context of the Semantic Web, the word semantic means machine processable. For data, the semantics convey what a machine can do with that data." He described the "semantic test," which is passed if, when you give data to a machine, it will do the right thing with it. He also underlined that the Semantic Web is, like XML, a declarative environment, where you say what you mean by some data, and not what you want to do with it.

Having outlined its scope, Berners-Lee explained each of the elements in the Semantic Web architecture. He explained the importance of RDF/RDF Schema as a language for the description of "things" (resources) and their types. Above this, he described the ontology layer. An ontology is capable of describing relationships between types of things, such as "this is a transitive property," but does not convey any information about how to use those relationships computationally. On top of the ontology layer sits the logic layer. This is the point at which assertions from around the Web can be used to derive new knowledge. The problem here is that deduction systems are not terribly interoperable. Rather than design one overarching reasoning system, Berners-Lee suggests a universal language for representing proofs. Systems can then digitally sign and export these proofs for other systems to use and possibly incorporate into the Semantic Web.

Most of the new work today is happening regarding ontologies. Practical solutions include the use of XSLT to derive RDF from XML sources, work on topic maps and RDF convergence, the emergence of general-purpose RDF databases and engines, and general and specific GUIs for RDF data.

The development of the Semantic Web involves the adoption of different technologies (Figure 7), which allow adding meaning to the structure of the XML documents and describing the necessary semantic information in order to be processed by the machines. For a long time, this problem has been dealt with by means of "ontologies" described as documents or files "that definitely define the relationships between the terms." The ontologies allow working with concepts, instead of key words, in the information retrieval systems. According to the information sources, the ontologies describe the content of

Figure 7. Semantic Web

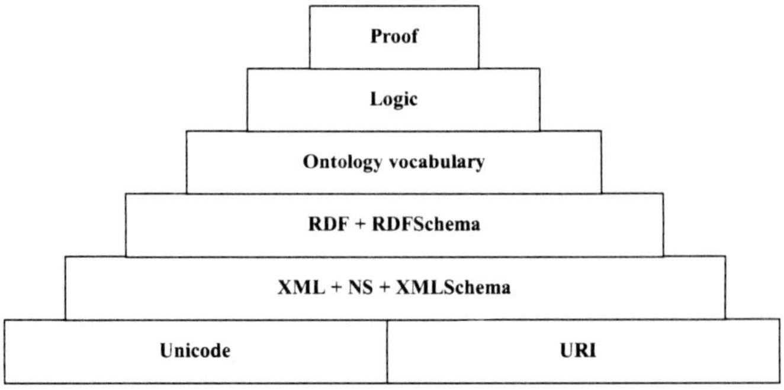

the data repositories regardless of their syntactic representation, enabling their semantic integration (Mena et al., 2000). A problem that will arise in the near future, due to the quick spreading of specific ontologies (and standards for the metadata), is the integration of such ontologies.

As a means to materialize a conceptualization or ontology, a language to represent that knowledge is required. Traditionally, these languages have been developed in the area of artificial intelligence and concentrate their formal base on paradigms such as: the first and second order predicate calculus, description logic or the object-oriented ones. It is the different computational and expressive properties that later differentiate these languages. Among the most outstanding ones, Ontilingua, Loom, OCML and Flogic can be mentioned.

XML invites the publication of ontologies using the syntax of such standard. This way, insofar as it is possible, the arduous task of having to define the parsers is avoided. Languages based on XML are ideal candidates for the Semantic Web. Simple HTML Ontology Extensions (SHOEs), Ontology Exchange Language (XOL), Ontology Mark-up Language (OML) and Resource Description Framework Schema Language (RDFS) are some of them. They inherit the labels of XML and incorporate new characteristics that improve the expressiveness of the initial data model. Other proposals, which extend RDF and RDFS, can be added to the previous list, such as: Ontology Interchange Language (OIL), DAML+OIL and its successor OWL.

Given that XML imposes the necessity of a structural restriction (a common core) to provide unmistakable methods of semantic expression, RDF isn't but the infrastructure that allows the codification, reuse and exchange of structured metadata. This way, RDF is the most promising model to associate information to the content of Web resources.

It is not likely that a single language may cover all the needs and requirements presented in the Semantic Web. An analysis of the most wished needs, regarding expressiveness and power of their reasoning mechanisms, will provide us with the profile of an efficient language for the Semantic Web. A clear distinction between the terms is established: representation of knowledge and reasoning. The formalization of knowledge is carried out, in most cases, throughout the use of concepts, n-ary relationships,

Table 1. Comparison of Languages According to the Elements to Represent the Field of Knowledge

	ONTO LINGUA	OCML	LOOM	FLOGIC	XOL	SHOE	RDF(S)	OIL
Concepts	+	+	+	+	+	+	+	+
N-ary relationships	+	+	+	+	+	+	+	+
Functions	+	-	-	+	+	-	-	+
Procedures	+	+	+	-	-	-	-	-
Instances	+	+	+	-	+	+	+	-
Axioms	+	-	-	+	-	+	-	+
Rules of Production	-	+	+	-	-	+	-	NA
Formal Semantics	+	+	+	+	+	-	-	-

functions, procedures, instances, axioms, rules of production—and we could add as well, throughout formal semantic. These parameters determine the expressiveness of the language. Table 1 shows a comparison according to these terms.

It can be noticed that the languages based on XML do not usually provide the possibility of defining functions, procedures and axioms, except some limited way of axiomatization such as the deductive rules in the case of SHOE. They also lack a formal semantics inherent to the language. This makes the implementation of efficient mechanisms of reasoning difficult. In this sense, Ontolingua is perhaps the most expressive of the formalisms presented, although at present there is no inference machine implementing it.

Other interesting comparison can be carried out according to the reasoning mechanisms that language allows. Table 2 includes these aspects.

OIL has an automatic system of classification (desirable in the case of the ontologies), Flogic implements the handling of exceptions, and both present sound and complete systems of inference. Compared to the languages based on XML, traditional languages support the implementation of procedures, the maintenance of restrictions, and both top-down and bottom-up evaluation. Thus, an important trade-off is settled between completeness and expressiveness of inference mechanisms used, and its efficiency. This trade-off makes very interesting the study and development of techniques for the distributed evaluation of logical programs in this context, techniques that provide support to the query processing based on ontologies in the Semantic Web.

The most ingenuous setting for the Semantic Web would be the one in which all the data sources commit with a very limited set of well-known, universally accepted ontologies. Furthermore, all the data sources would be universal and homogeneously acces-

Table 2. Language Reasoning Mechanisms (presented in Corcho & Gómez, 2000)

	ONTO LINGUA	OCML	LOOM	FLOGIC	XOL	SHOE	RDF(S)	OIL
Mechanisms of Inference								
Correct	-	+	+	+	-	-	-	+
Complete	-	-	-	+	-	-	-	+
Classification								
Automatic	-	-	+	-	-	-	-	+
Exceptions								
Use of exceptions	-	-	-	+	-	-	-	-
Inheritance								
Monotonic	+	+	+	+	NA	+	NA	+
No Monotonic	+/-	+/-	+	+	NA	-	NA	-
Simple Inheritance	+	+	+	+	NA	+	+	+
Multiple Inheritance	+	+	+	+	NA	+	+	+
Procedures								
Implementation	+	+	+	-	-	-	-	-
Restrictions								
Examination	+	+	+	+	-	-	-	-
Model of Evaluation								
Top-Down	-	+	+	+	-	NA	-	-
Bottom-Up	-	+	+	+	-	NA	-	-

sible. Thus, each system would collect the axioms and resources of its ontology quickly and would process them. It is evident that this scenario is not very realistic as a basic architecture for the Semantic Web. Everybody is not expected to commit with a limited group of ontologies, nor is an isolated system expected to process a whole ontology that involves a great amount of resources. It is easier to imagine that there will be many ontologies and many systems in charge of evaluating specific ontologies. This way, the evaluation should be made in a cooperative way, thanks to the interaction of these agents or systems. In this context, it is essential to respect the interoperability and autonomy of the system. This requires certain isolation at different levels, which we will analyze from three different dimensions. Each one of them presents a particular set of problems that must be dealt with in relation to privacy, heterogeneity and distribution.

From the point of view of privacy, a firm may want to isolate or protect the data sources and/or axioms that define the elements of the vocabulary of its ontology. Taking the three basic elements that make the model of an ontology, namely, the vocabulary, the axioms and the data sources committed with it, only the first of them must be necessarily public (totally or partially).

The second dimension mentioned is the heterogeneity, based on two key factors: the formalism and the inference mechanism. The extension of an ontology should be able to be feasible even when using two different formalisms to represent the axioms. In the same way, two systems based on ontologies can use different mechanisms of inference to compute the facts of such axioms.

In an ingenuous model of implementation, we could think — very much to the point — that the heterogeneity in the formalism can be solved introducing a translator. However, an extreme case (but real and usual) of heterogeneity corresponds to the declaration of Value Added Services (VAS). A VAS in an integration or mediation system can be interpreted as an extra functionality that incorporates to the system and whose semantics is not, and cannot be, expressed in the language used for its integration. The concept of VAS appears in multiple fields, such as the stored procedures and external procedures in relational DBMS, the external predicates in logical languages, etc.

The analysis of the third dimension, that we just have named distribution, is aimed at considering aspects that are of paramount importance for the real viability of the Semantic Web. There are two basic points of view in the distribution: the first one refers to the evaluation of the ontology and the second one refers to the optimization of such evaluation. Regarding the evaluation we run into important aspects such as replication, load balancing and level of tolerance to errors (errors attributable to losses — no accessibility — of data sources, as well as losses of systems or agents of evaluation). Secondly, optimization techniques change radically when considering aspects of opacity regarding the resources, axioms, etc.

DISCUSSION: A DATABASE PERSPECTIVE

Since Codd formally defined the relational model in the early 1970s, it has proved its expressiveness and efficiency, but also has presented limitations. This has motivated the definition of many extensions. Among these, two have shown an unusually high degree of success. Deductive and object-oriented database paradigms are attempts to introduce recursion and object orientation in databases. XML is a standard based on a semi-structured model that allows structural recursion. Its future algebra has functional language characteristics that support both static and dynamic type inference. This means that XML includes and extends the problems of distribution, recursion and object orientation in relational models.

Although XML, as a data model, is in its early stages, its general acceptance is focusing much research and development in both the industry and research communities. Even though not completely mature, it is being successfully used in the e-commerce field, B2B, data interchange and integration, etc.

Obviously, XML has inherited not only the advantages from its ancestors, but also many still open problems at both theoretical and practical levels, which affect many aspects, including constraints management and query processing issues.

It has been shown that there exist several ways to specify integrity constraints in XML, using DTDs or XML-Schema, among others. To avoid multiple fetching of constraints expressed in different formats during data management, it would be desirable to choose a unique format of constraints specification. The XML-Schema seems to be the best candidate due to its expressiveness, as is shown in recent studies (Lee & Chu, 2000).

Nevertheless, other standards, like RDF and RDF Schemas, are complementary and can be used together in a higher abstraction level, as proposed in the Semantic Web.

Almost all of the aspects related to maintenance and query optimization via integrity constraints are open in XML, because of its recent development.

Many frontiers are open to research and development. Moreover, we still cannot ensure that the W3C XML query language and algebra recommendations, in its current status, would be valid as a practical query language for data-intensive processing. Alternative proposals exist (see the comparative analysis of Bonifati & Ceri, 2000), although many of them conform to the W3C's proposal. A good example is the proposal (Beech, Malhotra & Rys, 1999) developed by three important W3C members: Oracle, IBM, and Microsoft. Together, they have developed a query language and algebra very close to SQL and relational algebra whose results are compatible with XQuery's, although these are especially oriented to data-intensive processing.

An update semantic model is still undefined revealing the amount of work yet to do. For a complete definition of the data manipulation language, it will be necessary to define new recommendations including the given update commands. Having finished the process of complete formalization of the language, the development of a transactional system for XML would be necessary. It would maintain data integrity under multiple concurrent accesses. This work is mainly related to the logical data schema. Improvements in the physical model will begin later on.

The current commercial interest and pressure for XML technology development has produced that almost all computer science disciplines converge to its study. An interesting example of this can be observed in the XML query algebra draft. This algebra is defined on a mathematical monad concept, which is usual in functional languages. This concept has been exhaustively studied for languages like Haskell, and has been applied to generate optimization mechanisms based on binding propagation. Magic rewriting techniques have proven their good results in query optimization on both deductive and relational databases. They are also based on binding strategies, called Sideway Information Passing, or *sip* strategies. The most sophisticated versions of these algorithms use integrity constraints to determine the binding strategy. Thus, optimization based on binding strategies could be approached in XML by both Datalog and Haskell developers.

As a result, we may note how many aspects of XML query processing, including integrity constraints management, would have to receive serious attention from the database community. New fields of research are open, and in-depth research on all aspects related to this new data model on the Web are of vital interest regarding its application to industry.

The Semantic Web will continue to be a model of growth similar to the Web, and its success depends on us being able to elaborate realistic techniques that make this development model feasible. The trade-off adopted between the concepts of expressive power, correctness, completeness and efficiency, for each one of the different mechanisms of inference, will open a wide range of study regarding new evaluation techniques — based on ontologies — for distributed logical programs within the context of the Semantic Web. On the other hand, the query and efficient management of huge distributed knowledge bases still have many unsolved aspects, related — among other things — with the efficient integration of information and the development of distributed mechanisms of inference.

REFERENCES

Abiteboul, S., Buneman, P. & Suciu, D. (2000). *Data on the Web. From Relations to Semi-Structured Data and XML.* Morgan Kaufmann Publishers.

Abiteboul, S., Hull, R. & Vianu, V. (1995). *Foundations of Databases.* Addison-Wesley.

Abiteboul, S., Quass, D., McHugh, J., Widom, J. & Wiener, J. (1997). The Lorel query language for semi-structured data. *International Journal on Digital Libraries,* 1(1), 68-88.

Arens, Y., Knoblock, C.A. & Shen, W.M. (1996). Query reformulation for dynamic information integration. *Journal of Intelligent Information Systems, Special Issue on Intelligent Information Integration,* 6(2/3), 99-130.

Arpirez, J.C., Corcho, O., Fernández-López, M. & Gómez-Pérez, A. (2001). WebODE: A scalable workbench for ontological engineering. *Proceedings of the First International Conference on Knowledge Capture (KCAP01),* Victoria, Canada.

Ashish, N. & Knoblock, C.A. (1997). Wrapper generation for semi-structured Internet sources. *SIGMOD Record,* 26(4), 8-15.

Bancilhon, F., Maier, D., Sagiv, Y. & Ullman, J.D. (1986). Magic sets and other strange ways to implement logic programs. *Proceedings of the ACM SIGMOD-SIACT Symposium on Principles of Database Systems,* 1-16.

Baris, G., Knoblock, C.A., Chen, Y.S., Minton, S., Philpot, A. & Shahabi, C. (2000). The theaterloc virtual application. Proceedings of the *Twelfth Annual Conference on Innovative Applications of Artificial Intelligence (IAAI-2000),* Austin, Texas.

Baru, C.K., Gupta, A., Ludäscher, B., Marciano, R., Papakonstantinou, Y., Velikhov, P. & Chu, V. (1999). XML-based information mediation with MIX. *Proceedings of the ACM SIGMOD Conference 1999,* 597-599.

Beech, D., Malhotra, A. & Rys, M. (1999). *A Formal Data Model and Algebra for XML.* Communication to the W3C. Available online at: http://www-db.stanford.edu/dbseminar/Archive/FallY99/malhotra-slides/malhotra.pdf.

Berners-Lee, T. (2000). *Semantic Web—XML2000.* At XML2000. Available online at: http://www.w3.org/2000/Talks/1206-xml2k-tbl/Overview.html.

Bernstein, P.A., Brodie, M.L., Ceri, S., DeWitt, D.J., Franklin, M.J., García-Molina, H., Gray, J., Held, G., Hellerstein, J.M., Jagadish, H.V., Lesk, M., Maier, D., Naughton, J.F., Pirahesh, H., Stonebraker, M. & Ullman, J.D. (1998). The Asilomar report on database research. *SIGMOD Record,* 27(4), 74-80.

Bonifati, A. & Ceri, S. (2000). Comparative analysis of five XML query languages. *SIGMOD Record,* 29(1), 68-79.

Bowers, S. & Delcambre, L. (2000). Representing and transforming model based information. *Proceedings of the International Workshop on the Semantic Web (SemWeb) at the 4th European Conference on Research and Advanced Technology for Digital Libraries (ECDL2000),* Lisbon, Portugal.

Buneman, P. (1997). Semi-structured data tutorial. The Sixth ACM SIGMOD Symposium on Principles of Database Systems (PODS'97). *SIGMOD Record,* 26(2).

Chakravarthy, U.S., Grant, J. & Minker, J. (1990). Logic-based approach to semantic query optimization. *ACM Transactions on Database Systems*, 15(2), 162-207.

Chawathe, S., Abiteboul, S. & Widom, J. (1998). Representing and querying changes in semi-structured data. *Proceedings of the International. Conference on Data Engineering,* 4-13.

Corcho, O. & Gómez, A. (2000). A Roadmap to ontology specification languages. *Proceedings of Knowledge Acquisition, Modelling and Managements, 12th International Conference (EKAW 2000)*. Lecture Notes in Computer Science 1937. Berlin, Germany: Springer.

Corcho, O., Fernández-López, M. & Gómez-Pérez, A. (2001). *Techical Roadmad v1.0. IST Proyect IST-2001-29243 OntoWeb.*

Document Object Model (DOM) Level 1 Specification (Second Edition) 2000. (2000). Available online at: http://www.w3.org/TR/2000/WD-DOM-Level-1-20000929/.

Fahl, G., Risch, T. & Sköld, M. (1993). AMOS—An architecture for active mediators. *Next Generation Information Technologies and Systems (NGITS 1993)*, 47-53.

Fan, W., Kuper, G.M. & Siméon, J. (2001). A unified constraint model for XML. *Proceedings of the 10th International World Wide Web Conference (WWW'10).*

Fernández, M. (1996). *UnQL Project.* Available online at: http://www.research.att.com/projects/unql/.

Fernández, M. & Suciu, D. (1998). Optimizing regular path expressions using graph schemas. *Proceedings of the International. Conference on Data Engineering,* 14-23.

García-Molina, H., Quass, D., Papakonstantinou, Y., Rajaraman, A., Sagiv, Y., Ullman J.D. & Widom, J. (1995). The TSIMMIS approach to mediation: Data models and languages. *Next Generation Information Technologies and Systems (NGITS 1995).*

Goldman, R., McHugh, J. & Widom, J. (1999). From semi-structured data to XML: Migrating the Lore data model and query language. *Proceedings of the Workshop on the Web and Databases (WebDB'99),* 25-30.

Grahne, G. & Thomo, A. (2000). An optimization technique for answering regular path queries. *International Workshop on the Web and Databases (WebDB 2000 Informal Proceedings),* 99-104.

Grahne, G. & Thomo, A. (2001). Algebraic rewritings for optimising regular path queries. *Proceedings of the International Conference on Database Theory (ICDT 2001),* 301-315.

Haas, L.M., Kossmann, D., Wimmers, E.L. & Yang, J. (1997). Optimizing queries across diverse data sources. *Proceedings of the 23rd Very Large Data Base Conference (VLDB 1997),* 276-285.

Haas, L.M., Miller, R.J., Niswonger, B., Roth, M.T., Schwarz, P.M. & Wimmers, E.L. (1999). Transforming heterogeneous data with database middleware: Beyond integration. *IEEE Data Engineering Bulletin,* 22(1), 31-36.

Heflin, J.D. (2001). *Towards the Semantic Web: Knowledge Representation in a Dynamic, Distributed Environment.* PhD Thesis.

Lakshmanan, L.V.S., Sadri, F. & Subramanian, I.N. (1996). A declarative language for querying and restructuring the Web. *Proceedings of the Workshop on Research Issues in Data Engineering,* 12-21.

Lee, D. & Chu, W.W. (2000). Comparative analysis of six XML schema languages. *SIGMOD Record,* 29(3), 76-87.

Lee, D. & Chu, W.W. (2000). Constraints-preserving transformation from XML document type definition to relational schema. *Proceedings of the International Conference on Conceptual Modeling (ER 2000),* 323-338.

Levy, A.Y., Mumick, I.S. & Sagiv, Y. (1994). Query optimization by Predicate Move Around. *Proceedings of the 20th Very Large Data Base Conference (VLDB 1994)*, 96-107.

McHugh, J. & Widom, J. (1999). Query optimization for XML. *Proceedings of the 25th Very Large Data Bases Conference (VLDB 1999)*, 315-326.

Mena, E., Illaramendi, A., Kashyap, V. & Sheth, A.P. (2000). OBSERVER: An approach for query processing in global information systems based on interoperation across pre-existing ontologies. *Distributed and Parallel Databases*, 8(2), 223-271.

Mihaila, G. (1996). *WebSQL: An SQL-Like Query Language for the WWW*. MSc Thesis, University of Toronto. Available online at: http://www.cs.toronto.edu/~websql/.

Nestorov, S., Abiteboul, S. & Motwani, R. (1998). Extracting schema from semi-structured data. *ACM SIGMOD*, 295-306.

Resource Description Framework (RDF) Model and Syntax Specification. (1999). Available online at: http://www.w3.org/TR/REC-rdf-syntax.

Resource Description Framework (RDF) Schema Specification 1.0. (2000). W3C Candidate Recommendation, 27 March 2000. Available online at: http://www.w3.org/TR/2000/CR-rdf-schema-20000327.

Rodríguez-Martínez, M. & Roussopoulos, N. (2000). MOCHA: Self-extensible database middleware system for distributed data sources. *Proceedings of the ACM SIGMOD Conference*, 213-224.

Roth, M.T. & Schwarz, P.M. (1997). Don't scrap it, wrap it! A wrapper architecture for legacy data sources. *Proceedings of the 23rd Very Large Data Base Conference (VLDB 1997)*, 266-275.

Roth, M.T., Arya, M., Haas, L.M., Carey, M.J., Cody, W.F., Fagin, R., Schwarz, P.M., Thomas II, J. & Wimmers, E.L. (1996). The Garlic Project. *Proceedings of the ACM SIGMOD Conference*, 557.

Sahuguet, A. & Azavant, F. (1999). Building light-weight wrappers for legacy Web data-sources using W4F. *Proceedings of the 25th Very Large Data Base Conference (VLDB 1999)*, 266-275.

Sahuguet, A. & Azavant, F. (1999). Web ecology: Recycling HTML pages as XML documents using W4F. *ACM SIGMOD Workshop on the Web and Databases (WebDB'99 Informal Proceedings)*, 31-36.

Silberschatz, A. & Zdonik, S.B. (1996). Strategic directions in database systems—Breaking out of the box. *Computing Surveys*, 28(4), 764-778.

Tamer Özsu, M. & Valduriez, P. (1999). *Principles of Distributed Database Systems (Second Edition*.

Tomasic, A., Raschid, L. & Valduriez, P. (1995). *Scaling Heterogeneous Databases and the Design of Disco*. Research Report No. 2704, Institudt National de Recherche en Informatique et en Automatique.

Ullman, J. (1989). *Principles of Database and Knowledge-Base Systems, Volumes 1 and 2*. New York: Computer Science Press.

XML 1.1. (2002). W3C Candidate Recommendation, October. Available online at: http://www.w3.org/XML/.

XML-Schema. (2001). W3C Recommendation, 2 May 2001. Available online at: http://www.w3.org/XML/Schema.

XQuery 1.0 and XPath 2.0 Formal Semantics. (2002). W3C Working Draft, 16 August 2002. Available online at: http://www.w3.org/TR/query-semantics/.

XSL. The eXtensible Stylesheet Language. (1999). W3C Recommendation, 16 November 1999. Available online at: http://www.w3.org/Style/XSL.

Chapter IX

Applying JAVA-Triggers for X-Link Management in the Industrial Framework

Abraham Alvarez
Laboratoire d'Ingénierie des Systèmes d'Information, INSA de Lyon, France

Y. Amghar
Laboratoire d'Ingénierie des Systèmes d'Information, INSA de Lyon, France

ABSTRACT

This chapter focuses on referential link integrity problems. In the industrial context, the life cycle of a document plays a central role in describing the "steps out" of a product. Users realize some manipulations like creation, edition, suppression and querying under a multi-user environment, risking possible destruction or the alteration of the document's integrity. A classical impact is the infamous "Error 404: file not found." However, the user needs a notification alert mechanism to prevent and warrant the coherence of manipulations over all the life cycle processes of a product. The main objective of this chapter is to provide a generic relationship validation mechanism to remedy this shortcoming. We believe in the combination of some standard features of XML, specifically XLL specification as a support for integrity management and Java-Triggers approach as an alert method. This study, compared with actual approaches, proposes a solution based on active functionalities.

INTRODUCTION

The business contributions of intranet applications have proven that this technology is a golden approach to support corporate Web-based systems (as stated in Balasubramanian et al., 1997, 1998). Increasing in number, all kinds of organizations are taking advantage of intranets to propagate structured documentation (e.g., technical, medical, academic, etc.). Intranet technology is well used to enhance organizations' business strategies (Bonifatti, 2000). The current Web and intranet services are short of referential integrity support. In this study, the coherence problem means that a link depends on the "state" of the referenced document. When documents are edited or revised, locations can probably be altered, with the potential risk of destroying the record of a linked text. Observable examples are broken links and dangling references, arguably two of the most unwanted problems in distributed domains.

Another frequent problem is resource migration. Experience has shown that Web resources often "migrate" during the reorganization of hardware resources (e.g., as a result of an increase in the volume of information published by a given site).

The question is how to preserve the link integrity when, at any time, document links can be altered in some way, with the potential risk of destroying the record of a linked text (broken links). The main purpose of this chapter is to provide a generic relationship validation mechanism to keep the link references in a "coherent state" over all processes involved. It proposes a solution based on active functionalities. Our approach is based both on the definition of ECA rules and Java-Triggers Technology; the rules are used as alert mechanisms. Therefore, some standard features of XML, highlighted in the XLL specifications (X-link and X-pointer) presented by the XML-Linking working group, will be considered in this work as a support for integrity management.

BACKGROUND

In the literature we have found several research and development projects addressed to referential link integrity problem; two main categories of solutions have been proposed: preventive and corrective solutions (Ashman, 1999, 2000).

Preventive Solutions

- **Forbidding changes:** is a preventive strategy, the modification of documents is not authorized (Thistlewaite, 1995). Links pointing to documents or part of documents should not fail.
  - This approach does not provide a protection in cases where the host information is changed. Addressed to link update problem only.
- **Versioning:** is one of the main issues in the hypermedia field adopted by Vitali (1999) and Nelson (Theodor, 1999). The changes in the document are permitted by the creation of a newer version and are notified to the reader. Thus, the document changes as new versions become the active document. In summary, versioning provides an easy and safe solution to the well-know problem of referential link integrity.

- Versioning is made at the document level, a fine-grained versioning is required, i.e., granularity on the node level. Therefore, versioning philosophy does not participate in the application « by default »; it needs to be implanted and maintained by the user.

- **Embedded links:** Davis proposes embedded links as a link integrity solution (Hugh, 1998). Embedded links are already familiar from the usual HTML link specification, where the source of the link and information about the destination are embedded into the data, using <A tag>. In contrast, one feature of the "open hypermedia systems" analyzed by Davis is that all link information is separated from the data and stored externally. Embedded linking avoids link errors in two ways. The first way is to embed the source end point of a link into a document, so that a wrong reference cannot occur (the link and its source end point are contained in the same part of the same file). While this solves the problem for the sources of links, it has no effect on the referential integrity of link destination end points because these usually refer to external files. The second way is embedding of name tags (e.g. <A name="xxx"> tags supported by HTML) to help with the referential integrity of destination end points at the part of the level. Instead of specifying internal points with byte-offsets, tags with names are embedded in the documents to demarcate the required segment of the document. This embedding of the demarcation specifiers in the destination end point can cure the problem caused by moving the end point within the document, but it fails when the end point is completely deleted or the file is renamed or deleted. Embedded links are not useful for data that cannot be overwritten, such as read-only data or data owned by others, and this is what motivates the use of externalized links in systems such as Microcosm (Hall, 1993), despite their greater chance of link error.
- **External links:** allow linking into resources that we have no writing access to — these are stored in a read-only medium or have been heavily linked by other users for other purposes. For example, in an insurance company, one may wish to link the client file; for legal reasons this correspondence must not be altered in any way. Hence, links coming from the correspondence must be maintained externally. Generally, they are stored in external databases, where each link is a record entry in a link table. Another case where documents must remain inviolate is for accountability purposes, i.e., links to previous versions of a product brochure must be maintained for historical, legal or temporal context. The idea of this approach has been exploited in many hypermedia systems, including Hyper-G (Andrews et al., 1995), Hyperware (Maurer, 1996) and Intermedia (Haan et al., 1992). One of the Hypermedia systems developed at Brown University's Institute for Research and Information and Scholarship (ISIS) was probably the first system to introduce this approach. A similar approach is described in Wilde (2000) where the authors consider a separation between the document content, links and their content. Moreover, they explain how X-link and X-pointer are used to implement a hypermedia model.

  - The weighty maintaining of external link bases is a disadvantage; whenever a link resource changes; external links risk pointing to the wrong reference place.
- **Link attributes:** the majority of hypertext links are simple references from a source to a destination node. Links mainly describe the target node and provide some

information concerning the location. Nevertheless, some information related to the semantic characteristics of the association that links designates lakes. For this reason, it is straightforward that by attaching semantic characteristics to the link, it is possible to enhance the hypertext link information or certain knowledge. Most hypermedia systems that provide semantic types such as SEPIA (Streiz et al., 1992) help authors to organize and structure information more effectively and readers to find their way through network of links by providing important context information. Oinas-Kukkonen (1998) proposes to integrate link attributes like semantic link types and link keywords. Link attribute properties associated with links provide knowledge about interrelationships between pieces of information. This preserves the context of information units and increases the local coherence of an information collection link; attributes also provide the user a way to know or preview the target before activating the link (Thüring et al., 1995).

- The main weakness of these approaches is the volatility of the medium (the moving or renaming of documents or host name machine, or domain name changes, etc.); the additional information helps readers with organization and knowledge. Moreover, for purposes of linking integrity, this is not really a full solution. On the other hand, we think another possible preventive solution to minimize "dead or broken links" is ensuring that authors and system administrators can correctly create links only to documents already existing in the document database.

- Another preventive solution is proposed by Davis (1999) introducing the concept called "**publishing**" solution.

Corrective Solutions

- **Forward mechanism:** is a method that informs readers that a link they have used has been corrupted and is to replace the specified end point with a "small note" that notifies the reader that the required end point has been moved or deleted. The note which replaces the expected end point actually assumes the end point's identity and is retrieved in place of the end point (Ingham et al., 1996). Forwarding mechanisms are well tried on the Web. Many readers will follow a link to a page, only to be sent a small note that tells them: the link they followed is not longer valid and sometimes will automatically point the reader to the new location. These forwarding pointers (also called "redirection" in the Web community) are enabled by HTTP protocol. Ingham et al. (1996) improved the usefulness of these forwarding mechanisms by replacing the small note with a computation that invisibly forwards the reader's document request to the new document location. For dealing with deleted documents, they propose the use of "gravestones," which are small documents that replace the deleted object and serve to notify a reader that the document has been removed. They also propose that a system administrator keep a count of the number of times a gravestone is accessed in a given time period, so that when the count drops to zero, it is reasonable to delete the gravestones as well. As Creech (1996) points out, these mechanisms do not repair any broken links in other documents; instead, they provide browsers with a means for rediscovering the correct end-point reference. If the mechanisms are sufficiently invisible, the reader may not even be aware that the link needs repairing. Some browsers will flash up the redirection notice only very briefly before automatically forwarding the reader to the new page.

- **Dereferencing (aliasing):** is one solution for managing links to a document that has been renamed or moved. Third-party dereferencing works by using a form of alias instead of a direct link end-point specification. Instead of giving the absolute address (e.g., a Universal Resource Locator in Web documents), which identifies the exact host and file name, an alias is created that will eventually resolve to the absolute address. Absolute addresses are paired with their aliases and kept in a registry. Resolving a link alias involves a lookup in this registry to find the corresponding absolute address. Whenever the absolute address of a link end-point changes, only a registry entry needs to be changed, instead of changing every link that points to that end point. A Uniform Resource Name provides a reliable and persistent address to a network resource. This strategy works well for modifications of documents, especially at the whole-document level. It can also work well at the part-of-file level if the named section of a document that is the actual end point is renamed. It does not work at all for deletions: if an entry is removed from the registry, recovery is not possible and an error message will be returned.
  - Aliasing has four main disadvantages. The first is that it requires a registry of aliases, which needs to be mirrored on a number of servers and kept accurate. Aliases must be governed by a naming authority that ensures the validity of selected aliases and assigns approved aliases (Ianella et al., 1996). The second disadvantage is that the strategy requires the cooperation of link creators to refer to the aliases instead of to the absolute address. If absolute addresses are used, the registry is completely bypassed. This could easily happen when readers "bookmark" an interesting page — they may inadvertently bookmark the absolute address rather than the alias. The third disadvantage is that it depends on the cooperation of alias owners to enter the initial aliases in the first place and then keep the aliases up to date. Finally, the redirection strategy is also slower than direct referencing, because each request for a document requires two retrievals, one for the dereferencing of the alias and a second for the actual document retrieval. The Web provides a number of example implementations. The first example is a formal proposal being developed by the Internet Engineering Task Force (IETF), where the aliases are called Uniform Resource Names (URNs) (Berners-Lee, 1996). URNs can specify files to be retrieved via HTTP, but they also function as an addressing scheme for almost any information for which a retrieval protocol exists; thus, the more a retrieval protocol exists, the broader the addressing scheme. The URN scheme comprehends a number of already-supported data addressing protocols such as ftp, gopher, e-mail, telnet and news. However, it could also support other protocols such as the telephone system and the International Standard Book Numbering (ISBN) system, with addresses such as urn:telecom:441159514237 or urn:isbn:0-19-861134-X. A similar naming system is Location Independent File Names (LIFNs), which is in principle the same as URNs although its primary purpose is for naming and sharing software components and other resources.
- **Relative references:** HieNet (Daniel, 1993) is a link mechanism conceived to generate new links based on previously created user links, i.e., in the links similarity

approach. Otherwise, HieNet takes into consideration two aspects for link generation: the link profile and the node size. This approach is inspired in Salton's (1989) Vector space model and the work of Bernstein (1990).

- **Paradigm of agents:** the most common conception is in the resource Discovery Domain. A resource discovery agent is a process that, either semi-autonomously or autonomously, searches for and presents new sources of relevant information to the user. How relevant this information is depends upon the accuracy of the agent's analysis process. Examples of this process type are WWW search robots. Another domain is Information Integrity. On the WWW the process must examine all of the HTML documents to locate the dangling links. Nevertheless, the integrity problem could be solved by agents autonomously interacting with the WWW servers: if an integrity problem is located, the agent could fix it by locating the missing document on the server. If the agent could not fix it, then it puts a flag, like broken link, etc. But the implementation of such repairing agents may require additional functionality to be incorporated into the WWW servers. The size and complexity of the WWW means that it is impossible to check information integrity when the documents are being edited and linked. A retrieval system that offers the ability to authors to attach additional information to hyperlinks, and also provides suggestions on the information to be attached as effort to increase the integrity of hyperlink information, is presented by Varlamis et al. (2001). While Leslie (1998) introduces a Distributed Link Service (DLS), the agent helps users with browsing and information discovery activities.

Finally, DeRose presents the most up-to-date overview of the X-link, X-pointer and X-path recommendations, explaining important features of hypertext systems not seen previously, e.g., one-to-many links, out-of-line or externalized links and calculations of links positions (DeRose et al., 2001). In a literature survey related to links history, Lewis et al. (1999) make a distinction between navigation and retrieval information handling. Nowadays, in the area of hypermedia research systems, we have found powerful systems such as MicroCosm (Hall, 1993), Hyperware (Maurer, 1996), linking Systems Dexter (Halasz, 1990; Debra et al., 1999) and Intermedia (Haan et al., 1992). However, these are still constrained by the limitations imposed by HTML. The OpenDoc architecture[1] (Killpack, 1994) is an answer to satisfy the interoperability problems in a hypermedia system.

MOTIVATION

One of the causes of broken links is the volatility of the medium. Thousands of manipulations are done within a very short time, users or owners of documents delete documents, often without preserving the old document. E-document includes structured or semi-structured documents in HTML, XML formats. Sometimes documents are deleted or the domain name of the document collection changes, or perhaps the directory structure of the documents is altered. In each case, the addresses of the documents are changed (URL addresses) and are no longer correct. Let us describe how some common Web operations can affect the author's link: deleting pages, splitting pages and changing page titles.

- **Deleting pages:** is very similar to moving pages; the links to the pages being deleted need to be updated. When pages are deleted, it is generally not possible to automatically update links as with pages that have moved, because the deletion of a page often requires more than deleting the links that make reference to it. This can be seen in the example of an HTML subsection with one bulleted item that contains a link reference. If the page referred to by the link is deleted, the author may want to delete the whole subsection, or restructure his document in some other way. Thus, the author must be notified and decide how to change the content manually.
- **Splitting pages:** means dividing a page into two or more pages. Many times this maps to narrowing the scope of an existing page. Since it is very difficult to know which one of the split pages we have to point to, it is generally not possible to automatically update links to split pages. Thus, the best we can do is to tell the author that a link may be incorrect and now points to a page that was split into the following set of pages. With this information, the author can determine how to update the link.
- **Renaming a file:** is just that — changing the "title" of the page, not changing the page's Uniform Resource Locator (URL). This frequently occurs when the contents of a page are broadened or narrowed. A page title change is not equivalent to moving a page because all the referencing links are still correct; however, each of the anchor names of these links may now be incorrect. Updating link anchors is not necessarily straightforward, because the link anchor title may be different from the title of the referenced page. In cases where the anchor is different, the author should be notified of this difference so that the anchor name can be changed. It may be possible to have link anchors changed automatically by having the author include some sort of extra attribute with their link. If this were the case, link management tools could automatically update the link anchor name.

Another cause of broken links is concurrence. Users can modify without willing it a link location (source or target) that makes reference to another document or to the same document (reference link). This alteration can impact over other department activities or tasks, i.e., to derive a chain reaction. For instance, once an author is satisfied with his or her work, a notification e-mail is sent to a group department. The design department writes requirements documents for the manufacturing department, who then writes documents for users or for other departments and so on. Figure 1 depicts this scenario.

Moreover, in the industrial context, the online technical documentation is a support describing and defining department activities of the overall manufacturing process, executed by several departments such as designing, manufacturing, maintaining and assembling areas. Considering this context and using intranet technology to deliver, share and connect documents to other departments, any change in the online documentation can impact over other department activities, notably in the whole cycle of a product's development. Under the previous context, the technical documentation projects in organization require coherent manipulations on the overall process involved.

Knowing the factors of risk, the user claims a reactive work environment including a notification mechanism like a "warning message" or "pop-up message" when an edition operation is done. Edition operations include changes in the link address and insertion

Figure 1. Major Phases of Product Manufacturing

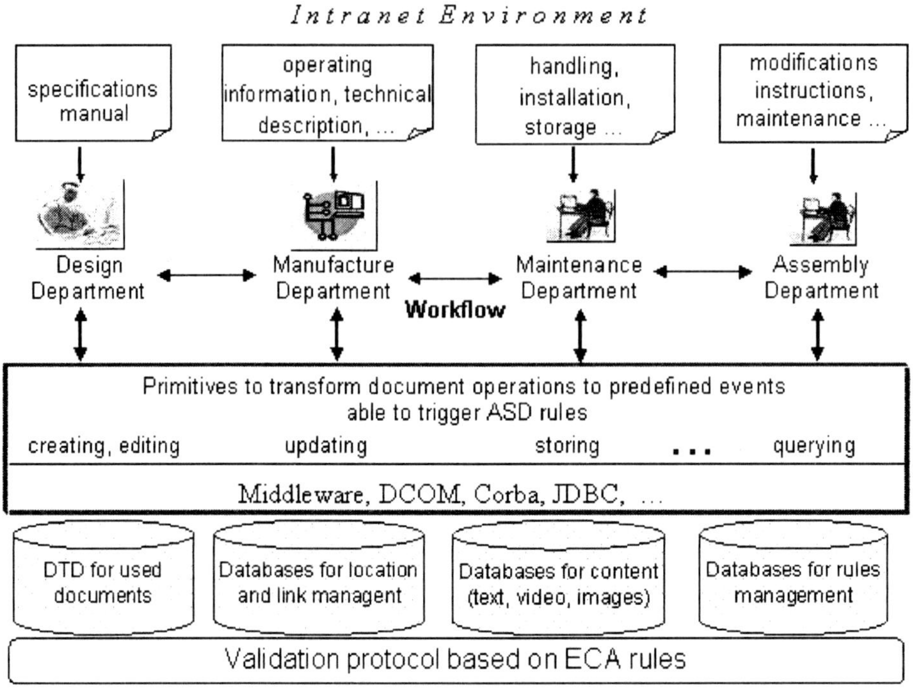

or deletion of text nodes. Finally, we could argue that existing solutions called "link managers" lack the active capabilities.

The main motivation of this study is to provide a dynamic mechanism based on active functionalities (triggers and rules definition) to warrant the link integrity. It is based both on the definition of ECA rules and Java-Triggers Technology. The rules are used as alert mechanisms, e.g., rules to notify when changes occurred in the data. Our approach compared to others approaches is very well situated in the Web-based information systems and Active Database Technology.

XML and Active Database Background

Definition 1. The technical documentation is the creation, control, delivery and maintenance of distributed information across the extended enterprise and a network that includes sources and users. The technical documentation is not a recent concept in the intranet environment (Albin, 1996). The online technical documentation serves as an interface between the user and the product. Using intranet technology, document workflow relates to the product's life cycle.

The set of relevant information for a particular task or a set of related tasks during the life cycle of the product is, e.g., manual specifications for a design department, modification instructions for maintenance department and so on.

- Users who create, use and maintain the information set are working under intranet environment. User manipulations are concurrent.
- All documents are interrelated by links over all processes.
- Changes can impact notably in other department activities.

Table 1 is addressing some limitations imposed by SGML and HTML. The World Wide Web Consortium (W3C, 2001) has developed an Extensible Markup Language (XML) to make up these limitations. XML is a subset of SGML that retains the SGML advantages of extensibility, structure and validation in a language that is designed to be easier to learn, use and implement than full SGML (DeRose, 2001).

Links Categories

Links come in many forms: they can embody the concrete connection between two adjacent pages, sections or footnotes in a document, or they can represent the organizational connection between a paragraph in a document and an annotation by a reviewer.

Table 1. XML Advantages vs. SGML & HTML

Features	SGML & HTML Limitations	XML
Extensibility Capacity to structure and validate documents	Fixed tags: not allowing users to specify their own tags or attributes in order to parameterize	Extensible set of tags
Views Applications that require the Web client to present different views of the same data to different users	Single presentation of each document: not supporting the specification of deep structures needed to represent database schemas	Multiple views of the same document (provided by XSL)
Query	Only query	Selective Query "sensitive-field"
Linking	Html links are limited because their semantics only allow pointing the whole document or pre-embedded "#section identifiers" to be addressed. Also, their syntax involve identification by location that has proven to be extremely fragile	XLL specification (X-Link & X-pointer), are used to support the integrity management

Table 2. Links Category

Services or Issues	**Navigation (transversal notion):** One of the main reasons for the web's success is "point and click." Linking forms the basis of hypertext functionality, is the most popular in the hypertext and hypermedia systems. This type of link is implicit. **Pattern matching or linguistic links:** First-class links type, they can be found easily using a simple pattern-matching technique. A fairly example is matching words in a document to entries in a dictionary. In almost all cases, these links are from a word or phrase of a small document. **Links denoting further information:** Another common use of links is to show that there is further information about some item "referential links," e.g., see more information, click here.
Structural Links: Structural links are those that represent a layout or possible logical structure of a document.	**Retrieval:** This can be the first step of any user interaction, where document itself is retrieved from the server. In structured documents represent the logical structure (DOM) selecting information by the nodes. **Browsing:** Links between documents provide a valuable browsing function within a document collection. **Citation linking:** Are used to provide additional context, Linking on references contained in research articles within the CiteSeer (ResearchIndex) database. Lawrence et al. (2000) attempt to relocate the missing URL address and discusses the persistent URL standards and usages.
Function	**Links representing actions:** A very common use of links is to represent actions. The action follows such links triggers: so, a link comprises a trigger in the main body of the text plus the retrieval action performed when that trigger is activated. Links used in this way facilitate a hands-free approach to information and display.
Protocol	This category is based on the type of documents they connect. We have included this links category because they are typically recognized by a "resource" that they connect.

We think of several ways and sorts of links classification (services, structural, function, protocol). Nevertheless, arbitrary divisions by four major groups allow a comprehensible taxonomy: service, structure, function and purpose.

Background of Active Database and Triggers Approach

This section shows the basic knowledge of the Active Databases and Triggers approach. An important functionality supported by many of the most recent relational and object-relational database systems is represented by triggers that enhance the database with reactive capabilities and that can be used to support integrity constraints, i.e., to maintain the integrity of the data, and maintaining long-running transactions. In Event-Condition-Action (ECA) formalism, the Event specifies when a rule should be triggered, the Condition is a query that is evaluated when the Event occurs, and the Action is executed when the Event occurs and the condition is satisfied.

The notion of trigger appeared in the seventies, and has been generalized with the notion of active rule that is based on the Event-Condition-Action (ECA) formalism. The semantic of an ECA rule is noted as follows: when an event E is produced, if the condition C is satisfied, then the action A is executed. Actions are initiated by the DBMS when appropriate events occur, independent of external requests. These rules allow database designers to specify the active behavior of a database application that provides the enforcement of database integrity. In the literature, several approaches were proposed to integrate active concepts into databases.

Several commercial database management systems (DBMSs) include an event/trigger mechanism that has been proposed by Kotz (1988) such as the Postgres rule system (Stonebraker, 1990), Starburst's production and alert rules (Lohman, 1991), Ariel's production rule system (Hanson, 1989), the ECA model of HiPAC (Dayal, 1988) and the event-action EA model of Ode (Gehani, 1992). Few researches have addressed the conceptual specification of behavioral aspects of applications independently from any active DBMS. To our knowledge, only IDEA (Ceri, 1993) and SORAC (Peckham, 1995) projects have treated the design of active databases. However, IDEA methodology is strongly linked to the Chimera DBMS. The SORAC model permits the schema designer to specify enforcement rules that maintain constraints on object and relationships to facilitate the task of the designer.

VALIDATION PROCESS

As a part of the preventive solution category, this study is notably related in the works of Thüring et al. (1995), Hugh (1999) and Oinas-Kukkonen (1998). We believe that these preventive techniques are an answer to link integrity problem but not a full solution. However, these works focus only on representation aspects. Our contribution proposes both coherence representation point of view and algorithmic points of view. This work allows the development of a new fundamental to enhance middleware of documents.

XML Specification

XLL allows XML tags to refer to other XML or HTML documents, as well as specific elements or data within those documents. In addition, X-link specifies a set of attributes in X-link namespace, and one can add element tag references to other documents, while X-pointer specifies a syntax to select specific elements within a document.

Validating Link Process

The mechanism to maintain the link integrity is described in this section. After the hypertext document creation, the next important steps are validating the document by a classical parser for XML-documents, making a recognition of links and finally, the referential links validation.

Step 1 — Parser Validation

This step consists of verifying the syntax and structure of documents before applying the process of validation (Step 3); we are using an evaluation copy of XML Spy 3.5 developed by IBM[2]. Two kinds of parsers are available for the validation of documents: a "non-validating processor" that makes sure that XML documents are **"well-formed-syntactically"** correct. The second is a "validating processor" that checks for much more, particularly the **document structure** against a set of declarations to be sure that the structure contains all the parts required by these declarations (Laurent, 1999). Unfortunately, both parsers are far less performing when it comes to checking the relationship coherence of structured documents. The importance of this step is to reduce potential syntax errors and check the document structure, for a more powerful analysis to the next step.

Step 2 — Links Recognition

In order to keep the reliability recognition, let us consider only "well-formed-syntactically" documents (Step 1). The next step is to detect the tags between the documents; this means, to identify the type of link. The simple and extended links are the classical links embedded in most of the structured documents. The simple link is used to "surf" or to navigate between the documents (transversal notion); this link is unidirectional. The extended link is multi-directional, allowing a multi-directional navigation and reference. The other types of links are not considered for the moment.

Figure 2.

To have a general panorama of X-link properties, a summary is considered. In this way, XLL language has two types of links: internal and external links. Internal links are "online" links (within the document), an advantage lies in the use of X-pointer; this means that we can point any portion of the document and identify the end-points of the link that work on the tree nodes (child, descendant, antecessor, etc.) e.g., HREF=http://lisi.insa-lyon.fr/~aalvarez/ #id(publications).child (3,item). External links are "out-of-line" (stored in a database).

Step 3 — Referential Links Validation

The existence of a link is asserted by a linking element. Linking elements are reliably recognized by software applications. When the user inputs the URL or file location, the application searches within documents all occurrences of type: *"A HREF=", "xmlns:xlink=", "<link target=", "<IMG SRC=", "<ID Ref=", etc.* We begin the validation link process "if the target link exists": validating the resources (start-point) to targets (end-point) for each type of link, i.e., the links relationships in the same document, in other documents. This step uses Java application displaying the valid and wrong links, i.e., find out if the links are valid or no longer valid.

Relationship Validation Mechanism

From now on, we will focus on describing the example. A small technical manual was chosen to illustrate the repercussion of any change during the life cycle of a product. The main purpose of producing the online technical documentation is to provide an easy way to find and update the information that is needed.

In this example, three types of links are considered in this chapter: composition, sharing and referential links.

Composition links represent the composition of a document structure by elements called nodes. The source corresponds to the root node, the target being a component of the source. Each anchor of the link is both source and target. This link is bi-directional. Moreover, it shows the hierarchical organization in order to retrieve the document structure.

Figure 3. Link Representation

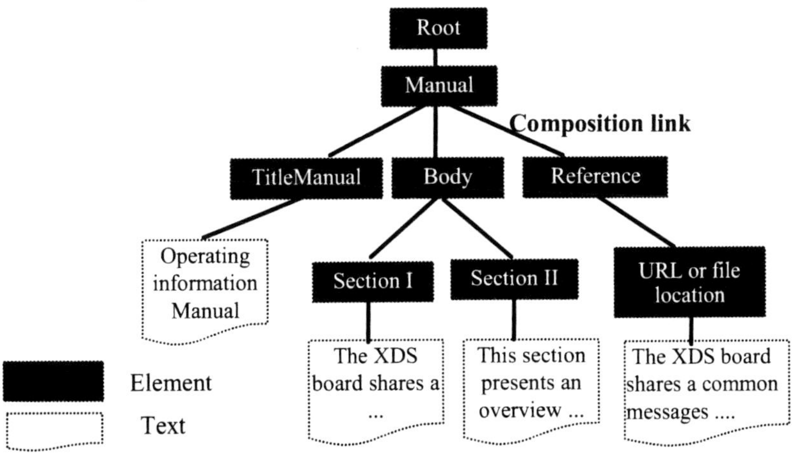

In Figure 3, "manual" represents the document type and the root element of the document: an article is composed by child elements called nodes; in this case, a manual is composed by a {ManualTitle} containing "Operating Information Manual," a {Body element} and afterwards a {Reference element}. {Section I}and {Section II} are children nodes of {Body element} and so on. Each anchor of the link is both source and target. This link is bi-directional and implicit. Moreover, it shows the hierarchical organization, generally to retrieve the document structure.

Reference links allow the establishment of a reference between documents and document fragments. These kinds of links are unidirectional, and are often represented by known expressions such as "see section 1," "for more information," etc.

Information sharing links allow the same information to be pointed between two or more fragments. This link is unidirectional and explicit.

Example

Considering a European manufacturing enterprise of video cassette recorders (VCRs), its products are manufactured with European electric characteristics, i.e., 220volts and 50Hz frequency. All the VCRs' operating manuals have a similar structure: a manual title, a body and its sections. Section I contains the Introduction and General Information, Section II Basic Operations, Section III corresponds to Technical Specifications and so on. A new project of expansion focuses on the North American area. Considering this expectation and the difference of American electric characteristics, i.e.,

Figure 4. Product Life Cycle, Related with Document Generation

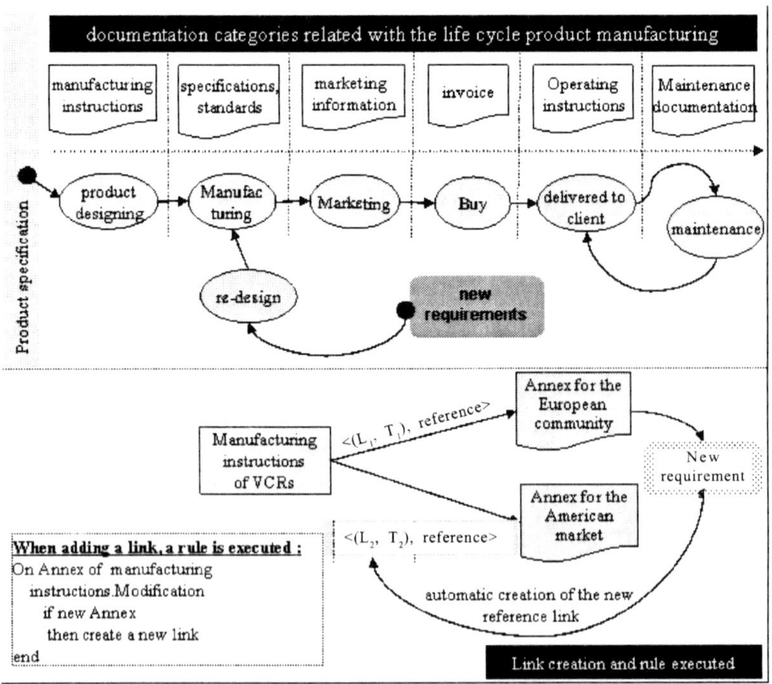

110volts and 60Hz., the company needs to think about the repercussions implied by this change in the related technical documentation across the product life cycle.

Figure 4 describes the processes of a product life cycle and the creation of a new link when a new requirement is claimed. If we consider that case, i.e., the quality service of documentation requires the addition of a new annex for previous manufacturing instructions manual.

This annex shall contain the new product specifications concerning the electric transformation to involve the North American sector. This new change on the technical annex has to be generated by the creation of a new "reference link," i.e., the original annex makes reference to a new technical annex. When the user modifies the original annex, the validation mechanism has to be executed by the system automatically creating the new reference link. Regarding Figure 4, a rule has been executed to create the link.

Now, the challenge is to keep the link references in a "coherent state" before and after manipulations; in addition, when documents are edited or revised, locations change, with the risk of potentially destroying a record of a linked text. In this level, our mechanism verifies if all links are valid or no longer valid.

Rules Definition

The components of a rule pattern are *event, condition* and *action.*

An *event* is an occurrence in the database or application's environment. In this way, "the detection of changes within the application's scope is performed using events," e.g., when a document is altered, the documents server reacts to this change, which is materialized with an event through the network. A type of event describes the situations that can be recognized by the system. These belong to one of the following classical database operations: insert, delete, update. For a document database, the set of operations is extended by the replace operation. These operations are generally described as follows:

- **Insertion:** Every time new resources (XML or HTML documents) are inserted, new target anchors are created containing a reference to the appropriate resource description.
- **Update:** Updating documents or link documents can lead to a global inconsistency's document database on the server.
- **Suppression:** Before the specified Web-based resources can actually be deleted, their entries in the resource description entity with the appropriate URLs have to be deleted.

For our purpose, primitive operations, which can be done on documents leading to potential inconsistencies document database:

- **Move or rename:** Moving a page involves physically moving the page in question, and keeping consistent, on the Web, links that refer to this page. It is possible to automatically update links that point to a moved page as long as the above restrictions or are honored when links can be automatically repaired.
- **Modification:** Document and link modifications can occur either at the whole-document level or at the internal level. Whole-document changes include the moving or renaming of documents or host machine, name or domain name changes. Internal changes include moving, editing, adding text, etc.

- **Deletion:** Document and link deletions also occur at the whole-document level or at the internal level. Whole-document deletions include the usual deletion. Internal deletions in documents can include the removal of fragments of text or other data.
- **Link missing:** Attempt to find the missing resource, such as href, ftp, http, telnet, etc.; they are typically recognized by a "mark up" code, i.e., "Tag" already embedded in the text.

A *condition* is a predicate or a query over a database (such as a comparison between object attributes). The condition consists of controlling the action execution. In the context of documentation coherence, conditions may concern link verifications. When document databases are structured through XML, a condition may result from X-path query (condition on document database) or an SQL query (condition on consistency).

```
Define rule Insertion_Link
On insert Document.Element
if (new.element = true)
   then add Document.Element
       where doc_status = valid
```

An *action* can produce one or more events. Corrective solution tries to solve situations when we move or delete a document. We have three ways of behaving responsibly:

1. We can leave some form of forward reference to the new document.
2. We can inform anything that points at us about the change.
3. We can update some name server through which our document is accessed.

The *algorithm* starts from an initial pass through an input URL-location or a file location (establish a connection to the specified URL, i.e., var stringURL) in order to search any text chains containing the referential tags as "<A HREF=", "XLINK:HREF","<LINK TARGET=","<IMG SRC=","<ID REF=" into a document in a recursive way. The verified links are stored in a table (Hastable class provided by Java.util;).

```
LinkValidation
Begin
   /* Variables definition */
        String stringURL;
        int i=1, line=1, lineNo=1;
        String[]linkStrings={"<A REF=","XLINK:HREF","<LINK TARGET= ",
        "<IMG SRC=","<ID REF=");
   /* Getting url-location */
        void clicked() {
        if ( stringURL == null ){
        showStatus("URL ENTRY IS EMPTY !");
            return;}
        . . .
```

```
startIndex=ret+1;
lineNo++;}
void CompareTo
for (int int i = 0; i < hash.size(); i++) {URL storedU =
(URL)en.nextElement();
if (u.sameFile(storedU) == true )
{s = new String ("already checked=>"+u );
    return}}
end
```

Application

The next figure depicts the parts of a running application. The input field takes the URL or file location to be verified, i.e., URL: http://lisi.insa-lyon.fr/~aalvarez/document_a.XML. (1) The Output window shows the status of each link and the links contained in the same document; (2) when the link address is valid, an OK message is displayed.

CONCLUSION AND FURTHER WORK

Link integrity and trigger concepts are the issues considered in this chapter. We have shown the different approaches to avoid the link reference problem. Two categories of solutions (the preventive and corrective) were discussed. The actual solutions are concentrated in representation aspects and are not full solutions. We have proposed a preventive mechanism to maintain the link reference integrity supported by a strong algorithm, moreover considering some XLL specifications from XML-Linking workgroup.

Figure 5. Running Application

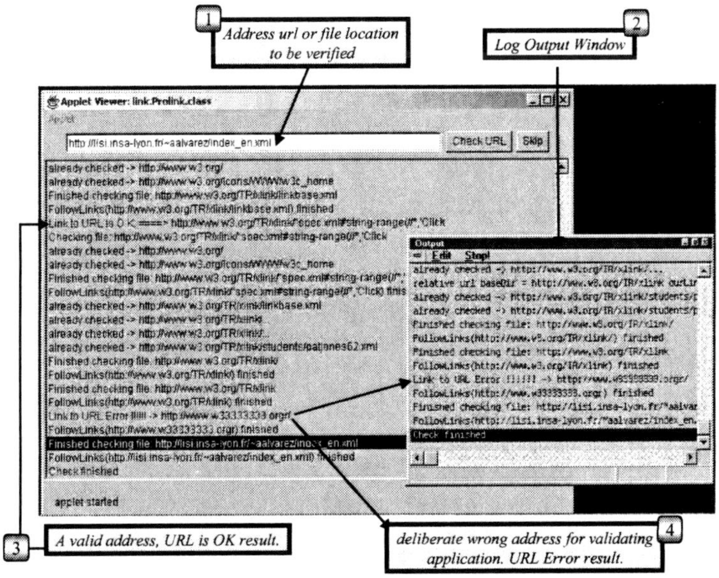

Further research should contain at least two future directions: management of document and fragment versions. Another direction is the DTD translation to schema XML. It would be beneficial to consider rules maintenance and allow addition, suppression or rules modification. The maintenance requires the development of algorithms, e.g., validation of the coherence rules. A detailed presentation of this work is presented in Alvarez (2002).

ACKNOWLEDGMENTS

I would like to thank The National Council for Sciences and Technology of MEXICO (CONACYT) for the financial support.

ENDNOTES

1 OpenDoc is a registered trademark of Apple Computer, Inc.

2 XML Spy 3.5 is an Integrated Development Environment (IDE) for the eXtensible Markup Language (XML). http://www.xmlspy.com.

REFERENCES

Albing, B. (1996). Process constraints in the management of technical documentation. *Proceedings of ACM SIGDOC'96.*

Alvarez, A & Amghar, Y. (2002). Active server for the management of structured documents link integrity. *Proceedings of EISIC: IFIP WG8.1 Working Conference on Engineering Information Systems in the Internet Context (EISIC 2002),* Kanazawa, Japan, September 25-27.

Andrews, K., Kappe F. & Maurer H. (1995). Hyper-G and harmony, towards the next generations of network information technology. *Information Processing and Management.* Special Issue: *Selected Proceedings of the Workshop on Distributed Multimedia Systems*, Graz, Austria.

Ashman, H. (2000). Electronic document addressing: Dealing with change. *ACM Computing Surveys,* 32.

Ashman, H. & Rosemary, M.S. (1999). Computing survey's electronic symposium on hypertext and hypermedia: Editorial. *ACM Computing Surveys,* 31.

Balasubramanian, V. & Alf, B. (1998). Document management and Web technologies. *Communications of the ACM,* 41(7).

Balasubramanian, V., Alf, B. & Daniel, P. (1997). A large-scale hypermedia application using document management and Web technologies. *Proceedings of Hypertext 97, The Eighth ACM Conference on Hypertext,* University of Southampton, UK, April 6-11. ACM Press.

Berners-Lee, T. (1996). *Universal Resources Identifiers in WWW: A Unifying Syntax for the Expression of Names and Addresses of Objects on the Network as Used in the WWW.* 59-94.

Bernstein, M. (1990). An apprentice that discovers hypertext links. *Hypertext: Concepts, Systems and Applications: Proceedings of the European Conference on Hypertext. INRIA,* Versailles, France, 212-223.

Bonifatti, A., Ceri, S. & Paraboschi, S. (2000) Active rules for XML: A new paradigm for e-services. *Proceedings of the First Workshop on E-Services, co-held with the 26th VLDB Journal,* 39-47.

Ceri, S. & Manthey, R. (1993). *First Specification of Chimera.* IDEA DD.2P.004.01.

Creech, M.L. (1996). Author-oriented link management. Proceedings of the 5th International WWW Conference. *Computer Networks and ISDN Systems,* 28, 1015-1025.

Daniel, T.C. (1993). HieNet: User-centered approach for automatic link generation. *Proceedings of Hypertext '93, Seattle, Washington, USA,* November 14-18, 256-259.

Dayal, U. (1988). The HiPAC Project: Combining active databases and timing constraints. *SIGMOD Record,* 17(1), 51-70.

Debra, P., Houben, G. & Wu, H. (1999). AHAM: A Dexter-based reference model for adaptative hypermedia. *Proceedings of Hypertext '99, the 10th ACM Conference on Hypertext and Hypermedia: Returning to Our Diverse Roots,* Darmstdt, Germany, 147-156.

Derose, S.J., Eve, M., David, O. & Jam, C. (2001). *XML Linking Language (XLink) Version 1.0.* W3C Recommendation, 27 June 2001.

Gehani, N.H. (1992). Composite event specification in active databases: Model & implementation. *Proceedings of the 18th VLDV Conference,* Vancouver, Canada.

Haan, B.J., Paul, K., Victor, A.R., James, H.C. & Norman, K.M. (1992). IRIS Hypermedia Services. *Communications of the ACM,* 35(1), 36-51.

Halasz, F.G. & Schwartz, M.D. (1990). The Dexter Hypertext Reference Model. Proceedings of the Hypertext Standardization Workshop by the National Institute of Science and Technology (NIST). *Communications of the ACM,* 37(2), 30-39.

Hall, W., Hill, G. & Davis, H. (1993). The Microcosm Link Service, Technical Briefing. *Proceedings of ACM Hypertext '93,* Seattle, Washington, USA, 256-259.

Hanson, E.N. (1989). An initial report on the design of Ariel: A DBMS with an integrated production rule system. *SIGMOD Record,* 18(3), 12-19.

Hugh, C.D. (1998). Referential integrity of links in open hypermedia systems. *Proceedings of ACM Hypertext '98,* 207-216.

Hugh, C.D. (1999). Hypertext link integrity. *ACM Computing Surveys,* 31.

Ianella, R., Sue, H. & Leong, D. (1996). BURNS: Basic urn service resolution for the Internet. *Proceedings of the Asia-Pacific World Wide Web Conference,* Beijing.

Ingham, D., Caughey, S. & Little, M. (1996). Fixing the broken-link problem: The W3Objects approach. Proceedings of the 5th International WWW Conference. *Computer Networks and ISDN Systems,* 28, 1255-1268.

Killpack, R.B. & Jaelynn, W. (1994). Interoperability: Rethinking the documentation paradigm. *Proceedings of SIGDOC94,* Banff, Alberta, Canada.

Kotz, A.M., Dittrich, K.R. & Mulle, J.A. (1988). Supporting semantic rules by a generalized event/trigger mechanism. Proceedings of EDBT'88, Venice, Italy. *Advances in Databases Technology,* 303, 76-91.

Laurent, S. & Biggar, R. (1999). Inside XML DTDs. McGraw-Hill.

Lawrence, S., Coetzee, F., Glover, E. & Flake, G. (2000) Persistence of information on the Web: Analyzing citations contained in research articles. *CIKM.*Leslie, A.C. (1998). Link services or links agents? *Proceedings of Hypertext'98, the Ninth ACM Conference on Hypertext and Hypermedia: Links, Objects, Time and Space—Structure in Hypermedia Systems,* June 20-24, Pittsburgh, PA, USA.

Lewis, H.P., Hall, W., Leslie A.C. & David, R. (1999). The significance of linking. *ACM Computing Surveys,* 31(4).

Lohman, G.M. (1991). Extensions of Starburst: Objects, types, functions and rules. *Communications of the ACM,* 34(10), 94-109.

Maurer, H. (1996). Hyperware, The next generation Web solution. Reading, MA: Addison-Wesley.

Oinas-Kukkonen, H. (1998). What is inside a link? *Communications of the ACM,* 41(7), 57-66.

Peckham, J., MacKeller, B. & Doherty, M. (1995). Data model for extensible support of explicit relationships in design databases. *VLDB Journal,* 4(1), 157-191.

Salton, G. (1991). The smart document retrieval project. *ACM Proceedings of the 4th International SIGIR Conference on Research and Development in Information Retrieval,* Chicago, IL, USA.

Stonebracker, M. (1990). On rules, procedures, caching and views in database systems. *Proceedings of the ACM SIGMOD,* Atlantic City, NJ, USA, 281-290.

Streiz, N., Haake, J.H., Andreas, L., Wolfgang, S., Schütt, H. & Thüring, M. (1992). SEPIA: A cooperative hypermedia authoring environment. *Proceedings of the Conference on Hypertext,* Milan, Italy, 11-22.

Theodor, H.N. (1999). Xanalogical structure, needed now more than ever: Parallel documents, deep links to content, deep versioning, and deep re-use. *ACM Computing Surveys,* 31(4).

Thistlewaite, P. (1995). Managing large hypermedia information bases: A case study involving the Australian Parliament. *Proceedings of Ausweb'95,* 223-228.

Thüring, M., Jörg, H. & Haake, J.M. (1995). Designing for comprehension: A cognitive approach to hypermedia development. *Communications of the ACM,* 38(8), 57-66.

Varlamis, I. & Vazirgiannis, M. (2001). Web document searching using enhanced hyperlink semantics based on XML. *IEEE.*

Vitali, F. (1999). Versioning hypermedia. *ACM Computing Surveys,* 31.

W3C. (2001). Available online at: http://www.w3.org/XML/. Last working draft: 16 May 2001.

Wilde, E. & Lowe, D. (2000). From content-centered publishing to a link-based view of information resources. *Proceedings of the International Conference on System Sciences,* Maui, Hawaii.

Section III

Advances in Database and Supporting Technologies

Chapter X

Metrics for Data Warehouse Quality

Manuel Serrano
University of Castilla-La Mancha, Spain

Coral Calero
University of Castilla-La Mancha, Spain

Mario Piattini
University of Castilla-La Mancha, Spain

ABSTRACT

This chapter proposes a set of metrics to assess data warehouse quality. A set of data warehouse metrics is presented, and the formal and empirical validations that have been done with them. As we consider that information is the main organizational asset, one of our primary duties should be assuring its quality. Although some interesting guidelines have been proposed for designing "good" data models for data warehouses, more objective indicators are needed. Metrics are a useful objective mechanism for improving the quality of software products and also for determining the best ways to help professionals and researchers. In this way, our goal is to elaborate a set of metrics for measuring data warehouse quality which can help designers in choosing the best option among more than one alternative design.

INTRODUCTION

It is known that organizations are very rich in data but poor in information. Today technology has made it possible for organizations to store vast amounts of data obtained at a relatively low cost; however, these data fail to provide information (Gardner, 1998).

Data warehouses have appeared as a solution to this problem, supporting decision-making processes and new kinds of applications as marketing.

A data warehouse is defined as a "collection of subject-oriented, integrated, non-volatile data that supports the management decision process" (Inmon, 1997). Data warehouses have become the key trend in corporate computing in the last few years, since they provide managers with the most accurate and relevant information to improve strategic decisions. Also the future for data warehoused is promising. Jarke et al. (2000) forecast a market of 12 millions American dollars for the data warehouse market for the next few years. However, the development of a data warehouse is a difficult and very risky task. It is essential that we can assure the information quality of the data warehouse as it became the main tool for strategic decisions (English, 1999).

Information quality of a data warehouse comprises data warehouse system quality and presentation quality (see Figure 1). In fact, it is very important that data in a data warehouse reflect correctly the real world, but it is also very important that data can be easily understood. In data warehouse system quality, as in an operational database (Piattini et al., 2000), three different aspects could be considered: DBMSs quality, data model quality and data quality.

In order to assess DBMS quality, we can use an international standard like ISO 9126 (ISO, 1999), or some of the existing product comparative studies. This type of quality should be addressed in the product selection stage of the data warehouse life cycle.

Data quality must address mostly the extraction, filtering, cleaning and cleansing, synchronization, aggregation, loading, etc., activities of the life cycle. In the last few years, very interesting techniques have been proposed to assure data quality (Bouzeghoub & Kedad, 2002).

Last, but not least, data warehouse model quality has a great influence in the overall information quality. The designer has to choose the tables, processes, indexes and data partitions, representing the logical data warehouse and facilitating its functionality (Jarke et al., 2000).

Figure 1. Information and Data Warehouse Quality

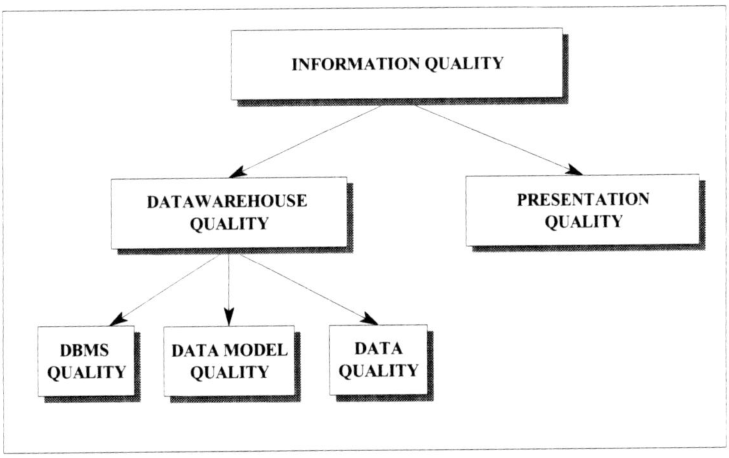

Figure 2. Example of a Multidimensional Data Model Design

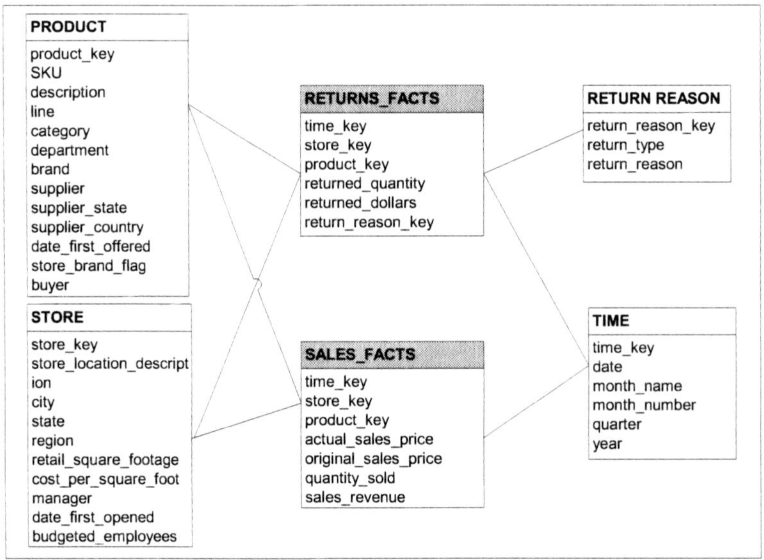

Multidimensional data models are used to design data warehouses (Petersen & Jensen, 2001). A multidimensional data model is a direct reflection of the manner in which a business process is viewed. It captures the measurements of importance to a business, and the parameters by which the measurements are broken out. The measurements are referred to as *fact* or *measures*. The parameters by which a fact can be viewed are referred to as *dimensions* (Adamson & Venerable, 1998).

Usually multidimensional data models are represented as star schemas, which consist of one central table and several dimensional tables. The measures of interest are stored in the fact table (e.g., sales, inventory). For each dimension of the multidimensional model, there exists a dimensional table (e.g., product, time) that stores the information about the dimensions (Jarke et al., 2000).

In Figure 2 we present an example of multidimensional data model design, in which we have two fact tables (Returns_Facts and Sales Facts) and four dimensional tables (Product, Store, Return_Reason and Time):

In recent years different authors have proposed some useful guidelines for designing multidimensional data models (Vassiliadis, 2000; Jarke et al., 2000; Bouzeghoub & Kedad, 2002). However, more objective indicators are needed to help designers and managers to develop quality multidimensional data models (Hammergren, 1996; Kelly, 1997; Kimball et al., 1998). Also, interesting recommendations for achieving a "good" multidimensional data model have been suggested (Kimball et al., 1998; Adamson & Venerable, 1998; Inmon, 1997), but quality criteria are not enough on their own to ensure quality in practice, as different people will generally have different interpretations of the same criteria. The goal should be to replace intuitive notions of design "quality" with formal, quantitative, objective metrics in order to reduce subjectivity and bias in the evaluation process.

The definition of a set of objective metrics for assuring multidimensional data model quality is the final aim of our work. As we know, quality depends on several factors and characteristics such as functionality, reliability, usability, understandability, etc. (external attributes) (ISO, 1999). Several of these characteristics are affected by the complexity (internal attribute) of the multidimensional data model.

However, it is not enough with proposing metrics and it is fundamental to be sure that these metrics are really useful for the goal they were conceived, through different kinds of validations.

In this chapter we will propose metrics for multidimensional data model quality, which can characterize their complexity and the different validations we have made with them.

In the next section we will present the framework followed to define and validate metrics. The third section summarizes the proposed metrics, and then the formal validation of these metrics is described. As a part of the empirical validations, a controlled experiment is presented, conclusions and future work will be presented in the last section.

A FRAMEWORK FOR DEVELOPING AND VALIDATING DATA WAREHOUSE METRICS

As we have said previously, our goal is to define metrics for controlling data warehouse complexity. Metrics definition must be done in a methodological way; it is necessary to follow a number of steps to ensure the reliability of the proposed metrics. Figure 3 presents the method we apply for the metrics proposal.

In this figure we have four main activities:

- **Metrics definition.** The first step is the definition of metrics. Although it looks simple, it is an important one in ensuring metrics are correctly defined. This definition is made, taking into account the specific characteristics of the multidi-

Figure 3. Steps Followed in the Definition and Validation of the Metrics

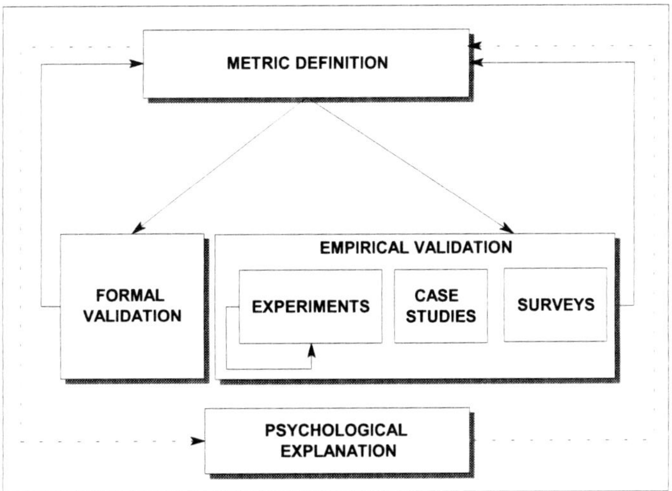

mensional data model we want to measure and the experience of database designers and administrators of these information systems.

- **Formal validation.** The second step is the formal validation of the metrics. The formal validation helps us to know when and how to apply the metrics. There are two main tendencies in metrics formal validation: the frameworks based on axiomatic approaches and the ones based on the measurement theory. The goal of the first ones is merely definitional. On this kind of formal framework, a set of formal properties is defined for a given software attribute and it is possible to use this property set for classifying the proposed metrics.
  The most well-known frameworks of this type are those proposed by Weyuker (1988), Briand et al. (1996) and Morasca and Briand (1997). The main goal of axiomatization in software metrics research is the clarification of concepts to ensure that new metrics are in some sense valid. However, if we cannot ensure the validity of the set of axioms defined for a given software attribute, we cannot use it to validate metrics. It cannot be determined whether a metric that does not satisfy the axioms has failed because it is not a metric of the class defined by the set of axioms (e.g., complexity, length) or because the axiom set is inappropriate. Since the goal of axiomatization in software metrics research is primarily definitional, with the aim of providing a standard against which to validate software metrics, it is not so obvious that the risks outweigh the benefits (Kitchenham & Stell, 1997).
  The measurement theory-based frameworks (such as Zuse, 1998; Withmire, 1998; or Poels & Dedene, 2000) specify a general framework in which metrics should be defined. The strength of measurement theory is the formulation of empirical conditions from which we can derive hypothesis of reality. Measurement theory gives clear definitions of terminology, a sound basis of software metrics, criteria for experimentation, conditions for validation of software metrics, foundations of prediction models, empirical properties of software metrics and criteria for measurement scales. However, most research in the software measurement area does not address measurement scales. Much of it argues that scales are not so important. These arguments do not take into account that empirical properties of software metrics are hidden behind scales. Units are also closely connected to measurement scales. The discussion of scale types is important for statistical operations. Because many empirical and numerical conditions are not covered by a certain scale type, the consideration of the empirical and numerical conditions is necessary and very important, too.
- **Empirical validation.** The goal of this step is to prove the practical utility of the proposed metrics. Although there are various ways of performing this step, basically we can divide the empirical validation into experimentation, case studies and surveys.
  - Experimentation is usually made using controlled experiments. These experiments are launched when we have control over the situation and want to manipulate behavior directly, precisely and systematically. Replication of the experiment is also necessary because it is difficult to understand the applicability of isolated results from one study and, thus, to assess the true contribution to the field (Basili et al., 1999).

- The case studies usually work with real data and are used for monitoring projects, activities or assignments. The case study is normally aimed at tracking a specific attribute or establishing relationships between different attributes.
- A survey is a comprehensive system for collecting information to describe, compare or explain knowledge, attitudes and behavior (Pfleeger & Kitchenham, 2001), and is often an investigation performed in retrospect, when for example a tool or technique has been used for a while. Surveys provide no control over the execution or the measurement, though it is possible to compare them to similar ones, but it is not possible to manipulate variables. The results from the survey are analyzed to derive descriptive or explanatory conclusions.

- **Psychological explanation.** Ideally we will be able to explain the influence of the values of the metrics from a psychological point of view. Some authors, such as Siau (1999), propose the use of cognitive psychology as a reference discipline in the engineering of methods and the studying of information modeling. In this sense, cognitive psychology theories such as the Adaptive Control of Thought (ACT) (Anderson, 1983) could justify the influence of certain metrics in data warehouse understandability. The knowledge of the limitation of human information processing capacity could also be helpful in establishing a threshold in the metrics for assuring the data warehouse quality.

As shown in Figure 3, the process of defining and validating metrics is evolutionary and iterative. As a result of the feedback, metrics could be redefined based on discarded formal, empirical validation or psychological explanation.

PROPOSED METRICS

In this section, we present the metrics we have proposed for multidimensional data models. As some metrics can be applied at the table, star and schema level, we present them separately.

Table-Level Metrics

In the last two years, we have researched different metrics for assuring relational database quality (Calero et al., 2001). Two of these metrics could be useful for data warehouses:

- **NA(T).** Number of attributes of a table.
- **NFK(T).** Number of foreign keys of a table.

In Table 1, we can found the values of the table metrics for the star schema shown in Figure 2.

Star-Level Metrics

- **NDT(S).** Number of dimensional tables of a star.
- **NT(S).** Number of tables of a star, which corresponds to the number of dimensional tables added the fact table.

Table 1. Values for Table Metrics

	NA	NFK
PRODUCT	13	0
STORE	10	0
RETURN REASON	3	0
TIME	6	0
RETURNS_FACTS	6	4
SALES-FACTS	7	3

$NT(S) = NDT(S) + 1$

- **NADT(S).** Number of attributes of dimensional tables of a star.
- **NAFT(S).** Number of attributes of the fact table of a star.
- **NA(S).** Number of attributes of a star.

$NA(S) = NAFT(FT) + NADT(S)$
Where FT is the fact table of the star S.

- **NFK(S).** Number of foreign keys of a star.

$$NFK(S) = NFK(FT) + \sum_{i=1}^{NDT} NFK(DT_i)$$

Where FT is the fact table of the star S and Dti is the dimensional table number i of the star S.

- **RSA(S).** Ratio of star attributes. Quantity of attributes of dimensional tables per number of attributes of the fact table of the star.

$$RSA(S) = \frac{NADT(S)}{NAFT(FT)}$$

Where FT is the fact table of the star S.

- **RFK(S).** Ratio of foreign keys. Quantity of the fact table attributes which are foreign keys.

$$RFK(S) = \frac{NFK(FT)}{NAFT(FT)}$$

Where FT is the fact table of the star S.

In Table 2, we find the values of the star metrics for the example shown in Figure 2.

Table 2. Values for Star Metrics

	Returns Facts	Sales Facts
NA	38	36
NFK	4	3
NDT	4	3
NT	5	4
NADT	32	29
NAFT	6	7
RSA	32/6	29/7
RFK	4/6	3/7

Schema-Level Metrics

- **NFT(Sc).** Defined as a number of fact tables of the schema.
- **NDT(Sc).** Number of dimensional tables of the schema.
- **NSDT(Sc).** Number of shared dimensional tables. Number of dimensional tables shared for more than one star of the schema.
- **NT(Sc).** Number of tables. Number of the fact tables plus the number of dimensional tables of the schema.

$$NT(Sc) = NFT(Sc) + NDT(Sc)$$

- **NAFT(Sc).** Number of attributes of fact tables of the schema.

$$NAFT(Sc) = \sum_{i=1}^{NFT} NA(FT_i)$$

Where FTi is the fact table i of the schema Sc.

- **NADT(Sc).** Number of attributes of dimensional tables of the schema.

$$NADT(Sc) = \sum_{i=1}^{NDT} NA(DT_i)$$

Where DTi is the dimensional table i of the schema Sc.

- **NASDT(Sc).** Number of attributes of shared dimensional tables of the schema.

$$NASDT(Sc) = \sum_{i=1}^{NSDT} NA(DTi)$$

Where DTi is the dimensional table i of the schema Sc.

- **NA(Sc).** Number of attributes of the schema.

$$NA(Sc) = NAFT(Sc) + NADT(Sc)$$

- **NFK(Sc).** Number of foreign keys in all the fact tables of the schema.

$$NFK(Sc) = \sum_{i=1}^{NFT} NFK(FT_i)$$

Where FTi is the fact table i of the schema Sc.

- **RSDT(Sc).** Ratio of shared dimensional tables. Quantity of dimensional tables, which belong to more than one star.

$$RSDT(Sc) = \frac{NSDT(Sc)}{NDT(Sc)}$$

- **RT(Sc).** Ratio of tables. Quantity of dimension tables per fact table.

$$RT(Sc) = \frac{NDT(Sc)}{NFT(Sc)}$$

- **RScA(Sc).** Ratio of schema attributes. Number of attributes in dimension tables per attributes in fact tables.

$$RScA(Sc) = \frac{NADT(Sc)}{NAFT(Sc)}$$

- **RFK(Sc).** Ratio of foreign keys. Quantity of attributes that are foreign keys.

$$RFK(Sc) = \frac{NFK(Sc)}{NA(Sc)}$$

- **RSDTA(Sc).** Ratio of shared dimensional tables attributes. Number of attributes of the schema that are shared.

$$RSDTA(Sc) = \frac{NASDT(Sc)}{NA(Sc)}$$

In Table 3, we find the values of the schema metrics for the star schema shown in Figure 2.

Table 3. Values for Data Warehouse Schema Metrics

Metric	Value
NA	45
NFK	7
NDT	4
NT	6
NADT	32
NAFT	13
RFK	7/45
NFT	2
NSDT	3
NASDT	29
RSDT	3/4
RT	4/2
RScA	32/13
RSDTA	29/45

METRICS FORMAL VALIDATION

As we have said, there are two basic tendencies in formal metrics validation: axiomatic approaches and measurement theory. In this section, we will present both validation techniques with an example of a formal framework. The formal framework proposed by Briand et al. (1996) is an example of axiomatic approach and Zuse's formal framework is based on measurement theory.

Briand et al. (1996) Formal Framework

The Briand et al. (1996) mathematical framework presents a series of properties that must be fulfilled by certain types of metrics. The different kinds of metrics, and the properties which identify every one, are applicable to modules and modular systems. The main elements of this framework are:

- A *System* is defined as a pair *(E,R)*, where *E* is the set of elements of *S*, and *R* is a binary relation among the elements of *E* $(R \subseteq E x E)$. From this point, we say that *m* is a *Module* of *S if and only if* $E_\mu \subseteq E$, $R_m \subseteq E_m x E_m$ and $R_m \subseteq R$.
- The elements of a module are connected with elements of other modules of the system with input and output relations. So, the following two sets are defined:

$$InputR(m)=\{(e_1,e_2)\in R \,/\, e_2\in E_m \wedge e_1\in E-E_m\}$$
$$OutputR(m)=\{(e_1,e_2)\in R \,/\, e_1\in E_m \wedge e_2\in E-E_m\}$$

- *MS=(E,R,M)* is a *Modular System* if *S=(E,R)* is a system according to the previous definition and *M* is a collection of modules of *S* with no common elements (they are disjoint).
- *IR* is the union of all the relations, which relate the entities of a concrete module (intramodule relationship). According to this definition, *R-IR* is the set of relations among elements of different modules (intermodule relationship).

Table 4. Measurement Concepts and their Properties (Briand et al., 1996)

	SIZE	LENGTH	COMPLEXITY	COHESION	COUPLING
Nonnegativity	X	X	X	X	X
Null value	X	X	X	X	X
(Disjoint) Module additivity	X		X		X
Nonincreasing monotonicity for nonconnected components		X			
Nondecreasing monotonicity for nonconnected components		X			
Disjoint modules		X			
Symmetry			X		
Module Monotonicity			X		
Normalization				X	
Monotonicity				X	X
Cohesive modules				X	
Merging of modules					X

This framework provides a set of mathematical properties that characterize and formalize several important measurement concepts: size, length, complexity, cohesion and coupling (see Table 4).

Zuse (1998) Formal Framework

This framework is based on an extension of the classical measurement theory. People are interested in establishing "empirical relations" between objects, such as "higher than" or "equally high or higher than." These empirical relations will be indicated by the symbols "• >" and "• >=" respectively. We called Empirical Relational System a triple: A = (A, • >=, o), where A is a non-empty set of objects, • >= is an empirical relation to A and o is a closed binary (concatenation) operation on A.

Zuse (1998) defines a set of properties for metrics, which characterize different measurement structures. The most important ones are shown in Table 5. In this table the mathematical structures proposed by the author are presented. Based on these structures it is possible to know to which scale a metric pertains (see Zuse, 1998, for more information).

When a metric accomplishes the modified extensive structure, it can be used on the ratio scale. If a metric does not satisfy the modified extensive structure, the combination rule (which describes the properties of the software metric clearly) will exist or not exist depending on the independence conditions. When a metric assumes the independence conditions but not the modified extensive structure, the scale type is the ordinal scale. Finally, if a metric accomplishes the modified relation of belief, it can be characterized above the ordinal scale (the characterization of metrics above the ordinal scale level is very important because we cannot do very much with ordinal numbers).

Table 5. Zuse's Formal Framework Properties

MODIFIED EXTENSIVE STRUCTURE	INDEPENDENCE CONDITIONS	MODIFIED RELATION OF BELIEF
Axiom1: (A, • >=) (weak order) **Axiom2**: A1 o A2 • >= A1 (positivity) **Axiom3:** A1 o (A2 o A3) ≈ (A1 o A2) o A3 (weak associativity) **Axiom4**: A1 o A2 ≈ A2 o A1 (weak commutativity) **Axiom5**: A1 • >= A2 ⇒ A1 o A • >= A2 o A (weak monotonicity) **Axiom6**: If A3 • > A4 then for any A1, A2, then there exists a natural number n, such that A1o nA3 • >A2 o nA4 (Archimedean axiom)	**C1**: A1 ≈ A2 ⇒ A1 o A ≈ A2 o A and A1 ≈ A2 ⇒ A o A1 ≈ A o A2 **C2**: A1 ≈ A2 ⇔ A1 o A ≈ A2 o A and A1 ≈ A2 ⇔A o A1 ≈ A o A2 **C3**: A1 • >= A2 ⇒ A1 o A • >= A2 o A, and A1 • >= A2 ⇒ A o A1 • >= A o A2 **C4**: A1 • >= A2 ⇔ A1 o A • >= A2 o A, and A1 • >= A2 ⇔A o A1 • >= A o A2 Where A1 ≈ A2 if and only if A1 • >= A2 and A2 • >= A1, and A1 • > A2 if and only if A1 • >= A2 and not (A2 • >= A1).	**MRB1**: ∀ A, B ∈ ℑ: A • >= B or B • >= A (completeness) **MRB2**: ∀ A, B, C ∈ ℑ: A • >= B and B • >= C ⇒ A • >= C (transitivity) **MRB3**: ∀ A ⊇ B ⇒ A • >= B (dominance axiom) **MRB4**: ∀ (A ⊃ B, A ∩ C = ϕ) ⇒ (A • >= B ⇒ A U C • > B U C) (partial monotonicity) **MRB5**: ∀ A ∈ ℑ: A • >= 0 (positivity)

Example

We present the formal validation made with the NFK metric on both formal frameworks

Briand et al. (1996)

To demonstrate that NFK is a complexity metric, we prove that it verifies the properties given by Briand et al. (1996) for this kind of metrics:

1. Nonnegativity. The complexity of a system $S=<E,R>$ is nonnegative. $\mathrm{Complexity}(S)\geq 0$
2. Null value. The complexity of a schema is null if it has no referential integrity relations.

   $$(R=\varnothing)\Rightarrow(\mathrm{Complexity}(S)=0)$$

3. Symmetry. The complexity of a schema does not depend on the convention chosen to represent the referential integrity relations between its elements.

   $$(S=<E,R> \text{ and } S^{-1}=<E,R^{-1}>)\Rightarrow \mathrm{Complexity}(S)=\mathrm{Complexity}(S^{-1})$$

   The definition of NFK is the same disregarding the direction of the reference.
4. Module monotonicity. The complexity of a schema $S=<E,R>$ is no less than the sum of the complexities of any two of its modules with no referential integrity relationships in common.

$$(S=<E,R> \text{ and } m_1=<E_{m1},R_{m1}> \text{ and } m_2=<E_{m2},R_{m2}> \text{ and } m_1 \cup m_2 \subseteq S \text{ and } R_{m1} \cap R_{m2}=\varnothing) \Rightarrow Complexity(S) \geq Complexity(m_1)+Complexity(m_2)$$

If the modules are no disjoint, this means that between elements of both modules, there is a relation of referential integrity, so NFK never decreases.

5. Disjoint module additivity. The complexity of a schema composed of two disjoint modules is equal to the sum of the complexities of the two modules.

$$(S=<E,R> \text{ and } S=m_1 \cup m_2 \text{ and } m_1 \cap m_2=\varnothing) \Rightarrow Complexity(S) \geq Complexity(m_1)+Complexity(m_2)$$

Every module will have a value for NFK. When modules are disjoint, neither a foreign key nor a table will be common to both modules. Therefore, the result of NFK of the system will be the sum of the NFK of the two modules.

Zuse (1998)

In order to obtain the combination rule for NFK, we can observe that the number of foreign keys—when we made a concatenation by a natural join—decreases when this join is made by foreign key and candidate key, and remains the same when the join is made in other way. So, we can characterize the combination rule for NFK as:

$$NFK(R_i o R_j) = NFK(R_i) + NFK(R_j) - v$$

NFK and the Modified Extensive Structure.

- *Axiom 1.* Weak order is fulfilled because it fulfills transitivity: NFK(R1)>=NFK(R2) or NFK(R2)>=NFK(R1) and completeness: NFK(R1)>=NFK(R2) and NFK(R2)>=NFK(R3) Þ NFK(R1)>=NFK(R3).
- *Axiom 2.* Positivity is not fulfilled because if R1 has one foreign key (which connects R1 with R2) and R2 has no foreign keys, the result of the R1oR2 is zero.
- *Axiom 3.* Weak associativity is fulfilled because the natural join operation is associative.

Figure 4. NFK does not Fulfill Weak Monotonicity

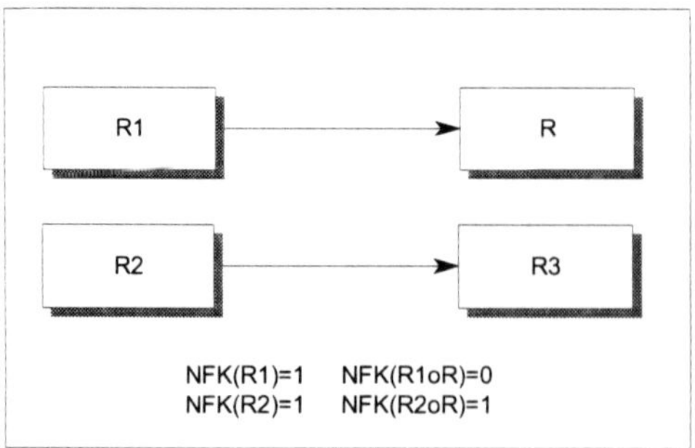

Figure 5. NFK does not Fulfill the Archimedean Axiom

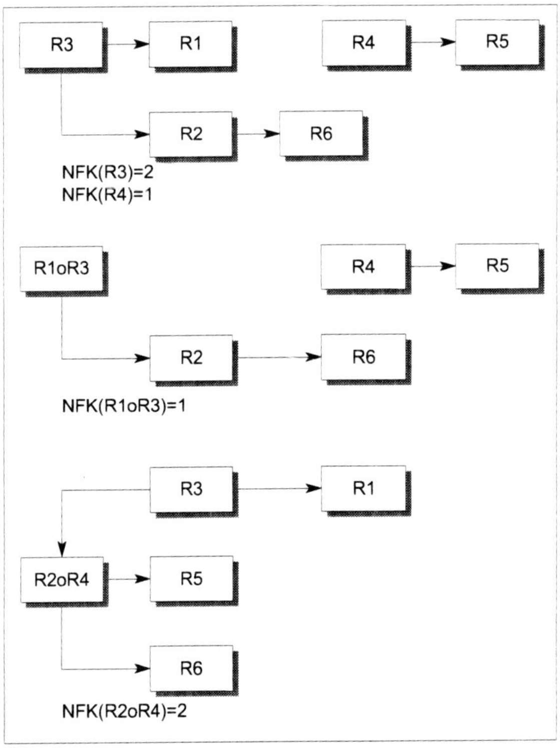

- *Axiom 4.* Weak commutativity is fulfilled because the natural join operation is commutative.
- *Axiom 5.* Weak monotonicity is not fulfilled as we can see in Figure 4.
- *Axiom 6.* Archimedean axiom is necessary to prove every axiom because, when we combine a table with itself, the number of foreign keys vary, then the metric is not idempotent. In order to prove that the Archimedean axiom is not fulfilled, we see Figure 5, where an example that does not fulfill the axiom is shown.

NFK and the Independence Condition Structure.

- C1 is not fulfilled. If we observe Figure 5, R2 and R4 have NFK=1, if we combine both tables with R5, we obtain that NFK(R2oR5)=1 and NFK(R4oR5)=0.
- C2. If the first is not fulfilled, the second is not fulfilled.
- C3. The third is not fulfilled because the weak monotonicity is not fulfilled.
- C4. If the third is not fulfilled, nor can the fourth be fulfilled.

NFK and the Modified Structure of Belief.

- As NFK fulfills weak order, it also fulfills conditions one and two.
- The third condition is also fulfilled because if all the foreign keys of B are in A, then it is clear that NFK(A)>=NFK(B).

- Regarding the fourth condition, if A⊃B, then NFK(A)>NFK(B), if there are neither common foreign keys between A and C, nor can be common foreign keys between B and C, then the condition is fulfilled.
- The last conditions are also fulfilled because if A has no foreign keys, NFK(A)=0 but it cannot be less than zero.

To summarize, we can characterize NFK as a metric above the level of the ordinal scale, assuming the modified relation of belief.

Summary of the Metrics Formal Validation

In Table 6, we present the results obtained for all the presented metrics on both formal frameworks.

With the axiomatic approach results, we can know, for example, that we need some metrics for capturing cohesion and coupling, and covering all the characteristics defined by the framework. From the measurement theory results, we can know what kind of operations it is possible to make with the defined metrics, what statistics it is possible to apply to them, etc.

Table 6. Summary of Metrics Formal Validation

	BRIAND ET AL. (1996)	ZUSE (1998)
NA	SIZE	ABOVE THE ORDINAL
NFK	COMPLEXITY	ABOVE THE ORDINAL
NDT	SIZE	ABOVE THE ORDINAL
NT	SIZE	RATIO
NADT	SIZE	ABOVE THE ORDINAL
NAFT	SIZE	ABOVE THE ORDINAL
NFT	SIZE	RATIO
NSDT	SIZE	ABOVE THE ORDINAL
NASDT	SIZE	RATIO
RSA	NOT CLASSIFIABLE	ABSOLUTE
RFK	NOT CLASSIFIABLE	ABSOLUTE
RSDT	NOT CLASSIFIABLE	ABSOLUTE
RT	NOT CLASSIFIABLE	ABSOLUTE
RSDTA	NOT CLASSIFIABLE	ABSOLUTE

METRICS EMPIRICAL VALIDATION

In the past, empirical validation has been an informal process relying on the credibility of the proposer. Often times, when a metric was identified theoretically as an effective metric of complexity, practitioners and researchers began to use the metric without questioning its validity. Today, many researchers and practitioners assume that validation of a metric (from a theoretical point of view) is not sufficient for widespread acceptance. They expect the empirical validation to demonstrate that the metric itself can be validated. Useful results of an experimentation depend on careful, rigorous and complete experimental design (see, for example, Wohlin et al., 1999). A claim that a metric is valid because it is a good predictor of some interesting attribute can be justified only by formulating a hypothesis about the relationship and then testing the hypothesis (Fenton & Pfleeger, 1997).

In the rest of this section, we will present an experiment we have done with some of the metrics discussed in this chapter. This initial experiment requires further experimentation in order to validate the findings. However, these results can be useful as a point of start for future research. A complete description of the experiment can be found in Serrano et al. (2002).

Our objective was to demonstrate that the schema-level metrics (NA, NFK, NDT, NT, NADT, NAFT, RFK, NFT, NSDT, NASDT, RSDT, RT, RscA and RSDTA) can be used for measuring the complexity of a data warehouse schema, which influences the data warehouse understandability (one quality factor, as remarked on the standard ISO 9126). The formal hypotheses were:

- *Null hypothesis, H_0:* There is not a statistically significant correlation between the structural complexity metrics and the understandability of the schemas.
- *Alternative hypothesis, H_1:* There is a statistically significant correlation between structural complexity metrics and the understandability of the schemas; that is also practically significant.

The participants of this study were 12 experts in database design (practitioners with an average of two years of experience on databases). To test the hypotheses, we handed 11 data warehouse schemas (each one with different metrics values) to the subjects. The schemas were given in different order and were general enough to be easily understood by each of the subjects. The subjects were asked to rank the complexity of each schema (from 1 = too easy to 7 = too complex).

Based on the results of this experiment, we can conclude that there is a high correlation between the complexity of the schemas and the metrics NFK, NFT, NT and NSDT. The correlation value between the metric NDT and the complexity was greater than the cutoff value for rejecting H_0; however, we cannot accept H_0 clearly due to the low distance between the obtained value and the cutoff value. The other metrics do not seem to be correlated with complexity.

In any case, to have more conclusive results about the usefulness of metrics as complexity indicators, it would be necessary to further experiment with the metrics.

CONCLUSIONS AND FUTURE WORK

If we really consider that information is "the" main organizational asset, one of our primary duties should be assuring its quality. Although some interesting guidelines have been proposed for designing "good" multidimensional models for data warehouses, more objective indicators are needed. Metrics are useful and objective mechanisms for improving the quality of software products and also for determining the best ways to help professionals and researchers.

In this way, our goal is to elaborate a set of metrics for measuring data warehouse quality which can help designers in choosing the best option among more than one alternative design.

As a start of this work, we have presented in this chapter some metrics we have defined for measuring the data warehouse star design complexity, we have presented the formal validation of these metrics and we have explained a first experiment we have developed in order to validate them.

As a conclusion of the formal validation, we have obtained that all the metrics are useful from the Zuse (1998) measurement theory framework point of view and most of them are classifiable by the Briand et al. (1996) axiomatic formal framework.

As a conclusion of our experiment, there seems to be a correlation between some of the metrics (NT, NFT, NSDT and, maybe, NDT) and the complexity of the data warehouse schema. Even though the results obtained in this experiment are encouraging, we cannot consider them conclusive. We are aware that it is necessary to replicate the experiment and to carry out new ones in order to confirm our results.

Following the MMLC (Measure Model Life Cycle) of Cantone and Donzelli (2000) with this and other experiments, our research can be classified into the creation phase. At this moment we are beginning different collaborations with companies in order to go to the acceptance phase through the systematic experimentation in a context suitable to reproduce the characteristics of the application environment, with real business cases and real users.

ACKNOWLEDGMENT

This research is part of the CALDEA project (TIC 2000-0024-P4-02) supported by the Subdireccion General de Proyectos de Investigación, Ministerio de Ciencia y Tecnologia of Spain.

REFERENCES

Adamson, C. & Venerable, M. (1998). *Data Warehouse Design Solutions*. New York: John Wiley & Sons.

Anderson, J.R. (1983). *The Architecture of Cognition*. Cambridge, MA: Harvard University Press.

Basili, V.R., Shull, F. & Lanubille, F. (1999). Building knowledge through families of experiments. *IEEE Transactions on Software Engineering*, (4), 456-473.

Bouzeghoub, M. & Kedad, Z. (2002). Quality in data warehousing. In *Information and Database Quality*. Kluwer Academic Publisher, 163-198.

Briand, L.C., Morasca, S. & Basili, V. (1996). Property-based software engineering measurement. *IEEE Transactions on Software Engineering*, 22(1), 68-85.

Calero, C., Piattini, M. & Genero, M. (2001). Empirical validation of referential integrity metrics. *Information and Software Technology*, 43(15), 949-957.

Cantone, G. & Donzelli, P. (2000). Production and maintenance of software measurement models. *Journal of Software Engineering and Knowledge Engineering*, 5, 605-626.

English, L.P. (1999). *Improving Data Warehouse and Business Information Quality: Methods for Reducing Costs and Increasing Profits*. New York: John Wiley & Sons.

Fenton, N. & Pfleeger, S.L. (1997). *Software Metrics: A Rigorous Approach* (2nd edition). London: Chapman & Hall.
Gardner, S.R. (1998). Building the data warehouse. *Communications of the ACM*, 41(9), 52-60.
Hammergren, T. (1996). *Data Warehousing: Building the Corporate Knowledge Base.* Milford: International Thomson Computer Press.
Inmon, W.H. (1997). *Building the Data Warehouse* (2nd edition). New York: John Wiley & Sons.
ISO. (1999). *Software Product Evaluation—Quality Characteristics and Guidelines for Their Use.* ISO/IEC Standard 9126, Geneva.
Jarke, M., Lenzerini, M., Vassilou, Y. & Vassiliadis, P. (2000). *Fundamentals of Data Warehouses.* Berlin: Springer.
Kelly, S. (1997). *Data Warehousing in Action.* New York: John Wiley & Sons.
Kimball, R., Reeves, L., Ross, M. & Thornthwaite, W. (1998). *The Data Warehouse Lifecycle Toolkit.* New York: John Wiley & Sons.
Kitchenham, B. & Stell, J.G. (1997). The danger of using axioms in software metrics. *IEEE Proceedings on Software Engineering,* 144(5-6), 279-285.
Morasca, S. & Briand, L.C. (1997). Towards a theoretical framework for measuring software attributes. *Proceedings of the Fourth International Software Metrics Symposium*, 119-126.
Petersen, T.B. & Jensen, C.S. (2001). Multidimensional database technology, *Computer*, 34(12), 40-46.
Pfleeger, S.A. & Kitchenham, B.A. (2001). Principles of survey research. *Software Engineering Notes*, 26(6), 16-18.
Piattini, M., Genero, M., Calero, C., Polo, M. & Ruiz, F. (2000). Database quality. In Diaz, O. & Piattini, M. (Eds.), *Advanced Database Technology and Design.* London: Artech House.
Poels, G. & Dedene, G. (2000). Distance-based software measurement: Necessary and sufficient properties for software measures. *Information and Software Technology*, 42(1), 35-46.
Serrano, M. Calero, C. & Piattini, M. (2002). Validating metrics for data warehouses. *Proceedings of the Conference on Empirical Assessment in Software Engineering (EASE 2002),* Keele, UK, April 8-10.
Siau, K. (1999). Information modeling and method engineering: A psychological perspective. *Journal of Database Management,* 10(4), 44-50.
Vassiliadis, P. (2000). *Data Warehouse Modeling and Quality Issues.* PhD Thesis, Department of Electrical and Computer Engineering.
Weyuker, E.J. (1988). Evaluating software complexity measures. *IEEE Transactions on Software Engineering,* 14(9), 1357-1365.
Whitmire, S.A. (1997). *Object-Oriented Design Measurement.* New York: John Wiley & Sons.
Wohlin, C., Runeson, P., Höst, M., Ohlson, M., Regnell, B. & Wesslén, A. (2000). *Experimentation in Software Engineering: An Introduction.* Kluwer Academic Publishers.
Zuse, H. (1998). *A Framework of Software Measurement.* Berlin: Walter de Gruyter.

Chapter XI

Novel Indexing Method of Relations Between Salient Objects

R. Chbeir
Laboratoire Electronique Informatique et Image, Université de Bourgogne, France

Y. Amghar
Laboratoire d'Ingénierie des Systèmes d'Information, INSA de Lyon, France

A. Flory
Laboratoire d'Ingénierie des Systèmes d'Information, INSA de Lyon, France

ABSTRACT

Since the last decade, images have been integrated into several application domains such as GIS, medicine, etc. This integration necessitates new managing methods particularly in image retrieval. Queries should be formulated using different types of features such as low-level features of images (histograms, color distribution, etc.), spatial and temporal relations between salient objects, semantic features, etc. In this chapter, we propose a novel method for identifying and indexing several types of relations between salient objects. Spatial relations are used here to show how our method can provide high expressive power to relations in comparison to the traditional methods.

INTRODUCTION

During the last decade, a lot of work has been done in information technology in order to integrate image retrieval in the standard data processing environments. Image retrieval is involved in several domains (Yoshitaka, 1999; Rui, 1999; Grosky, 1997;

Smeulders, 1998) such as GIS, medicine, surveillance, etc., where queries' criteria are based on different types of features such as metadata (Trayser, 2001; Sheth, 1998; Duncan, 2000), low-level features (Wu, 1995; Berchtold, 1997; Veltkamp, 2000), semantic features (Oria, 1997; Mechkour, 1995; Chu, 1998), etc.

Principally, relations between salient objects are very important. In medicine, for instance, the spatial data in surgical or radiation therapy of brain tumors is decisive because the location of a tumor has profound implications on a therapeutic decision (Chbeir, 2000, 2001). Hence, it is crucial to provide a precise and powerful system to express spatial relations.

In the literature, three major types of spatial relations are proposed (Egenhofer, 1989):

- *Metric relations* measure the distance between salient objects (Peuquet, 1986). For instance, the metric relation "far" between two objects A and B indicates that each pair of points A_i and B_j has a distance greater than a certain value d.
- *Directional relations* describe the order between two salient objects according to a direction, or the localization of a salient object inside images (El-kwae, 1999). In the literature, 14 directional relations are considered:
  - Strict: north, south, east, and west
  - Mixture: north-east, north-west, south-east and south-west
  - Positional: left, right, up, down, front and behind

  Directional relations are *rotation variant* and there is a need to have referential base. Furthermore, directional relations do not exist in certain configurations.
- *Topological relations* describe the intersection and the incidence between objects (Egenhofer, 1991, 1997). Egenhofer (1991) has identified six basic relations: *disjoint, meet, overlap, cover, contain* and *equal.* Topological relations present several characteristics that are *exclusive* to two objects (i.e., there is one and only one topological relation between two objects). Furthermore, topological relations have *absolute* value because of their constant existence between objects. Another interesting characteristic of topological relations is that they are transformation, translation, scaling and zooming *invariant.*

In spite of all the proposed work to represent complex visual situations, several shortcomings exist in the methods of spatial relation computations. For instance, Figure 1 shows two different spatial situations of three salient objects that are described by the same spatial relations in both cases: topological relations — a1 Touch a2, a1 Touch a3, a2 Touch a3; and directional relations — a1 Above a3, a2 Above a3, a1 Left a2.

The existing systems do not have the required expressive power to represent these situations. Thus, in this chapter, we address this issue and propose a novel method that

Figure 1. Two Different Spatial Situations

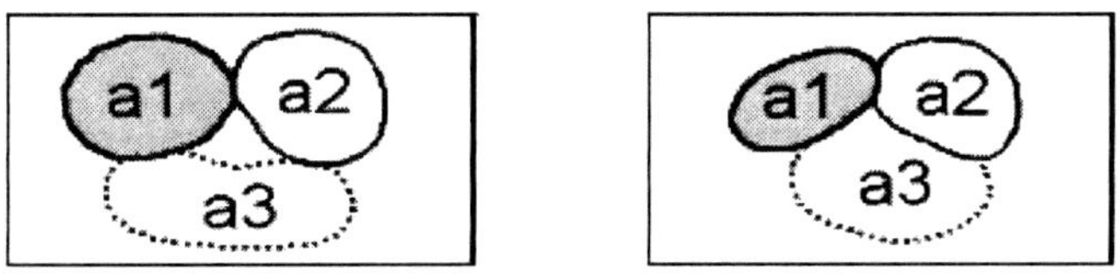

can easily compute several types of relations between salient objects with better expressions. The rest of this chapter is organized as follows. First we present our method for identifying relations, followed by a discussion of how our method gives better results using spatial features. Finally, conclusions are given.

PROPOSITION

The 9-Intersection model proposed by Egenhofer (1991) represents each shape "A" as a combination of three parts: *interior* **A°**, *boundary* **∂A** and *exterior* **A⁻**. The topological relations between two shapes are obtained by applying an intersection matrix between these parts (Figure 2). Each intersection is characterized by an empty (∅) or non-empty (¬∅) value.

Our proposal represents an extension of this 9-Intersection model. It provides a general method for computing not only topological relations but also other types of relations such as temporal, spatial, etc. The idea shows that the relations are identified in the function of the features of shape, time, etc. The shape feature gives spatial relations, the time feature gives temporal relations and so on. To identify a relation between two salient objects, we propose the use of an intersection matrix between sets of features.

Definition

Let us first consider a feature F. We define its intersection sets as follows:

- The ***interior*** **F^{Ω}** contains all elements that cover the interior or the core of F. In particular, it contains the barycentre of F. The definition of this set has a great impact on the other sets. F^{Ω} may be empty (∅).
- The ***boundary*** **∂F** contains all elements that allow determining the frontier of F. ∂F is never empty (¬∅).
- The ***exterior*** **F^-** is the complement of $F^{\Omega} \cup \partial F$. It contains at least two elements ⊥ (the minimum value) and ∞ (the maximum value). F^- can be divided into several disjoint subsets. This decomposition depends on the number of the feature dimensions.

For instance, if we consider a feature of one dimension i (such as the acquisition time of an image), two intersection subsets can be defined (Figure 3):

Figure 2. The 9-Intersection Model: The Topological Relation Between Two Shapes is Based on the Comparison of the Three Parts of Each One

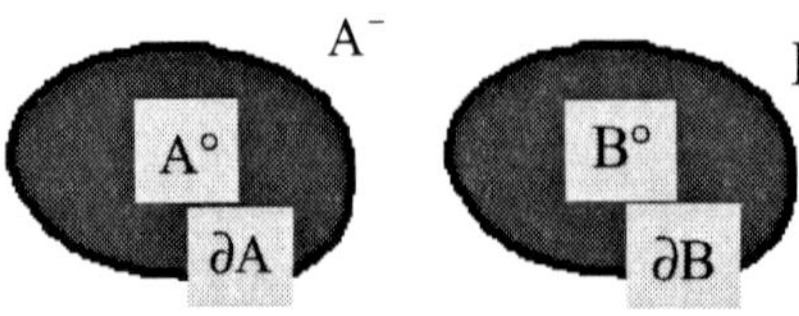

$$R(A,B) = \begin{pmatrix} A^\circ \cap B^\circ & A^\circ \cap \partial B & A^\circ \cap B \\ \partial A \cap B^\circ & \partial A \cap \partial B & \partial A \cap B \\ A^- \cap B^\circ & A^- \cap \partial B & A^- \cap B \end{pmatrix}$$

Figure 3. Intersection Sets of One-Dimensional Feature

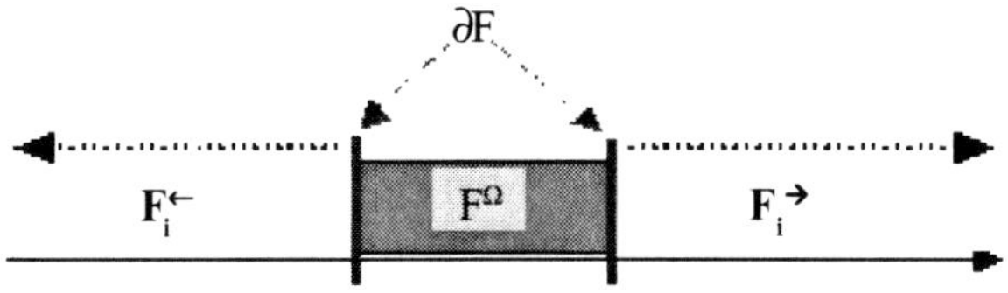

- **$F_i^{\leftarrow}$ (or inferior)** contains elements of F^- that do not belong to any other intersection set and inferior to ∂F elements on the basis of i dimension.
- **$F_i^{\rightarrow}$ (or superior)** contains elements of F^- that do not belong to any other intersection set and superior to ∂F elements on the basis of i dimension.

If we consider a feature of two dimensions i and j (as the shape in a 2D space), we can define four intersection subsets (Figure 4):

- **$F_i^{\leftarrow} \cap F_j^{\leftarrow}$ (or inferior)** contains elements of F^- that do not belong to any other intersection set, and are inferior to F^{Ω} and ∂F elements on the basis of i and j dimensions.
- **$F_i^{\leftarrow} \cap F_j^{\rightarrow}$** contains elements of F^- that do not belong to any other intersection set and, are inferior to F^{Ω} and ∂F elements on the basis of i dimension, and superior to F^{Ω} and ∂F elements on the basis of j dimension.
- **$F_i^{\rightarrow} \cap F_j^{\leftarrow}$** contains elements of F^- that do not belong to any other intersection set and are superior to F^{Ω} and ∂F elements on the basis of i dimension, and inferior to F^{Ω} and ∂F elements on the basis of j dimension.
- **$F_i^{\rightarrow} \cap F_j^{\rightarrow}$ (or superior)** contains elements of F^- that do not belong to any other intersection set and are superior to F^{Ω} and ∂F elements on the basis of i and j dimensions.

More generally, we can determine intersection sets (2^n) of n dimensional feature. In addition, we use a tolerance degree in the feature intersection sets definition in order to represent separations between sets. For this purpose, we use two tolerance thresholds:

- internal threshold ε^i that defines the distance between F^{Ω} and ∂F,
- external threshold ε^e that defines the distance between subsets of F^-.

Figure 4. Intersection Sets of Two-Dimensional Feature

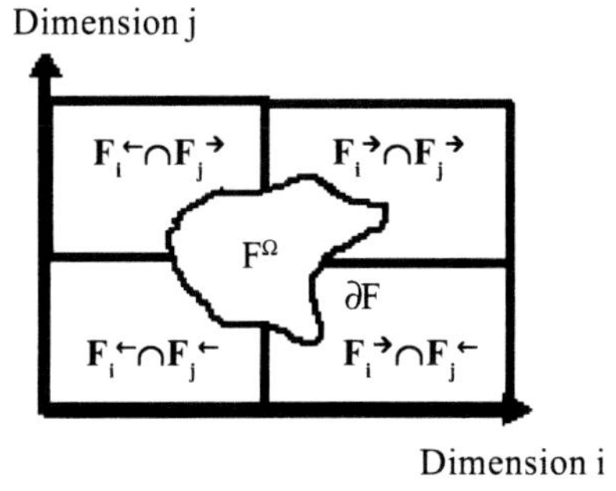

Figure 5. Intersection Matrix of Two Objects A and B on the Basis of One-Dimensional Feature

$$
R(A,B) = \begin{array}{|c|c|c|c|}
\hline
A^{\Omega} \cap B^{\Omega} & A^{\Omega} \cap \partial B & A^{\Omega} \cap B^{\leftarrow} & A^{\Omega} \cap B^{\rightarrow} \\
\hline
\partial A \cap B^{\Omega} & \partial A \cap \partial B & \partial A \cap B^{\leftarrow} & \partial A \cap B^{\rightarrow} \\
\hline
A^{\leftarrow} \cap B^{\Omega} & A^{\leftarrow} \cap \partial B & A^{\leftarrow} \cap B^{\leftarrow} & A^{\leftarrow} \cap B^{\rightarrow} \\
\hline
A^{\rightarrow} \cap B^{\Omega} & A^{\rightarrow} \cap \partial B & A^{\rightarrow} \cap B^{\leftarrow} & A^{\rightarrow} \cap B^{\rightarrow} \\
\hline
\end{array}
$$

To calculate the relation between two salient objects, we establish an intersection matrix of their corresponding feature intersection sets. Matrix cells have binary values:

- 0 whenever intersection between sets is empty,
- 1 otherwise.

For a one-dimensional feature (such as the acquisition date), the intersection matrix of Figure 5 is used to compute relations between two salient objects A and B.

For a two-dimensional feature (such as the shape) of two salient objects A and B, we obtain the intersection matrix shown in Figure 6.

Example

Table 1 shows several spatial situations and their distinguished corresponding intersection matrixes. This demonstrates that each situation is identified by a different relation contrarily to traditional methods that consider all situations as similar (topological: "B disjoint A"; directional: "B is below A"). Gray cells contain variant values in these situations; black cells contain invariant values in any situation; white cells may vary according to the situations. In fact, there are a number of hypotheses and rules used to eliminate impossible or invariant situations such as the intersection of two inferiors that is always not empty. This issue is not detailed in this chapter.

Figure 6. Intersection Matrix of Two Objects A and B on the Basis of Two-Dimensional Feature

$A^{\Omega}\cap B^{\Omega}$	$A^{\Omega}\cap\partial B$	$A^{\Omega}\cap B_1^{\leftarrow}\cap B_2^{\leftarrow}$	$A^{\Omega}\cap B_1^{\leftarrow}\cap B_2^{\rightarrow}$	$A^{\Omega}\cap B_1^{\rightarrow}\cap B_2^{\rightarrow}$	$A^{\Omega}\cap B_1^{\rightarrow}\cap B_2^{\leftarrow}$
$\partial A\cap B^{\Omega}$	$\partial A\cap\partial B$	$\partial A\cap B_1^{\leftarrow}\cap B_2^{\leftarrow}$	$\partial A\cap B_1^{\leftarrow}\cap B_2^{\rightarrow}$	$\partial A\cap B_1^{\rightarrow}\cap B_2^{\rightarrow}$	$\partial A\cap B_1^{\rightarrow}\cap B_2^{\leftarrow}$
$A_1^{\leftarrow}\cap A_2^{\leftarrow}\cap B^{\Omega}$	$A_1^{\leftarrow}\cap A_2^{\leftarrow}\cap\partial B$	$A_1^{\leftarrow}\cap A_2^{\leftarrow}\cap B_1^{\leftarrow}\cap B_2^{\leftarrow}$	$A_1^{\leftarrow}A_2^{\leftarrow}\cap B_1^{\leftarrow}\cap B_2^{\rightarrow}$	$A_1^{\leftarrow}\cap A_2^{\leftarrow}\cap B_1^{\rightarrow}\cap B_2^{\rightarrow}$	$A_1^{\leftarrow}\cap A_2^{\leftarrow}\cap B_1^{\rightarrow}\cap B_2^{\leftarrow}$
$A_1^{\leftarrow}\cap A_2^{\rightarrow}\cap B^{\Omega}$	$A_1^{\leftarrow}\cap A_2^{\rightarrow}\cap\partial B$	$A_1^{\leftarrow}\cap A_2^{\rightarrow}\cap B_1^{\leftarrow}\cap B_2^{\leftarrow}$	$A_1^{\leftarrow}A_2^{\rightarrow}\cap B_1^{\leftarrow}\cap B_2^{\rightarrow}$	$A_1^{\leftarrow}\cap A_2^{\rightarrow}\cap B_1^{\rightarrow}\cap B_2^{\rightarrow}$	$A_1^{\leftarrow}\cap A_2^{\rightarrow}\cap B_1^{\rightarrow}\cap B_2^{\leftarrow}$
$A_1^{\rightarrow}\cap A_2^{\rightarrow}\cap B^{\Omega}$	$A_1^{\rightarrow}\cap A_2^{\rightarrow}\cap\partial B$	$A_1^{\rightarrow}\cap A_2^{\rightarrow}\cap B_1^{\leftarrow}\cap B_2^{\leftarrow}$	$A_1^{\rightarrow}A_2^{\rightarrow}\cap B_1^{\leftarrow}\cap B_2^{\rightarrow}$	$A_1^{\rightarrow}\cap A_2^{\rightarrow}\cap B_1^{\rightarrow}\cap B_2^{\rightarrow}$	$A_1^{\rightarrow}\cap A_2^{\rightarrow}\cap B_1^{\rightarrow}\cap B_2^{\leftarrow}$
$A_1^{\rightarrow}\cap A_2^{\leftarrow}\cap B^{\Omega}$	$A_1^{\rightarrow}\cap A_2^{\leftarrow}\cap\partial B$	$A_1^{\rightarrow}\cap A_2^{\leftarrow}\cap B_1^{\leftarrow}\cap B_2^{\leftarrow}$	$A_1^{\rightarrow}A_2^{\leftarrow}\cap B_1^{\leftarrow}\cap B_2^{\rightarrow}$	$A_1^{\rightarrow}\cap A_2^{\leftarrow}\cap B_1^{\rightarrow}\cap B_2^{\rightarrow}$	$A_1^{\rightarrow}\cap A_2^{\leftarrow}\cap B_1^{\rightarrow}\cap B_2^{\leftarrow}$

Table 1. Several Spatial Situations with Corresponding Intersections Matrix

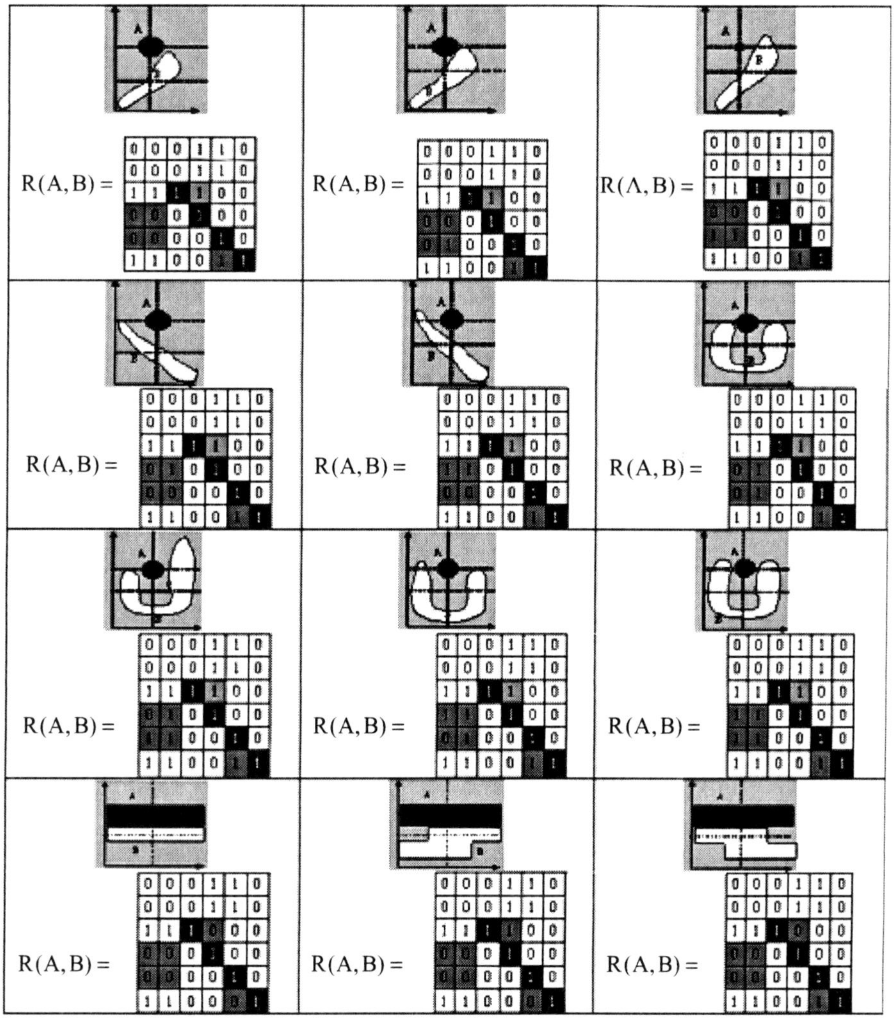

DISCUSSION

Using our method, we are able to provide a high expression power to spatial relations that can be applied to describe images and formulate complex visual queries in several domains. For example, for Figure 1 that shows two different spatial situations between three salient objects a1, a2 and a3, our method expresses the spatial relations as shown in Figure 7. The relations R(a1, a2) and R'(a1, a2) are equal, but the relations R(a1, a3) and R'(a1, a3) are clearly distinguished. Similarly, we can express relations between a2 and a3 in both situations.

Moreover, our method allows combining both directional and topological relation into one *binary* relation, which is very important for indexing purposes. There are no

Figure 7. Identified Spatial Relations Using our Method

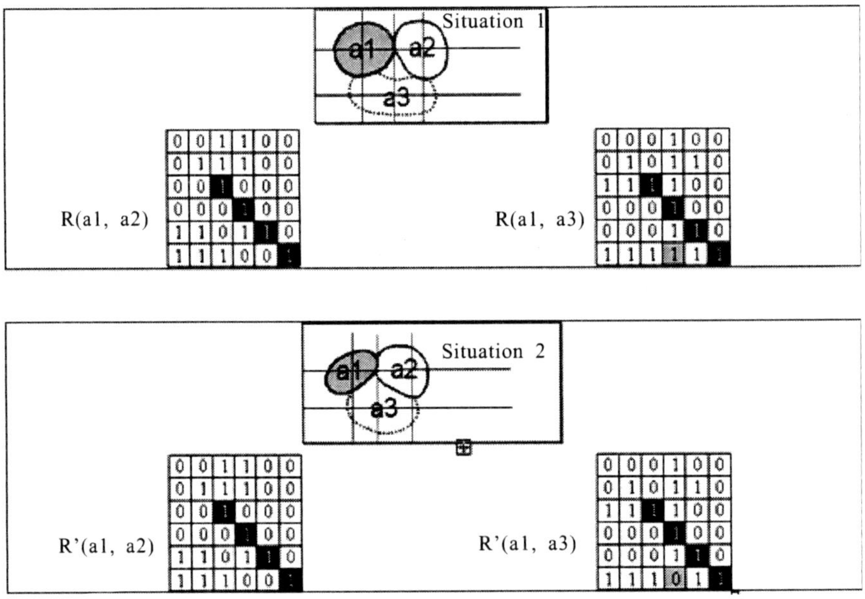

directional and topological relations between two salient objects, but only one spatial relation. Hence, we can propose a 1D-String to index images instead of 2D-Strings (Chang, 1987).

CONCLUSION

In this chapter, we presented our method to identify relations between two salient objects in images. We used spatial relations as a support to show how relations can be powerfully expressed within our method. This work aims to homogenize, reduce and optimize the representation of relations. It is not limited to spatial relations, but is also applicable to other types of relations (temporal, semantic, spatio-temporal, etc.).

However, in order to study its efficiency, our method requires more intense experiments in a complex environment where a great number of feature dimensions and salient objects exist. Furthermore, we are currently working on its integration in our prototype MIMS (Chbeir, 2001) in order to improve image storage and retrieval.

REFERENCES

Berchtold, S., Boehm, C., Braunmueller, B., et al. (1997). Fast parallel similarity search in multimedia databases. *Proceedings of the SIGMOD Conference,* Arizona, USA, 1-12.

Chang, S.K., Shi, Q.Y. & Yan, C.W. (1987). Iconic indexing by 2-D Strings. *IEEE Transactions on Pattern Analysis and Machine Intelligence,* PAMI-9(3), 413-428.

Chbeir, R. & Favetta, F. (2000). A global description of medical image with a high precision. *Proceedings of the IEEE International Symposium on Bio-Informatics and Biomedical Engineering (IEEE-BIBE'2000),* Washington, DC, USA, 289-296.

Chbeir, R., Amghar, Y. & Flory, A. (2001). A prototype for medical image retrieval. *International Journal of Methods of Information in Medicine,* (3), 178-184.

Chu, W.W., Hsu, C.C., Cárdenas, A.F., et al. (1998). Knowledge-based image retrieval with spatial and temporal constraints. *IEEE Transactions on Knowledge and Data Engineering,* 10(6), 872-888.

Duncan, J.S. & Ayache, N. (2000). Medical image analysis: Progress over two decades and the challenges ahead. *IEEE Transactions on Pattern Analysis and Machine Intelligence,* 22(1).

Egenhofer, M. (1997). Query processing in spatial query by sketch. *Journal of Visual Language and Computing,* 8(4), 403-424.

Egenhofer, M. & Herring, J. (1991). *Categorising Binary Topological Relationships Between Regions, Lines, and Points in Geographic Databases, A Framework for the Definition of Topological Relationships and an Algebraic Approach to Spatial Reasoning Within this Framework.* Technical Report 91-7, National Center for Geographic Information and Analysis, University of Maine, Orono.

Egenhofer, M., Frank, A. & Jackson, J. (1989). A topological data model for spatial databases. *Proceedings of the Symposium on the Design and Implementation of Large Spatial Databases,* Santa Barbara, CA. *Lecture Notes in Computer Science,* 409, 271-286.

El-kwae, M.A. & Kabuka, M.R. (1999). A robust framework for content-based retrieval by spatial similarity in image databases. *ACM Transactions on Information Systems,* 17(2), 174-198.

Grosky, W.I. (1997). Managing multimedia information in database systems. *Communications of the ACM,* 40(12), 72-80.

Mechkour, M. (1995). EMIR2. An Extended Model for Image Representation and Retrieval. *Database and EXpert system Applications (DEXA),* 395-404.

Oria, V., Özsu, M.T., Liu, L., et al. (1997). Modeling images for content-based queries: The DISMA approach. *Proceedings of VIS'97,* San Diego, California, USA, 339-346.

Peuquet, D.J. (1986). The use of spatial relationships to aid spatial database retrieval. *Proceedings of the Second International Symposium on Spatial Data Handling,* Seattle, Washington, USA, 459-471.

Rui, Y., Huang, T.S. & Chang S.F. (1999). Image retrieval: Past, present, and future. *Journal of Visual Communication and Image Representation,* 10, 1-23.

Sheth, A. & Klas, W. (1998). *Multimedia Data Management: Using Metadata to Integrate and Apply Digital Media.* San Francisco, CA: McGraw-Hill.

Smeulders, A.W.M., Gevers, T. & Kersten, M.L. (1998). Crossing the divide between computer vision and databases in search of image databases. *Proceedings of the Visual Database Systems Conference,* Italy, 223-239.

Trayser, G. (2001). *Interactive System for Image Selection.* Digital Imaging Unit Center of Medical Informatics University Hospital of Geneva. Available online at: http://www.expasy.ch/UIN/html1/projects/isis/isis.html.

Veltkamp, R.C. & Tanase, M. (2000). *Content-Based Image Retrieval Systems: A Survey*. Technical Report UU-cs-2000-34, Department of Computer Science, Utrecht University.
Wu, J.K., Narasimhalu, A.D., Mehtre, B.M., et al. (1995). CORE: A Content-based retrieval engine for multimedia information systems. *Multimedia Systems,* 3, 25-41.
Yoshitaka, A. & Ichikawa, T. (1999). A survey on content-based retrieval for multimedia databases. *IEEE Transactions on Knowledge and Data Engineering,* 11(1), 81-93.

Chapter XII

A Taxonomy for Object-Relational Queries

David Taniar
Monash University, Australia

Johanna Wenny Rahayu
La Trobe University, Australia

Prakash Gaurav Srivastava
La Trobe University, Australia

ABSTRACT

A comprehensive study of object-relational queries gives not only an understanding of full capability of object-relational query language but also a direction for query processing and optimization. This chapter classifies object-relational queries into REF queries, aggregate queries and inheritance queries. REF queries are queries involving REF pointers, whereas aggregation queries use either nested table structures or index on clusters. Finally, inheritance queries are queries on inheritance hierarchies.

INTRODUCTION

There have been many notions in recent times about Object Relational Database Management Systems (ORDBMS), but still different people have different understandings of the concept (Dorsey & Hudicka, 1999). ORDBMS is based on SQL3, which consists of a basic relational model along with objects, row types, collections and abstract data types (Fuh et al., 1999). Incorporation of a new object feature has given rise to object thinking in which data, its associated operations and methods are considered together while designing and developing the system. The increase in the size and complexity in the data is demanding a new type of database, which should efficiently handle both the issues without affecting the overall performance. The advantage associated with a database based on the SQL3 model is that the system is more flexible and robust so that the changes in the business process or newly discovered requirements can be accommodated easily (Fuh et al., 1999).

The Relational Database Management System (RDBMS) has been investigated well; yet, in all respects the same has not been done for ORDBMS. Most papers have only introduced the new data structures in SQL3 (Carey, 1992; Stonebraker & Moore, 1996; Fuh et al., 1999). These new data structures have given rise to new types of queries, an area that has not been investigated much. This chapter attempts to develop a framework of queries which arise due to new data structures that have been introduced in SQL3. The aim of this chapter is not to introduce the new object features, but to give a clear understanding of the full capability of the new queries that arise due to new data structures.

The chapter is organized as follows. The first section gives a brief introduction about the new data structures and the way they are implemented in SQL 3 standards. Next, the various types of object relational queries based on new data structures are described, and finally, we discuss the essence of this chapter and how the work in this chapter can be extended so as to cover various other areas in object relational queries.

NEW DATA STRUCTURES IN SQL3

The model given in Figure 1 is the base model for the work, which has been carried out in this chapter. The model reflects the database schema of a Web-based tutor payment system for a given university. The data model given in Figure 1 will be used for all our running example queries in this chapter.

The new data structures that have been introduced in Object Relational Databases can be broadly classified into REF, nested tables, index on clusters and inheritance. Nested tables and clusters are commonly used to implement the aggregation concepts.

REF Structure

REF is similar to pointers in object-oriented programming language and is used to define the link between two tables. REF is essentially a logical pointer, which can be used outside the scope of the database (Dorsey & Hudicka, 1999). It is incorporated into a database by defining one attribute in the table, which holds the REF information of the attribute, which belongs to the other table. REF is used when there is an association relationship between two objects. Association relationships can be of three types: *many to many*, *one to many*, and *one to one* (Loney & Koch 2000). REF is used in different ways to establish an association relationship depending on the type of association relationship. The general syntax for implementing REF is given in

An example of *REF* implementation is between Person and Login in Figure 1. This relationship can be implemented in ORDBMS, which in our case is Oracle 9i by the following syntax (see Figure 2).

Figure 1. Database Schema for Tutor Payment System of a University

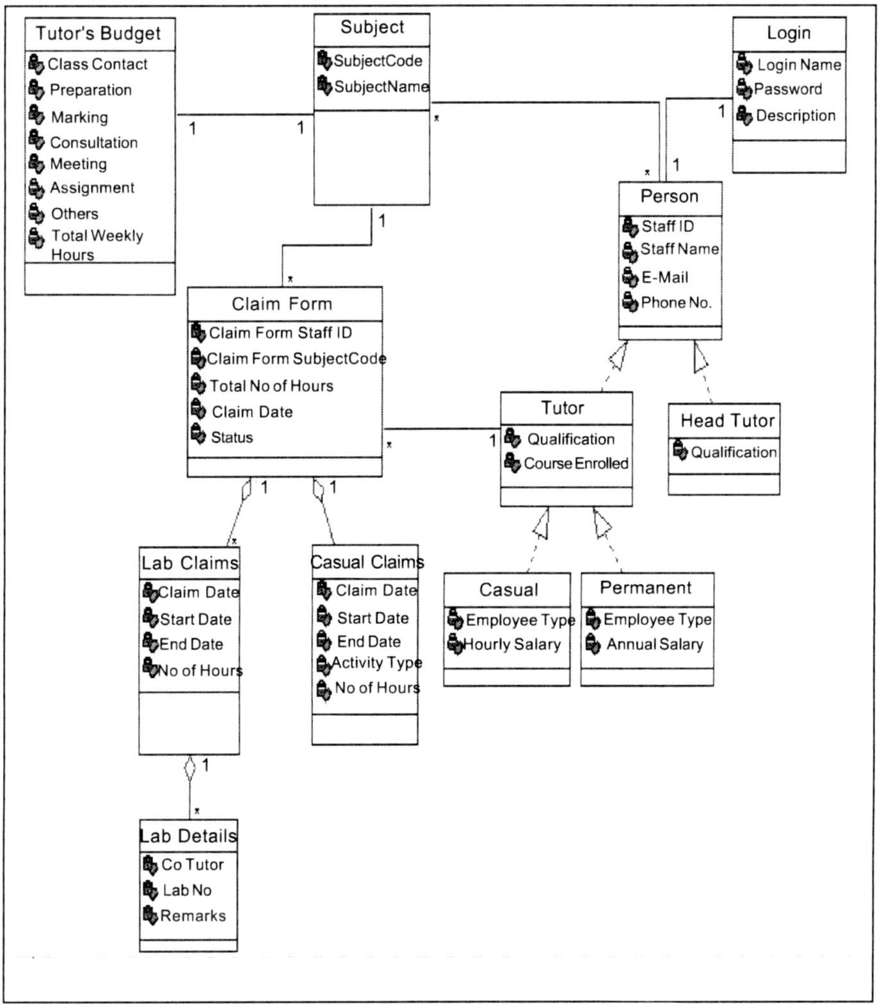

Figure 2. General Syntax for Implementing REF

```
CREATE OR REPLACE TYPE <Object Name 1> AS OBJECT
(<attribute name1>   <datatype>,
 <attribute name2>   <datatype>,
 <...................>   <...........>) /

CREATE OR REPLACE TYPE <Object Name 2> AS OBJECT
(<attribute name1>      <datatype>,
 <attribute name2>      <datatype>,
 <...................>      <...........>,
 <attribute name3> REF   <Object Name1>) /
```

```
CREATE OR REPLACE TYPE Person AS OBJECT
   (Staffid          number,
   Staff_name        varchar2(50),
   E_mail            varchar2(50),
   Phone_no          number) /

CREATE TABLE Person_t OF Person
   (Staffid          NOT NULL PRIMARY KEY);

CREATE OR REPLACE TYPE Login AS OBJECT
   (Loginname        varchar2(20),
   Password          varchar2(20),
   Description       varchar2(20),
   Loginstaff_id     REF Person) /

CREATE TABLE Login_t OF Login
   (Loginname        NOT NULL PRIMARY KEY,
   Password          NOT NULL,
   Loginstaff_id     SCOPE IS Person_t);
```

Execution of the above syntax creates two tables: Person_t and Login_t. The attribute which holds the REF value is called the *ref attribute* (e.g., Loginstaff_id in Login_t table), and the attribute to which the ref attribute points is called the *referred attribute* (e.g., staffid in person_t table). The data in the corresponding table can be entered by the following syntax.

```
INSERT INTO Person_t
VALUES (123002,'Prakash', 'pgsrivas@cs.latrobe.edu.au',946710);

INSERT INTO Login_t
VALUES   ('pgsrivas','prakash', 'tutor',
         (SELECT REF(a) FROM person_t a
         WHERE a.Staffid=123002));
```

Collection Types

Collection types give the flexibility of storing a series of data entries that are jointly associated to a corresponding row in the database. They can be further classified into two: *VARRAYS, Nested Tables.* We will not be discussing VARRAYS in this chapter, since at the moment we cannot write SQL statements to access the elements of the VARRAYS. The elements of the VARRAYS can only be accessed through PL/SQL block, hence it is out of the scope of this chapter.

Nested table is one of the ways for implementing aggregation. Nested table data is stored in a single table, which is then associated with the enclosing table or object type. In nesting technique, the relationship between *"part"* and *"whole"* is the existence dependent type. If the data for the whole object is removed, all of its part objects are removed as well. Nested table is a user-defined datatype, which is linked to the main table

Figure 3. General Syntax for Implementing Homogeneous Nested Table

```
CREATE OR REPLACE TYPE <Object Name1> AS OBJECT
(<attribute name1>  <datatype>,
 <attribute name2>  <datatype>,
 <....................>  <...........>,
 <....................>  <...........>) /

CREATE OR REPLACE TYPE <Object Name2>
  AS TABLE OF <Object Name1> /

CREATE OR REPLACE TYPE <Object Name3> AS OBJECT
(<attribute name>  <datatype>,
 <attribute name>  <datatype>,
 <..................>  <...........>,
 <attribute name>  <Object Name2>) /
```

in which it is nested. Generally, nesting technique is of two types: *homogeneous* and *heterogeneous*, depending upon the number of the parts that the main table has.

Homogeneous Aggregation

Homogeneous aggregation is the type of aggregation in which each whole has one and only one part. Current ORDBMS supports multilevel nesting as well (i.e., one whole can have one part and that part can also have another part). The general syntax for implementing homogeneous nested table is given in Figure 3.

Multilevel nesting in ORDMBS such as Oracle 9i is restricted to two levels only. Homogeneous aggregation in Figure 1 is between Claim Form, Lab Claims and Lab Details. Multilevel nesting can be viewed as single-level nesting with two levels, i.e., one level between Claim Form and Lab Claims, and another level between Lab Claims and Lab Details. Table creation is as follows (written in Oracle 9i syntax).

```
CREATE OR REPLACE TYPE lab_details AS OBJECT
   (co_tutor              varchar2(20),
   lab_no                 number,
   remarks                varchar2(50)) /

CREATE OR REPLACE TYPE lab_details_t
       AS TABLE OF lab_details /

CREATE OR REPLACE TYPE lab_claims AS OBJECT
   (claim_date            date,
   start_time             varchar2(10),
   end_time               varchar2(10),
   no_of_hours            number,
   details                lab_details_t) /
```

```
CREATE OR REPLACE TYPE lab_claims_t
      AS TABLE OF lab_claims /

CREATE OR REPLACE TYPE claim_form AS OBJECT
   (claim_id                  number,
   claimformstaffid           number,
   claimformsubject_code      varchar2(10),
   tot_no_of_hours            number,
   claim_date                 date,
   status                     varchar2(10),
   lab                        lab_claims_t) /

CREATE TABLE claim_form_t OF claim_form
   (claim_id                  not null primary key,
   claimformstaffid           not null,
   claimformsubject_code      not null)
NESTED TABLE lab STORE AS lab_tab
   (NESTED TABLE details STORE AS details_tab);
```

The nested table can only be accessed from the respective whole table (i.e., Lab Details table can only be accessed by lab, and lab_tab can only be accessed by claim_form_t). Data in the nested table is not inserted in the nested table but in the object of the nested table. The data in the above tables can be inserted by the following syntax.

```
INSERT INTO claim_form_t
VALUES(2,123002,'cse42ADB',16,'29-Aug-02','A',
   lab_claims_t(lab_claims('16-aug-01','10:00','12:00',2,
      lab_details_t(lab_details('Thiru',1,'Good'),
         lab_details('Prakash',1,'Good'))),
   lab_claims('16-aug-01','12:00','02:00',2,
      lab_details_t(lab_details('Niel',1,'Average'),
         lab_details('Prakash',1,'Good'))),
   lab_claims('17-aug-01','10:00','12:00',2,
      lab_details_t(lab_details('Thiru',1,'Good'),
         lab_details('Prakash',1,'Good'))),
   lab_claims('18-aug-01','02.00','04:00',2,
      lab_details_t(lab_details('Thiru',1,'Good'),
         lab_details('Dennis',1,'Good')))
));
```

Heterogeneous Aggregation

Heterogeneous aggregation is a type of aggregation in which a whole has multi parts associated with it, and each part belongs to one and only one whole. The general syntax for implementing heterogeneous aggregation is given in Figure 4.

Heterogeneous aggregation in Figure 1 is between Claim Form, Lab Claims and Casual Claims. The tables are created as follows:

Figure 4. General Syntax for Implementing Heterogeneous Nested Table

```
CREATE OR REPLACE TYPE <Object Name1> AS OBJECT
   (<attribute name1>              <datatype>,
   <attribute name2>               <datatype>,
   <.......................>       <.................>,
   <.......................>       <.................>) /

CREATE OR REPLACE TYPE <Object Name2>
   AS TABLE OF <Object Name1> /

CREATE OR REPLACE TYPE <Object Name3> AS OBJECT
   (<attribute name1>              <datatype>,
   <attribute name2>               <datatype>,
   <.......................>       <....................>,
   <.......................>       <....................>) /

CREATE OR REPLACE TYPE <Object Name4>
   AS TABLE OF <Object Name3> /

CREATE OR REPLACE TYPE <Object Name5> AS OBJECT
   (<attribute name1>              <datatype>,
   <attribute name2>               <datatype>,
   <.......................>       <....................>,
   <.......................>       <....................>,
   <attribute name3>               <Object Name2>,
   <attribute name4>               <Object Name4>) /
```

```
CREATE OR REPLACE TYPE lab_claims AS OBJECT
   (claim_date              date,
   start_time               varchar2(10),
   end_time                 varchar2(10),
   no_of_hours              number) /

CREATE OR REPLACE TYPE lab_claims_t
         AS TABLE OF lab_claims /

CREATE OR REPLACE TYPE casual_claims AS OBJECT
   (claim_date              date,
   start_time               varchar2(10),
   end_time                 varchar2(10),
   activity_type            varchar2(20),
   no_of_hours              number) /
```

```
CREATE OR REPLACE TYPE casual_claims_t
        AS TABLE OF casual_claims /

CREATE OR REPLACE TYPE claim_form AS OBJECT
  (claim_id                  number,
  claimformstaffid           number,
  claimformsubject_code      varchar2(10),
  tot_no_of_hours            number,
  claim_date                 date,
  status                     varchar2(10),
  lab                        lab_claims_t,
  casual                     casual_claims_t) /

CREATE TABLE claim_form_t OF claim_form
  (claim_id                  not null primary key,
  claimformstaffid           not null,
  claimformsubject_code      not null)
  NESTED TABLE lab STORE AS lab_tab,
  NESTED TABLE casual STORE AS casual_tab;
```

The execution of the above statement will create one whole table (i.e., claim_form_t) and two nested tables lab_tab and casual_tab embedded in claim_form_t table. The whole table claim_form_t is linked to lab_tab and casual_tab through lab and casual attributes, respectively. An important point to notice in the above implementation is that we are not creating tables to store nested data; instead we are only creating a datatype and are storing an attribute of that datatype with a different name. Hence while inserting data into nested table, we actually store data in the object rather than in the table. The syntax for inserting data in the above implemented structure is as follows.

```
INSERT INTO claim_form_t
VALUES (2,123002,'cse42ADB',22,'29-Aug-02','A',
  lab_claims_t
    (lab_claims('16-Jul-02','09.00','10:00',1),
    lab_claims('16-Jul-02','12:00','02:00',2),
    lab_claims('17-Jul-02','04:00','06:00',2),
    lab_claims('18-Jul-02','02.00','04:00',2),
    lab_claims('23-Jul-02','09:00','10:00',1),
    lab_claims('23-Jul-02','12:00','02:00',2),
    lab_claims('24-Jul-02','04:00','06:00',2),
    lab_claims('25-Jul-02','02:00','04:00',2)),
  casual_claims_t
    (casual_claims('14-Jul-02', '10.00','04.00', 'Assignment',6),
    casual_claims('12-Jul-02','03.00', '04.00', 'Meeting',1),
    casual_claims('26-Jul-02','10.00','11.00', 'Tutorial',1)));
```

Clustering

Clustering gives the flexibility of storing the "*whole-part*" type of information in one table. This technique is used when there is aggregation (i.e., the whole is composed of parts). This enforces a dependent type of relationship and each (i.e., either whole or part) has a unique ID (Loney & Koch, 2002). Clustering can be further classified into homogeneous and heterogeneous clustering aggregation.

Homogeneous Clustering Aggregation

Homogeneous clustering aggregation is one in which each whole has one and only one part. In Figure 1 homogeneous aggregation is between Claim Form and Lab Claims and between Claim Form and Casual Claims. The general syntax for implementing homogeneous clustering technique is given in Figure 5.

An example of the homogeneous clustering technique is between Claim Form and Lab Claims. This is implemented in ORDBMS, which in our case is Oracle 9i by the following syntax.

Figure 5. General Syntax for Implementing Homogeneous Clustering Technique

```
CREATE CLUSTER <Cluster Name>
(<attribute name>                    <datatype>);

CREATE OR REPLACE TYPE <Whole Object Name> AS OBJECT
(<attribute name1>                   <datatype>,
 <attribute name2>                   <datatype>,
 <....................>              <...........>) /

CREATE OR REPLACE TYPE <Part Object Name> AS OBJECT
(<whole attribute name>              <datatype>,
 <attribute name>                    <datatype>,
 <...................>               <...........>,
 <...................>               <...........>) /

CREATE INDEX <Index Name> ON CLUSTER <Cluster Name> ;
```

```
CREATE CLUSTER claim_cluster
   (staffid                number);
```

```
CREATE OR REPLACE TYPE claim_form_c AS OBJECT
    (staffid              number,
    subject_code          varchar2(10),
    tot_no_of_hours       number,
    claim_date            date,
    status                varchar2(10)) /

CREATE TABLE claim_form_c_t OF claim_form_c
    (staffid              not null,
    subject_code          not null)
Cluster claim_cluster(staffid);

CREATE OR REPLACE TYPE lab_claims_c AS OBJECT
    (staffid              number,
    lab_id                number,
    claim_date            date,
    start_time            varchar2(10),
    end_time              varchar2(10),
    no_of_hours           number) /

CREATE TABLE lab_claims_c_t OF lab_claims_c
    (staffid              not null)
Cluster claim_cluster(staffid);

CREATE INDEX cluster_index ON Cluster claim_cluster;
```

The execution of the above statement implements an aggregation relationship between Claim Form and Lab Claims using a clustering technique. The tables are populated by the following syntax.

```
Insert into claim_form_c_t
Values (123002,'cse42ADB',16,'29-Aug-02','A');

Insert into lab_claims_c_t
Values(123002,101,'24-aug-02','12:00','02:00',2);

Insert into lab_claims_c_t
Values(123002,101,'27-aug-02','10:00','12:00',2);

Insert into lab_claims_c_t
Values(123002,101,'29-aug-02','02:00','04:00',2);
```

Heterogeneous Clustering Aggregation

Heterogeneous clustering aggregation is one in which each whole has two or more parts. In Figure 1 the heterogeneous aggregation is between Claim Form, Lab Claims and Casual Claims. This type of relationship is implemented in ORDBMS, which in our case is Oracle 9i by the following syntax.

```
CREATE CLUSTER claim_cluster
   (staffid number);

CREATE OR REPLACE TYPE claim_form_c AS OBJECT
   (staffid             number,
   subject_code         varchar2(10),
   tot_no_of_hours      number,
   claim_date           date,
   status               varchar2(10)) /

CREATE TABLE claim_form_c_t OF claim_form_c
   (staffid             not null,
   subject_code         not null)
   Cluster claim_cluster(staffid);

CREATE OR REPLACE TYPE lab_claims_c AS OBJECT
   (staffid             number,
   lab_id               number,
   claim_date           date,
   start_time           varchar2(10),
   end_time             varchar2(10),
   no_of_hours          number) /

CREATE TABLE lab_claims_c_t OF lab_claims_c
   (staffed not null)
Cluster claim_cluster(staffid);

CREATE OR REPLACE TYPE casual_claims_c AS OBJECT
   (staffid             number,
   casual_id            number,
   claim_date           date,
   start_time           varchar2(10),
   end_time             varchar2(10),
   activity_type        varchar2(20),
   no_of_hours          number) /

CREATE TABLE casual_claims_c_t of casual_claims_c
   (staffed not null)
Cluster claim_cluster(staffid);

CREATE INDEX cluster_index ON Cluster claim_cluster;
```

The execution of the above statements implements heterogeneous clustering aggregation between Claim Form, Lab Claims and Casual Claims. The tables are populated by the following syntax.

```
Insert into claim_form_c_t
Values(123002,'cse42ADB',14,'29-Aug-02','A');

Insert into lab_claims_c_t
Values(123002,101,'24-aug-02','12:00','02:00',2);

Insert into lab_claim_c_t
Values(123002,101,'27-aug-02','10:00','12:00',2);

Insert into lab_claims_c_t
Values(123002,101,'29-aug-02','02:00','04:00',2);

Insert into casual_claims_c_t
Values(123002,001,27-aug-02,'09.00','10.00',Meeting,1);

Insert into casual_claims_c_t
Values(123002,001,'28-aug-02','10.00','04.00','Assignment', 6);

Insert into casual_claims_c_t
Values(123002,001,'28-aug-02','04.00','05.00','Meeting',1);
```

Inheritance

Inheritance is a relationship between entities, which gives the flexibility to have the definition and implementation of one entity be based on other existing entities. The entities are typically organized into hierarchy consisting of parent and child (Loney & Koch, 2002). The child inherits all the characteristics of its parent and can also add new characteristic of its own. A parent can have many children, but each child will have only one parent. There can be multilevels of inheritance (i.e., a parent can have many other children as well). Basically in Object Relational Database System, inheritance can be of three types: *union inheritance*, *mutual exclusion inheritance* and *partition inheritance*. The basic difference between three types of inheritance is in implementation, but for querying purposes they are basically the same. In this chapter we have only taken union inheritance into consideration for writing SQL statements, as the only difference between different types of inheritance is the way they are implemented in the database and not in terms of writing SQL. The general syntax for implementing an inheritance relationship is as follows.

An example of inheritance relationship is depicted in Figure 1 between Person, Tutor, Head Tutor, Permanent and Casual object types. For experimentation purposes we have implemented the above relationship in Oracle 9i. The type of implementation definition used is union inheritance. The above tree hierarchy is implemented by the following syntax.

Figure 6. General Syntax for Implementing Inheritance

```
CREATE OR REPLACE TYPE <Parent Object Name> AS OBJECT
(<attribute name1>  <datatype>,
 <attribute name2>  <datatype>,
 <...................>  <...........>,
 <attribute name>   <datatype>) NOT FINAL /

CRAETE TABLE <Parent Table Name> OF <Parent Object Name>
(<attribute name1>   not null primary key);

CREATE OR REPLACE TYPE <Child1 Object Name>
  UNDER <Parent Object Name>
(<attribute name1>  <datatype>,
 <attribute name2>  <datatype>,
 <...................>  <...........>,
 <...................>  <...........>) /

CREATE OR REPLACE TYPE <Child2 Object Name>
  UNDER <Parent Object Name>
(<attribute name1>  <datatype>,
 <attribute name2>  <datatype>,
 <...................>  <...........>,
 <...................>  <...........>) /

CREATE OR REPLACE TYPE <Child11 Object Name>
  UNDER <Parent Object Name>
(<attribute name1>  <datatype>,
 <attribute name2>  <datatype>,
 <...................>  <...........>,
 <...................>  <...........>) /
```

```
CREATE OR REPLACE TYPE person AS OBJECT
   (staffid              number,
   staff_name            varchar2(50),
   e_mail                varchar2(50),
   phone_no              number) NOT FINAL /

CREATE TABLE person_t OF person
   (staffid              not null primary key);

CREATE OR REPLACE TYPE tutor UNDER person
   (qualification        varchar2(50),
   course_enrolled       varchar2(30)) NOT FINAL /
```

```
CREATE OR REPLACE TYPE head_tutor UNDER person
   (qualification           varchar2(20)) /

CREATE OR REPLACE TYPE permanent UNDER tutor
   (employement_type    varchar2(20),
   annual_salary            number) /

CREATE OR REPLACE TYPE casual UNDER tutor
   (employement_type    varchar2(20),
   hourly_rate              number) /
```

The execution of the above statements implements inheritance hierarchy. The only table that is created in the entire hierarchy is for the supertype, which in our case is person_t. Each type is populated by inserting data in the object of the type. The above relationship is populated as follows.

```
Insert into person_t
Values(person(123024,'Pauline',
   'pauline@cs.latrobe.edu.au',94671001));

Insert into person_t
Values(head_tutor(123006,'Anne',
   'anne@latrobe.edu.au',94671006,'GDICP'));

Insert into person_t
Values(tutor(123007,'Dennis',
   'dennis@latrobe.edu.au',94671007,'B.Sc.'));

Insert into person_t
values(permanent(123002,'Prakash',
   'pgsrivas@cs.latrobe.edu.au',94064891,
   'Bachelor of Comp. Sci.', 'Master of Comp. Sci.',
   'Full Time',20000));

Insert into person_t
Values(casual(123013,'Thiru','Thiru@latrobe.edu.au',
   94671002,'Bachelor of Comp. Sci.',
   'Master of Comp. Sci.','Part Time',23.24));
```

QUERIES IN OBJECT RELATIONAL DATABASE

Object Relational Queries are the queries that exploit the basic object relational model, thus allowing the user to retrieve data from the new data structures that have been

Figure 7. General Classification of the ORDBMS Queries

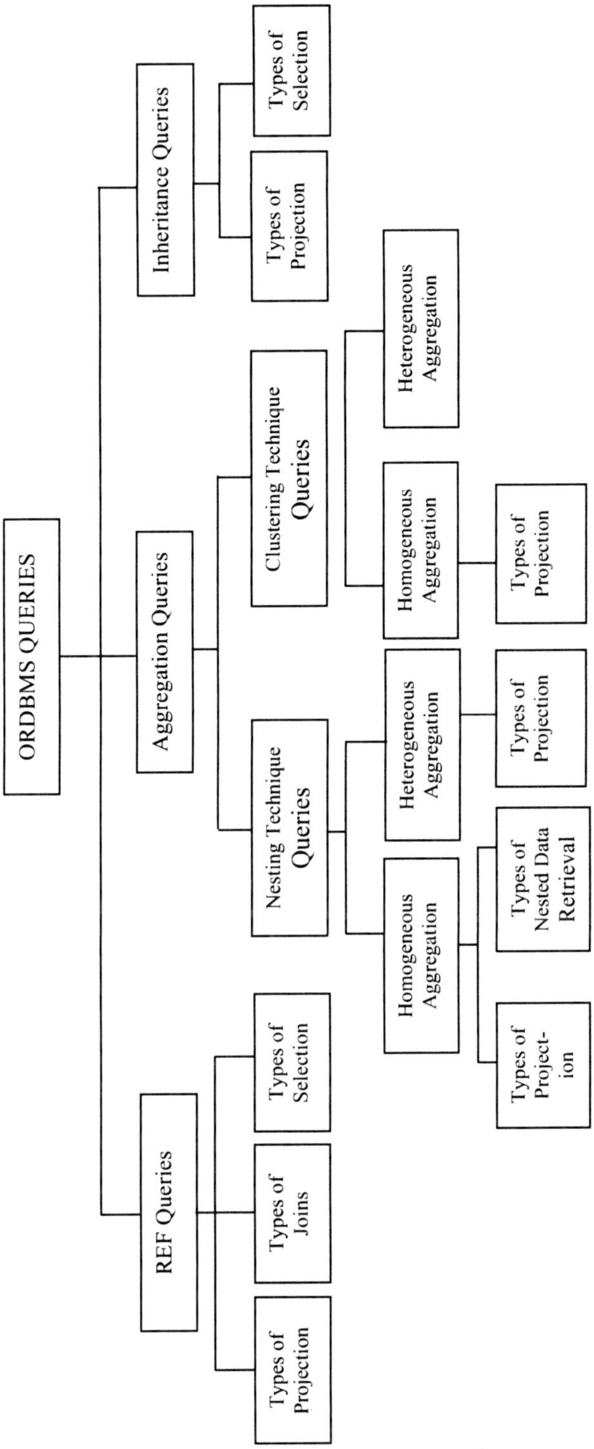

introduced in the model. Object Relational Queries can be broadly classified into: *queries having REF, queries for nested table structure, queries using index cluster and queries for inheritance relationship.* The basic difference between these four types of queries is that they are associated with different data structures in ORDBMS. ORDBMS used for implementing the model given in Figure 1 and executing the SQL statements on the model is Oracle 9i. A classification of the queries in this chapter is in Figure 7. Each of the groups refers to one of the new data structures that we have in the Object Relational Database System.

REF QUERIES

REF queries are the type of queries that involve REF either in projection or join or selection. REF is a logical pointer that creates a link between two tables so that integrity in data can be maintained between the two tables. The attribute which holds the REF value is called as *ref attribute* (e.g., Loginstaff_id in Login_t table) and the attribute to which ref attribute points is called as *referred attribute* (e.g., staffid in person_t table). Ref attributes store the pointer value of referred attribute as its real data value. The most important thing to keep in mind is that whenever we refer to REF, we always give the alias of the table, which holds the referred attribute and not the table name. REF takes as its argument a correlation variable (table alias) for an object table. Generally, REF query consists of projection, joins and selection. The general syntax of a REF query is given below.

```
SELECT <Projection List>
FROM <Table1>, <Table2>, ... ... ...
WHERE <Join>
[And <Selection>];
```

Projection refers to what we to get as a result of the execution of the query. Joins are the links that are responsible for maintaining integrity in data, which is common to two tables. Selection is the condition based on which we do projection. Different types of selection, projection and join for REF queries are as follows.

Types of Selection

Selection is user defined conditional predicate form the problem definition database domain. The result of the execution of the query conforms to the selection criterion defined by the user. In REF queries, selection can be done in the following three different ways.

Simple Selection

Simple selection is a condition, which is placed on a non-REF attribute of the table, and the conditional value is given directly for an attribute in the query. The general syntax of such a type of query is as follows.

```
SELECT <Projection List>
FROM <table1> <alias1>, <table2> <alias2>,... ... ...
WHERE <Join>
AND <alias1>.<attribute name> = <condition>;
```

An example of the query with simple condition is as follows: "Retrieve the Staff Name and Password for the Staff whose ID is 123002." This query can be written as follows.

```
Select p.staff_name, l.password
From person_t p, login_t l
Where l.loginstaff_id = REF(p)
And p.staffid =123002;
```

Nested Selection

In a nested condition query, the condition is applied using nested query. This type of query is written when the condition has to be applied on the REF attribute. The result of the execution of the nested query is a system-generated REF value corresponding to the condition, which is applied to the referred attribute.

The general syntax of such a type of query is as follows.

```
SELECT <Projection List>
FROM <table1> <alias1>, <table2> <alias2>
WHERE <Join>
AND <alias2>.<ref attribute> =
   (SELECT REF(<alias3>)
   FROM tabel1 <alias3>
   WHERE <alias3>.<attribute name> = <condition>);
```

Consider the following query as the example: "Retrieve the Staff Name and Password for the Staff whose ID is 123002." This query is similar to the one we have in simple selection. Hence the same query can be rewritten as follows.

```
Select p.staff_name, l.password
From person_t p, login_t l
Where l.loginstaff_id = REF(p)
And l.loginstaff_id =
   (Select REF(a)
   From person_t a
   Where a.staffid =123002);
```

Path Expression Selection

In path expression selection query condition is applied on the referred attribute traversing through to the REF attribute. This can only be used if the attribute on which the condition is to be applied is a REF attribute. The general syntax for such a type of query is as follows.

```
SELECT <Projection List>
FROM <table1> <alias1>, <table2> <alias2>
WHERE <Join>
AND <alias2>.<ref attribute>.<referred attribute> = <condition>;
```

Using the previous example, the SQL for this can be rewritten using path expression selection as follows.

```
Select p.staff_name, l.password
From person_t p,login_t l
Where l.loginstaff_id = REF(p)
And l.loginstaff_id.staffid = 123002;
```

Types of Projection

Projection is defined as the list of attributes, which a user wants to display as a result of the execution of the query. In REF queries, projection can be done in two ways.

Simple Projection

Simple projection is the projection where we select an attribute from a table predefined by the alias of the table from which we are selecting the attribute. General syntax for simple projection query is as follows.

```
SELECT   <alias1>.<attribute name>,
         <alias2>.<attribute name>
FROM     <table1> <alias1>, <table2> <alias2>,... ... ...
WHERE    <join>;
```

Consider the following query as an example: "Retrieve StaffName and Password of all the employees in the department." The SQL for the query can be written as follows.

```
Select p.staff_name, l.password
From person_t p, login_t l
Where l.loginstaff_id = REF(p);
```

Path Expression Projection

Path expression projection is a type of projection in which we project the REF attribute and select the value of the referred attribute using path expression. The general syntax of such a query is as follows.

```
SELECT   <alias1>.<ref attribute>.<referred attribute>,
         <alias1>.<attribute name>, ... ...
FROM     <table1> <alias1>;
```

The above query (i.e., the one in which we have to select Staff Name and Password of all the employees from the database) can be rewritten as follows using path expression in projection.

```
Select l.loginstaff_id.staffid, l.password
From login_t l;
```

The execution of the query is based on the concept that REF actually creates a virtual link between the REF attribute and referred attribute. Path expression projection is merely traversing the link starting from the table, which holds the REF attribute, and going to the referred attribute in the other table.

Types of Joins

Join can be defined as the logical link between two attributes, each belonging to different table. Joins in an Object Relational Database System are established by using REF. They enforce integrity constraint on the table, which has the REF column, so that the value of the REF column has to be from the list of values of referred column. Joins can be written in the following three types.

REF Join

Each real data of the referred attribute has a unique REF value associated to it and it is a system-allocated value. REF value is different from the real data that the referred attribute actually holds. Whenever a REF attribute is created, it stores the REF value of the referred attribute as a real data. Hence each of the REF attribute's real data is one of the REF values of the referred attribute. The general syntax for the REF join query is as follows.

```
SELECT <Projection List>
FROM <table1> <alias1>, <table2> <alias2>, ... ... ...
WHERE <alias2>.<ref attribute> = REF(<alias1>) ;
```

An example of REF join query using REF is as follows: "Retrieve the Staff Name and Password of all the employees in the department." This query can be written as follows.

```
Select p.staff_name, l.password
From person_t p, login_t l
Where l.loginstaff_id = REF(p);
```

Path Expression Join

Path expression join is a join in which the value of the REF attribute is directly taken from the referred attribute. The data in the REF attribute is a logical pointer, which is generated by the system. Each time REF data is referred to, Oracle optimizer takes the pointer value and searches for the same value in the other table to which the REF attribute has been defined as a scope of. After locating the pointer value, optimizer looks for the data that the attribute actually holds and returns it. Hence every time a path expression is used, the result of the path expression is the value of the referred attribute. The general syntax for the query using path expression join is as follows.

```
SELECT   <Projection List>
FROM     <table1> <alias1>, <table2> <alias2>
WHERE    <alias1>.<referred attribute> =
         <alias2>.<ref attribute>.<referred attribute>;
```

Consider the previous join example. The same query can be rewritten using path expression join as follows.

```
Select p.staffid, l.password
From person_t p, login_t l
Where p.staffid = l.loginstaff_id.staffid;
```

DEREF and VALUE Join

In this type of join, two key words are used. The DEREF returns the object instance corresponding to a REF (i.e., it returns the corresponding row from the object and not from the table). The VALUE function takes as its argument a correlation variable (table alias) for an object table and returns object instances corresponding to rows of the table. Hence both DEREF and VALUE are basically same, and both are applied to objects and not the tables. The general syntax of such a type of query is:

```
SELECT <Projection List>
FROM <table1> <alias1>, <table2> <alias2>
WHERE DEREF(ref attribute) = VALUE(<alias1>);
```

Considering our running example, this query can be rewritten as follows.

```
Select p.staffid, l.password
From person_t p, login_t l
Where DEREF(l.loginstaff_id) = VALUE(p);
```

There are two limitations of this type of join: First, we cannot use this join if we are joining tables on any attribute which is not a REF attribute. Suppose in our sample schema in Login object we would have staff name as one of the attributes so that both the participating tables have staff name as one of their attributes. In traditional join approach we could have joined both the tables on staff name attribute. With this type of join approach, we cannot join both tables on staff name attribute because staff name is not a REF attribute.

Second, this join does not work with Nested Table, VARRAYS and LOB. Suppose if in our sample schema, person object phone number has been implemented as VARRAY rather than traditional number datatype, then this query would have given error because of the presence of VARRAY in the implementation structure.

AGGREGATE QUERIES

Aggregation is an abstraction concept for the building composite objects from their component objects. Participating entities have a "*Whole-Part*" type of relationship and the part is tightly coupled with the whole. Aggregation can be done in the following two ways: nesting technique and clustering technique. Both the techniques store aggregate data efficiently, but the degree of cohesiveness between whole and part data is more in nesting technique than in clustering technique. Nesting and clustering technique can further be classified into *Homogeneous* and *Heterogeneous Aggregation* depending upon the number of parts they have.

NESTING TECHNIQUE AGGREGATION QUERIES

Nesting technique is an existence-dependent type of aggregation where the existence of part is fully dependent on the whole object. The main advantage of nested aggregation is that part information is tightly coupled with whole information. If the data of the whole object is removed, then its part information is automatically removed.

Homogeneous Aggregation Queries Using Nesting Technique

Current ORDBMSs support multilevel nesting as well, i.e., one whole can have one part and that part can also have another part. Multilevel nesting in an ORDMBS such as Oracle 9i is restricted to two levels only. The general syntax for query of homogeneous nesting technique is as follows.

```
SELECT <Projection List>
FROM <[part table name/whole table name/part & whole table name]>;
```

The projection list can be list of attributes from part or whole or both. Depending upon the type of projection, we can also have different types of table names. We can either select only from part or from whole or from both.

Types of Projection — Homogeneous

Aggregation is basically a composition of different components so as they form the whole system. Hence in aggregation, data is viewed at three levels. The first is projecting data only from the child. The second is projecting data only from the parent, and the third is projecting data from both. Hence in aggregation, projection can be further classified into: single-level projection and multilevel projection. Single-level projection is when we project attributes only from one component (i.e., from whole or from any one of the parts). Multilevel projection is when we project more than one component in one projection list (i.e., either two parts, or whole along with one of the parts, or whole along with both the parts).

Single-Level Projection

Single-level projection is defined as the list of values for the attributes from any one part or whole, which a user wants to display as a result of the execution of the query.

Generally, single-level projection can be divided into the following two types: *simple projection* and *cursor-based projection.*

Simple projection refers to the projection of any one part or whole attributes preceded by the table alias. The general syntax for such a type of projection is as follows.

```
SELECT   <alias2>.<attribute name1>,
         <alias2>.<attribute name2>,... ... ...
FROM     <whole table> <alias1>,
         TABLE(<alias1>.<nested attribute>) <alias2>
[WHERE <condition>] ;
```

Consider the following example for simple projection query: "Retrieve the lab claim details of all the tutors in the department." This query can be written as follows.

```
Select   l.claim_date,
         l.start_time,
         l.end_time,
         l.no_of_hours
From     claim_form_t c,
         Table(c.lab) l;
```

Cursor-based projection is like executing two queries in one query. The SQL written in cursor block executes and gets the result, but the final result is displayed based on the outer syntax of the query. The important thing to keep in mind is that the final result as a result of the execution of the query not only depends on the SQL written in cursor block, but also on the SQL in which this cursor block is embedded. The general syntax of such type of projection is as follows.

```
SELECT CURSOR
   (SELECT <Projection List>
   FROM TABLE(<alias2>.<nested attribute>)) <alias1>
FROM <whole table> <alias2>
[WHERE <condition>];
```

The same query as above can be rewritten using the cursor clause as follows.

```
Select Cursor (Select * from Table(c.lab)) Lab
From claim_form_t c;
```

Multilevel Projection

Multilevel projection is basically projecting attributes from either two parts or from whole and both parts. Like for single level, multilevel projection is divided into *simple* and *cursor-based projection*.

Simple projection is projection of all the attributes from all the components. There are two limitations in this type of projection: first, we cannot select attribute by naming them; and second, we cannot have a formatted output, instead we have a nested output. The output of the query is the output of all the levels starting from the level on which

Table 1.

```
Select *
From claim_form_t ;
CLAIM_ID CLAIMFORMSTAFFID CLAIMFORMS TOT_NO_OF_HOURS CLAIM_DATE STATUS
---------- ---------------- ---------- --------------- --------- --------
LAB(CLAIM_DATE, START_TIME, END_TIME, NO_OF_HOURS,DETAILS(CO_TUTOR, LAB_NO, REMARKS)
--------------------------------------------------------------------------------
2 123002 cse42ADB 22 29-AUG-02 A
LAB_CLAIMS_T(LAB_CLAIMS('16-AUG-01', '10:00', '12:00', 2,LAB_DETAILS_T(LAB_DETAILS('Thiru', 1,'Good'),
LAB_DETAILS('Prakash', 1, 'Good'))),
LAB_CLAIMS('16-AUG-01', '12:00', '02:00', 2,LAB_DETAILS_T(LAB_DETAILS('Thiru', 1, 'Good'),
LAB_DETAILS('Dennis', 1, 'Good'))),
LAB_CLAIMS('17-AUG-01', '10:00', '12:00', 2,LAB_DETAILS_T(LAB_DETAILS('Thiru', 1, 'Good'),
LAB_DETAILS('Prakash', 1, 'Good'))),
LAB_CLAIMS('18-AUG-01', '02.00', '04:00',2,LAB_DETAILS_T (LAB_DETAILS('Thiru', 1, 'Good'),
LAB_DETAILS('Niel', 1, 'Good'))),
LAB_CLAIMS('19-AUG-01', '10:00', '12:00', 2,LAB_DETAILS_T(LAB_DETAILS('Prakash', 1, 'Good'),
LAB_DETAILS('Dennis', 1, 'Good'))),
LAB_CLAIMS('22-AUG-01', '10:00', '12:00', 2,LAB_DETAILS_T(LAB_DETAILS('Prakash', 1, 'Good'),
LAB_DETAILS('Niel', 1, 'Good'))),
LAB_CLAIMS('24-AUG-01', '12:00', '02:00', 2,LAB_DETAILS_T(LAB_DETAILS('Thiru', 1, 'Good'),
LAB_DETAILS('Ann', 1, 'Good'))),
LAB_CLAIMS('27-AUG-01', '10:00', '12:00',2,LAB_DETAILS_T (LAB_DETAILS('Wenny', 1, 'Good'),
LAB_DETAILS('Dennis', 1, 'Good'))),
LAB_CLAIMS('29-AUG-01', '02:00', '04:00', 2,LAB_DETAILS_T(LAB_DETAILS('Prakash', 1, 'Good'),
LAB_DETAILS('Ann', 1, 'Good'))))
```

we have asterisk mark (*). If we have an asterisk on the whole table, then the output would be the whole table along with the entire nested table, and if it is on the first nested table, then the output would be the first nested table along with the second nested table. The general syntax for such a query is as follows.

```
SELECT *
FROM <whole table name >;
```

Consider an example "Retrieve the details of all the claims for all the tutors along with the Subject Code and Staff ID." The SQL for this query and output of the query is as shown in Table 1.

The result of the execution of this query is a nested output. For each row of the whole table, in this case claim_form_t table, all the corresponding rows from nested table in this case lab_tab are displayed as nested data in whole table row. If it is multilevel nesting, then for each main table row (i.e., claim_form_t), all the corresponding first-level nested table rows, i.e., lab_tab, and for each of the nested table rows, all the rows of the second-level nested table, i.e., details_tab, are displayed.

Another example of simple projection is: "Retrieve the details of all the claims submitted to the department." The SQL for this query and output of this query is as follows.

```
Select l.*
From claim_form_t c, Table(c.lab) l;
```

CLAIM_DAT	START_TIME	END_TIME	NO_OF_HOURS
16-JUL-02	09:00	10:00	1
16-JUL-02	12:00	02:00	2
17-JUL-02	04:00	06:00	2
18-JUL-02	02.00	04:00	2
23-JUL-01	09:00	10:00	1
23-JUL-02	12:00	02:00	2
24-JUL-02	04:00	06:00	2
25-JUL-02	02:00	04:00	2

8 rows selected.

The result of this query will be all the rows from the first nested table along with all the corresponding rows from second nested table if any.

Cursor-based projection for multilevel nesting can only be used to extract data form parts and not from whole along with parts. This type of projection query in cursor is executed separately and the final result is displayed based on the query definition outside the cursor clause. General syntax for such a query is as follows.

```
SELECT CURSOR
   (SELECT <Projection List>
   FROM TABLE(<alias2>.<nested attribute>)) <alias1>
FROM <whole table> <alias2>
[WHERE <condition>];
```

Consider the following query as an example: "Retrieve the details of the claims for all the tutors for the department." This query can be written using cursor as follows. Query syntax is followed by output of the query.

```
Select CURSOR(Select * from Table(c.lab) l) part
From claim_form_t c ;
```

PART

CURSOR STATEMENT : 1

CURSOR STATEMENT : 1

CLAIM_DAT	START_TIME	END_TIME	NO_OF_HOURS
16-JUL-02	09:00	10:00	1
16-JUL-02	12:00	02:00	2
17-JUL-02	04:00	06:00	2

18-JUL-02	02.00	04:00	2
23-JUL-01	09:00	10:00	1
23-JUL-02	12:00	02:00	2
24-JUL-02	04:00	06:00	2
25-JUL-02	02:00	04:00	2

8 rows selected.

The output of this query will depend on the type of nesting. If it is single-level nesting, then the output will be formatted output and in case of multilevel nesting, it will be nested output.

Types of Nested Data Retrieval — Homogeneous

Data from nested table cannot be queried directly. It can only be queried from the main table in which it is nested. Mostly definition of nested data retrieval is accompanied by selection predicate defined on the whole table because retrieving nested data without associating it with the main data would be useless. Hence all types of nested data retrieval are associated with the main table in some way or another. Types of nested data retrieval can be categorized into three groups: un-nesting, THE clause and TABLE clause.

Un-Nesting Nested Table

Un-nesting nested table gives the flexibility to break the coupling bond between whole table and part tables during run time only (i.e., un-nesting is effective during the execution of the SQL). This gives the flexibility to have selection criterion on the part. The general syntax for this query is as follows.

```
SELECT   <alias2>.<attribute name1>,
         <alias2>.<attribute name2>, ... ... ...
FROM     <whole table> <alias1>,
         TABLE (<alias1>.<nested attribute>) <alias2>
[WHERE <condition>];
```

Consider the example: "Retrieve the Staff ID and their Subject Code for all the tutors who were lab in-charge on 17 Aug 2002 in the department." The SQL for the query is as follows.

```
Select   c.claimformstaffid,
         c.claimformsubject_code
From     claim_form_t c,
         Table(c.lab) l
Where    l.claim_date = '17-Aug-02';
```

Consider the following example of multilevel nesting: "Retrieve the lab details of Staff ID 123002 for Subject cse42ADB for the lab of which he was in charge on 17 Aug 2002." The SQL for this query is as follows.

```
Select    d.co_tutor,
          d.lab_no,
          d.remarks
From      claim_form_t_mn c,
          Table(c.lab) l,
          Table(l.details) d
Where     c.claimformstaffid = 123002
And       c.claimformsubject_code='cse42ADB'
And       l.claim_date = '17-Aug-02';
```

THE Clause

THE is the keyword used to refer nested table. THE retrieves the data from the nested table based on the selection predicate on the whole table. It enables one to query a collection in the FROM clause like a table. The limitation associated with THE is that the selection predicate should be on the primary key of the whole table, and this type of selection cannot be applied with cursor-based projection. The general syntax for this type of query is.

```
SELECT    <nested table attribute1>,
          <nested table attribute2>, ... ... ...
FROM THE        (SELECT <nested attribute>
                FROM <whole table> <alias1>
                WHERE <primary key condition>);
```

Consider the following example: "Retrieve the Claim Details of the claim whose ID is 2 in the department." The SQL for this is:

```
Select claim_date, start_time, end_time, no_of_hours
From THE (Select lab
          From claim_form_t c
          Where c.claim_id = 2);
```

TABLE Clause

A TABLE expression un-nests or flattens the collection attribute of a row into one or more relational rows. It enables one to query a collection in the FROM clause like a table. The TABLE expression can be used to query any collection value expression, including transient values such as variables and parameters. TABLE expression is similar to THE subquery expression. The limitation associated with TABLE clause is that the selection predicate should be on the primary key of the whole table and this type of selection cannot be applied with cursor-based projection. The general syntax for this type of query is.

```
SELECT    <nested table attribute1>,
          <nested table attribute2>, ... ... ...
FROM TABLE      (SELECT <nested attribute>
                FROM <whole table> <alias1>
                WHERE <primary key condition>);
```

Consider our running example, as in the THE clause above, the SQL for this is:

```
Select claim_date, start_time, end_time, no_of_hours
From TABLE
   (Select lab
   From claim_form_t c
   Where c.claim_id = 2);
```

Heterogeneous Aggregation Queries — Nesting Technique

Heterogeneous aggregate query consists of projection and selection predicate. Projection in heterogeneous aggregate query can be divided into simple projection and cursor-based projection. Selection predicate does not have any variation; it is just a simple conditional retrieval. The general syntax for heterogeneous aggregate query is as follows.

```
SELECT <Projection List>
FROM <whole table>
WHERE [<condition>];
```

Simple Projection

Simple projection's projection list can only have an asterisk (*). This type of projection can be used to project data simultaneously from whole and both parts. The output of the execution of such a type of query is a nested output. General syntax of such a type of query is as follows.

```
SELECT *
FROM <whole table name>;
```

An example of heterogeneous aggregate simple projection is: "Retrieve the details of all the claims along with the Staff ID and Subject Code for each claim." The SQL for this query is given below.

```
Select *
From claim_form_t;
```

Cursor-Based Projection

Cursor-based projection can only be used for projecting attributes from both the parts simultaneously. The limitation associated with cursor-based projection is that we cannot project attributes from whole along with parts. The general syntax for cursor-based projection is as follows.

```
SELECT
   CURSOR(SELECT <Projection list>
            FROM TABLE(<alias3>.<nested attribute>))<alias1>,
   CURSOR(SELECT <Projection list>
```

```
            FROM TABLE(<alias3>.<nested attribute>))<alias2>
FROM <whole table name> <alias3>
WHERE [<condition>];
```

Consider the following example: "Retrieve all the claim details, i.e., lab and casual, for the Staff ID 123002 for cse42ADB Subject in the department." The SQL for the query and output for the query is as follows.

```
Select
   Cursor (Select * from Table(c.lab)) "Lab Details",
   Cursor (Select * from Table(c.casual)) "Casual Details"
From claim_form_t c
Where c.claimformstaffid=123002
And c.claimformsubject_code='cse42ADB';
```

Lab Details	Casual Details
CURSOR STATEMENT : 1	CURSOR STATEMENT : 2

CURSOR STATEMENT : 1

CLAIM_DAT	START_TIME	END_TIME	NO_OF_HOURS
16-JUL-02	09:00	10:00	1
16-JUL-02	12:00	02:00	2
17-JUL-02	04:00	06:00	2
18-JUL-02	02.00	04:00	2
23-JUL-01	09:00	10:00	1
23-JUL-02	12:00	02:00	2
24-JUL-02	04:00	06:00	2
25-JUL-02	02:00	04:00	2

8 rows selected.

CURSOR STATEMENT : 2

CLAIM_DAT	START_TIME	END_TIME	ACTIVITY_TYPE	NO_OF_HOURS
14-JUL-02	10.00	04.00	Assignment	6
12-JUL-02	03.00	04.00	Meeting	1
26-JUL-02	10.00	11.00	Tutorial	1

3 rows selected.

The output is a formatted output, and for each corresponding row satisfying the selection predicate, the output will have two cursors — one for Lab Details and one for Casual Details.

CLUSTERING TECHNIQUE AGGREGATION QUERIES

Clustering technique implements the participating tables in a "*Whole-Part*" type of relationship. The part information is tightly coupled with the corresponding whole record. For each whole info, we have many corresponding parts, and this is achieved by creating cluster on the whole key. Index creation improves the performance of the whole clustering structure. Clustering can also be divided into two types depending upon the number of participating subtypes: *homogeneous clustering* and *heterogeneous clustering*.

Homogeneous Clustering Aggregation Queries

The general syntax for homogeneous clustering query is as follows.

```
SELECT <Projection List>
FROM <table name>
WHERE <Join>
AND [<condition>] ;
```

Generally, SQL for these queries is same as relational queries. This type of query can be divided into two parts: projection and selection. Selection is simple selection as we have in relational queries. Projection can be of the following types.

Simple Projection

Simple projection is projecting attributes preceded by the table alias to which they belong. The limitation associated with this type of projection is that attributes from only one table can be projected at a time (i.e., attributes from whole and part cannot be projected simultaneously). The general syntax of such a type of query is as follows.

```
SELECT   <alias1>.<attribute name>,
         <alias1>.<attribute name>, ... ... ...
FROM     <whole table name> <alias1>,
         <part table name> <alias2>
WHERE    <join>
AND      [<condition>];
```

Consider the following query as an example: "Retrieve the lab claim details for the Staff whose ID 123002 for the Subject cse42ADB." The SQL for this query is as follows.

```
Select   l.claim_date,
         l.start_time,
         l.end_time,
         l.no_of_hours
From     claim_form_C_t c,
         lab_claim_c_t l
```

```
Where     c.staffid = l.staffid
And       c.staffid=123002
And       c.subject_code='cse42ADB';
```

Cursor-Based Projection

Cursor-based projection gives the flexibility of projecting attributes from whole along with part. Query in the cursor clause is executed and the result is fetched based on the selection predicate. The final result of the execution of the query is based on the selection predicate of the main query. The general syntax for such a type of query is as follows.

```
SELECT CURSOR         (SELECT <Projection List>
                       FROM <main table name>
                       WHERE Join AND[<condition>]),
CURSOR                (SELECT <Projection List>
                       FROM <part table name>
                       WHERE Join AND [<condition>])
FROM <whole table name> <alias1>,
   <part table name> <alias2>
WHERE <alias1>.<attribute name> = <alias2>.< attribute name >
AND [<condition>] ;
```

An example of cursor-based projection can be: "Retrieve the details of the claims submitted by Staff whose ID is 123002 for the Subject whose code is cse42ADB." The SQL for this query and output of the query is as follows.

```
Select
   Cursor(Select *
          From claim_form_c_t c
          Where c.staffid=123002
          And c.subject_code='cse42ADB') Main,
   Cursor(Select l.claim_date, l.start_time,
                 l.end_time,l.no_of_hours
          From claim_form_c_t c, lab_claim_c_t l
          Where c.staffid = l.staffid
          And c.staffid=123002
          And c.subject_code='cse42ADB') Lab
From claim_form_C_t c
Where c.staffid=123002
And c.subject_code='cse42ADB';
```

```
        MAIN                                  LAB
-----------------------          -----------------------
CURSOR STATEMENT : 1             CURSOR STATEMENT : 2
```

CURSOR STATEMENT : 1

STAFFID	SUBJECT_CO	TOT_NO_OF_HOURS	CLAIM_DAT	STATUS
123002	cse42ADB	22	29-AUG-02	A

CURSOR STATEMENT : 2

CLAIM_DAT	START_TIME	END_TIME	NO_OF_HOURS
16-JUL-02	09:00	10:00	1
16-JUL-02	12:00	02:00	2
17-JUL-02	04:00	06:00	2
18-JUL-02	02.00	04:00	2
23-JUL-01	09:00	10:00	1
23-JUL-02	12:00	02:00	2
24-JUL-02	04:00	06:00	2
25-JUL-02	02:00	04:00	2

8 rows selected.

Heterogeneous Clustering Aggregation Queries

The general syntax for heterogeneous clustering query is as follows.

```
SELECT   <Projection List>
FROM     <table name>
WHERE    <Join>
AND      <Join>
AND      [<condition>] ;
```

Number of joins in the query depends upon the number of components that we have in the clustering structure. Generally, SQL for these queries is the same as relational queries. The query belonging to this category does not have any variation. This query gives the flexibility of selecting data from whole along with both the parts. If we want to retrieve data from any two components of the clustering structure, then we need to write a cursor only for those components (i.e., the number of cursor's in the projection depends upon the components that we want to have in the projection statement). Consider the following as an example for heterogeneous query: "Retrieve all the types of claims that have been claimed by Staff whose ID is 123002 for the Subject whose code is cse42ADB." The SQL of such a query and output of the query is given below.

```
Select
   Cursor
     (Select c.staffid, c.subject_code,
          c.tot_no_of_hours,c.claim_date,c.status
     From claim_form_C_t c
     Where c.staffid=123002
     And c.subject_code='cse42ADB') Main,
```

```
    Cursor
        (Select l.claim_date, l.start_time,
            l.end_time,l.no_of_hours
        From claim_form_c_t c, lab_claim_c_t l
        Where c.staffid = l.staffid
        And c.staffid=123002
        And c.subject_code='cse42ADB') Lab,
    Cursor
        (Select ct.claim_date, ct.start_time, ct.end_time
        From claim_form_c_t c,casual_claims_c_t ct
        Where c.staffid = ct.staffid
        And c.staffid=123002
        And c.subject_code='cse42ADB') Casual
From claim_form_C_t c
Where c.staffid=123002
And c.subject_code='cse42ADB';
```

MAIN	LAB	CASUAL
CURSOR STATEMENT : 1	CURSOR STATEMENT : 2	CURSOR STATEMENT : 3

CURSOR STATEMENT : 1

STAFFID	SUBJECT_CO	TOT_NO_OF_HOURS	CLAIM_DAT	STATUS
123002	cse42ADB		22	29-AUG-02 A

CURSOR STATEMENT : 2

CLAIM_DAT	START_TIME	END_TIME	NO_OF_HOURS
16-JUL-02	09:00	10:00	1
16-JUL-02	12:00	02:00	2
17-JUL-02	04:00	06:00	2
18-JUL-02	02.00	04:00	2
23-JUL-01	09:00	10:00	1
23-JUL-02	12:00	02:00	2
24-JUL-02	04:00	06:00	2
25-JUL-02	02:00	04:00	2

8 rows selected.

CURSOR STATEMENT : 3

CLAIM_DAT	START_TIME	END_TIME
14-JUL-02	10.00	04.00

12-JUL-02	03.00	04.00
26-JUL-02	10.00	11.00

3 rows selected.

INHERITANCE QUERIES

Generally, inheritance queries consist of projection and selection. SQL for inheritance queries is the same irrespective of type of inheritance or number of levels in the tree hierarchy unless mentioned specifically. The general syntax for inheritance queries is as follows.

```
SELECT <Projection List>
FROM<table name>
WHERE [<condition>];
```

Types of Projection

Projection in inheritance relationship can be either projecting from supertype or projecting from subtype or a combination of both. Projection from different types can be achieved by using the combination of the different types of projection described below.

Simple Projection

Simple projection's projection list has the name of the attributes belonging to the supertype only. The result of the execution of the query retrieves the data from all the subtypes along with the supertype. The general syntax of such a query is:

```
SELECT <Projection List>
FROM <table name>;
```

Consider the following query as an example: "Retrieve the details of all the employees who work in the department." The SQL for this query and output for the query is as follows.

```
Select *
From person_t;
```

STAFFID	STAFF_NAME	E_MAIL	PHONE_NO
123002	Prakash	pgsrivas@cs.latrobe.edu.au	94064891
123006	Anne	anne@latrobe.edu.au	94671006
123007	Dennis	dennis@cs.latrobe.edu.au	94671007
123013	Thiru	thiru@latrobe.edu.au	94671002
123024	Pauline	pauline@latrobe.edu.au	94671001

5 rows selected.

TREAT-Based Projection

TREAT expression tries to modify the object type into the declared type in the query. It tries to convert all the objects that it encounters during the execution of the query into the one, which is defined in the projection list of the query. It retrieves the data for all the rows that match the defined object in the query and returns NULL rows for all the unmatched objects. The limitation associated with this type of projection is that it retrieves data not only from the defined object in the projection list but also from all the subtypes of that object if any. The general syntax of such type of query is as follows.

```
SELECT TREAT(VALUE(<alias>) AS <object name>)
FROM <table name> <alias>;
```

An example of TREAT-based projection can be: "Retrieve the Staff ID, Staff Name along with their qualification for all the Head Tutors and Tutors in the department." This query can be written as follows. Query syntax is followed by output of the query.

```
Select     Treat(Value(p) as person).staffid ID,
           Treat(Value(p) as tutor).staff_name NAME,
           Treat(Value(p) as tutor).qualification "Qualification",
           Treat(Value(p) as head_tutor).qualification "Head Tutor"
From person_t p;
```

ID	NAME	Qualification	Head Tutor
123002	Prakash	Bachelor of Comp. Sci.	
123006	Anne	GDICP	
123007	Dennis	B.Sc.	
123013	Thiru	Bachelor of Comp. Sci.	
123024			

5 rows selected.

VALUE-Based Projection

Value-based projection is a type of projection in which a VALUE function takes as its argument a correlation variable (table alias) of an object table and returns object instances corresponding to rows of the table. The limitation associated with it is that it can be used to project attributes from the supertype only, or in other words only those attributes can be projected that belong to the supertype object table. We cannot use this type of projection to project attributes that are specific to any of the subtypes. The general syntax of such a type of query is as follows.

```
SELECT  VALUE(<alias>).<supertype attribute name1>,
        VALUE(<alias>).<supertype attribute name2>, ... ... ...
FROM <table name> <alias> ;
```

Consider the following query as an example: "Retrieve the details of all the employees who work in the department." The SQL for this is.

```
Select    Value(p).staffid,
          Value(p).staff_name,
          Value(p).e_mail
From person_t p;
```

VALUE(P).STAFFID	VALUE(P).STAFF_NAME	VALUE(P).E_MAIL
123002	Prakash	pgsrivas@cs.latrobe.edu.au
123006	Anne	anne@latrobe.edu.au
123007	Dennis	dennis@cs.latrobe.edu.au
123013	Thiru	thiru@latrobe.edu.au
123024	Pauline	pauline@latrobe.edu.au

5 rows selected.

Types of Selection

Because of tree type hierarchy, these selection predicates can be of any type in the hierarchy. Selection predicates can be broadly categorized as follows.

Simple Selection

Simple selection is applying selection predicate on the attribute of the table. The limitation associated with it is that since we don't have tables for types except for the supertype, we cannot apply selection predicate on any attribute that belongs to a specific subtype. The general syntax of such a type of query is as follows.

```
SELECT <Projection List>
FROM <table name> <alias>
WHERE <alias>.<parent attribute name> = <condition>;
```

Consider the following query as an example for simple projection: "Retrieve the details of the employee whose ID is 123002." The SQL and output for this is.

```
Select    Value(p).staffid,
          Value(p).staff_name,
          Value(p).e_mail
From person_t p
Where p.staffid = 123002;
```

VALUE(P).STAFFID	VALUE(P).STAFF_NAME	VALUE(P).E_MAIL
123002	Prakash	pgsrivas@cs.latrobe.edu.au

TREAT-Based Selection

Treat-based selection can be used to apply selection predicate on any type (i.e., can have selection predicate on supertype or subtype). The general syntax of such a type of query is as follows.

```
SELECT < Projection List>
FROM <table name>
WHERE
   TREAT(VALUE(<alias>) AS <type name>).<type attribute name>
   =<condition>;
```

An example of TREAT-based selection can be: "Retrieve the details of all the Tutors who have enrolled for the course Master of Computer Science in the department." The SQL and output of the query is.

```
Select p.staffid,
   Treat(Value(p) as tutor).staff_name NAME,
   Treat(Value(p) as tutor).qualification QUALIFICATION
From person_t p
Where Treat(Value(p) as tutor).course_enrolled
   = 'Master of Comp. Sci.';
```

STAFFID	NAME	Qualification
123002	Prakash	Bachelor of Comp. Sci.
123007	Dennis	B.Sc.
123013	Thiru	Bachelor of Comp. Sci.

3 rows selected.

VALUE-Based Selection

Value-based selection is the type of selection in which selection predicate is defined on the attributes of the table. The limitation associated with it is that the selection predicate can be applied only on the table. Since we have one table in the tree hierarchy, we cannot apply selection predicates on the attributes, which are specific to the subtypes. The general syntax for such a query is as follows.

```
SELECT <Projection List>
FROM <table name>
WHERE VALUE(<alias>).<supertype attribute name> = <condition>;
```

Consider the following query as an example: "Retrieve the details of the employee whose ID is 123002." The SQL and output for this query is as follows.

```
Select    Value(p).staffid,
          Value(p).staff_name,
          Value(p).e_mail
From person_t p
Where Value(p).staffid = 123002;
```

VALUE(P).STAFFID	VALUE(P).STAFF_NAME	VALUE(P).E_MAIL
123002	Prakash	pgsrivas@cs.latrobe.edu.au

Subtype-Based Selection

Subtype-based selection is a type of selection which uses the keyword IS OF. The IS OF type predicate tests object instances for the level of specialization of their type along with any other further subtype of the subtype. Subtype of the subtype, which in our case is Permanent or Casual type, is a more specialized version of the subtype, in our case Tutor type. The general syntax of such a query is.

```
SELECT <Projection List>
FROM <table name> <alias>
WHERE VALUE(<alias>) IS OF (Subtype name);
```

Consider the following as an example: "Retrieve the details of all the staff who are working as tutor in the department." The query can be written as.

```
Select Value(p).staffid,
 Value(p).staff_name,
 Value(p).e_mail
From person_t p
Where Value(p) is of (tutor_in);
```

VALUE(P).STAFFID	VALUE(P).STAFF_NAME	VALUE(P).E_MAIL
123002	Prakash	pgsrivas@cs.latrobe.edu.au
123007	Dennis	dennis@cs.latrobe.edu.au
123013	Thiru	thiru@latrobe.edu.au

3 rows selected.

The results of the execution of the query contain all the records, which are in Tutor object along with the records, which are in permanent and casual object. Hence with this type of selection predicate, it retrieves records not only from the object on which we have selection predicate, but also from all the objects, which are subtype to it.

Specific Subtype-Based Selection

Specific subtype-based selection is a specialized version of subtype-based selection. This type of selection gives the flexibility to restrict the result of the execution of the query to one level of subtype if there is more than one level in the tree hierarchy. The general syntax of this type of query is.

```
SELECT <Projection List>
FROM <table name>
WHERE Value(<alias>) IS OF (ONLY <subtype's name>);
```

An example of such a type of query can be: "Retrieve the details of all the staff who are working only as tutors in the department." The query can be written as:

```
Select   Value(p).staffid,
         Value(p).staff_name,
         Value(p).e_mail
From person_t p
Where Value(p) is of (ONLY tutor_in);
```

VALUE(P).STAFFID	VALUE(P).STAFF_NAME	VALUE(P).E_MAIL
123007	Dennis Wollersheim	dennis@cs.latrobe.edu.au

The result of the execution of this query is all the records that belong to tutor only and not from permanent and casual objects.

CONCLUSIONS AND FUTURE WORK

The above classification of the queries covers generally all the different types of queries that can occur because of new data structures in ORDBMS. The broad classification of the queries covers the new data structures, and each sub-classification covers the different ways of writing queries. Each query can be divided into projection, join and selection. Each sub-classification of projection or selection or join can be combined with any sub-classification of projection or selection or join to form a new query unless written specifically.

This chapter explores the taxonomy of the ORDBMS queries, which is the first step. Query optimization has been left for future work. The work would aim at finding out a most optimized query structure among the ones discussed in this chapter. The other aspect would also be to find out when one should use object relational queries versus relational queries. Query rewriting can also be one area in which future work can be carried out. This step involves rules for transformation of a given query structure into optimized structure.

REFERENCES

Carey, M. et al. (1999). O-R, what have they done to DB2? *Proceedings of the Very Large Databases International Conference (VLDB).*

Dorsey, P. & Hudicka, J.R. (1999). *Oracle 8 Design Using UML Object Modeling.* Oracle Press, McGraw Hill.

Fortier, P.J. (1999). *SQL3 Implementing the SQL Foundation Standard.* McGraw Hill.

Fuh, Y.-C. et al. (1999). Implementation of SQL3 structured types with inheritance and value substitutability. *Proceedings of the Very Large Databases International Conference (VLDB).*

Loney, K. & Koch, G. (2000). *Oracle 8i: The Complete Reference.* Osborne McGraw-Hill.

Loney, K. & Koch, G. (2002). *Oracle 9i: The Complete Reference.* Oracle Press.

Stonebraker, M. & Moore, D. (1996). *Object Relational DBMSs: The Next Great Wave.* Morgan Kaufmann.

Chapter XIII

Re-Engineering and Automation of Business Processes: Criteria for Selecting Supporting Tools

Aphrodite Tsalgatidou
University of Athens, Greece

Mara Nikolaidou
University of Athens, Greece

ABSTRACT

Re-engineering of business processes and their automation is an activity very common in most organizations in order to keep or create a competitive business advantage in the changing business environment. Business Process Modeling Tools (BPMTs) and Workflow Management Systems (WFMSs) are the most popular tools used for business process transformation and automation of the redesigned business processes within and outside organization's boundaries. This chapter describes a set of criteria for selecting appropriate BPMTs and WFMSs among the diversity of the tools offered in the market in order to assist the interested manager or business process engineer to more successfully manage the business process transformation. While establishing the proposed criteria, we considered currently available technology and standards for visual enterprise support and inter-organizational business process modeling and automation.

INTRODUCTION

An important aspect for every business, in order to be competitive, is the re-engineering of its business processes (see the two seminal papers by Hammer, 1990, and Davenport & Short, 1990, for an introduction to business process re-engineering) and their automation. Many enterprises have already started re-engineering efforts in order to keep or create a competitive advantage in a changing business environment, to address the rapid growth of the Internet market, to cross the chasm between organizational structures and e-commerce, and so on.

For a successful business transformation, new frameworks are needed for understanding the emerging organizational structures supporting new services (see for example the framework proposed by Schlueter & Shaw, 19970, as well as appropriate tools to support the whole business process lifecycle, i.e., every step and activity from capturing, modeling and simulating existing, redesigned or new business processes to their automation. Currently available commercial Business Process Modeling Tools (BPMTs) aim at supporting the first steps of the business process life cycle, i.e., the modeling and evaluation of business processes for improvement and re-engineering purposes (Enix, 1997).

The later steps of business process life cycle, i.e., implementation and automation, can be supported by a number of available technologies and tools like commercial groupware tools, Workflow Management Systems (WFMSs) or commercial transaction processing systems, depending on the type of process and on the degree to which a process depends on humans or software for performing and coordinating activities. Among these tools, the most popular for business process automation and implementation are the WFMSs. (See Georgakopoulos et al., 1995, for an overview on WFMSs and Dogac et al., 1998, for a collection of papers on a number of interesting issues related to WFMSs and interoperability.)

The rapid growth of the Internet and the provision of e-business services to increase sales and productivity introduced the need to model inter-organizational processes and consequently the support of inter-organizational workflows (i.e., the ability to model and automate processes that span several organizations). When dealing with inter-organizational processes, model interoperability becomes more of an issue. Relevant international standard organizations, such as the Workflow Management Coalition Group (WfMC, 2002), are currently dealing with the provision of protocols enabling the interaction and data exchange based on widely acceptable standards as the Extensible Markup Language — XML (WfMC, 2001). Thus, BPMTs and WFMSs should efficiently address interoperability issues to deal with inter-organizational processes.

A number of evaluation reports of existing BPMTs and WFMSs are being produced and updated regularly mainly by consulting companies such as SODAN, OVUM, Datapro, etc. These reports lean more towards the evaluation of specific products than the provision of a comprehensive framework for evaluation. This chapter aims at filling this gap by presenting a set of criteria to be taken into account by the person embarking on a search for suitable BPMTs/WFMSs and highlighting additional features they should support to conform with e-business requirements. Although the simultaneous attainment of all requirements is — and is likely to remain — moot, their awareness is likely to inform advantageously their prospective users, while being of use to developers/researchers, too.

The following sections provide a definition of business process, business process and workflow models, BPMTs and WFMSs, and subsequently discuss some classes of selection criteria.

BUSINESS PROCESS MODELS, WORKFLOW MODELS AND SUPPORTING TOOLS

A business process is a set of *activities* that are executed in order to achieve a business objective; this objective is usually to offer the right product or service to a customer with a high degree of performance measured against cost, longevity, service and quality (Jacobson et al., 1995). For a complete description of a business process, aside from the information describing constituent business process activities, we need information related to *resources* assigned to activities, i.e., objects necessary for the execution of activities, like actors, documents, data and so on; *control* of a business process which describes 'when' and 'which' activity will be executed; the *flow* of data in the process; and the *organizational structure* which consists of organizational units, people, roles, competence and so on. Consequently, business process modeling approaches should enable the modeling of all these types of information while at the same time providing facilities for tracing, simulating and graphically animating the constructed business process models.

A business process *model* is a process abstraction that depends on the intended use of the model. In the rest of the chapter, when a process model is intended for business process analysis, improvement and re-engineering, it will be called *business process model*. When such a model is intended for business process implementation and automation, it will be called *workflow model*.

In other words, a business process model can be seen at two levels: at the re-engineering level and at the automation (implementation) level. Thus, the model produced at the re-engineering level is later transformed to another model at the automation level in order to be used by application development programs or to be directly executed in an existing working environment. Each model captures level-specific information; however, there is some core business process information, like activities, resources, control information, flow of data and organizational structure, which has to be modeled at both modeling levels. Information — like execution time and cost of each activity, activity waiting time, cost of people, laws governing the organization, etc. — is information captured in the model at the re-engineering level. Information — like information technology required, details about the working environment and any other information necessary for the implementation of the business process — is captured in the workflow model at the automation level (see Figure 1). More about business process modeling may be found in Tsalgatidou and Junginger (1995).

Popular tools supporting the modeling, re-engineering and automation of a business process are *Business Process Modeling Tools (BPMTs)* and *Workflow Management Systems (WFMSs)*. More specifically:

- *BPMTs* aim at the development of business process models for management, documentation or re-engineering purposes. They focus on capturing and modeling details that are essential for business process analysis and simulation, like for example time, cost, resources, etc., the results of which can then be used for business process re-engineering and subsequent automation. Examples of BPMTs are the ARIS Toolset (IDS-Scheer, 2002), the Workflow-BPR (Holosofx, 2002), the Workflow Analyzer (Metasoftware, 2002), the Process Wise (ICL & Fujitsu, 2002) or even UML (Jacobson, 2001), to name a few.

- *WFMSs* aim at the development and subsequent automation of workflow models and thus, they differ in the level of detail in which their scope is located and their focus of attention: while BPMTs focus on higher-level chunks of business operations and their re-engineering, WFMSs aim mainly at transferring the process models (usually developed previously by BPMTs) in real-world settings. In order to accomplish that, they may interoperate with databases, LANs, document handling and imaging systems, legacy applications, etc. Examples of WFMSs are the FlowMark (IBM, 1999), Visual Workflow (FileNet, 2002), InConcert (InConcert, 1999), etc.

Therefore, it seems that an organization, in order to successfully support the whole business process life cycle (from modeling of a process to its automation) and efficiently cooperate with other organizations, needs to use appropriate BPMT and WFMS tools. A very important issue that arises here is the integration between BPMTs and WFMSs so that business process models developed by a BPMT can be then transformed in workflow models and utilized by a WFMS. We call this issue vertical interoperability, which is one of the main criteria for selecting appropriate tools. This, along with other criteria — which are based on the above intended functionality of BPMTs and WFMSs, and can assist in the selection of appropriate commercial tools — are presented in the following section. Especially when dealing with modeling and technical and process automation aspects, interoperability is considered as the key issue to enable inter-organizational processes. The conformance to standards, as those proposed by WfMC, facilitate such characteristics.

Figure 1. Business Process Modeling for Re-Engineering and Automation Purposes

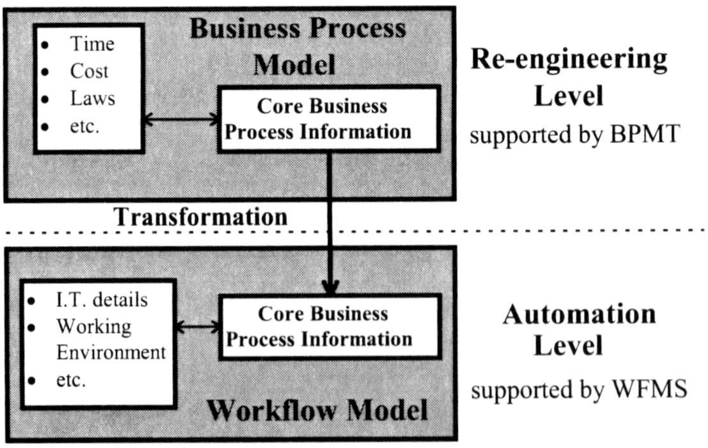

CRITERIA FOR SELECTING BPMTS AND WFMSS

The criteria are classified into the following categories: *user interface, modeling, analysis and validation, technical and process automation aspects*. They are presented as follows: in each category, the requirements concerning both categories of tools are presented first; these are then followed by a description of requirements specific for BPMT or WFMS, if any. The first three sets of criteria concern both categories of tools and mainly BPMTs, while the automation aspects mainly concern WFMSs.

User Interface Aspects

Requirements on user interface aspects can be classified into two categories: user interface requirements related to users and user interface requirements related to machines.

User Interface Requirements Related to Users

These concern mainly the provision of a highly interactive and graphical user interface (GUI), which, in the current state of the art, is more or less a truism. However, the provision of a GUI does not imply that all aspects of the process analysis and design can be carried out graphically. It is usually the case that a broad solution can be graphically designed, while the details must be filled in using some kind of high-level programming language script. Therefore, an additional requirement for *entire GUI definition* is set here. Support for efficient *GUI navigation* in the process models produced is also required. This support must be in accordance with the conceptual modeling mechanisms provided by the tool. *End user customization* facilities should also be provided.

Machine-Related User Interface Requirements

Portability and *adaptability* of the user interfaces are key issues here. Given the fact that the hardware infrastructure of business environments consists of diverse hardware architectures and operating systems, and that a large number of employees is likely to access business computing resources from different access points, e.g., desktop PCs, portable PCs, etc., the user interface should be portable across these diverse access points. This should affect neither the functionality of the interface itself nor its user friendliness. Portable languages such as Sun's Java Programming Language combined with CGI techniques enable the fulfillment of this criterion. Furthermore, given the ongoing increase of interest for intranet-related technologies, it is highly unlikely that BPMTs and WFMSs will escape the need to adapt to business intranets. As intranets promote the interoperability of diverse software platforms and since an increasing number of intranet applications provide a Web accessible gateway, it is a natural consequence that the user interface of the tools this chapter is dealing with should be adaptable to the changing intranet environment. The possibility of dynamically downloading user interfaces from central interface repositories should not be excluded as an option.

Modeling Aspects

Modeling Philosophy

The modeling philosophy employed by a tool is often advertised as the major feature of a BPMT. Actually, the model provided is the single most important founding principle of a BPMT since all analysis and subsequent benefits provided by a tool are based on the model expressiveness and its properties. For example, if a process is not accurately modeled in a BPMT, no analysis facilities can serve any useful purpose. Additionally, a BPMT without sufficient modeling depth can be counter-productive, since conclusions will be reached based on incomplete or inaccurate information. The Conversation for Action Model (Winograd & Flores, 1987) used in the Action Workflow (Medina-Mora et al., 1992), Petri Nets (Tsalgatidou et al., 1996) or some form of data flow diagrams (Jacobson, 2001; DeMarco, 1979) enriched with control information, are popular approaches. Assuming that BPMTs are used to model business processes, and that BPMTs and WFMSs interoperate, the role of a WFMS in workflow modeling is limited, since either the entire workflow model or a significant part of it is usually performed at the BMPT. In order to effectively automate a business process, the model adopted must facilitate its accurate and complete description. Thus, it is important to support a concise method for process modeling within the BPMT and WFMS environment. If similar models are not supported, a systematic transformation algorithm to depicted business process modeling entities within the WFMS is needed (Nikolaidou, 1999). Related interoperability issues are discussed in a following paragraph.

Conceptual Modeling Mechanisms

Business process and workflow modeling results in the construction of conceptual models of a given part of reality. Hence, requirements on conceptual modeling tools apply to BPMTs and WFMSs as well, the most prevalent being: abstraction mechanisms (classification, aggregation, generalization/specialization) and structuring mechanisms (for example, a model may be structured in terms of the processes investigated, the stakeholders involved, etc.). In many cases, workflow implementation is performed without studying the involved business processes, resulting in poor performance. This is due to the inefficient modeling constructs provided by WFMSs compared to BPMTs. The ability to integrate aggregated models and the provision of different abstraction levels for process description are essential features for inter-organization process support.

Flexible and Explicit Time Modeling

Despite long and intense efforts, time has proved especially difficult to be effectively modeled; the repeated attempts of the database community bear witness to this. BPMTs and WFMSs could not be exceptions; thus, a fitting representation of time, along with constraints, precedences and antecedences is invariably needed in business process and workflow modeling.

Model Annotations

No modeling formalism can capture all relevant details and pertinent facts. Process models often need to be annotated with extra-model information such as designer comments and rationale, analysis and validation statements, etc.

Organizational Structure Modeling

The modeling of human resources in a business process as simple agents may not be enough for conveying all relevant information. A more rigorous modeling of the organizational structure is in need, encompassing entities such as departments, actors, roles and so forth. The resulting organization models must be suitable for integration with the process models per se, so that actor participation in specific activities, actor permissions on specific resources, along with more general security specifications, could be specified accordingly. Object-based representation is usually adopted by existing BPMTs and WFMSs, enabling abstract representation of entities and the formation of hierarchies. Besides the ability to accurately represent the organizational structure, the interaction with external tools where relevant information is kept is considered as an additional feature. The conformance with existing (i.e., UML) or emerging standards (i.e., WfMC Entity Representation Model) contributes to this direction.

Resource Modeling

Resources can be modeled simply as input and/or outputs of process steps. A more economic and comprehensive approach is to create a model of the resources in use, for example creating a document type ontology, placing documents in a hierarchy, etc. Resource modeling should acquire the same features as organizational structure modeling.

Representation of Control, Data and Materials

Representation of data flow as well as materials and control flow among process steps is essential. The conformance with existing or emerging standards enables the interaction between different process models which is essential for inter-organizational process support.

Flow Type

Most existing BPMTs and WFMSs are built around a well-structured process paradigm (sequential or if-the-else-based flow), that is, process steps are modeled as following each other in a well-ordered succession. This usually fails to capture the dynamics of a real business environment. Although no final propositions have been made, some rule-based formalisms (rule-based flow) do offer a plausible alternative.

Analysis and Validation

- *Business process and workflow models should be formal, or amenable to formal analysis, for static analysis and validation.* Static analysis and validation of a model refer to the study of the derived models using specific algorithms and analysis approaches (not simulation). Such analysis and validation should be able to derive results on process metrics, identification of constraints and resource cost evaluation, among others. This entails some kind of mathematical formalism along which the relevant models are structured. Absence of such a foundation does not render static analysis and validation infeasible; they are, however, more difficult to use and more dependent on ad hoc approaches. Analytical tools used by BPMTs usually include: case analysis, weighted average analysis, critical path analysis, throughput analysis, resource utilization, value chain analysis and activity-based costing.

- *Executable business process and workflow models for dynamic analysis and validation.* Dynamic validation refers to the study of the derived models by way of their dynamic behavior. Simulation of the model specification is the main approach used for dynamic validation. By varying rates of input, a BPMT can simulate activities and assess performance issues, such as bottlenecks in a process. Procedures can then be developed based on these simulations to successfully plan for and manage uncontrollable variations of input. What-if analysis and if-what analysis of changes in business process and workflow models should also be provided. Most WFMSs provide workflow process animation tools but depend on external BPMTs for simulation and analysis. Therefore, the sophistication of analysis and simulation provided by BPMTs, as well as the degree of integration and interoperability between BPMTs and WFMSs, have a direct impact on the ability to validate and evaluate workflow process models.

Technical Aspects

Vertical Interoperability

As discussed in the second section, one of the major objectives of BPMTs, apart from assisting the re-engineering process, is to provide for implementation and automation of business processes through integration with WFMSs. For example, consider a situation where the business process model used by a BPMT is different than the workflow process model utilized by a WFMS. In such a case, their integration involves filtering business process model objects, validating the resulting workflow process model and placing it in the representation used by the WFMS engine. Therefore, BPMTs must export and possibly translate their process definitions to WFMSs or share process models and definitions with WFMSs. More detailed discussion on this may be found in Georgakopoulos and Tsalgatidou (1998).

Horizontal Interoperability

At the business process modeling level, this refers to the ability of the product to handle models created by other BPMTs. At the workflow level, this refers to the interoperability between various WFMSs, and between WFMSs and various heterogeneous systems participating in the workflow process. Connectivity to database systems used in the organization as well as to mainframes is also required here. Furthermore, interoperability at the workflow level requires additional technology and standards that exploit and extend current industry solutions for interoperability, such as those developed by the Object Management Group (OMG, 2002b), the World Wide Web Consortium and the Workflow Management Coalition Group (WfMC, 2002). Although there are emerging standards for WFMS interoperability and data exchange, one should note the lack of similar efforts for BPMTs. This is due to the different models used to represent different aspects of the same process, while studying it. Workflow interoperability is essential to build and support the cooperation of processes belonging in different organizations and the data exchange between them. BPMT interoperability, although a useful feature, does not directly affect inter-organization workflow support.

Object-Oriented Toolset

The usefulness of object orientation in process modeling rests in its potential for developing intuitive and economical conceptual models of the real world. An object-oriented toolset should provide the ability to model processes, resources and organization structure in an object-oriented framework, thus reducing redundancy and enhancing re-use of model components. The object-oriented paradigm is also adopted by existing and emerging standards for process and data representation, e.g., XML.

Process Models Repository

All business process modeling tools offer some kind of repository for storing and retrieving the constructed models. The functionality offered by such repositories may vary considerably, ranging from simple storage schemes to full database management systems. In the case of an object-oriented toolset, an underlying object-oriented database can improve the tool's capabilities and consolidate smoothly conceptual models and physical storage. Actually, the repository is a critical component in such systems and often distinguishes between a system that can be used in business production and one that simply cannot. Important issues here are concurrency control, recovery and advanced transactions. Therefore, it seems that there must be a database management system as part of the WFMS, even if this increases the cost of the system.

Integration With Other Tools

Communication software (like, for example, mail systems) becomes an indispensable component of corporate-wide networking. Smooth integration between workflow and communication tools should therefore be demanded. This has actually been followed in cases where companies sell workflow products to be embedded in a larger communication system, thus viewing flow of work as a special kind of communication-coordination among agents. Interoperability with other similar product families (e.g., document management systems, text retrieval or imaging systems, editing tools, fax, or payment packages if we are talking about electronic commerce applications, etc.) is required, too.

API Support

Although graphical specifications of workflow are user friendly and usually effective, the need for fine tuning or a more detailed specification than the one carried out graphically frequently arises. APIs can also be used to introduce specialized user interfaces or tools to meet specific application requirements. Furthermore, APIs can promote integration of favorable functionally equivalent components. For example, if the WFMS cooperates with a word processor, this should not be necessarily provided as part of the WFMS, but instead provide APIs for integrating the word processor the customer prefers. Workflow vendors provide APIs to accommodate such needs. Such APIs can be judged in terms of comprehensiveness, ease of use, libraries provided, etc.

Concurrency Control, Recovery and Advanced Transactions

WFMSs should support concurrency control and recovery. These are well-understood issues in database and transaction processing products, but current approaches followed by WFMSs (e.g., check-in/check-out, pass-by-reference/pass-by-value, etc.)

are primitive when compared to the concurrency support provided by database management systems.

Robustness and Availability

Continuous availability of WFMSs is crucial especially for critical systems. WFMSs should be resilient to failures and provide mechanisms for backup and efficient recovery. According to Alonso et al. (1997), the lack of robustness and the very limited availability constitute one of the major limitations of existing WFMSs, which lack the redundancy and flexibility necessary to replace failed components without having to interrupt the function of the system. Therefore, special attention should be paid on this aspect when selecting a WFMS.

High-Volume Processing, Performance and Scalability

High-volume processing is a key requirement for WFMSs. Many business processes require handling of a large number of workflow instances. Performance of a WFMS should be independent of the workload in the sense that many workflow instances could be created and processed when needed, without penalties to system performance. The use of more powerful computers may not necessarily yield corresponding improvements in WFMS throughput. Therefore, scalability of the workflow engine (server) and work list handler to deal with load balancing is an important requirement.

General Requirements

Both BPMTs and WFMSs share some requirements in common with most industrial-strength software products, such as availability in specific platforms usually encountered in business environments. UNIX, Windows NT, OS/2 and AIX are among the most popular server platforms, while Windows95 is the platform usually encountered by clients. Compliance to industry standards (e.g., CORBA (OMG, 2002b)), version update and customer support, ready case studies and product maturity is also required.

Process Automation Requirements

These requirements concern mainly WFMSs used for the automation of business processes and are the following:

- *Work-in-Process Tracking.* All objects of a workflow must be monitored by the system so that the process status is visible to management whenever required.
- *Automatic Resource Allocation.* This refers to an intelligent balancing of work among different employees, depending on particular persons' or groups' workload and responsibilities. This may, for example, involve task monitoring and "pushing" tasks to employees, as well as identification of inactive human resources.
- *Manual Resource Allocation.* It is clear that automatic resource allocation cannot be a surrogate for human control; the complexity of an organizational setting, along with the exigencies of a competitive business environment, often require human intervention. Such intervention may take the following forms: "pull applications" (employees may choose their next piece of work from a pool of tasks) to be completed, negotiation of work among people in the organization (including the

exchange of allocated work chunks, the splitting and/or sharing of work among related agents, etc.) and assignment of specific tasks to specific employees (usually carried out by the management).

- *Security*. Permissions must be potentially granted for initiating workflow processes, viewing status reports, re-routing a document, end-user customization, etc.
- *Statistics*. Already hinted to above, comprehensive statistical measures and status reports are indispensable for giving a clear and succinct picture of workflow execution. Such statistics and execution data should be possible to be fed back to a BPMT and facilitate process evaluation and improvement. This feature is essential for business process re-engineering. Thus, graphical representation of results and statistical processing of data could be useful.
- *Information Routing*. At least two kinds of information routing can be discerned: static routing, which involves information transfer from one person to the next according to a predefined schedule (and cannot be altered at will while in operation), and dynamic routing, which attempts to bring feedback concepts and responsiveness to information flow; techniques (like rule-based routing related to specific events) may be used to describe not a mere sequential list of actions, but situations along with the system responses.
- *Parallel Processing*. A prerequisite for modern multi-user systems, parallel processing allows work to be routed to multiple queues or in-baskets for simultaneous processing by distinct agents; priority and version control is essential, as well as handling of multi-user access problems, also encountered in the database community.
- *Document Rendezvous*. The term refers to the automatic matching of new incoming documents with existing documents pertaining to them already in the workflow; the resulting set of documents is then clipped together before being routed to the next action step.
- *Setting and Handling of Deadlines*. This can refer to setting and handling deadlines for task completion (task deadline), or for the termination of a specific activity carried out by a specific employee (employee deadline).
- *Tracing and Reporting*. Generation of reports with data about the business process from different perspectives (e.g., from enterprise perspective, resource flow perspective or from an activity perspective, including scheduling and costing information) are very useful for analysis of the business process at hand and for re-engineering purposes. Such reports can also be used for business process documentation, management presentations, user training or ISO 9000 certification and should be provided by BPMTs. Furthermore, workflow monitoring facilities should be provided by WFMSs, in order to give information about workflow execution and illustrate which activities are currently active, by whom they are performed, priorities, deadlines, duration and dependencies. Such data are very useful as they can be fed back to BPMTs and facilitate process evaluation and improvement. Reporting involving OLAP (On-Line Analytical Processing) tools, in case they are integrated with the WFMS, is also critical, as it helps managers to make critical decisions based on the comprehensive facts of their business.

CONCLUSIONS

Successful business process re-engineering and automation in an organization depends on the selection of appropriate supporting software tools. This chapter attempted to give a description of the intended functionality of supporting tools and subsequently provide a set of criteria to help the interested engineer to select appropriate BPMTs and WFMSs among the diversity of tools offered by software vendors. While establishing the proposed criteria, we considered essential inter-organizational process requirements to support e-commerce. The existence of emerging standards for vertical and horizontal interoperabilities, especially for WFMSs (e.g., WfMC), should also be taken into account.

In order to achieve business process re-engineering, the processes supported by an organization should be constantly monitored. Process automation may increase productivity, if workflows are implemented as the result of business process modeling and exploration. Thus, WFMSs should be used in cooperation with BPMTs.

It should be noted that we could not have aimed, nor have achieved, a perfect or complete set of requirements. The result can be therefore judged in terms of pragmatics; that is, its utility to the users, purchasers and researchers in the area. Being the outcome of our own involvement in the field, we believe that the experience gained will be of help to others.

ACKNOWLEDGMENT

The authors would like to thank Dr. Panos Louridas, from the University of Manchester Institute of Science and Technology, Manchester, UK, for his contribution in this work.

REFERENCES

Alonso, G. & Mohan, C. (1997). Workflow management systems: The next generation of distributed processing tools. Chapter 1 in *Advanced Transaction Models and Architectures*. Kluwer Academic Publishers, 35-62.

Davenport, T.H. & Short, J.E. (1990). The new industrial engineering: Information technology and business process redesign. *Sloan Management Review,* (Summer), 11-27.

DeMarco, T. (1979). *Structured Analysis & System Specification.* Englewood Cliffs, NJ/ London: Prentice Hall.

Dogac, A., Kalinichenko, L., Oszu, T. & Sheth, A. (Eds.). (1998). *Workflow Management Systems and Interoperability*. NATO ASI Series F. Springer-Verlag.

Enix. (2002). *Behaviour Modelling Techniques for Organisational Design.* Available online at: http://www.enix.co.uk/behmod.htm.

FileNet. (2002). Available online at: http://www.filenet.com.

Georgakopoulos, D. & Tsalgatidou, A. (1998). Technology and tools for comprehensive business process lifecycle management. In Dogac, A., Kalinichenko, L., Oszu, T. & Sheth, A. (Eds.), *Workflow Management Systems and Interoperability*. NATO ASI Series F. Springer-Verlag.

Georgakopoulos, D., Hornick, M. & Sheth, A. (1995). An overview of workflow management: From process modeling to workflow automation infrastructure. *Distributed and Parallel Databases,* 3(1), 119-153.

Hammer, M. (1990). Re-engineering work: Don't automate, obliterate. *Harvard Business Review,* (July-August), 104-112.

Holosofx. (2002). Available online at: http://www.holosofx.com.

IBM. (1999). *White Paper on Functional Assessment of IBM MQSeries FlowMark 3.1.*

ICL & Fujitsu. (2002). Available online at: http://services.fujitsu.com.

IDS-Scheer. (2002). Available online at: http://www.ids-scheer.de.

InConcert. (1999). Available online at: http://www.inconcertsw.com.

Jacobson, I. (2001). *Modeling Business Processes Using UML.* Technical Report, Rational Software.

Jacobson, I., Ericsson, M. & Jacobson, A. (1995). *The Object Advantage: Business Process Re-Engineering with Object Technology.* ACM Press.

Medina-Mora, R., Winograd, T., Flores, R. & Flores F. (1992). The action workflow approach to workflow management technology. *Proceedings of CSCW'92,* November, 281-288.

Metasoftware. (2002). Available online at: http://www.metasoftware.com.

Nikolaidou M., Tsalgatidou A. & Pirounakis (1999). A systematic approach to organisational workflow application development. *Proceedings of ECEC'99,* Society for Computer Simulation (SCS).

Object Management Group — OMG. (2002a). Available online at: http://www.omg.org/technology/documents/ modeling_spec_catalog.htm.

Object Management Group — OMG (2002b). Available online at: http://www.omg.org/technology/documents/ corba_spec_catalog.htm.

Schlueter, C. & Shaw, M. (1997). A strategic framework for developing electronic commerce. *IEEE Internet Computing,* 1(6), 20-28.

Tsalgatidou, A. & Junginger, S. (1995). Modeling in the re-engineering process. *ACM SIGOIS Bulletin,* 16(1), 17-24.

Tsalgatidou, A., Louridas, P., Fesakis, G. & Schizas, T. (1996). Multilevel petri nets for modeling and simulating organizational dynamic behaviour. *Simulation & Gaming, Special Issue on Simulation of Information Systems,* 27(4), 484-506.

WfMC. (2001). Workflow standard – workflow process definition interface. *XML Process Definition Language.* TC-1025.

WfMC. (2002). Available online at: http://www.wfmc.org.

Winograd, T. & Flores, F. (1987). *Understanding Computers and Cognition: A New Foundation for Design.* Addison-Wesley.

Chapter XIV

Active Rules and Active Databases: Concepts and Applications

Juan M. Ale
Universidad de Buenos Aires, Argentina

Mauricio Minuto Espil
Universidad de Buenos Aires, Argentina

ABSTRACT

This chapter surveys the topic of active rules and active databases. We analyze the state of the art of active databases and active rules, their properties and applications. In particular, we describe the case of triggers following the SQL-1999 Standard Committee point of view. Then, we consider the case of dynamic constraints for which we use a temporal logic formalism. Finally, we discuss the applicability, limitations and partial solutions found when attempting to ensure the satisfaction of dynamic constraints.

INTRODUCTION

Databases are essentially large repositories of data. From the mid-1980s to the mid-1990s, a considerable effort has been paid to incorporate reactive behavior to the data management facilities available (Dayal et al., 1988; Chakravarthy, 1989; Stonebraker, 1986). Reactive behavior is seen as an interesting and practical way for checking satisfaction of integrity constraints. Nevertheless, constraint maintenance is not the only area of application of data repositories with reactive behavior. Other interesting applications areas are materialized view maintenance (especially useful in the warehousing area), replication of data for audit purpose, data sampling, workflow processing, implementation of business rules, scheduling and many others. In fact, practically all products offered today in the marketplace support complex reactive behavior on the client side. Nevertheless, the reactive behavior supported by these products on the server side is in fact quite poor. Recently, the topic has regained attention because of the inherent reactive nature demanded in Web applications, and the necessity of migrating many of their functionality from browsers to active Web servers (Bonifati et al., 2002).

We can find several applications in the electronic commerce arena. In Abiteboul et al. (1999), the authors present the Active Views system, which can be seen as an application generator oriented to solve the problems faced in application development in an electronic commerce environment. In this system, an Active View specification is a declarative description of an application. The authors consider that an electronic commerce application involves several types of actors, for instance customers and sellers. Basically, a specification includes, for each type of actor: (a) the data and operations available, (b) the activities and (c) active rules specifying the sequence of activities and events about which the actor wants to be notified. Even though the rules are very simple, interesting is the novel way the rules are integrated in a general framework, and how they are used for sequencing activities, notification and tracing. In particular, an active rule in Active Views has the following components:

- *Events:* method calls, operations on instance variables and detection of change.
- *Conditions:* XML queries returning a Boolean value.
- *Actions:* method calls, operations on instance variables, notification or traces.

In Bailey et al. (2001), the authors describe an event-condition-action (ECA) rule language in XML to provide reactive functionality on XML repositories. The language is based on fragments of the XPath and XQuery standards, and the components of an ECA are, again, *events*, *conditions* and *actions*. The event part of a rule is an expression <operation> *e*, where e is a simple XPath expression. The condition part of a rule is either the constant TRUE or one or more Xpath expressions connected by Boolean connectives **and**, **or**, **not**, and it is evaluated on XML documents that have been changed by the event specified in the event part of the rule. Finally, the action part of the rule specifies actions to be executed on one or more XML documents which have been changed as a consequence of the event and for which the condition part of the rule evaluates to TRUE. An action is an expression of the form:

Insert *r* below e [before|after *q*] or delete *e*

where r, e and q are a simple XQuery expression, a simple XPath expression, either the constant TRUE or an Xpath qualifier, respectively.

Bonifati et al. (2001a) study the problem of pushing information to clients in the case when the pushing logic is distributed. They propose a class of Internet services that are performed by means of active rules in a remote site. The active rules monitor the events that happen at remote sites and notify the interested clients. The rules represent diverse e-services. These kinds of active rules simplify the original problem of active rules for XML (Bonifati et al., 2001), since the rules can just notify remote users and, consequently, cannot trigger each other.

Supporting reactive behavior implies that a database management system has to be viewed from a production rule system perspective (Baralis et al., 1996). Production rule definitions must be supported therefore by an active database system. These production rules are well known nowadays, in database terminology, as active rules or simply triggers.

Undesired behavioral characteristics have been observed related to production rule systems. For example, termination is not always guaranteed, non-determinism can be expected in the results and confluence with respect to a desired goal cannot be achieved (Aiken, Hellerstein & Widom, 1995; Baralis & Widom, 2000b). Since triggers and declarative integrity constraints definitions may appear intermingled in a concrete application, an integrating model is needed to soften, to some extent, the effects of this undesirable behavior, ensuring that, no matter what the nature of the rules involved is, integrity is always preserved.

Active rules and integrity constraints are related topics (Ceri, Cochrane & Widom, 2000). Systems do not support both completely, but partially, in its kernels. When a constraint must be enforced on data, if such constraint cannot be declared, it may be implemented by means of triggers. Studying the relationships between constraints and triggers from this point of view is therefore mandatory. In simple words, we need methods to check and enforce constraints by means of triggers.

From a user point of view, reactivity is a concept related to object state evolution over time. Dynamic constraints — constraints making assertions on the evolution of object states — may be needed to control changes in the state of data objects (Sistla & Wolfson, 1995a). Dynamic constraints are mandatory in the correct design of applications, particularly for workflow processing and for the Web. Actual products support some kind of functionality in this area, allowing triggers to refer to transitions, the relations existent between states, when an atomic modification operation is executed. Supporting such types of constraints by means of handcrafted triggers written by a novice, without any method in mind, may result in potentially dangerous effects from the perspective of correctness. Formal methods guaranteeing correctness are thus needed for a good deploying of such triggers.

The main goal of this chapter is to analyze the concepts related to active rules and active databases. In particular, we focus our discussion on the interaction between active rules and declarative constraints from both static and dynamic perspectives.

BACKGROUND

Usually, a database system performs its actions in response to requests from the users in a passive way. In some cases it is highly desirable that actions could be taken with no human intervention, that is, automatically responding to certain events.

Traditionally, the latter has been obtained embedding that behavior into the applications, that is, the application software recognizes some happenings and performs some actions in response.

On the necessity of such reactive behavior, obviously, it would be desirable that such functionality would be provided by the database system. A database with the capability to react to stimulus, be these external or internal, is called an *active database.*

Among the applications we can find are inventory control systems, online reservation systems and portfolio management systems, just to name a few (Paton & Diaz, 1999).

An *active database system* can be thought of as coupling databases and rule-based programming. The active database rules enable many desired database features such as integrity constraint checking and enforcement, derived data maintenance, alerts, authorization checking and versioning.

Knowledge Model

A central issue in the knowledge model of active databases is the concept of *active rule*. An active rule can be defined throughout three dimensions: *event*, *condition* and *action*. In this case, the rule is termed an ECA or event-condition-action rule, which specifies an action to be executed upon the happening that is to be monitored, provided a condition holds.

An event is defined as something that happens at a point in time. The source of the event determines how the event can be detected and how it can be described. We have several alternative sources, such as *transactions,* where the event is originated by transaction commands *abort, commit* and *begin-transaction.* Other sources are *operations on structure*, where the event is raised by an operation such as insert, delete or update, on some components of the data structure; *clock* or temporal, where the event raises at a given point in time; *external*, in the case that the event is raised by something happening outside the database. An example of the latter is the level of water reaching some specified height.

An event can be either *primitive*, in which case it is raised by a single occurrence in one source, or *composite*, in which case it is raised by a combination of events, be they primitive or composite.

A condition, i.e., a situation with respect to circumstances, is the second component of an active rule. We must consider the context in which the condition is evaluated. In general, we can associate three different database states with the condition in the processing of a rule, i.e., the database at:

- the start of the current transaction,
- the time when the event took place,
- the time the condition is evaluated.

Moreover, since the state before and after the occurrence of an event may be different, the condition can require the access to a previous or a new value.

An action consists of a sequence of operations. There are several options or possible actions, such as update the structure of the database, make an external call, abort a transaction or inform the user about some situation. The action has similar context to that of the condition. The context, in this case, determines which data are available to the action.

In general, an event can be explicit or implicit. In the first case, the event must always be given in a rule. It is said that the system supports ECA rules. If the event is not specified, the rules are called condition-action.

In ECA rules the condition can be optional. Then, if no condition is given, we have event-action rules.

Execution Model

The execution model determines how the rules are managed at execution time. This model is strongly dependent on the particular implementation, however, it is possible to describe it in general using a set of common activities or phases:

- *Signaling* begins when some source causes an event occurrence.
- *Triggering* analyzes the event signaled and triggers the rules associated with that event. This is called rule instantiation.
- *Evaluation* evaluates the condition part of instantiated rules. In this phase the *rule conflict set* is built containing every rule with satisfied conditions.
- *Scheduling* determines how the conflictive rules will be processed.
- *Execution* runs the corresponding actions from the instantiated rules with satisfying conditions.

How these phases are synchronized depends on the so-called coupling modes of ECA rules. There are two coupling modes: Event-Condition (E-C) and Condition-Action (C-A). We describe them as follows:

1. *E-C coupling mode* determines when the condition is evaluated, considering the triggering event produced by some source. In this case, we have three different options available:
   - Immediate coupling, where the condition is evaluated as soon as the event has happened.
   - Delayed coupling, where the evaluation of the condition part of the rule is not performed immediately after the event triggering, but is delayed until something happens before the commit of the transaction.
   - Detached coupling, where the condition is evaluated in a different transaction from the one triggering the event.
2. *C-A coupling mode* determines when the action is executed, considering the condition evaluation.

The same options are applicable in the C-A mode as are in the E-C mode.

Activation time is a concept that fixed the position of the signaling phase with respect to the event occurrence. It can be expressed by using a temporal modal operator such as *before*, *after*, *while* and so on.

Transition granularity *is a concept used in analyzing the relationship between event occurrences and rule instantiations. This relationship can be one-to-one, when the transition granularity is* elementary. *In this case, one event occurrence triggers one rule. The relationship can also be many-to-one, when the transition granularity is* complex. *In this case, several event occurrences trigger one rule.*

Net effect policy is a feature that indicates if the net effect of several event occurrences or each individual occurrence should be considered. The prototype database system Starburst, as an example, computes the net effect of event occurrences as follows:

- If an instance is created and possibly updated, and then deleted, the net effect is null.

- If an instance is created and then updated several times, the net effect is the creation of the final version of the instance.
- If an instance is updated and then deleted, the net effect is the deletion of the instance.

Cycle policy is related to what happens when an event is signaled as a consequence of a condition evaluation or an action evaluation in a rule. We consider two options: iterative and recursive. In the former case, the events signaled by a condition or an action evaluation are combined with those generated from the event sources and, consequently, are then consumed by the rules. In the latter case, the events signaled by a condition or an action evaluation cause the condition or action to be suspended in such a way that the rules monitoring the events can be processed immediately.

In the scheduling phase the order of rule execution is to be determined when multiple rules are triggered simultaneously. Hence, the scheduler must consider the choice for the next rule to be fired, applying some conflict resolutions policies, and the number of rules to be fired. The latter presents several options such as: (a) to fire all rules sequentially; (b) to fire all rules in parallel; (c) to fire all instantiations of a rule, before considering any other rule.

Termination and Confluence

Even though active database systems are very powerful, the developing of applications can be difficult, mainly because the behavior of rules is hard to understand and control (Baralis et al., 1993). Rule interaction is one of the most important aspects related to rule set behavior. Two important properties related to this problem are *termination* and *confluence*. It is said that a rule set is guaranteed to terminate if, for any database state, and initial modification, rule processing cannot continue forever. A rule set is confluent if, for any database state, and initial modification, the final database state after rule processing is independent of the order in which activated rules are executed.

In the last few years, many researchers have developed techniques that allow knowing in advance if a rule set has the properties of termination and confluence (Aitken et al., 1995; Bailey et al., 2000; Baralis & Widom, 1994, 2000a, 2000b; Baralis et al., 1998; Comai & Tanca, 1997; Karadimce & Urban, 1996; Zimmer et al., 1996). There are methods that perform basically termination analysis of a rule set and because of the undecidability of the problem (Bailey et al., 1998), we cannot expect full precision.

According to the time when the methods are applied, they can be classified in *static*, if the rule set is analyzed at compile time, or dynamic, if the rule set behavior is analyzed at run time. In the first case, these techniques statically analyze a rule set before setting the rules in the database. In particular Baralis and Widom (2000a) analyze some techniques for performing static analysis of Event-Condition-Action and Condition-Action rules. In that work, the authors propose a Propagation Algorithm that determines when the condition of one rule is affected by the action of other rules, and when two rule actions commute. Basically, the algorithm propagates the action of one rule through the condition of another rule, in order to determine how the action affects the condition. Since this algorithm can determine when one rule may activate another rule, it becomes valuable in analyzing termination. Also, because the algorithm can determine when the execution order of two rules is significant, it is useful in analyzing confluence. In addition, the proposed techniques are able to identify the responsible rules in the case termination or confluence is not guaranteed. These techniques appear implemented partially in the context of the Chimera project (Widom & Ceri, 1996).

Bailey et al. (2000) describe a dynamic approach to the problem of termination analysis. It is based on a variable upper limit for the number of recursive rules being fired. A previous analysis to the rule set execution allows us to estimate a suitable limit for that execution. The aforementioned estimation is computed using some historical information about the rules, i.e., data about the past execution behavior of the rule set. This differs from commercial products where termination is enforced by limiting the allowed number of recursive rules firing to a fixed upper limit. When that limit is reached, the actions of all the rules are rolled back. By estimating the limit dynamically, it is possible to allow that more terminating rule sets proceed, avoiding being aborted unnecessarily.

Finally, Baralis et al. (1998) present a combined approach between static termination analysis at compile-time and runtime detection of rule execution forever. The former is based on the separation of notions of rule triggering and rule activation. In the case of triggering, it occurs when a database update generates an event that triggers a rule. In rule activation, it occurs when a database update causes the condition of the rule to become true. On the other hand, The authors propose a technique for detecting cycles at runtime based on the history: if a certain situation has occurred in the past, it will occur in the future.

In the commercial systems side, the approach consists of imposing syntactic limitations, in order to guarantee termination or confluence at runtime, although in other cases counters are used to prevent infinite execution.

INTEGRATING ACTIVE RULES AND DECLARATIVE CONSTRAINTS

Let's get started describing how kernels of present commercial DBMSs support active rules and declarative constraints together.

Today, almost every commercial relational DBMS to some degree adheres to the proposal of the SQL-1999 standard. This standard establishes, in a more or less accurate way, how active rule mechanisms and declarative constraints should be defined and integrated.

Declarative Constraints

We assume the reader is already familiar with SQL constraints, so we simply start with a brief introduction here, to ease further comprehension. In an SQL-1999-compliant system, four classes of declarative constraints are supported: *check predicate constraints*, *referential constraints*, *assertions* and *view check options*. Check predicate constraints aim at validating conditions against the actual state of *one* table in the database, and include *primary key* and *unique* definitions, *not null* column definition and *explicit check* clauses that validate general predicates on the values of some of the columns of the table. Referential constraints aim at guaranteeing that a many-to-one relationship holds on the actual state of two tables: the *referencing* or *child* table, and the *referenced* or *parent* table. A many-to-one relationship ensures that the column values of a foreign key (a list of columns of the referencing table) match the column values of a candidate key (a list of columns of the referenced table). Assertions aim at validating general predicates on rows in *different* tables. View check options deal with the problem of admitting modification operations through cascade defined views, yet retaining the natural meaning of the operations.

A declarative constraint can be declared as having a deferrable or a non-deferrable activation time. However, we limit our analysis in this chapter to non-deferrable constraints only. The reader interested in a more thorough vision of constraint activation time may refer to the standard documents. For example, suppose we have defined the following table schemas:

invoice (invoice_number, customer, date, item_total);
detail (invoice_number, item_id, quantity);
goods (item_id, price, quantity).

Declarative constraints for these tables could be:

c1: PRIMARY KEY (invoice_number), on table invoice;
c2: PRIMARY KEY (invoice_number, item_id), on table detail;
c3: PRIMARY KEY (item_id), on table goods;
c4: invoice_number REFERENCES INVOICE (invoice_number), on table detail CASCADE;
c5 item_id references GOODS (item_id), on table detail RESTRICT.

Most of the declarative constraints included in the standard are currently supported by almost every SQL-1999-compliant DBMS in the marketplace. Exceptions arise, however. Complex conditions on rows in a table, like nested predicates and predicates involving aggregation, although allowed to appear in explicit check clauses by the standard, are rarely supported nowadays in commercial systems. Assertions are scarcely seen in commercial systems, either. We put off these exceptions for the moment.

Triggers

In SQL-1999 an active rule defined by the user is called a *trigger*, which is a schema object in a database (Ceri et al., 2000). The trigger structure is defined as follows:

CREATE TRIGGER *<trigger_name>* [BEFORE | AFTER] [*<event>* | *<events>*] ON *<table>*
REFERENCING NEW AS *<new_value>* OLD AS *<old_value>*
NEW TABLE AS *<new_table>* OLD TABLE AS *<old_table>*
FOR EACH [ROW | STATEMENT] WHEN *<condition>* *< action >*

Events can be statements INSERT, DELETE or UPDATE *<list>*; *<table>* must be the name of a defined base table or view name, *<list>* a list of column names of table *<table>*. When understood from the context, the list of columns in UPDATE statements is omitted. As we have pointed out before, we do not treat triggers on views here. From now on, a trigger event is therefore a modification operation on a base table. The activation time is specified by keywords BEFORE or AFTER, thus yielding before and after triggers. Before triggers fire immediately before the operation specified as the trigger event has been issued. After triggers fire immediately upon operation completion. The referencing clause admits defining correlation variables for transition values and transition tables, which allow the trigger to access column values in the affected rows before and after the execution of the modification operation. The transition granularity is specified by the clause ON EACH, and can be either set to ROW or STATEMENT. Hence, row-level and statement-level triggers can be defined. Row-level triggers fire one instantiation for each row affected by the modification operation. Provided no row is affected, a row-level trigger is never instantiated. Statement triggers fire only once per statement invocation and are evaluated even in the case the event does not happen to affect any row. For example, triggers for the tables defined above are:

TRIGGER t1: AFTER DELETE ON invoice
REFERENCING OLD AS old_inv_t FOR EACH STATEMENT
WHEN **exists** (**select** * **from** old_inv_t **where** old_inv_t.date > actual_date)
raise error and undo the delete operation;

Trigger t1 prevents the user from removing future pendant invoices.

TRIGGER t2: AFTER DELETE ON detail
REFERENCING OLD AS dtl FOR EACH ROW
update goods **set** quantity = goods.quantity - dtl.quantity
where goods.item_id=dtl.item_id.;

Trigger t2 updates the stock of an item whenever the item is removed from the detail of an invoice.

Viewing Constraints as Rules

Integrating triggers with declarative constraints has proved to be a non-simple task, due to subtleties present in actual implementations. Signaling, triggering and scheduling models for active rules turn out to be non-uniform among database vendors, thus compromising the clear understanding of the meaning of active rules in general.

Moreover, an SQL constraint, although specified in a declarative manner, cannot be regarded simply as a passive component. A declarative constraint includes explicitly or implicitly the specification of repairing actions. Hence, declaring an SQL constraint may be thought of as entailing the activation of internal active rules that enforce repairing actions whenever the constraint is violated. Bulk data import and load operations are different matters, of course, but these operations are normally supported by special utility packages and not supported by the kernel itself. Concede us putting away import-export operations, therefore.

In summary:

c- Once a *check* constraint is declared, two after rules for events INSERT and UPDATE candidate key, respectively, become active on the (target) table where the constraint is defined, with statement-level granularity, and a condition defined so as to be satisfied whenever the associated predicate is violated. The action part for both rules consists in the execution of a controlled rollback undoing the effects of the application of the modification operation. For instance, constraint c1 implies that a constraint rule with statement-level granularity becomes active, having INSERT as the rule event, invoice as the target table and predicate:

exists (**select** * **from** invoice, Δ(invoice,insert)^{new}
where invoice.invoice_number = Δ(invoice,insert)^{new}.invoice_number
and not (invoice.ROWID = Δ(invoice,insert)^{new}.ROWID))

as the rule condition. In the predicate above, Δ(invoice,insert)^{new} stands for the new transition table, and ROWID stands for a dummy column containing the identifier of each row in the table.

2- Whenever a referential integrity constraint is declared, the activation of the following internal active rules are generated:

c- Two after rules for events INSERT and UPDATE foreign key, respectively, on the referencing table, with statement-level granularity, and a condition stating that there exists at least one row in the new transition table whose foreign key value does not match the candidate key value of any row in the referenced table. As is the case with check constraints, the action prescribed by these rule specifies a controlled rollback. For instance, constraint c4 entails the activation of a rule for event UPDATE invoice_number on table detail, with predicate:

exists (**select** * **from** Δ(detail,update)^{new}

where Δ(detail,update)^{new}.invoice_number **not in** (**select** invoice_number **from** invoice)), as the rule condition. Δ(detail,update)^{new} above stands for the new transition table.

b- Providing that the repairing action for constraint violation is neither RESTRICT nor NO ACTION, two after rules for events UPDATE candidate key and DELETE, respectively, on the referenced table, with row-level granularity, and a condition stating that there exists at least one (dangling) row in the referencing table whose foreign key value matches the old value of the row instantiating the rule. For instance, constraint c4 entails the activation of a rule for event DELETE on table invoice, with row granularity, and predicate:

exists (**select** * **from** detail **where** θ(invoice,delete)^{old}.invoice_number = detail.invoice_number)

as the rule condition. θ(invoice,delete)^{old} above stands for the old value of each row.

The firing of any of these rules would carry out the execution of an UPDATE operation that sets the foreign key value of each dangling row in the referencing table to null or a default value (options SET NULL and SET DEFAULT, respectively), or the execution of a DELETE operation, removing all dangling rows from the referencing table (option CASCADE). For instance, the constraint rule for event DELETE on table invoice associated with constraint c4 has the SQL command:

delete from detail **where** detail.invoice_number = θ(invoice,delete)^{old}.invoice_number

as the rule action. Again, θ(invoice,delete)^{old} stands for the old value of the row being deleted.

c- Providing the repairing action for constraint violation is RESTRICT or NO ACTION, two after triggers on the referenced table, for events UPDATE candidate key and DELETE, respectively, with statement-level granularity, and a condition stating that there exists at least one row in the referencing table whose foreign key value matches the candidate key of a row in the old transition table. For instance, constraint c5 implies the activation of a rule for event DELETE on table goods, with predicate:

exists (**select** * **from** detail, δ_k(goods,delete)^{old}
where δ_k(goods,delete)^{old}.item_id = detail.item_id)

as the rule condition. δ_k(detail,delete)^{old} stands here for the old transition table (the notation will be clarified later). The firing of any of these rules would carry out the failure of the modification operation, and a controlled rollback undoing all changes.

Up to this point, the reader may wonder if declarative constraints and triggers are all the same thing. Despite their similarities, declarative constraints and constraint rules must be distinguished.

First, declarative constraints should be processed only after all changes entailed by an SQL modification statement are effectively applied. This is not an arbitrary policy, if we reckon that a modification statement in SQL may affect many rows at once and some declarative constraints as primary and foreign key definitions involve the analysis of many rows, too.

Second, it is unlikely to suppose a rule designer being aware, when writing a trigger, of all possible inconsistent states the database could reach. Hence, admitting a lack of consistence when firing a trigger would introduce unpredictable behavior in user applications. The query optimizer could also outperform due to lack of consistency, when a query is prepared for execution in the body of a rule, because the optimizer usually makes use of constraints to simplify execution plans. A declarative constraint, on the contrary, is meant as dealing with inconsistent database states. Consequently, a trigger should not be exposed to an inconsistent database state when the evaluation phase of a rule instantiation comes around, while constraint would.

Moreover, a particular user would expect that the success or failure of the execution a particular statement could be predicted, particularly in the presence of triggers. In a sense, she requires the process to be confluent. Unfortunately, this is not a simple goal to achieve. The outcome of a modification statement may be affected in many ways: by the order in which the rows involved in the modification are processed, by the particular ordering chosen when applying cascade repairing actions to enforce multiple integrity constraints, by the firing of triggers and so on.

The considerations above imposed the obligation of producing a precise specification on how declarative integrity constraints and constraint rules should be integrated.

The actual accepted specification produced by the SQL-1999 standardization committee is based on a proposal submitted by a research group in the IBM Almaden Research Center (Cochrane, Pirahesh & Mattos, 1996). We proceed now to review the set of recommendations the standard draft establishes on how to proceed when triggers and declarative constraints are specified together.

Binding Variables to Transitions

The execution of an operation e affecting one row of a table t in the database (an elementary modification operation) can be abstracted by the existence of a *transition*, a pair consisting of the state $\theta(t,\varepsilon)^{old}$ of the row immediately before the execution starts, and the state $\theta(t,\varepsilon)^{new}$ reached when the execution is complete (considering meaningless values as old values in insert operations and new values in delete operations as nulls). Since we have already established that old and new transition variables are defined along with a trigger, and since they can be referred by the condition and action parts of the trigger, transition values have to be saved in memory. A binding has to be provided therefore for each affected row that links the trigger transition variables to the area in memory that stores the values.

SQL modification operations are essentially bulk operations, so they can be abstracted as sets of elementary transitions. Since the sets of transitions describing the SQL operation must become available for use whenever firing a trigger or a constraint rule, transition tables $\Delta(t,\varepsilon)^{old}$ and $\Delta(t,\varepsilon)^{new}$ have to be created so as to store these sets of transitions. A separate working area organized as forming a stack of storage space slots must be provided to hold transition tables.

Evaluating Constraints and Triggers

Suppose an SQL modification operation e, as an INSERT, UPDATE or DELETE statement, has been issued on a table t. The following steps are followed:

1) The transition old and new values implied by operation e are computed and stored in tables $\Delta(t,\varepsilon)^{old}$ and $\Delta(t,\varepsilon)^{new}$ placed in the working space slot on top of the stack. For example, suppose we have the statement:

   delete invoice **where** invoice_number=15932;

   and the database instance:

   invoice = { ..., ρ_1(15932, 'A&R Lmtd', 10-2-2001, 2), ... }
   detail = { ..., ρ_2(15932, 'AZ532', 15), ρ_3(15932, ' BD225', 3), ... }
   goods = { ..., ρ_4('AZ532', U$S45, 15751), ρ_5('BD225', U$S18, 2769), ... }
   ρ_i standing for row numbers.

   The transition tables computed for this operation are:

   Δ(invoice,delete)^{old} = { ρ_1(15932, 'A&R Lmtd', 10-2-2001, 2) } and
   Δ(invoice,delete)^{new} = { ρ_1(- , - , - , -) }

2) A variable k, denoting the round number, is set to 0. Old and new transition tables $\Delta(t,\varepsilon)^{old}$ and $\Delta(t,\varepsilon)^{new}$, currently on top of the stack, are given aliases $\delta_0(t,\varepsilon)^{old}$ and

$\delta_0(t,\varepsilon)^{new}$, respectively, for round 0. Note that, when k=0, it turns out to be one pair of tables $\delta_0(t,\varepsilon)^{old}$ and $\delta_0(t,\varepsilon)^{new}$ only, that corresponds to the transitions computed for SQL statement e.

3) For each pair of tables $\delta_k(t,\varepsilon)^{old}$ and $\delta_k(t,\varepsilon)^{new}$, before triggers with e in <*events*> and t as <*table*> are considered for application, on a one-by-one basis, according to a global ordering criteria, and enter their signaling phase. Statement triggers are considered first whether a currently selected table $\delta_k(t,\varepsilon)^{old}$ is empty or not, providing that they have not been fired yet. Row-level triggers are fired next, once for each row in table $\delta_k(t,\varepsilon)^{old}$, on a row-by-row basis. Each row in table $\delta_k(t,\varepsilon)^{old}$ generates an instantiation of the trigger, and is attached to the trigger old transition variable. If the event is INSERT or UPDATE, and the trigger action updates its new transition variable, the corresponding row in table $\delta_k(t,\varepsilon)^{new}$ is updated. If an error occurs or is raised when executing the action part of the trigger, or an attempt to modify the database is made, the entire process breaks down, all changes to the database are undone and an error is reported. If $\delta_k(t,\varepsilon)^{old}$ is empty, no before trigger is instantiated.

4) The database is modified according the contents in table $\delta_k(t,\varepsilon)^{new}$. Inserts are carried out first, updates are performed next and deletes are postponed to the end. In our example, row ρ_1 is removed from table invoice. Note that any row in $\delta_k(t,\varepsilon)^{new}$, modified in the previous step, due to the execution of a before trigger action that modifies its new transition variable, implies that a modification to the corresponding database table applies here.

5) The constraints must be checked, as the database state remains consistent. Recall that constraints are viewed as rules. The first rules to be selected for constraint satisfaction checking are the rules corresponding to referential constraints on table t that match the event ε, and have RESTRICT specified as its repairing action. The reason for this preemption criterion is that referential constraints with RESTRICT semantics are meant to be checked before any cascade action has taken place. Because RESTRICT semantics prescribe undoing all work performed in association with a modification operation that brings out a dangling foreign key, no harm is done if the constraints are chosen on an arbitrary order basis. If the condition in any constraint rule is satisfied (the constraint is violated), the process ends in an error.

6) Rules generated by referential constraints on table t having cascade repairing actions as SET DEFAULT, SET NULL or CASCADE are considered now. Because repairing actions ε' (an update statement for SET DEFAULT, a delete statement for CASCADE) refer to the parent table, let's call it t', new intermediate transition tables $\delta_{k+1}(t',e')^{old}$ and $\delta_{k+1}(t',\varepsilon')^{new}$ are generated in the working storage, before any change is effectively made to the database. Many new intermediate transition tables may appear as a result. In our example, when k=0, constraint c4 activates an instantiation of a rule that entails the execution of the SQL command:

delete from detail **where** detail.invoice_number = $\theta(\text{invoice,delete})^{old}$. invoice_number

with row ρ_1 in $\delta_0(\text{invoice,delete})^{old}$ replacing $\theta(\text{invoice,delete})^{old}$, so yielding the transient tables $\delta_1(\text{detail,delete})^{old}$ as consisting of rows ρ_2 (15932, 'AZ532', 15) and

ρ_3 (15932, ‘ BD225’, 3), and δ_1(detail,delete)^{new} as consisting of rows ρ_2 (- , - , -) and ρ_3 (- , - , -).

7) The contents of all tables $\delta_k(t,\varepsilon)^{old}$ and $\delta_k(t,\varepsilon)^{new}$ are appended to the contents of tables $\Delta(t,\varepsilon)^{old}$ and $\Delta(t,\varepsilon)^{new}$, as long as k>0. Tables $\Delta(t,\varepsilon)^{old}$ and $\Delta(t,\varepsilon)^{new}$ are created and allocated in the current working area (on top of the stack), on the condition that they do not already exist. If no transient table with subscript k+1 exists, then there are no pending cascade actions to be applied, so the resultant state of the database must be checked over for constraints not entailing cascade actions nor restrict semantics. This checking processing is described in the next step. If at least one transient table with subscript k+1 exists, variable k is updated to k+1, and the process is resumed at step 3.
In our example, when k=1:
   - Step 3 performs no action, because no before triggers are associated with table detail.
   - Rows ρ_2 and ρ_3 are removed from table detail in step 4.
   - No constraint with restrict semantics is violated, so step 5 performs no action.
   - No referential constraint with cascade action is defined in table detail, so no transient table is generated with subscript 2.

8) Check constraints and referential constraints with NO ACTION semantics are considered. The associated rules are fired then, as long as the rule target table matches the table argument t of any transient table $\Delta(t,\varepsilon)^{new}$, and the event argument ε is the firing event in the rule. If the condition of any of these rules holds (the constraint is violated), then the entire process fails, all modifications to the database are undone and an error is returned. If none of the conditions are satisfied, then the database is consistent, and after triggers would apply safely. In our example, when k = 0, no rules for primary key constraints c1, c2 and c3 are fired, because, whereas constraint c1 matches the table argument in transient table Δ(invoice,delete)^{new} and constraint c2 matches the table argument in transient table Δ(detail,delete)^{new}, their event argument is neither UPDATE not INSERT.

9) After triggers call for attention now. For each pair of existing tables $\Delta(t,\varepsilon)^{old}$ and $\Delta(t,\varepsilon)^{new}$, after triggers with ε in *<events>* and t as *<table>* are considered for application, on a one-by-one basis again, according to the global ordering. Row-level triggers are considered first in this case, once for each row in the current table $\Delta(t,\varepsilon)^{old}$, on a row-by-row basis. As was the case with before triggers, each row in table $\Delta(t,\varepsilon)^{old}$ generates an instantiation of the trigger, and a binding to the trigger old transition variable is established for each row. If table $\Delta(t,\varepsilon)^{new}$ is empty, no row-level trigger is instantiated and subsequently fired. Statement triggers on table t for event e are fired providing that they have not been fired before, table $\Delta(t,\varepsilon)^{new}$ exists and all row-level after triggers have been already instantiated and fired. The new transition variable is useless in the case of after triggers; issuing an update of such a variable makes no sense. Whereas failure is treated identically as it was treated in the case with before triggers, attempts to execute SQL modification operations against the database must receive a different treatment; they are allowed to occur in the action part of after triggers. Hence, if we recall that an SQL modification operation e‘ on a table t’, occurring in the action part of the trigger,

entails the presence of transitions, and these transitions should be saved, tables $\delta(t,\varepsilon)^{old}$ and $\delta(t,\varepsilon)^{new}$ are created to contain the new transitions.
In our example, trigger t2 is instantiated twice, because table D(detail,delete) has two rows (ρ_2 and ρ_3). The instance of t2 corresponding to row r_2 entails the execution of the update statement:

t2(ρ_2) : **update** goods **set** quantity = goods.quantity - 15
where goods.item_id = 'AZ532';

The instance of t2 corresponding to row ρ_3 entails the execution of the update statement:

t2(ρ_3): **update** goods **set** quantity = goods.quantity - 3
where goods.item_id = 'BD225';

Update statements t2(ρ_2) and t2(ρ_3) produce the tables:

- δ(goods,update)^{old} = { ρ_4('AZ532', U$S45, 15751), ρ_5('BD225', U$S18, 2769) }
- δ(goods,update)^{new} = {ρ_4('AZ532', U$S45, 15736), ρ_5('BD225', U$S18, 2766) }

On the contrary, trigger t1 enters its signaling phase, table variable old_inv_t is bound to table Δ(invoice,delete)^{old} and no action is executed, for condition:

exists (**select** * **from** Δ(invoice,delete)^{old} **where** Δ(invoice,delete)^{old}.date > actual_date)

does not hold.

10) Finally, if no pair of tables $\delta(t,\varepsilon)^{old}$ and $\delta(t,\varepsilon)^{new}$ exists, or, if there exists any, the tables' results are both empty, the process ends successfully. Otherwise, the top of the stack is advanced, each pair of non-empty tables $\delta(t,\varepsilon)^{old}$ and $\delta(t,\varepsilon)^{new}$ become the new $\Delta(t,\varepsilon)^{old}$ and $\Delta(t,\varepsilon)^{new}$ on top of the stack, and the process is resumed at step 2.
In our example, tables δ(goods,update)^{old} and δ(goods,update)^{new} are non-empty, so they become the sole tables Δ(goods,update)^{old} and Δ(goods,update)^{new} on top of the stack. A new pass is accomplished, starting at step 2. During this second pass, updates to rows ρ_4 and ρ_5 are applied to the database (step 4), and because no constraint is now violated, step 10 ends successfully.

GENERAL STATIC CONSTRAINTS AS ACTIVE RULES

As it was pointed out in the previous section, highly expressive declarative static constraints, as general check conditions and assertions, are rarely supported in commercial systems. Hence, a question is imposed: how can we enforce such constraints, since they are not supported by vendors in the kernel of their products? Fortunately, we have seen that a declarative static constraint, in general, can be viewed as a generator of active rules. We simply need to code appropriate triggers therefore, in order to enforce general static constraints. The transcription of constraints into triggers has received considerable attention in the last decade, and a body of work has dealt with the problem, focusing particularly on SQL (Ceri & Widom, 1990; Ceri, Fraternali, Paraboschi & Tanca, 1995; Baralis & Widom, 2000b).

We will present the main underlying ideas herein. First, we proceed to negate the assertion required to hold, and embed the resultant formula as the condition of a trigger template. If the database product does not allow complicated formulas to appear in the condition part of a trigger, a conditional statement on the result of the evaluation of the formula can be introduced instead in the body of the rule, as a guard for the action to be fired. A trigger template is thus generated for each constraint with this technique in mind.

There is a problem, however, if we follow such an approach. It is necessary to determine which events are candidates to fire the trigger and which tables are the target for these events. An extremely cautious and conservative approach would see any modification operation as potentially able to produce values violating the constraint, and would lead to the generation of many triggers as there are modification operations checking for event occurrences on every table that appear in the formula. This approach can be improved considerably, if we think that there exists a close relationship between modification operations and query predicates, thus indicating that certain modification operations might not affect the result of certain queries. If these relationships could be analyzed in a systematic manner, the number of triggers to generate in order to emulate the behavior of an assertion could be considerably reduced.

A good method for studying relationships between modification operations and queries is to analyze *propagation*. Propagation consists essentially of treating modification as queries. The fact must not surprise the reader, as long as he/she realizes that transition tables may be computed by executing a select query on the instance of the table that has been modified, with the arguments of the modification statement interspersed along the from and where clauses. For example, suppose we have a table USER with column names NAME and PASSWORD in its schema. Now suppose we have the following modification statement Upd:

Upd: **update** USER
set PASSWORD=""
where NAME=:input_name

The transition table for this statement can be computed by executing the select statement:

ΔUpd: **select** NAME **as** $NAME^{old}$, PASSWORD **as** $PASSWORD^{old}$,
NAME **as** $NAME^{new}$, "" **as** $PASSWORD^{new}$
from USER
where NAME=:input_name

The new state of table USER after the modification can be then computed as the result of:

```
( select NAME, PASSWORD
    from USER
 where not NAME=:input_name )
    union
( select NAME^new as NAME, PASSWORD^new as PASSWORD
    from ΔUpd )
```

If we have a constraint involving a complex SQL **where** condition *q* on table USER, we can replace references to table USER by the last SQL expression, to form the propagation of the modification Upd in the query *q*. We can study if: (a) the query may contain more data after the modification, an *insert* propagation case; (b) the query may contain less data after the modification, a *delete* propagation case; (c) the query may contain updated data after the modification, an *update* propagation case; (d) the query remains unchanged, a *null-effect* propagation case. Cases (a) and (c) lead to the generation of a trigger for the event UPDATE PASSWORD on the table USER. Cases (b) and (d) do not lead to generate any trigger.

Several propagation analysis techniques has been devised and developed: algebraic, syntactical and rule-based. Many of them have been incorporated in products for automatic generation of constraint maintenance, especially for SQL database products. Because these techniques are applied at design time, a certain degree of conservatism is imposed, in the sense of considering the generation of more triggers than what is strictly necessary. Study and improvements consider reducing conservatism.

DYNAMIC CONSTRAINTS ENFORCEMENT AND ACTIVE RULES

A different situation arises when a constraint is to be imposed on the evolution of database states, not on single states. Demand of support for dynamic constraint enforcement thus arises. Again, as was the case of static constraints, several attempts have been made to describe and formalize dynamic constraints (Chomicki, 1992), all aiming to capture accurately the meaning of such constraints, thus implementing mechanisms for checking and enforcing the constraints properly. When the approach chosen is to support dynamic constraints directly in the kernel of the database system, a certain modal temporal formalism is needed to describe the meaning of the constraints. If the formalism implies the existence of a user language, the developer would be able to express the constraints in a declarative manner, thus simplifying a good deploying of a complex system.

Declarative dynamic constraints are not supported in SQL-1999 at present, so conformant products do not provide any help in the matter. However, a simple family of dynamic constraints, *transition* or *two-state constraints*, can be easily emulated by means of triggers, with almost no cost (Widom & Finkelstein, 1990). Let's see how.

Transition Constraints

A transition constraint can be expressed in a declarative manner, associated to a CREATE TABLE statement, by a construct of the form:

> **referencing old as** T ^{old}
> **new as** T ^{new}
> **check** C (T ^{old}, T ^{new}) **on** [modified rows | table]

where T ^{old} denotes the state of the table, on which the constraint should be checked, immediately before the *transition event* occurrence; T ^{new} denotes the state of the table, immediately after the event has occurred; and C is an SQL **where** condition on tuples from T^{old} and T^{new}. *<action>* stands for an optional line of action to be followed in order to enforce consistency when a violation has taken place. The **on** clause in the constraint specification, the *granularity*, shows to what extent the table must be checked through (modified rows or the entire table). As was the case with static check constraints, the repairing action to be followed when the constraint is violated consists simply of undoing all changes introduced by the transition event. For example, suppose we have a table SPEED_LIMIT with a single column VALUE. We can assert a transition constraint saying that the speed limit value must remain unchanged. The constraint for table SPEED_LIMIT in this case would be:

> **referencing old as** old_spl
> **new as** new_spl
> **check** old_spl.VALUE = new_spl.VALUE **on modified rows**

It is necessary to analyze first which kind of operations may potentially produce a violation of the constraint, in order to check this constraint by means of triggers, as was the case with static constraints. We do not treat the subject here. We simply assume that all modification operations on the table SPEED_LIMIT excepting deletions are potentially dangerous for constraint preservation. Note that this is an extremely conservative position. In our case, insertions do not affect the result of the constraint evaluation; only updates may imply a potential violation.

It's easy to see that the constraint check and enforcement process can be emulated by the trigger:

```
after update on SPEED_LIMIT
referencing old_table as old_spl
new_table as new_spl
for each statement
when exists
     (select *
     from new_spl, old_spl
    where old_spl.ROWID = new_spl:ROWID and
     not old_spl.VALUE = new_spl.VALUE )
undo all changes
```

The reader may wonder why the granularity specified in the trigger is statement and not row. The reason is that a row-level trigger fires independently for each row present in the transition tables; while a row change may violate the constraint, another row may satisfy it, thus making it impossible to determine the precise point when the repairing action specified in the constraint should start up.

Note that the trigger can be easily built upon a trigger template if the problem of deciding which events should fire the trigger is solved.

A table granularity can be specified in the constraint, indicating that the constraint must be checked against the entire table instead of the affected rows. A more involved translation is needed in this case. The trigger would be:

```
after update on SPEED_LIMIT
referencing old_table as old_spl
for each statement
when exists
(select *
 from SPEED_LIMIT new_spl, old_SPEED_LIMIT old_spl
    where old_spl.ROWID = new_spl:ROWID and
            not old_spl.VALUE = new_spl.VALUE )
    undo all changes
with old_SPEED_LIMIT standing for:
    ( select * from old_spl ) union
    ( select * from SPEED_LIMIT where SPEED_LIMIT.ROWID not in
                ( select ROWID from old_spl ) )
```

The reason for this apparently complicated query is that, because of the granularity specified in the constraint, we need to check the constraint on the entire table, not only on the rows affected by the update. The rows not affected by the update, that is, not satisfying the predicate in the update statement, remain unchanged. Thus, we must test the constraint against them (recall that the constraints refer to transitions, not to states, and some condition may violate them). Note that, in the example before, the constraint is trivially satisfied on non-changing rows, but this is not the general case (note that if the check condition would have been old_spl.VALUE > new_spl.VALUE, the constraint would not have been satisfied in the entire table). Nevertheless, an optimization is only possible if we are able to prove that the situation arising when no change is made on the table always entails the constraint satisfaction, as is the case in the example. The condition in the trigger becomes the same condition as was the case for a row-level granularity constraint. On the other hand, if a proof exists that the situation of no change always entails that the constraint is not satisfied, we can simplify the trigger by eliminating the condition part. In this almost rare case, the trigger will always be fired after an update. Unfortunately, the implication problem is undecidable in general, so the technique of simplification shown above can be attempted only when the class of the conditions involved guarantees decidability.

A More General Approach: Active Rules as Temporal Logic Expressions

We have hitherto presented constructs expressing declarative transition constraints in a rather intuitive manner. No formal meaning has been produced yet. Now, we must consider the topic in a more formal manner. The semantics of declarative transition constraints should be built upon some temporal formalism. Actually, a class of dynamic constraints broader than transition constraints may be needed and methods for emulation should be developed. We must warn the reader, though, that because the concepts involved are not quite well understood, and performance payoffs for these emulating methods seem to be huge up to now, all these efforts have not entirely succeed in introducing products and solutions into the marketplace. Nevertheless, we choose to present an attempt in such a direction, to serve as a good example of the problem and the proposed solutions.

A good starting point is to think that every time a modification statement is executed, the state produced by the statement execution is *remembered*. A history *h* is thus maintained, defined as the sequence of pairs (E_i, S_i), $i \geq 0$ (the *transitions* in *h*), with E_i an *event* (the name of a modification operation, for instance), and S_i the state of the database immediately before the event occurrence has taken place. Then, we can use a language to express conditions on *h* itself, rather than on states. Languages expressing conditions on histories (linear discrete structures) have been extensively studied (Manna & Pnueli, 1992, 1995; Sistla, 1983; Wolper, 1983). We follow the language style of PTL (Sistla & Wolfson, 1995a ,1995b) in the chapter, because it has been conceived with an active database in mind and serves well the purpose of introducing the reader to the topic. Other similar approaches can be found in Chomicki (1992) and Lipeck and Saake (1987). We have augmented its constructs to support the specific events needed to modify data in an SQL-like database, and the concept of transition tables.

In PTL, the syntax of a first-order language expressing conditions (SQL **where** clauses, for instance) is augmented with two *modal past temporal* constructs: φ_1 **since** φ_2 , and **last time** φ_1, and with an *assignment* construct φ_1 **provided** q **as** X. φ_1, φ_2 stand for well-formed formulae in the language, X stands for a query variable, and q stands for a query, a function on states in the history. A special query name is provided, **modified rows**, such that, when evaluated on a state in position i of the history *h*, it returns the identification of all rows affected by the occurrence of E_i. A set of 0-ary predicates, *event* or *location predicates* such as **inserting**, **updating** and **deleting**, optionally qualified with a table name, is also supported. Variables appearing in a PTL formula are considered *bound*, provided they appear in the leftmost part of an assignment sub-formula or are table name alias in a first-order sub-formula (table names in from clauses can be regarded as the identity query). Otherwise, a variable is considered to be *free*. A constraint in PTL is a formula with no free variables.

The semantics for PTL formulas is defined with respect to a history and an evaluation function r which maps variables appearing free in the formula into domain values of the appropriate sort. Satisfaction of a PTL formula in a history *h* with respect to an evaluation ρ is defined inductively as follows:

- If φ is an event formula, then φ is satisfied by *h* with respect to r if and only if the event of the last transition in history *h* agrees with the event formula.
- If φ is a non-event atomic formula, then φ is satisfied by *h* with respect to r if and only if j holds, in a first-order sense, in the database state of the last transition in history *h*.
- If a formula is built upon the usual first-order connectives as **not**, **and**, **or** and so on, a first-order criteria for satisfaction is applied.
- If φ is a formula of the form φ_1 **provided** q **as** X, then *h* satisfies φ with respect to ρ if and only if *h* satisfies φ with respect to an evaluation ρ_1 such that $\rho_1(X) = q(S_i)$, the query predicate evaluated over the state of the transition, and $\rho_1(Y) = r(Y)$ for each variable $Y \neq X$ appearing free in φ_1.
- If j is a formula of the form **last time** φ_1, then *h* satisfies φ with respect to ρ if and only if φ_1 satisfies *h'* with respect to ρ, with *h'* resulting from deleting the last transition from history *h*.
- If φ is a formula of the form φ_1 **since** φ_2, then *h* satisfies φ with respect to ρ if and only if there exists a $j \leq i$, such that history *h* up to position j satisfies φ_2 with respect to ρ, and for all positions $k > j$ up to the last position, history *h* up to k satisfies φ_1 with respect to ρ.

Other useful modal constructs can be obtained, from the basic ones. For example, the modal operator **first** can be obtained as synonymous of **not last time true**. Hence, the constraint studied in the previous section can be expressed in PTL as follows:

```
first or
( last time not exists
(select *
   from SPEED_LIMIT old_spl, new_spl
where old_spl.ROWID=new_spl.ROWID
   and not old_spl.VALUE=new_spl.VALUE))
provided modified rows as new_spl
```

It is not easy to appreciate the real expressive power of this language. It is sufficient to say that it can express not only transition predicates, but more powerful conditions on the whole previous history of the database changes, as complex events and deadlines (conditions on time). The problem here is not merely to determine the real power of a language like the one presented here, but how to detect efficiently eventual violations, and how to repair these violations accurately. The issue is not completely solved nowadays, and is an interesting open area of research. We will postpone the treatment of these problems to an upcoming section, and we will concentrate on presenting the sketch of a correct algorithm that checks for constraint violations.

Checking for Satisfaction of Temporal Logic Constraints

An algorithm has been devised to enforce constraints expressed in PTL. The key idea is to fire a trigger after each modification statement execution, so as to produce and maintain sufficient auxiliary information to detect a constraint violation and react in consequence.

The first step in the devising process of the method is to proceed to negate the temporal formula, to obtain a monitoring formula. For example, the formula in the example above is now presented by its opposite, the monitoring formula f:

```
not first and
(last time exists
(select *
   from SPEED_LIMIT old_spl, new_spl
where old_spl.ROWID = new_spl.ROWID
   and not old_spl.VALUE = new_spl.VALUE))
provided modified rows as new_spl
```

When a modification statement is executed, a trigger is fired and proceeds to compute, for each sub-formula g in the main formula f, a Boolean expression $F_{g,i}$ (a SQL where clause), the *firing formula*, where i is the position in the history of the modification transition. If the firing formula $F_{g,i}$ evaluates to false, then the constraint is satisfied by state S_i. If the state reached after the execution of the i-th modification. $F_{g,i}$ evaluates to true, then the constraint is violated and a correcting action is fired. Note that the trivial correcting action "undo the last modification" actually works well as a correcting action. It preserves the satisfaction of the constraint.

When the formula contains temporal past operators, such as **last time** and **since**, $F_{g,i}$ must be evaluated inductively, referencing previous transitions in the history. To reduce the potentially huge amount of space needed to "remember" the whole previous history of the evolution of the database to a minimum, a technique is needed: an auxiliary historic table q^h is maintained for each different query q appearing in the formula. The historic table schema is formed by adding a timestamp column (a position number) and an event name column to the query schema. In what follows, we will denote by q^h_i the table containing the result of query q at past state s_i, for any query q appearing in the formula. Tables q^h_i could be easily reconstructed by examining the content of historic tables q^h.

The idea in the computation is to proceed with the elimination of temporal operators, by means of a careful rewriting process of $F_{g,i}$. $F_{g,i}$ is then evaluated inductively as follows:

- If g is an event formula and i > 0, $F_{g,i}$ = true if the event formula agrees with the event name firing the trigger, otherwise it evaluates to false.
- If g is a non-event atomic formula (an SQL where clause), two cases must be distinguished. If g has at least one free variable, $F_{g,i}$ = g' where g' is a Boolean expression involving free and bound variables. Otherwise, if all variables are bound in g, $F_{g,i}$ results in the formula evaluated in the database state s_i (true or false).
- If g = g1 **and** g2, g1 **or** g2, or **not** g1, $F_{g,i}$ must evaluate to $F_{g1,i} \wedge F_{g2,i}$, $F_{g1,i} \vee F_{g2,i}$ or $\neg F_{g1,i}$.
- If g = **last time** g1, two cases arise: if i = 0 then $F_{g,i}$ evaluates always to false; otherwise, if i > 0, $F_{g,i} = F_{g,i}[q_1 / q_1{}^h{}_{i-1}] \ldots [q_k / q_k{}^h{}_{i-1}]$, for all queries q_j, $1 \leq j \leq k$, in g, e [X / Y] stands for the substitution of all free occurrences of variable X in e by Y.

- If g = g1 **since** g2, it can be reduced to the case of **last time**. $F_{g,i} = F_{g2,i}$ **or** ($F_{g1,i}$ **and last time** $F_{g,i}$.
- If g = g_1 **provided** q **as** X, then $F_{g,i}$ turns out to be simply g_1 [X / q].

If f is a temporal formula, when i > 0 and before any $F_{g,i}$ has been computed, rows appearing in the old transition table ΔT^{old}_i are appended to the auxiliary historic tables, timestamped with i - 1. Once any of the $F_{g,i}$ has been computed, all rows associated with queries on states up to the first state mentioned in the newly computed $F_{f,i}$ are deleted from the historic tables. Note that this case arises provided that no **since** operator appears in the formula f.

We will continue with the constraint formula in the example, to see how the algorithm works.

Suppose we have a sequence of two update statements on the table SPEED_LIMIT. The first of these update statements actually happens to produce no change in the column VALUE. The second update, however, changes the column value. The sequence is shown graphically, as follows (Figure 1).

U_1 and U_2 in the figure represent the updates. T_1 and T_2 represent the transition tables, with old and new values of modified rows. The current position in the history is indicated by i (in this initial case, we are placed in the situation before any update has been issued, so i = 0). The syntactic structure of the formula f is:

g1 **and** g2; g1 is: **not** g2; g2 is: **first**; g3 is: g4 **provided modified rows as** new_spl;
g4 is: **last time** g5;
g5 is: **exists** (**select** * **from** SPEED_LIMIT old_spl, new_spl
where old_spl.ROWID=new_spl.ROWID
and not old_spl.VALUE=new_spl.VALUE).

Variables appearing bound in f are old_spl and new_spl. Because both refer to the same query, the identity function applied on table SPEED_LIMIT, only one historic table is needed. We will name this table $SPEED\_LIMIT^h$. In what follows, we will denote the state of rows in the query SPEED_LIMIT, relevant to state s_i, as $SPEED\_LIMIT^h_i$. As it was pointed out before, this state can be reconstructed from table $SPEED\_LIMIT^h$.

Now, we advance the actual position to 1 (after the execution of update U_1). Real firing of the monitoring trigger is produced. We have the situation shown in Figure 2.

All rows in ΔT^{old}_1 are appended to the table $SPEED\_LIMIT^h$, with value 0 in the timestamp column, and value **update** in the event name column.

Figure 1. Sequence of Two Update Statements on the Table SPEED_LIMIT

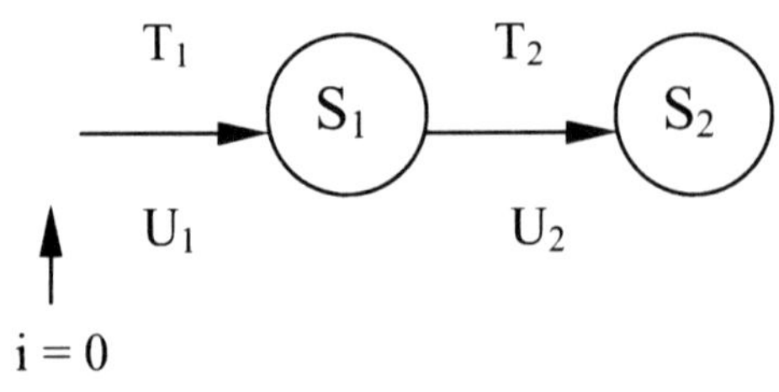

Figure 2. Situation After a Real Firing of the Monitoring Trigger is Produced

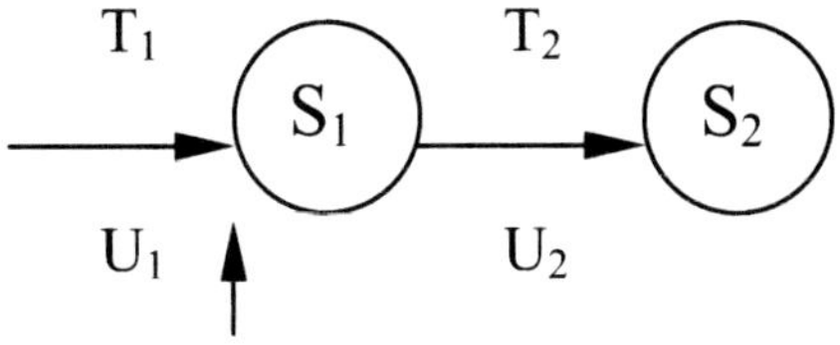

$F_{f,1} = F_{g1,1}(S_1) \wedge F_{g3,1}(S_1) = \text{false} \wedge \text{false} = \text{false}$
$F_{g1,1} = \neg F_{g2,1} = \text{false};$
$F_{g2,1} = \text{true};$
$F_{g3,1} = F_{g4,1}[\text{new\_spl} / \Delta T^{new}_1];$
$F_{g4,1} = F_{g5,1}[\text{SPEED\_LIMIT} / \text{SPEED\_LIMIT}^h_0];$
and $F_{g5,1} = g_5;$

$F_{g2,1}$ = true because i points to the first position in the sequence. $F_{g3,1}$ evaluates to false in state S_1 because the rows modified by U_1 agree in the column VALUE with the contents of SPEED_LIMIT $^h_0 = \Delta T^{old}_1$. Recall that update U_1 does not produce any change in the column VALUE of the table SPEED_LIMIT at the initial state. The formula $F_{f,1}$ evaluates to false in S_1, then the constraint is not violated in state S_1. The rows in the table SPEED_LIMIT^h corresponding to position 0 can be deleted safely. This is the first position number mentioned in a query, present in $F_{g3,1}$ (SPEED_LIMIT $^h_0$).

Let's go on now with position 2 as the current position. This is illustrated in Figure 3.

All rows in ΔT^{old}_2 are appended to the table SPEED_LIMIT ^{h}, with value 1 in the timestamp column, and value **update** in the event name column.

$F_{f,2} = F_{g1,2}(S_2) \wedge F_{g3,2}(S_2) = \text{true} \wedge \text{true} = \text{true}$
$F_{g1,2} = \neg F_{g2,2} = \text{true};$
$F_{g2,2} = \text{true},$
$F_{g3,2} = F_{g4,2}[\text{new\_spl} / \Delta T^{old}_2];$
$F_{g4,2} = F_{g5,2}[\text{SPEED\_LIMIT} / \text{SPEED\_LIMIT}^h_1];$
and $F_{g5,2} = g_5;$

$F_{g2,1}$ = false because i does not point to the first position in the sequence. $F_{g3,2}$ evaluates to false in state S_2 because the rows modified by U_2 does not agree in the column

Figure 3.

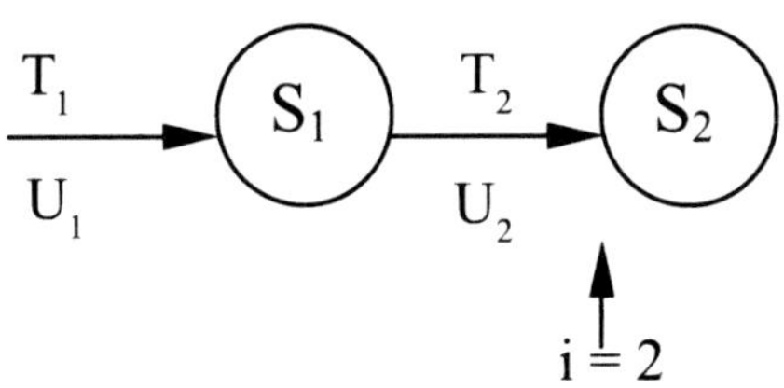

VALUE with the contents of SPEED_LIMIT $^{h}_{1}$. Recall that update U_2 changes the column VALUE of at least one row of the table SPEED_LIMIT at the previous state. The formula $F_{f,2}$ evaluates to true in S_2, then the constraint is violated in state S_2 and a correcting action is needed. Note that in the case we undo the changes introduced by the last update, the state S_1 is reached again and the constraint is satisfied at position 1.

Also note that, neither in the composition of $F_{g3,\ 2}$ nor in $F_{g1,\ 2}$, is a reference to position 0 present. The rows in the table SPEED_LIMIT ^{h}, corresponding to position 1, can be deleted. This is the first position number mentioned in a query present in $F_{g3,\ 2}$ (SPEED_LIMIT$^{h}_{1}$).

It is clear that this deletion can be done because no **since** operator appears in the formula, otherwise a reference to the deleted position would be present.

Applicability, Drawbacks and Partial Remedies

Several drawbacks in the above techniques appear when the main issue is applicability.

1) The processing effort paid off in each instantiation of a rule may compromise seriously the throughput and response time of the system. Recall that the monitoring of the constraint satisfaction is accomplished every time a modification operation is executed.
2) The amount of space required to store auxiliary historic tables is limited. Formulas with constructs equivalent to **since** are good examples of this.
3) The relationship between constraint satisfaction and transaction processing is not quite clearly established. For example, if several transactions can run concurrently, and some of them do not prevent the others from seeing uncommitted data, repeatable reads isolation level is not granted.

The question is not entirely solved. Partial remedies to the first problem have been outlined. Monitoring of constraint satisfaction may be postponed up to specific event occurrences, and only updating of historic tables is issued in the meantime. Deferring the checking process to commit time or supporting extra-system time events is a possibility. New event types are needed, such as **attempting to commit**, **at time** t or pseudo queries returning time values. Logical or net-effect modification operations may also be supported, in opposition to physical operations. An automata-based approach has been devised to recognize such logical events from patterns of physical events. This approach could be observed in the ODE object database system from AT&T Bell Laboratories (Gehani & Jagadish, 1991) and in the prototype database rule-oriented system Ariel (Hanson, 1992), where so-called Ariel-TREAT discrimination networks serve the purpose of testing complex historic patterns. More recent works focused on the specification and detection of complex events (Chakravarthy, Krishnaprasad, Anwar & Kim, 1994; Chakravarthy & Mishra, 1994; Chakravarthy, 1997; Yang & Chakravarthy, 1999), but constraints have not received special attention therein. The second problem has received less attention than the first, but again attempts to solve the space problem have been addressed. For example, in Ariel some query results could be maintained intentionally, specially when the selection factor is low. The efforts paid in that direction in the early nineties have not been reflected in the database marketplace, but increasing interest is regained presently, specifically in the area of Web servers, and particularly when e-commerce is the issue. The concept of elapsed time and expiration time serves, in this area, to prevent histories from growing indefinitely.

The third problem is the most problematic. Sistla and Wolfson (1995) have defined the concepts of *off-line* and *online* satisfaction of a constraint with respect to transactions. A constraint is said to be *off-line satisfied* if it is satisfied at the commit point of all transactions, considering, up to these points, all modification operations of committed transactions. A constraint is said to be *online satisfied* if it is satisfied at the commit point of all transactions, considering only modification operations of committed transactions with commit point reaching up to these points. These two notions of satisfaction differ with respect to which modifications a transaction could see. *Off-line* implies that a transaction sees all committed work, independently of the commit point. This notion is closer to the notion of a transaction manager guaranteeing cursor stability. *Online* satisfaction implies that a transaction only sees all previously committed work. This last notion of satisfaction is closer to the notion of a system guaranteeing a repeatable reads isolation level.

CONCLUDING REMARKS

In this chapter, we have presented a brief survey of the interaction between active rules and integrity constraints. We have discussed the current proposed techniques to deal with situations when both declarative static constraints and triggers are defined. We have shown that the main problem consists of ensuring that the constraints are preserved in the presence of cascade firing of before and after triggers. The perspective of our treatment follows the SQL-1999 Standard Committee point of view, which constitutes the state of the art in that matter. We have given a brief sketch on how to generate triggers for integrity constraint maintenance, manually or automatically, for the static case when such a constraint definition is not supported by database kernels. Then, we have addressed the problem of ensuring satisfaction of dynamic constraints, and we review a formal approach based on temporal logic formalism. We have shown that if the dynamic constraints are simply two-state or transition constraints, the satisfaction problem can be easily implemented by means of triggers. We have also seen that the approach, although formal, can be implemented as well for the general case of actual systems. Some issues concerning applicability related with the last techniques remain open to researchers and practitioners, and improvements in these techniques are expected in the future.

REFERENCES

Abiteboul, S., Cluet, S., Mignet, L., Amann, B., Milo, T. & Eyal, A. (1999). Active views for electronic commerce. *Proceedings of the International Conference on Very Large Data Bases*, 138-149.

Aiken, A., Hellerstein, J. & Widom, J. (1995). Static analysis techniques for predicting the behavior of active database rules. *ACM Transactions on Database Systems*, 20(1), 3-41.

Bailey, J., Dong, G. & Ramamohanarao, K. (1998). Decidability and undecidability results for the termination problem of active database rules. *Proceedings of ACM PODS'98*.

Bailey, J., Poulovassilis, A. & Newson, P.(2000). A dynamic approach to termination analysis for active database rules. *Proceedings of the International Conference on Computational Logic,* 1106-1120.

Bailey, J., Poulovassilis, A. & Wood, P. (2001). An event-condition-action language for XML. *Proceedings of the ACM Conference, WWW2001.*

Baralis, E., Ceri, S. & Paraboschi, S. (1998). Compile-time and runtime analysis of active behaviors. *IEEE Transactions on Knowledge and Data Engineering,* 10(3), 353-370.

Baralis, E. & Widom, J. (1994). An algebraic approach to rule analysis in expert database systems. *Proceedings of the 20th International Conference on Very Large Data Bases.*

Baralis, E. & Widom, J. (2000a). *Better Static Rule Analysis for Active Database Systems.* Stanford University Research Report 02/06/2000.

Baralis, E. & Widom, J. (2000b). An algebraic approach to static analysis of active database rules. *ACM Transactions on Database Systems,* 25(3), 269-332.

Baralis, E., Ceri, S. & Paraboschi, S. (1996). Modularization techniques for active rules design. *ACM Transactions on Database Systems,* 21(1), 1-29.

Baralis, E., Ceri, S. & Widom, J. (1993). Better termination analysis for active databases. *Proceedings of the International Workshop on Rules in Database Systems,* 163-179.

Bonifati, A., Braga, D., Campi, A. & Ceri, S. (2002). Active XQuery. *Proceedings of ICDE 2002.*

Bonifati, A., Ceri, S. & Paraboschi, S.(2001). Active rules for XML: A new paradigm for e-services. *VLDB Journal,* 10(1), 39-47.

Bonifati, A., Ceri, S. & Paraboschi, S. (2001a). Pushing reactive services to XML repositories using active rules. *Proceedings of the 10th WWW Conference.*

Ceri, S. & Widom, J. (1990). Deriving production rules for constraint maintenance. *Proceedings of the International Conference on Very Large Data Bases,* 566-577.

Ceri, S., Cochrane, R. & Widom, J. (2000). Practical applications of triggers and constraints: Successes and lingering issues. *Proceedings of the International Conference on Very Large Data Bases.*

Ceri, S., Fraternali, P., Paraboschi, S. & Tanca, L. (1995). Automatic generation of production rules for integrity maintenance. *ACM Transactions on Database Systems,* 19(3), 367-422.

Chakravarthy, S. (1989). Rule management and evaluation: An active DBMS perspective. *SIGMOD Record,* 18(3), 20-28.

Chakravarthy, S. (1997). SENTINEL: An object-oriented DBMS with event-based rules. *Proceedings of the ACM International Conference, SIGMOD,* 572-575.

Chakravarthy, S. & Mishra, D. (1994) Snoop: An expressive event specification language for active databases. *Data and Knowledge Engineering,* 14(1), 1-26.

Chakravarthy, S., Krishnaprasad, V., Anwar, E. & Kim, S. (1994). Composite events for active databases: Semantic contexts and detection. *Proceedings of the International Conference on Very Large Data Bases,* 606-617.

Chomicki, J. (1992) History-less checking of dynamic constraints. *Proceedings of the International Conference on Data Engineering.* IEEE Computer Society Press.

Cochrane, R., Pirahesh, H. & Mattos, N. (1996). Integrating triggers and declarative constraints in SQL database systems. *Proceedings of the International Conference on Very Large Data Bases.*

Comai, S. & Tanca, L. (1997). Active database specification. *Proceedings of the 3rd International Workshop on Rules in Database Systems (RIDS).*

Dayal, U. et al. (1988). The HiPAC project: Combining active databases and timing constraints. *SIGMOD Record*, 17(1), 51-70.

Gehani, N. & Jagadish, H. (1991). ODE as an active database: Constraints and triggers. *Proceedings of the International Conference on Very Large Data Bases*, 327-336.

Hanson, P. (1992). Rule condition testing and action execution in Ariel. *Proceedings of the ACM International Conference, SIGMOD*, 49-58.

Karadimce, A. & Urban, S. (1996). Refined triggering graphs: A logic-based approach to termination analysis in an object-oriented database. *Proceedings of the 12th ICDE.*

Lipeck, U. & Saake, G. (1987). Monitoring dynamic integrity constraints based on temporal logic. *Information Systems*, 12(3), 255-266.

Manna, Z. & Pnueli, A. (1992). *The Temporal Logic of Reactive and Concurrent Systems: Specification.* Springer-Verlag.

Manna, Z. & Pnueli, A. (1995). *The Temporal Logic of Reactive Systems: Safety.* Springer-Verlag.

Paton, N. & Diaz, O. (1999). Active database systems. *ACM Computing Surveys*, 31(1), 63-103.

Sistla, A.P. (1983). *Theoretical Issues in the Design of Distributed and Concurrent Systems.* PhD Thesis, Harvard University, Cambridge, Massachusetts.

Sistla, A.P. & Wolfson, O. (1995a). Temporal triggers in active databases. *IEEE Transactions on Knowledge and Data Engineering*, 7, 471-486.

Sistla, A.P. & Wolfson, O. (1995b). Temporal conditions and integrity constraints in active databases. *Proceedings of the ACM International Conference, SIGMOD*, 269-280.

Stonebraker, M. (1986). Triggers and inference in database systems. In Brodie, M. & Mylopoulos, J. (Eds.), *On Knowledge Base Management Systems.* Springer-Verlag.

Widom, J. & Ceri, S. (1996). Active database systems: Triggers and rules for advanced database processing. Morgan Kaufmann.

Widom, J. & Finkelstein, S. (1990). Set-oriented production rules in database management systems. *Proceedings of the ACM International Conference, SIGMOD*, 259-270.

Wolper, P. (1983). Temporal logic can be more expressive. *Information and Cont****, 56, 72-99.

Yang, S. & Chakravarthy, S. (1999). Formal semantics of composite events for distributed environment. *Proceedings of the International Conference on Data Engineering.* IEEE Computer Society Press, 400-407.

Zimmer, D., Meckenstock, A. & Unland, R. (1996). Using petri nets for rule termination analysis. *Proceedings of the 2nd ARTBD.*

Section IV

Advances in Relational Database Theory, Methods and Practices

Chapter XV

On the Computation of Recursion in Relational Databases

Yangjun Chen*
University of Winnipeg, Canada

ABSTRACT

*A composite object represented as a directed graph is an important data structure which requires efficient support in CAD/CAM, CASE, office systems, software management, Web databases and document databases. It is cumbersome to handle such an object in relational database systems when it involves recursive relationships. In this chapter, we present a new encoding method to support the efficient computation of recursion. In addition, we devise a linear time algorithm to identify a sequence of reachable trees (w.r.t.) a directed acyclic graph (DAG), which covers all the edges of the graph. Together with the new encoding method, this algorithm enables us to compute recursion w.r.t. a DAG in time O(*e*), where* e *represents the number of edges of the DAG. More importantly, this method is especially suitable for a relational environment.*

* *The author is supported by NSERC 239074-01 (242523) (Natural Science and Engineering Council of Canada)*

INTRODUCTION

It is a general opinion that relational database systems are inadequate for manipulating composite objects which arise in novel applications such as Web and document databases (Mendelzon, Mihaila & Milo, 1997; Abiteboul et al., 1997; Chen & Aberer, 1998, 1999), CAD/CAM, CASE, office systems and software management (Banerjee et al., 1988; Teuhola, 1996). Especially when recursive relationships are involved, it is cumbersome to handle them in a relational system. To mitigate this problem to some extent, many methods have been proposed, such as *join index* (Valduriez & Borel, 1986) and *clustering of composition hierarchies* (Haskin & Lorie, 1982), as well as the encoding scheme (Teuhola, 1996).

In this chapter, we present a new encoding method to facilitate the computation of recursive relationships of nodes in a DAG. In comparison with Teuhola's, our method is simple and space-economical. Specifically, the problem of Teuhola's, the so-called *signature conflicts*, is removed.

BACKGROUND

A composite object can be generally represented as a directed graph. For example, in a CAD database, a composite object corresponds to a complex design, which is composed of several subdesigns (Banerjee et al., 1988). Often, subdesigns are shared by more than one higher-level design, and a set of design hierarchies thus forms a directed acyclic graph (DAG). As another example, the citation index of scientific literature, recording reference relationships between authors, constructs a directed cyclic graph. As a third example, we consider the traditional organization of a company, with a variable number of manager-subordinate levels, which can be represented as a tree hierarchy. In a relational system, composite objects must be fragmented across many relations, requiring joins to gather all the parts. A typical approach to improving join efficiency is to equip relations with hidden pointer fields for coupling the tuples to be joined (Carey et al., 1990). Recently, a new method was proposed by Teuhola (1996), in which the information of the ancestor path of each node is packed into a fix-length code, called the *signature*. Then, the operation to find the transitive closure w.r.t. a directed graph can be performed by identifying a series of signature intervals. No joins are needed. Using Teuhola's method, CPU time can be improved up to 93% for trees and 45% for DAGs in comparison with a method which performs a SELECT command against each node, where the relation to store edges is equipped with a clustering index on the parent nodes (Teuhola, 1996).

In this chapter, we follow the method proposed in Teuhola (1996), but using a different encoding approach to pack "ancestor paths." For example, in a tree hierarchy, we associate each node v with a pair of integers (α, β) such that if v', another node associated with (α', β'), is a descendant of v, some arithmetical relationship between α and α' as well as β and β' can be determined. Then, such relationships can be used to find all descendants of a node, and the recursive closure w.r.t. a tree can be computed very efficiently. This method can be generalized to a DAG or a directed graph containing cycles by decomposing a graph into a sequence of trees (forests), in which the approach described above can be employed. As we will see later, a new method can be developed based on the techniques mentioned above, by which recursion can be evaluated in $O(e)$

time, just as an algorithm using *adjacency lists*. The adjacency list is a common data structure to store a graph in computational graph theory (see Mehlhon, 1984). However, our method is especially suitable for the implementation in a relational environment. More importantly, the proposed encoding scheme provides a new way to explore more efficient graph algorithms to compute transitive closures.

TASK DEFINITION

We consider composite objects represented by a directed graph, where nodes stand for objects and edges for parent-child relationships, stored in a binary relation. In many applications, the transitive closure of a graph needs to be computed, which is defined to be all ancestor-descendant pairs. A lot of research has been directed to this issue. Among them, the semi-naive (Bancihon & Ramakrishnan, 1986) and the logarithmic (Valduriez & Boral, 1986) are typical *algorithmic* solutions. Another main approach is the materialization of the closure, either partially or completely (Agrawal & Jagadish, 1990). Recently, the implementation of the transitive closure algorithms in a relational environment has received extensive attention, including performance and the adaptation of the traditional algorithms (Abiteboul et al., 1990; Agrawal, Dar & Jagadish, 1990; Ioannidis, Ramakrishnan & Winger, 1993; Dar & Ramakrishnan, 1994; Teuhola, 1996).

The method proposed in this chapter can be characterized as a partial materialization method. Given a node, we want to compute all its descendants efficiently based on a specialized data structure. The following is a typical structure to accommodate part-subpart relationship (Cattell & Skeen, 1992):

- Part(Part-id, Part-rest),
- Connection(Parent-id, Child-id, Conn-rest),

where Parent-id and Child-id are both foreign keys, referring to Part-id. In order to speed up the recursion evaluation, we'll associate each node with a pair of integers which helps to recognize the ancestor-descendant relationships.

In the rest of the chapter, the following three types of graphs will be discussed.

i) Tree hierarchy, in which the parent-child relationship is of one-to-many type, i.e., each node has at most one parent.
ii) Directed acyclic graph (DAG), which occurs when the relationship is of many-to-many type, with the restriction that a part cannot be sub/superpart of itself (directly or indirectly).
iii) Directed cyclic graph, which contains cycles.

Later we'll use the term *graph* to refer to the *directed graph*, since we do not discuss non-directed ones at all.

LABELLING A TREE STRUCTURE

In the method proposed in Teuhola (1996), each node v is associated with an interval (l, h), where l and h *are* two signatures each consisting of a bit string. These bit strings are constructed in such a way that if the interval associated with a descendant of v is $(l',$

h'), then $l \leq l'$ and $h \geq h'$ hold. Although this method is incomparably superior to a trivial method, it suffers from the follows disadvantages:

1) This method is space-consuming since signatures tend to be very long.
2) The size of signatures has to be pre-determined. Different applications may require different signature lengths. This can be tuned only manually.
3) There may exist the so-called signature conflicts, i.e., two nodes may be assigned the same signature.

In the following, we search for remedies for these three drawbacks. First, we discuss a tree labeling method to demonstrate the main idea of the improvement in this section. The discussion on general cases will occur later on.

Consider a tree *T*. By traversing *T* in *preorder*, each node *v* will obtain a number *pre*(*v*) to record the order in which the nodes of the tree are visited. In the same way, by traversing *T* in *postorder*, each node will get another number *post*(*v*). These two numbers can be used to characterize the ancestor-descendant relationship as follows.

Proposition 1. Let *v* and *v*' be two nodes of a tree *T*. Then, *v*' is a descendant of *v* if *pre*(*v*') > *pre*(*v*) and *post*(*v*') < *post*(*v*).
Proof. See Knuth (1973).

If *v*' is a descendant of *v*, then we know that *pre*(*v*') > *pre*(*v*) according to the preorder search. Now we assume that *post*(*v*') > *post*(*v*). Then, according to the postorder search, either *v*' is in some subtree on the right side of *v*, or *v* is in the subtree rooted at *v*', which contradicts the fact that *v*' is a descendant of *v*. Therefore, *post*(*v*') must be less than *post*(*v*).

The following example helps for illustration.

Example 1

See the pairs associated with the nodes of the graph shown in Figure 1(a). The first element of each pair is the preorder number of the corresponding node and the second is the postorder number of it. Using such labels, the ancestor-descendant relationship can be easily checked.

Figure 1. Labeling a Tree

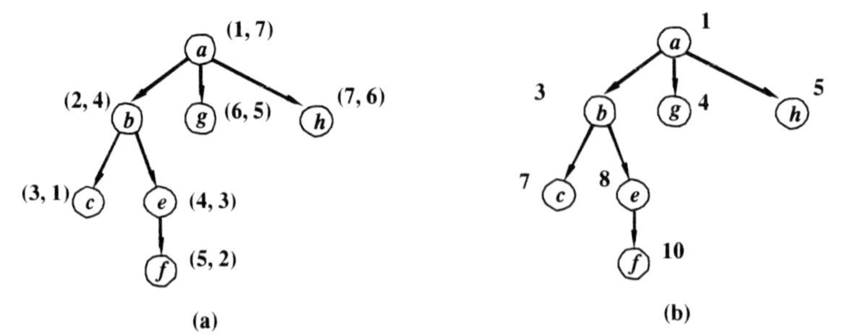

For example, by checking the label associated with *b* against the label for *f*, we know that *b* is an ancestor of *f* in terms of Proposition 1. We can also see that since the pairs associated with *g* and *c* do not satisfy the condition given in Proposition 1, *g* must not be an ancestor of *c* and vice versa.

According to this labeling strategy, the relational schema to handle recursion can consist of only one relation of the following form:

Node(Node_id, label_pair, Node_rest),

where label_pair is used to accommodate the preorder number and the postorder number of each node, denoted label_pair.preorder and label_pair.postorder, respectively. Then, to retrieve the descendants of node *x*, we issue two queries. The first query is very simple as shown below:

```
SELECT    label_pair
          FROM  Node
          WHERE Node_id = x
```

Let the label pair obtained by evaluating the above query be *y*. Then, the second query will be of the following form:

```
SELECT    *
          FROM  Node
          WHERE label_pair.preorder > y.preorder
   and    label_pair.postorder < y.postorder
```

From the above discussion, we can see that the three drawbacks of Teuhola's method (Teuhola, 1996) mentioned above can be eliminated: 1) each node is associated with only a pair of integers and therefore the space overhead is low; 2) the size of each label pair remains the same for all applications; 3) there are no signature conflicts since each label pair is different from the others.

In the following, we show two other important techniques to identify the sibling relationship and the parent-child relationship.

For the first task, consider a new labeling method as shown in Figure 1(b). First we assign 1 to the root; then during the breadth-first traversal, we number the children of each node consecutively from $x + 2$, where x is the largest number assigned so far. We call such a labeling method the *sibling-code*. Then, we can associate each parent node with an interval $[a, b]$ such that each child's sibling-code $s \in [a, b]$. Therefore, two nodes are siblings if their sibling-codes belong to the same interval.

To identify the parent-child relation, we associate each node with a level number. The root has the level number 0. All the children of the root have the level number 1, and so on. Then, if node x is the ancestor of y and at the same time $l(x) = l(y) - 1$ ($l(x)$ stands for the level number of x), then we know that x is the parent of y.

GENERALIZATION

Now we discuss how to treat the recursion w.r.t. a general structure: a DAG or a graph containing cycles. First, we address the problem with DAGs. Then, the cyclic graphs will be discussed.

Recursion W.R.T. DAGs

We want to apply the technique discussed above to a DAG. To this end, we define the following concept (Shimon, 1979).

Definition 1. A subgraph $G'(V, E')$ of a finite DAG $G(V, E)$ is called a *branching* if $d_{in}(v) \leq 1$ for every $v \in V$ ($d_{in}(v)$ represents the in-degree of v).

For example, the graph shown in Figure 2(b) is a branching of the graph shown in Figure 2(a).

Let each edge $e \in E$ have a cost $c(e)$. A branching $G'(V, E')$ is a called a *maximal branching* if $\sum_{e \in E'} c(e)$ is maximum. In addition, a tree appearing in a branching and rooted at a node r is called a reachable-tree from r.

In the following, we will divide a DAG into a set of reachable trees. This method shares the flavor of Teuhola's (1996). But our decomposition strategy is quite different from Teuhola's. In his method, a DAG is decomposed into a set of reachable trees which are separated from each other, i.e., there are no common nodes between any two reachable trees, while in ours two reachable trees may have common nodes. The advantage of our method can be seen in the following discussion.

Below we concentrate only on single-root graphs for simplicity. But the proposed method can be easily extended to normal cases. We construct a sequence of reachable trees for a DAG G with the single-root r_0, which covers all the reachable edges from r_0 in G. For our problem, we assume that each edge e in G is associated with a cost $c(e) = 1$. Given r_0, we are interested in the maximal branching B in G, and the reachable tree from r_0 in B, denoted $T_{max}(G)$. First, we recognize $T_{max}(G)$ from G. Then, we remove $T_{max}(G)$ and subsequently all isolated nodes from G, getting another graph G_1. Next, for a leaf node r_1 in $T_{max}(G)$, we construct another reachable tree from r_1 in G_1: $T_{max}(G_1)$ and remove $T_{max}(G_1)$ and all isolated nodes from G_1. Next, for a node r_2, which is a leaf node of $T_{max}(G)$ or $T_{max}(G_1)$, we construct a third reachable tree. We repeat this process until the remaining graph becomes empty. It is therefore easy to see that all $T_{max}(G_i)$'s can be obtained in O(k(n +

Figure 2. A DAG and One of its Brachings

e)) time by repeating graph search procedure k times, where n and e represent the number of the nodes and the edges of the DAG, respectively, and k is the number of trees into which G can be decomposed. However, this time complexity can be reduced to $O(n + e)$ by implementing an algorithm which computes such a sequence in a single-scan.

For a DAG $G = (V, E)$, we represent the sequence of reachable trees $T_{max}(G_i)$ ($i = 0, 1, ..., m; G_0 = G$) as follows:

$T_{max}(G_0) = (V_1, E_1)$,
$T_{max}(G_1) = (V_2, E_2)$,
$T_{max}(G_2) = (V_3, E_3)$,
… …
$T_{max}(G_m) = (V_{m+1}, E_{m+1})$,

where V_1 stands for the set of nodes in G, V_i ($i = 2, ..., m+1$) for the set of nodes in $G - E_1 \cup E_2 \cup ... \cup E_{i-1}$, and m is the largest in-degree of the nodes of G.

In the following, we give a linear time algorithm to compute all $T_{max}(G_i)$'s.

The idea is to construct all $E_1, E_2, ... E_m$ in a single scan. During the graph search we compute, for each edge e being scanned, the i satisfying $e \in E_i$. Such i can be defined to be the smallest such that if e is put in E_i, the condition: each node in any E_j ($j = 1, ..., i$) is visited only once, is not violated, where E_i denotes the edge sets constructed so far. In the algorithm, we always choose an unvisited edge e that is adjacent to edge $e' \in E_i$ with the largest i. In the algorithm, we associate each node v with a label $l(v)$: $l(v) = i$ indicates that v has been reached by an edge of the forest $T_{max}(G_{i-1}) = (V_i, E_i)$. In the following algorithm, we assume that the nodes are numbered in terms of the depth-first search.

```
Algorithm find-forest
input: G = (V, E)
output: E_1, E_2, ..., E_m
   begin
      E_1 := E_2 := ... := E_m := ∅;
      Mark all nodes v ∈ V and all edges e ∈ E "unvisited";
      l(v) := 0 for all v ∈ V;
      while there exist "unvisited" nodes do
          begin
          choose an "unvisited" node v ∈ V with the largest l and the smallest
          "depth-first" number;
          for each "unvisited" edge e incident to v do
              begin
                 Let u be the other end node of e (≠ v);
*                E_{l(u)+1} := E_{l(u)+1} ∪ {e};
**               l(u) := l(u) + 1;
***              if l(v) < l(u) then l(v) := l(u) - 1;
                 Mark e "visited";
              end
```

Mark x "visited";
end
end

For example, by applying the above algorithm to the graph shown in Figure 2(a), we will obtain the edges of three reachable trees shown in Figure 3(b). In the Appendix, we will trace the execution of the algorithm against Figure 3(a) for a better understanding.

In the above algorithm, each edge is visited exactly once. Therefore, the time complexity of the algorithm is bounded by $O(n + e)$. In the following, we prove a theorem to establish the correctness of the algorithm.

Proposition 2. Applying Algorithm "*find-forest*" to a DAG G, a sequence of reachable trees w.r.t. G will be found, which covers all of its edges.

Proof. First, we note that by the algorithm, each edge will be visited exactly once and put in some E_i. Therefore, the union of all E_is will contains all edges of G. To prove the theorem, we need now to specify that in every E_i, except the root node of E_i, each node can be reached along only one path, or say, visited exactly one time w.r.t. E_i. Pay attention to the lines marked with * and **. If a node u is visited several times along different edges, such edges will be put in different E_is. Therefore, in each E_i, u can be visited only once. By the line marked with ***, if an edge (v, u) is put in some E_i, then an unvisited edge reaching v afterwards will be put in E_i or E_{i+1}. If in E_i there is no edge reaching v up to now (in this case, $l(v) < l(u)$ holds), the label of v will be changed to $i - 1$. Then, if afterwards an unvisited edge reaches v, it will be put in E_i. Otherwise, $l(v) = l(u)$ and there must already be an edge in E_i reaching v. Thus, if afterwards an unvisited edge reaches v, it will be put in E_{i+1}. In this way, in E_i, v can be visited only once, which completes the theorem proof.

Now we can label each E_i in the same way as discussed in the previous section. (A forest can be regarded as a tree with a virtual root which has a virtual edge linking each tree root of the forest.) In addition, we notice that a node may appear in several E_is. For example, in Figure 3(b), node 6 appears in E_1 and E_2 while node 4 occurs in all the three reachable trees. Then, after labeling each E_i, each node v will get a pair sequence of the form: $(pre_{i_1}, post_{i_1}).(pre_{i_2}, post_{i_2}). \ldots .(pre_{i_j}, post_{i_j})$, where for each $i_k \in \{1, ..., m\}$ (m

Figure 3. DAG and its Node-Disjunct Maximal Trees

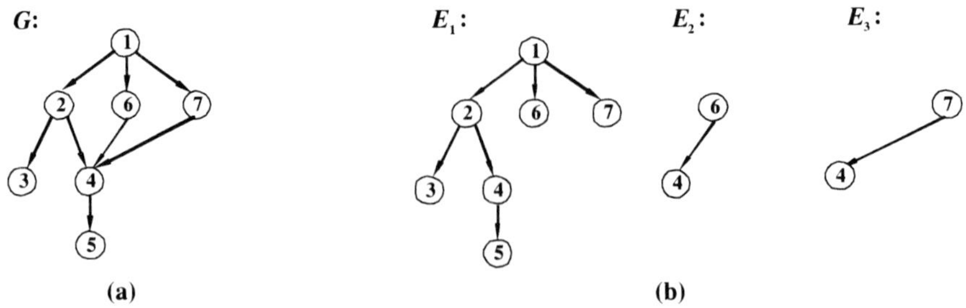

is the in-degree of v) and (pre_{i_k} , $post_{i_k}$) stands for the preorder number and postorder number of v w.r.t. E_{i_k} . In the subsequent discussion, we also say that a label belongs to some E_i, referring to the fact that this pair is calculated in terms of E_i. In terms of such a data structure, we give a naive algorithm below.

```
Δ_global := ∅;
Δ_local := ∅;
S := {x};                  (* The descendants of x will be searched. *)
function recursion(S)
begin
   for each x ∈ S do {
        let p_1.p_2. ... p_m be the pair sequence associated with x;
        for i = m to 1 do {
*            let Δ be the set of descendants of x w.r.t. E_i (evaluated using p_i);
**           for each y ∈ Δ, remove the pair belonging to E_i from the pair sequence
             associated with y;
             Δ_local := Δ_local ∪ Δ;}}
Δ_local := Δ_local - Δ_global;
Δ_global := Δ_global ∪ Δ_local;
call recursion(Δ_local);
end
```

In the above algorithm, pay attention to the line marked with *, by which all the descendants of x will be evaluated in E_i, using p_i. Since these descendants may appear also in other E_js, they should be used for the further computation. But the pair belonging to E_i has to be eliminated from the pair sequences associated with these nodes to avoid the repeated access to the edges in E_i, which is done by the line marked with **.

The above algorithm suffers, however, from redundancy as discussed next.

The graph shown in Figure 4(a) can be decomposed into two reachable trees as shown in Figure 4(b). Applying *recursion*(7) to this graph, the descendant set found in the first **for** loop is {4, 5}. In the second **for** loop, the descendants of nodes 4 and 5 will be found, which are s_1 = {5, 6} (the descendants of node 4) and s_2 = {6} (the descendants of node 5), respectively. Obviously, s_2 is completely covered by s_1. Therefore, the work of producing s_2 can be saved. To this end, we associate each E_i with a bit string of size

Figure 4. Illustration of Redundancy of Recursion (S)

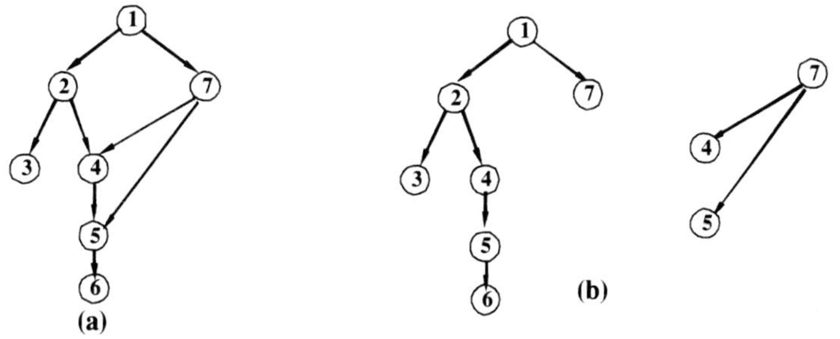

n, denoted B_i. If some node j is a descendant evaluated w.r.t. E_i, the jth bit of B_i will be set to 1, i.e., $B_i[j] = 1$. If the descendants of a node k w.r.t. E_i will be found, we first check $B_i[k]$ to see whether it is equal to 1. If so, the corresponding computation will not be made. Another problem is that if s_2 is produced first, the redundant work cannot be avoided even though the checking is performed. Thus, the order of the nodes whose descendants will be found is important. With respect to an E_i, the nodes with smaller preorder numbers will be treated earlier than those with a larger preorder number. It is because a node with a larger preorder number may be a descendant of a node with a smaller one, but not vice versa. In order to sort the nodes in this way, we have to change the control method of the above algorithm. Assume that each node v is associated with a pair sequence of the form: $p_1.p_2. \ldots p_m$, where m is the largest in-degree of the graph. If v does not appear in E_i, p_i will be of the form: (_, _) and will be ignored by sorting. The nodes, whose descendants w.r.t. E_i are going to be found, will first be sorted in terms of p_i. Then, the descendants of these nodes w.r.t. E_i will be produced. In a second loop, the nodes will be sorted again in terms of p_{i-1}. This process repeats until all p_i's are handled. Below is the corresponding algorithm with the checking mechanism used.

$\Delta_{global} := \emptyset$;
$\Delta_{local} := \emptyset$;
$S := \{x\}$; (* The descendants of x will be searched. *)
let $p_1.p_2. \ldots p_m$ be the pair sequence associated with each node of the graph;
for $i = 1$ to m **do** $B_i = 0$;
function *refined-recursion*(S)
begin
  for $i = m$ to 1 **do** {
    sort S in terms of p_is;
    let the sorted S be $\{v_1, \ldots, v_k\}$;
    for $j = 1$ to k **do** {
    if $B_i[v_j] = 0$ then $\Delta :=$ the set of descendants of v_j w.r.t. E_i (evaluated using p_i);
    for each $v_j \in \Delta$ **do** $\{B_i[v_j] := 1\}$
    $\Delta_{local} := \Delta_{local} \cup \Delta$;}}
  $\Delta_{local} := \Delta_{local} - \Delta_{global}$;
  $\Delta_{global} := \Delta_{global} \cup \Delta_{local}$;
  call *refined-recursion*(Δ_{local});
end

Note that we take only O(1) time to check a bit in the bit string. For each newly evaluated node set (each time stored in Δ_{local} in the above algorithm), sorting operations will be performed. But each node v in Δ_{local} can take part in the sorting only d times, where d represents the in-degree of v, since for each node v only d pairs in the pair sequence associated with it is not of the form: (_, _). Assume that each time only Δ_{ij} from $\Delta_i (= \Delta_{local})$ participates in the sorting. Then, the total cost for sorting is:

$$\sum_i \sum_j |\Delta_{ij}| \cdot \log |\Delta_{ij}| \leq e \times \log n.$$

Since each edge is visited at most once, the traversal of the graph needs only O(e) time. Therefore, the time complexity of the algorithm is bounded by O($e \times \log n$), a little bit less than the time required by an algorithm using an adjacency list. More importantly, this algorithm is quite suitable for a relational environment. Furthermore, we can store the data in a special way to support the sorting operation so that no extra time is required. For example, we can define two simple relations to accommodate the graph and its pair sequences as follows:

node(Node_id, Node_rest),
reachable_forest(E_num, label_pair, Node_id).

The first relation stores all the nodes of the graph. The second relation stores all the reachable trees, in which "E_num" is for the identifiers of the reachable trees. If for each of them the label pairs are stored in the increasing order of their preorder numbers, the sorting operations in the algorithm *refined-recursion*() can be removed. Then, the time complexity of the algorithm can be reduced to O(e). This can be done as follows. Whenever some E_i is considered during the execution, we take the tuples with E_num = i from the relation "reachable_forest." Then, we scan these tuples and check, for each tuple, to see whether B_i[node_id] = 1. If it is the case, the corresponding label pair will be put in a list (a temporary data structure) sequentially. Obviously, the list constructed in this way is sorted into the in-creasing order of the preorder numbers w.r.t. E_i.

Recursion W.R.T. Cyclic Graphs

Based on the method discussed in the previous section, we can easily develop an algorithm to compute recursion for cyclic graphs. We can use Tarjan's algorithm for identifying strong connected components (SCCs) to find cycles of a cyclic graph (Tarjan, 1973) (which needs only O($n + e$) time). Then, we take each SCC as a single node (i.e., condense each SCC to a node). The resulting graph is a DAG. Applying the algorithm *find_forest*( ) to this DAG, we will get a set of forests. For each forest, we can associate each node with a pair as above. Obviously, all nodes in an SCC will be assigned the same pair (or the same pair sequence). For this reason, the method for evaluating the recursion at some node x should be changed. For example, if a graph becomes a tree after condensing each SCC to a node, the select-from-where statements like those given in the third section (against this graph) can be modified as follows. The first query is quite the same as that shown in the third section:

```
SELECT   label_pair
FROM     Node
WHERE    Node_id = x
```

But the second is changed slightly:

```
SELECT   *
FROM     Node
WHERE    label_pair.preorder ≥ y.preorder
   and   label_pair.postorder ≤ y.postorder
```

By the second query, the nodes in the same SCC as x will be regarded as the descendants of x.

For general cases, the method for checking ancestor-descendant relationship applies. No extra complexity is caused. Since Tarjan's algorithm runs in $O(n + e)$ time, computing recursion for a cyclic graph needs only $O(e)$ time.

CONCLUSION

In this chapter, a new labeling technique has been proposed. Using this technique, the recursion w.r.t., a tree hierarchy can be evaluated very efficiently. In addition, we have introduced a new algorithm for computing reachable trees, which requires only linear time. Together with the labeling technique, this method enables us to develop an efficient algorithm to compute recursion for directed graphs in $O(e)$ time, where e represents the number of the edges of the DAG. More importantly, this method is especially suitable for relational databases and much better than the existing methods.

REFERENCES

Abiteboul, S., Cluet, S., Christophides, V., Milo, T., Moerkotte, G. & Simon, J. (1997). Quering documents in object databases. *International Journal of Digital Libraries*, 1(1), 5-19.

Agrawal, A., Dar, S. & Jagadish, H.V. (1990). Direct transitive closure algorithms: Design and performance evaluation. *ACM Transactions of Database Systems,* 15(3), 427-458.

Agrawal, R. & Jagadish, H.V. (1989). Materialization and incremental update of path information. *Proceedings of the 5th International Conference on Data Engineering*, Los Angeles, CA, USA, 374-383.

Agarawal, R. & Jagadish, H.V. (1990). Hybrid transitive closure algorithms. *Proceedings of the 16th International VLDB Conference*, Brisbane, Australia, 326-334.

Bancihon, F. & Ramakrishnan, R. (1986). An amateur's introduction to recursive query processing strategies. *Proceedings of the ACM SIGMOD Conference*, Washington, DC, USA, 16-52.

Banerjee, J., Kim, W., Kim, S. & Garza, J.F. (1988). Clustering a DAG for CAD databases. *IEEE Transactions on Knowledge and Data Engineering*, 14(11), 1684-1699.

Carey, M. et al. (1990). An incremental join attachment for Starburst. *Proceedings of the 16th VLDB Conference,* Brisbane, Australia, 662-673.

Cattell, R.G.G. & Skeen, J. (1992). Object operations benchmark. *ACM Transactions on Database Systems*, 17(1), 1-31.

Chen, Y. & Aberer, K. (1998). Layered index structures in document database systems. *Proceedings of the 7th International Conference on Information and Knowledge Management (CIKM)*, Bethesda, MD, USA, 406-413.

Chen, Y. & Aberer, K. (1999). Combining pat-trees and signature files for query evaluation in document databases. *Proceedings of the 10th International DEXA Conference on Database and Expert Systems Application*, Florence, Italy, September. City: Springer Verlag, 473-484.

Dar, S. & Ramarkrishnan, R. (1994). A performance study of transitive closure algorithm. *Proceedings of the SIGMOD International Conference*, Minneapolis, MN, USA, 454-465.

Haskin, R.L. & Lorie, R.A. (1982). On extending the functions of a relational database system. *Proceedings of the ACM SIGMOD Conference*, Orlando, FL, USA, 207-212.

Ioannidis, Y.E., Ramakrishnan R. & Winger, L. (1993). Transitive closure algorithms based on depth-first search. *ACM Transactions on Database Systems*, 18(3), 512-576.

Jagadish, H.V. (1990). A compression technique to materialize transitive closure. *ACM Transactions on Database Systems*, 15(4), 558-598.

Knuth, D.E. (1973). *The Art of Computer Programming: Sorting and Searching*, London: Addison-Wesley.

Mehlhorn, K. (1984). *Graph Algorithms and NP-Completeness: Data Structure and Algorithm 2.* Berlin: Springer-Verlag.

Mendelzon, A.O., Mihaila, G.A. & Milo, T. (1997). Querying the World Wide Web. *International Journal of Digital Libraries*, 1(1), 54-67.

Shimon. E. (1979). *Graph Algorithms.* City, MD: Computer Science Press.

Tarjan, R. (1972). Depth-first search and linear graph algorithms. *SIAM Journal of Computing,* 1(2), 146-140.

Teuhola, J. (1996). Path signatures: A way to speed up recursion in relational databases. *IEEE Transactions on Knowledge and Data Engineering*, 8(3), 446-454.

Valduriez, P. & Boral, H. (1986). Evaluation of recursive queries using join indices. *Proceedings of the 1st Workshop on Expert Database Systems*, Charleston, SC, USA, 197-208.

APPENDIX

In this appendix, we trace the algorithm *find-reachable-tree* against the tree shown in Figure 3(a).

See Figure 5. At the beginning, every $r(v)$ is set to 0. After the first loop, the l-value of node 1 remains 0. But the l-values of 2, 6 and 7 are changed to 1. Moreover, node 1 and edge (1, 2), (1, 6) and (1, 7) are marked with "v" to indicate that they have been visited. In addition, part of E_1 has been generated. The rest of the steps are listed in Figures 6, 7 and 8.

Figure 5. The First Execution Step of Find-Node-Disjunct-Forest

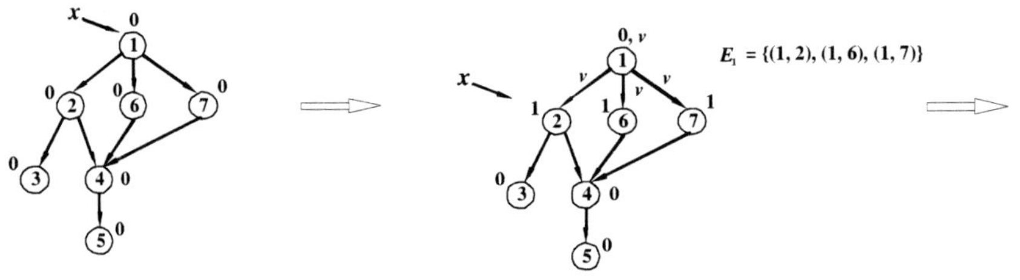

Figure 6. The Second and Third Execution Step of Find-Node-Disjunct-Forest

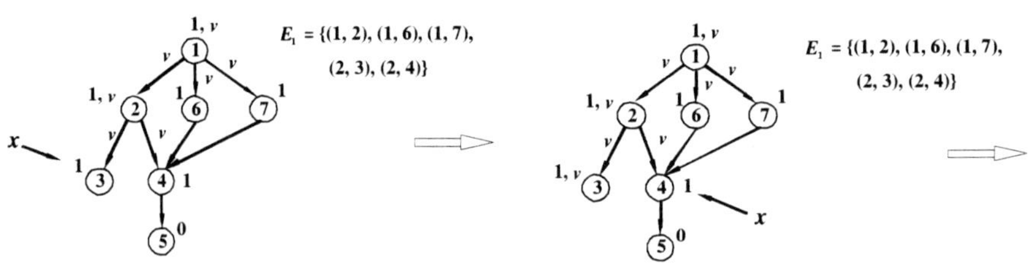

Figure 7. The Fourth and Fifth Execution Step of Find-Node-Disjunct-Forest

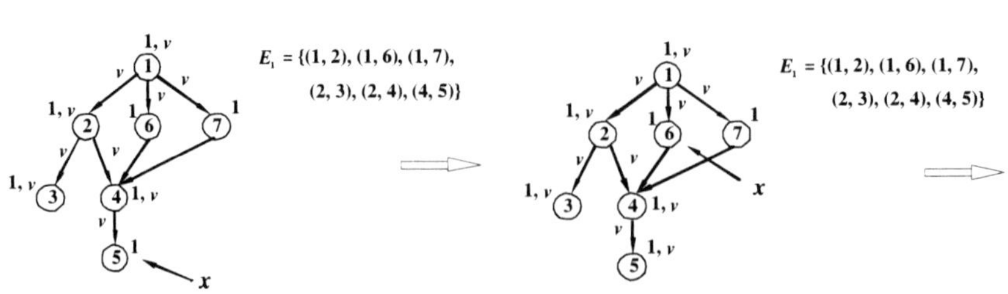

Figure 8. The Sixth and Seventh Execution Step of Find-Node-Disjunct-Forest

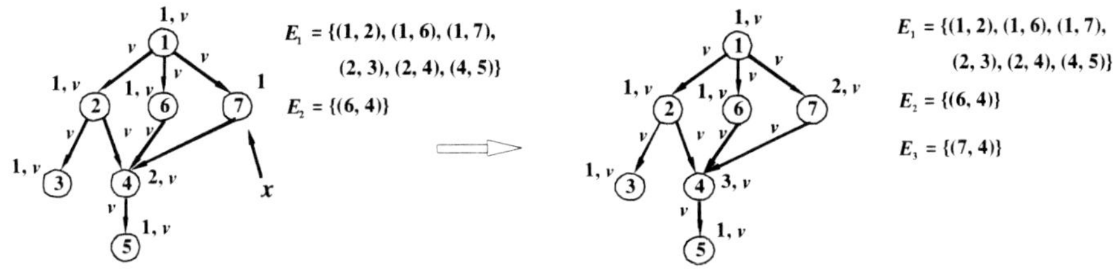

Chapter XVI

Understanding Functional Dependency

Robert A. Schultz
Woodbury University, USA

ABSTRACT

In explaining functional dependency to students, I have noticed in texts a mixture of two types of elements: intensional (or psychological or meaning) and extensional (patterns of repetition in the data). In this chapter I examine whether it is possible to consider functional dependency, in particular, in second and third normal forms, solely on an extensional basis. The Microsoft Access Analyzer utility seems to do so. I illustrate the mix of intensional and extensional elements in textbook definitions of functional dependency. I conclude that although in principle first, second and third normal form can be done solely by extensional means, in practice intensional considerations are indispensable. Finally, I discuss these questions with respect to the "higher order" normal forms, namely Boyce-Codd, fourth, fifth and Domain/Key normal form.

INTRODUCTION

In attempting to explain the process of normalization of databases to students, I have noticed that texts differ in small but significant ways in how they explain the concept of *functional dependency*, which is necessary to define and to implement the normal forms.

I think this disparity is due to a problem in the concept of functional dependency itself. Although intuitively clear, it is actually a mixture of two quite different elements:

- Psychological or meaning elements involving dependencies in knowledge — for example, we need to know customer name in order to know customer address. (I will call these *intensional* elements.)
- Objective elements derived solely from the data about the objects represented in the database in some way reflected in tables. (I will call these *extensional* elements. The idea is that an extensional element must be based on differences in the way data appear in the table — most notably, patterns of repetition of field values.)

The main motivation for normalization and the normal forms is the elimination of "bad" data redundancies in the database. A tool such as Analyzer in Microsoft Access is able to accomplish this without using any intensional elements or indeed without even considering the meaning of the field names. In logical terminology, its procedures are purely extensional. All that Analyzer uses are patterns of repetition of field values.

We can use repetitions in the data to determine first, second and third normal forms once primary keys are determined. Of course this depends on the data not being misleading. I will discuss whether the following extensional conjecture is true.

The Extensional Conjecture: All possible combinations of the data allow normalization (first, second and third normal form) on the basis of repetitions in the data alone (supposing primary keys are given).

Seemingly, identifying the primary key from existing fields involves intensional elements. Just looking at a table filled with data doesn't decide whether the customer social security number or customer credit card number is to be the primary key. Nevertheless, it is an extensional matter whether or not a field or fields can be a primary key — in other words, whether the field or fields is a candidate key. If there are (genuine) duplications in the values for the field, we do not have a candidate key.

Analyzer usually does not identify primary keys for tables from field values. Instead, for each table it often assigns a new field with non-repeating incremental numerical values, or it allows the user to pre-identify one or more fields in a table as the primary key. The situation here will turn out to mirror the situation with first, second and third normal forms: all can be defined extensionally, but in practice, intensional elements may be all but indispensable because we are normally not in possession of all possible combinations of field values.

Near the end of the chapter, I will comment on the applicability of my conclusions to the "higher" normal forms, namely Boyce-Codd, fourth, fifth and domain-key normal forms.

My procedure will first be to recap material from standard logical works on the distinction between intension and extension. Then I will examine several sample definitions of functional dependency from popular texts on database design to show how intensional and extensional elements are mixed. Following that, I will examine the issue of whether the Extensional Conjecture is true. I will conclude by discussing the implications both for teaching and for using the concept of functional dependency and the normal forms.

INTENSION AND EXTENSION

The distinction between extensional and intensional elements is familiar in logic. See, for example, Lewis and Langford:

> *[A] proposition may be taken as asserting a relation between the concepts which the terms connote, or between the classes which the terms denote... The laws governing the relations of concepts constitute the logic of the* connotation or intension *of these terms; those governing the relations of classes constitute the logic of the* denotation *or* extension *of these terms. (Lewis & Langford 1959, p. 27)*

Thus, intension has to do with the meanings of the terms involved, and extension with what objects are denoted by or referred to by the terms. In general, if two terms have the same intension or meaning, they have the same extension; but two terms can have the same extension but different meanings or intensions. The classic example is 'the morning star' and 'the evening star' which have the same extension — the heavenly body Venus — but clearly have different meanings or connotations (Frege, 1892).

It is this last fact which makes intensions difficult to use in mathematical or scientific or technical contexts — in fact we don't have clear criteria for when intensions are the same. The same applies to terms expressing psychological attitudes, such as *knowing*. I can fail to know that the evening star is the same as the morning star. Yet I cannot fail to know that the evening star is the same as the evening star. What we know about, the objects of knowing, are therefore not extensional but intensional in nature. If we speak about conventions or conventional connections, the result is the same: we are dealing with non-extensional contexts.

It would thus be better if normalization, as an important feature of database design, could be done without the use of intensional elements. In fact we will see that use of the first three normal forms can be extensional in nature. This means that the only features of fields appealed to is extensional — the frequency of their appearance with other fields, and that therefore the meanings or connotations of those fields are not used. This also means that connections between fields having to do with knowledge about the meanings of field names or about business rules or conventions connecting field values are intensional as well.

However, intensional elements may be almost indispensable shortcuts. If we actually had available all the data elements in a database, there would be no question about using extensional methods, for example, the Analyzer function in Microsoft Access. But when the full (extensional) database is not available, we may need to turn to intensional elements to determine functional dependency and hence database design. Let us look at some textbook accounts of functional dependency.

DEFINITIONS OF FUNCTIONAL DEPENDENCY

Textbook definitions of functional dependency differ in various ways. Let us start with a recognized database guru. James Martin's definition of functional dependency is:

Data item B of record R is functionally dependent on data item A of record R if, at every instant of time, each value in A has no more than one value of B associated with it in record R. (Martin, 1983, p. 208)

This definition is both extensional and clear: all one needs to do is to examine the pattern of repetitions in the record. If there are multiple values of B for one value of A in a record instance at any time, then, according to Martin's definition, B is not functionally dependent on A.

However, it is easy to be less clear. The authors of a popular recent textbook attempt to provide an extensional definition by utilizing the mathematical concept of *function*. The authors of *Systems Analysis in a Changing World* propose the following definition: "A functional dependency is a one-to-one relationship between values of two fields." Formally stated, "Field A is functionally dependent on field B if for each value of B there is only one corresponding value of A" (Satzinger et al., 2002, p. 404).

The author's statement is somewhat misleading. In terms of file and record relationships, a one-to-one relationship is always symmetrical, which would mean that A is functionally dependent on B if and only if B is functionally dependent on A. This is clearly not so for functional dependencies among fields.

The authors probably have in mind the concept of one-to-one used with mathematical functions: a function is one-to-one if there is one value in the range of the function for each value in the domain of the function. The less misleading definition of functionally dependent would thus be:

Field A is functionally dependent on Field B if for each value of B there is at most *one value of A.*

This clarification is very similar to James Martin's definition, with the variables A and B reversed. Having to add the "at most" clause draws attention to an odd consequence, both of this revision and the original Martin definition: *any* field A, with nothing but null values in rows where B has a value, is functionally dependent on B. I think we have to live with this. If any values of A do appear, there can be at most one for each value of B.

The authors of Satzinger et al. pretty much stick to extensional considerations in the normalization examples which follow. Intensional elements are mentioned as shortcuts:

The correct answer [to a functional dependency question between catalog and product price]...depends on [the company's] normal conventions for setting product prices in different catalogues. (Satzinger, 2002, p. 406)

As mentioned earlier, conventions are intensional elements.

Many other authors similarly begin with extensional definitions and then use intensional elements as intuitive shortcuts. Thus, Shelly Cashman Rosenblatt (1998, p. 8.16):

Do any of the fields in the...STUDENT record depend on only a portion of the primary key? The student name, total credits, GPA, advisor number and advisor name all relate only to the student number, and have no relationship to the course number.

Awad and Gotterer (1992, pp. 221-222) actually define functional dependency with intensional elements:

> *A* ***functional dependency*** *occurs when a unique value of one attribute can always be determined if* we know (*my italics) the value of another.*

Also Gibson and Hughes (1994, pp. 501-502):

> *A* ***functional dependency*** *is a relation that exists between data items wherein data values for one item are used to identify data values for another data item. Stated another way, if you know the value for data item X, you can functionally determine the value(s) for data item Y.*

Allowing the possibility of multiple values is of course incorrect. Otherwise this is a completely intensional definition of functional dependency.

Whitten, Bentley and Barlow (1989) actually do not use the term functional dependency in defining the normal forms:

> *An entity is in 2NF if it has a* combination *key and all non-key elements are derived by the full key, not part of it. PRODUCT (1989, p. 255)*

And in working out an example, non-key elements are said to be:

> *...elements [that] truly describe a PRODUCT, not an ORDERED PRODUCT (1989, p. 255)*

and thus are to be put into the PRODUCT table rather than the ORDERED PRODUCT table. These authors depend completely upon the intuitive intensional notions of "derivation" and "truly describing" to characterize second and third normal form.

Finally, Kroenke, in *Database Processing,* again explicitly defines functional dependency using intensional terms:

> *If we are given the value of one attribute, we can obtain (or look up) the value of another attribute...In more general terms, attribute Y is functionally dependent on attribute X if the value of X determines the value of Y. Stated differently, if we know the value of X, we can obtain the value of Y. (2002, p. 122)*

It is very easy to fall into the view that some field values have some sort of power to determine other values. Even in mathematics, it is easy to think of a function as "acting" on a set of values (the domain) to produce another set of values (the range). But such thoughts are at best metaphors, because we know that a (mathematical) function is simply a set of ordered pairs with certain properties (Halmos, 1960, pp. 30-31). So, should similar talk of field values "determining" other field values also be taken as metaphors?

THE TRUTH ABOUT FUNCTIONAL DEPENDENCY

I am inclined to believe that the situation with functional dependency is parallel to that of the intension of a term in general: the most promising modern theory of the relation of intension and extension identifies the intension of a term with its extension in all possible worlds (Lewis, 1969, pp. 171-173). The meaning or intension of a term may indeed be exhausted by the extension of that term in all possible worlds. But we do not have access to all possible worlds. Thus, functional dependency may be fully determined by all possible (extensional) combinations of data. But we may not have access to all possible data combinations.

Thus the usefulness of intensional elements in determining normal forms lies in the fact that they allow us to anticipate what further data elements will behave like. However, whether a given set of tables is in first, second or third normal form, at a given moment, depends completely on the extensional pattern of repetitions of data items.

Thus it is possible for a utility such as Analyzer in Microsoft Access to normalize tables without access to the actual meanings of the data items. We can tell that Analyzer is using extensional methods when there are "unusual" repetitions in the data and Analyzer makes the "wrong" choice in dealing with them. Consider Table 1.

We know it is an "accident" that only Fall class information appears here, but Analyzer does not, so it proposes the table structure in Figure 1.

OTHER MATTERS

There are a few other related matters which need to be discussed: first, to what extent primary keys are extensional; second, how this discussion applies to *first* normal form, which, after all, is defined in terms of repeating groups rather than functional dependency; and finally, what are the implications for the *other* normal forms/.

Analyzer's analysis above raises some of the issues. Since a primary key is defined as a unique identifier, we can have extensional criteria for assigning a candidate primary key: The candidate field(s) must not have recurring values anywhere in the table. From an intensional point of view, Analyzer makes a poor decision in choosing StudentFirstName as the primary key. We know that a composite key of StudentFirstName

Table 1.

Class ID	ClassName	DepartmentN	Term	StudentFirstName	StudentLastName	Grade
1	Comp & Lit	English	Fall	Margaret	Peacock	C
1	Comp & Lit	English	Fall	Tim	Smith	A
1	Comp & Lit	English	Fall	Brandon	Coake	B
1	Comp & Lit	English	Fall	Nancy	Davolio	A
1	Comp & Lit	English	Fall	Helvetius	Nagy	B
2	Coll Algebra	Math	Fall	Nancy	Davolio	A
2	Coll Algebra	Math	Fall	Margaret	Peacock	B
2	Coll Algebra	Math	Fall	Matthew	Dunn	B
2	Coll Algebra	Math	Fall	Helvetius	Nagy	B+
2	Coll Algebra	Math	Fall	Deborah	Peterson	A
3	Databases	Compu Inf	Fall	Tim	Smith	A
3	Databases	Compu Inf	Fall	Margaret	Peacock	A
3	Databases	Compu Inf	Fall	Helvetius	Nagy	A
3	Databases	Compu Inf	Fall	Nancy	Davolio	A
3	Databases	Compu Inf	Fall	Matthew	Dunn	A

Figure 1.

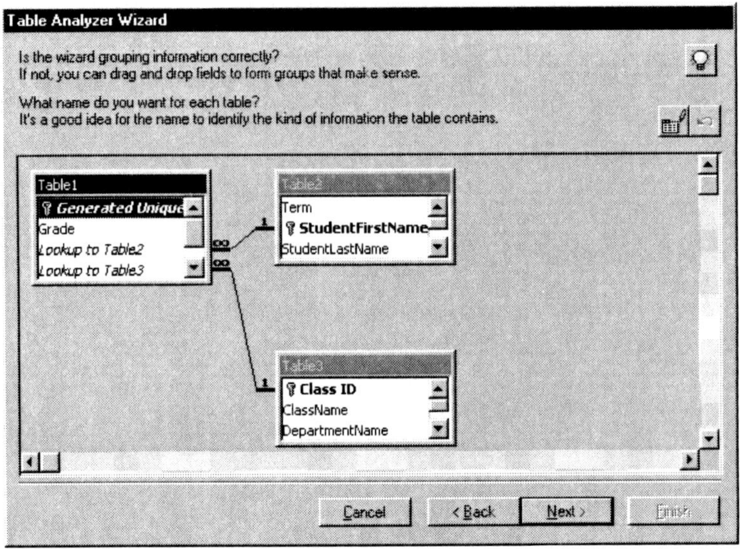

and StudentLastName would be better, and that an assigned ID key would be best. Once again, if we had all the data, Analyzer would get it right.

If one is dealing only with extensional patterns of repetition, functional dependency itself is a matter of repeating groups. Thus we see Analyzer treat all issues such as choice of primary key, repeating groups and functional dependencies as a matter of repetitions of field values within a table. Since these days all database design is likely to take place in a table environment, the older characterization of first normal form as extra sub-rows within a row can't be directly represented. Instead, to make the data fit in a table, the (formerly) non-repeating information repeats. Thus in the StudentClass table above, either ClassID-ClassName-DepartmentName-Term could be viewed as a repeating group, or StudentFirstName-StudentLastName could be viewed as a repeating group.

Or, instead, one could simply begin with the table above and check for second and third normal form. Satzinger et al. (2002, pp. 406-409) are very good at doing this, but they do explicitly suggest that using only extensional methods is "tricky" and recommend looking for intensional information about the underlying entities.

Alternatively, I will outline at the end of the chapter what I call "Quick and Dirty Normal Form," which is intended to be an extensional method of reaching third normal form from an initial table in a relational database. It suffers, of course, from our recognized limitation that if the data is incomplete in the wrong way, the results may not be good.

Finally, there remain the implications of what I have said for the "higher" normal forms, that is, fourth normal form, fifth normal form, Boyce-Codd normal form and domain key normal form. Since Boyce-Codd normal form uses the concept of functional dependency in its formulations, I need to say something about it. Although the topic of this chapter is functional dependency, which is not a primary element in the formulation of fourth and fifth normal form and domain key normal form, it makes sense to ask whether the additional concepts used in these "higher" normal forms are also fundamentally extensional in nature.

For Boyce-Codd normal form, we need to check whether every field, on which other fields are functionally dependent, is potentially a key (that is, has unique values for each record). Since, as we have seen, functional dependency and primary keys are extensional matters, so also should be ascertaining Boyce-Codd normal form.

Fourth normal form adds the concept of *multi-valued dependency*. One definition: in a table R with columns A, B and C, B is multi-valued dependent on A if there is more than one value of B for a single value of A. IF C is also multi-valued dependent on A, anomalies (mainly update anomalies) arise. (In fact, three is smallest set of attributes exhibiting multi-valued dependencies.) A set of tables is in fourth normal form if there are no multi-valued dependencies present. Thus multi-valued dependency is clearly an extensional matter, having to do with whether or not there are certain repetitions of values in a table or not. So even though multi-valued dependency is different from functional dependency, it can be defined and treated using only extensional considerations.

Fifth normal form uses the concept of join dependency rather than functional dependency. Join dependency states that any decomposition of tables must be able to be rejoined to recover the original table. Tables in fifth normal form are join dependent. Failure to achieve fifth normal form is normally uncovered when data is added to the decomposed tables. Then it is discovered that the rejoined tables contain spurious data.

The discussion likely to take place concerning join dependency is similar to that which takes place when design decisions are made on the basis of the "wrong" set of data. It seems even more likely that intensional characteristics will help with fifth normal form than the other normal forms, because join dependency cannot be determined by simply looking at the data. It is not clear whether anything other than an iterative trial-and-error procedure is possible for detecting join dependency. These considerations are clearly extensional, since they depend only upon patterns of field values in joined and unjoined tables. But that does not make the process of determining fifth normal form any easier.

Domain key normal form (DK/NF) is different. There is no algorithm for doing DK/NF. DK/NF seems to be motivated by an attempt to formalize an intensional definition of functional dependency. The actual concepts involved, however, are extensional. My conclusions about what this means are tentative.

The definition of domain key normal form (DK/NF) is that every constraint on the values of attributes is a logical consequence of the definition of keys and domains (Kroenke, 2002, p. 134). What is being formalized is the picture of field values "determining" others by relations of meaning or knowledge. This was exactly what we found to be the use of intensional elements in doing the lower-order normal forms.

However, in the original formulation of DK/NF by Fagin (1981), all the central concepts needed are defined extensionally. It is worth looking at these definitions to see whether the result is still extensional or not, especially since Fagin is explicitly trying to replace the notion of functional dependency with a broader notion. Also, it is universally acknowledged that there is no algorithm for putting a set of tables into DK/NF. Yet if all the concepts involved are extensional, it would seem as though an algorithm should be possible. Fagin's concepts as used in DK/NF are different enough from functional dependency to require a more extensive examination than is possible here. I hope to complete this examination in the near future.

CONCLUSIONS

My conclusions:

1) Normalization (1nf, 2nf, 3nf) can be done of the basis of (extensional) patterns of repetitions in field values alone.
2) However, intensional elements (meanings or definitions of field names, conventions, business rules, definitions of domains) are indispensable in practice because we usually do not have access to all possible data.
3) The higher-order normal forms, Boyce-Codd normal form and fourth normal form use straightforward extensions of the (extensional) concept of functional dependency.
4) The concept of join dependency underlying fifth normal form also seems to be extensional but quite a bit more difficult to apply, because it depends not only on all possible data, but on all possible decompositions and recompositions of groups of tables.
5) Domain key normal form seems to be a formulation of an intensional view of dependencies between field values. As such, it seems to function more as a guiding ideal than as a practically usable formulation.

QUICK & DIRTY NORMAL FORM (FOR USE WITH MICROSOFT ACCESS)

1) Put all fields into one table using "create table by entering data."
2) Make a couple of backups of the table.
3) Enter a fair amount of data, probably 10-20 records.
4) Use a (select) query to select any group of fields that repeat together, with Unique Values property set to Yes.
5) Rerun the query as a make-table query.
6) Select or add a primary key for the new table.
7) Remove all non-key duplicated fields from the old table.
8) Repeat Steps three through five until only primary keys are redundant when original datasheet is displayed.
9) Set concatenated primary key in original table.
10) Run Analyzer on a backup and compare results.

REFERENCES

Awad & Gotterer (1992). *Database Management.* Danvers, MA: Southwest.

Fagin, R. (1981). A normal form for relational databases that is based on domains and keys. *ACM Transactions on Database Systems,* 6(3), 387-415.

Frege, G. (1892). On sense and reference. In Geach, P.T. & Black, M. (Eds.). (1952). Translation of "Ueber Sinn und Bedeutung." *Zeitschrift fuer Philosophie und Philosophische Kritik,* 100, 25-50.

Geach, P.T. & Black, M. (Eds.). (1952). *Translations from the Philosophical Writings of Gottlob Frege.* Oxford: Blackwell.

Gibson & Hughes (1994). *Systems Analysis and Design*. Danvers, MA: Boyd & Fraser.
Halmos, P. (1960). *Naive Set Theory*. Princeton: Van Nostrand.
Kroenke, D. (2002). *Database Processing* (8th edition). Upper Saddle River, NJ: Prentice-Hall.
Lewis, C.I. & Langford, C.H. (1959). *Symbolic Logic*. New York: Dover.
Lewis, D. (1969). *Convention*. Cambridge, MA: Harvard.
Martin, J. (1983). *Managing the Database Environment*. Englewood Cliffs, NJ: Prentice-Hall.
Satzinger, Jackson & Burd (2002). *Systems Analysis in a Changing World* (2nd edition). Cambridge, MA: Course Technology.
Shelly, Cashman & Rosenblatt (1988). *Systems Analysis and Design* (3rd edition). Cambridge, MA: Course Technology.
Whitten, Bentley, & Barlow (1989). *Systems Analysis and Design Methods* (2nd edition). Boston, MA: Irwin.

Chapter XVII

Dealing with Relationship Cardinality Constraints in Relational Database Design

Dolores Cuadra Fernández
Universidad Carlos III de Madrid, Spain

Paloma Martínez Fernández
Universidad Carlos III de Madrid, Spain

Elena Castro Galán
Universidad Carlos III de Madrid, Spain

ABSTRACT

Conceptual models are well-known tools to achieve a good design of information systems. Nevertheless, the understanding and use of all the constructs and constraints which are presented in such models are not an easy task and sometimes it is cause of loss of interest.

In this chapter we have tried to study in depth and clarify the meaning of the features of conceptual models. The disagreements between main conceptual models, the confusion in the use of some of their constructs and some open problems in these models are shown. Another important topic treated in this chapter is the conceptual-to-logic schemata transformation process.

Some solutions are presented in order to clarify the relationship construct and to extend the cardinality constraint concept in ternary relationships. How to preserve the cardinality constraint semantics in binary and ternary relationships for their implementation in a DBMS with active capabilities has also been developed.

INTRODUCTION

Database modeling is a complex task that involves conceiving, understanding, structuring and describing real Universes of Discourse (UD) through the definition of schemata using abstraction processes and data models. Traditionally, three phases are identified in database design: conceptual, logical and physical design. The conceptual modeling phase represents the most abstract level since it is independent of any Database Management System (DBMS) and, consequently, it is very close to the user and allows him to collect almost completely the semantics of the real world to be modeled.

A conceptual schema, independently of the data formalism used, plays two main roles in the conceptual design phase: a *semantic* role, in which user requirements are gathered together and the entities and relationships in a UD are documented, and a *representational* role that provides a framework that allows a mapping to the logical design of database development. Three topics are involved in the database conceptual modeling process: data modeling formalism, methodological approach and CASE tool support. One of the most extended data modeling formalisms, the Extended Entity Relationship (EER) model has proven to be a precise and comprehensive tool for representing data requirements in information systems development, mainly due to an adequate degree of abstraction of the constructs that it includes. Although the original ER model was proposed by Chen (1976), many extensions and variations as well as different diagrammatic styles have been defined (Hull & King, 1987; McAllister, 1998; Peckhan & Maryanski, 1988).

In database conceptual analysis, among the most difficult concepts to be modeled are relationships, especially higher-order relationships, as well as their associated cardinalities. Some textbooks (Boman et al., 1997; Ullman & Widom, 1997) assume that any conceptual design can be addressed by considering only binary relationships since its aim is to create a computer-oriented model. We understand the advantages of this approach although we believe that it may produce certain loss of semantics (some biases are introduced in user requirements) and it forces one to represent information in rather artificial and sometimes unnatural ways.

Concerning the logical design, the transformation process of conceptual schemata into relational schemata should be performed trying to completely preserve the semantics included in the conceptual schema; the final objective is to keep the semantics in the database itself and not in the applications accessing the database. Nevertheless, sometimes a certain loss of semantics is produced, for instance, foreign key and not null options in the relational model are not enough to control ER cardinality constraints.

This chapter is devoted to the study of the transformation of conceptual into logical schemata in a methodological framework focusing on a special ER construct: the relationship and its associated cardinality constraints. The section entitled "EER Model Revisited: Relationships and Cardinality Constraint" reviews the relationship and cardinality constraint constructs through different methodological approaches in order to establish the cardinality constraint definition that will follow. In this section a cardinality constraint definition is adopted and some extensions are proposed in order to collect more semantics in a conceptual schemata that incorporates higher-order relationships. The "Transformation of EER Schemata into Relational Schemata" section is related to the transformation of conceptual relationships into the relational model following an active rules approach. Finally, several practical implications are offered, and future research is discussed.

EER MODEL REVISITED: RELATIONSHIPS AND CARDINALITY CONSTRAINTS

This section reviews entity, relationship and cardinality constraint constructs of different data models in order to highlight some special semantic problems derived from the different methodological approaches given to them. The EER model (Teorey, Yang & Fry, 1986) is considered as the basic framework to study the different meanings of cardinality constraints. The objective is to make a profound study of the different cardinality constraints definitions as well as the implications of their usage.

Basic Concepts: Entities, Relationships and Cardinality Constraints

The central concepts of the ER model are entities and relationships; these constructs were introduced by Chen (1976) and have been incorporated in other conceptual models although with different names[1]: class, type, etc., for entities and associations for relationships. Nevertheless, those concepts do not have a precise semantics and, consequently, it is necessary to fix their meaning.

In spite of the fact that the entity concept is widely used and accepted, there is no agreement on a definition; for instance, Thalheim (2000) collects 12 different entity denotations. Although experts are not able to give a unique definition, the underlying concept is coincident in all of them and its usage as a design element does not suppose great disadvantages. An extensive entity definition is not given here, but to highlight: according to Thalheim (2000) an entity is a *representation* abstraction with modeling purposes. Date (1986) adds that the represented concept is a distinguishable object, but we do no consider this feature essential because it depends on the designer point of view.

The relationship concept is more confusing; it is defined as an *association* among entities. This definition offers many interpretations; for instance, in several design methods there are some differences depending on whether relationships can participate in other relationships as in HERM (Thalheim, 2000), by means of association entities as in UML, OMG (2000) or by grouping as clusters a set of entities and relationships (Teorey, 1999). These differences are due to the fact that a relationship combines *association* features with *representation* features and therefore it might be considered as a relationship (if association aspects are highlighted) or as an entity (if representation aspects are emphasized). For instance, a marriage can be seen as a relationship (association between two people) or as an entity (representation of a social and legal concept) and both of them are possible. This duality is a source of design problems.

Previous comments are based on several experiments described in Batra and Antony (1994) and Batra and Zanakis (1994), proving that novice designers do not have any difficulty representing entities and attributes because they are simple concepts and easily identifiable from specifications. However, the identification of relationships and their properties is more complicated. They argue that the large number of combinations for a given set of entities is an obstacle in detecting relationships and, consequently, more design errors appear.

Apart from these definitions, the linguistic level applied to these concepts is very important; it is required to distinguish between entity/relationship and occurrences of an entity/relationship. In the first case, there is an algebraic or abstract data type perspective that groups a set of possible values that are being represented (or associated) and, in the second case, an occurrence references a specific value of an entity or relationship.

Finally, depending of the number of entities related, we distinguish binary relationships if they associate two entities and higher-order relationships if they associate three or more entities.

The definition of the relationship concept is very important in order to interpret the corresponding cardinality constraints; below, the most relevant definitions and their similarities are exposed. In this section the definition of relationship is equivalent to the definition of relationship type that appears in almost textbooks concerning the EER model; this relationship construct has a name and a set of properties. The values associated to a relationship are called instances. In order to simplify the explanation of this section, the attributes of a relationship are not considered.

McAllister (1998) defines a relationship as the need of storing associations among entity instances. Each relationship has two or more roles that specify the link between the entity and the relationship.

For example, the relationship *Provide* (Figure 1) has three roles and consequently is a ternary relationship. Usually, the names of the roles do not appear in the representation of a relationship type excepting if an entity participates with different roles in the same relationship.

An instance of a relationship is a tuple (e_1, e_2, ..., e_n) where *n* represents the number of roles and each e_i is a key instance for the entity participant in the i-th role. In the example of Figure 1, several examples of relationship instances are shown in Table 1.

Another way of defining a relationship is through the *links* (Elmasri & Navathe, 2000). A link R among *n* entities $E_1 \ldots E_n$ represents a set of associations among these

Figure 1. Ternary Relationship Example

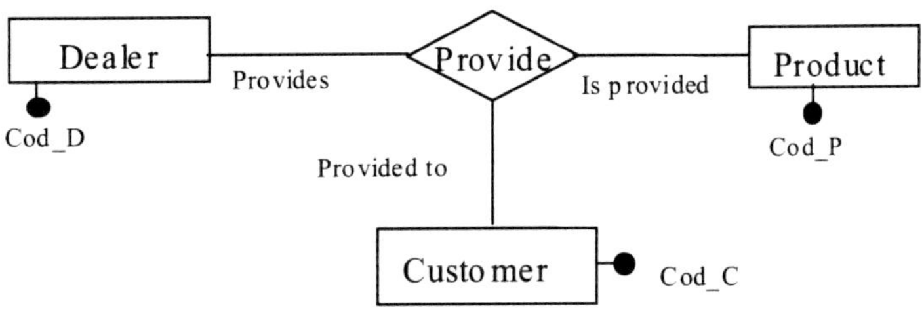

Table 1. Examples of Relationship Instances

Cod_D	Cod_P	Cod_C
100	P01	3000
100	P02	3000
200	P01	1000

entities. In a formal way, R is a set of link instances r_i where each r_i associates *n* individual entities (e_1, ..., e_n) and each e_j of r_i is a member of entity E_j, $1 \leq j \leq n$. In summary, a link is a subset of the Cartesian product E_1 x...x E_n. In the example of Figure 1, a link instance could be $Provide_j$ = (100, P01, 3000).

In fact, the only difference among the two previous definitions is the way of naming the relationship. Another important aspect concerns the multiple participation of an entity in an n-ary relationship (n>2). In both definitions it is allowed, but in McAllister (1998) this multiple participation is more clear due to different roles that could be associated to the entity in order to distinguish different participations in the relationship.

A more general and less restricted definition is given in Thalheim (2000) where relationships are decomposed in two types: first and higher order. A first-order relationship has the form R = ({E_1, ..., E_n}), where R is the name of the relationship and {E_1, ..., E_n} is a sequence of entities or entity *clusters.*[2] An instance of R, taking into account that only entities participate in the relationship, in a given moment t, E_1^t, ..., E_n^t is called r and is an element of the Cartesian product $R^t \subset E_1^t$x...x E_n^t. This definition is very similar to McAllister (1998) but includes a new element, the cluster, that extends the definition.

The (i+1)-order relationship is defined as the association of a set of entities and relationships or cluster of order not higher than i for i>0. Formally, R = (ent(R), rel(R)) where R is the name of the (i+1)-order relationship, ent(R) is a sequence of entities or entity clusters {E_1, ..., E_k} and rel(R) is a sequence of relationships of order not higher than i or clusters of the set {E_1, ..., E_k, R_1, ..., R_j} with at least a relationship. An instance of an (i+1)-order relationship where only entities and relationships, in a given moment t, is defined as an element of the Cartesian product $R^t \subset E_1^t$x...x E_n^t x R_1^tx...x R_j^t.

The ORM model (Halpin, 2001) does not use the relationship construct; the associations among objects are represented as a set of predicates that are distinguished by a name and are applied to a set of roles forming a set of *facts*. Although the representation is different, the concept itself is the same; the definition of association is similar to McAllister (1998).

The four previous approaches share a common view that consists of presenting the instances of a relationship as elements of the Cartesian product of participant entity instances, although Thalheim (2000) includes a new constructor, the cluster, and allows associations among relationships. In our exposition we will adopt the work of McAllister (1998) that allows us to present the cardinality constraints in the next section.

MAIN CARDINALITY CONSTRAINT APPROACHES

In this section, the most extended data models with their corresponding cardinality constraint approaches are studied. Two main approaches are discussed:

1) Chen's constraint is one extension of the mapping constraint (a special case of cardinality constraint that considers only the maximum cardinality and that for binary relationships can be 1:1, 1:N or N:M) (Chen, 1976). This constraint has been adopted or extended in different data models and methodologies.
2) The MERISE approach (Tardieu, 1989) incorporates the participation semantics.

These two approaches meet each other when cardinality constraints for binary relationships are defined (excepting the natural differences in graphical notations). Both of them represent the same semantics in binary relationships although the way of expressing it is different.

Binary Relationships

Figure 2 shows an example of cardinality constraint over a binary association using UML notation (OMG, 2000); it is called multiplicity constraint and it represents that an employee works in one department (graphically denoted by a continuous line) and that at least one employee works in each department (graphically denoted by a black circle with the tag +1). Minimum multiplicity of 1 in both sides forces all objects belonging to the two classes to participate in the association. Maximum multiplicity of *n* in *Employee* class indicates that a department has n employees, and maximum multiplicity of 1 in *Department* means that for each employee there is only one department. Consequently, UML multiplicity follows Chen's style because to achieve the cardinality constraints of one class, the process is to fix an object of the other class and to obtain how many objects are related to it.

Figure 3 illustrates the same example but using MERISE methodology (Tardieu, 1989); cardinality constraints represent that an occurrence of Employee entity participates once in the *Works* relationship and an occurrence of Department entity participates at least once in the relationship.

Figure 2. Cardinality Constraints Using XML

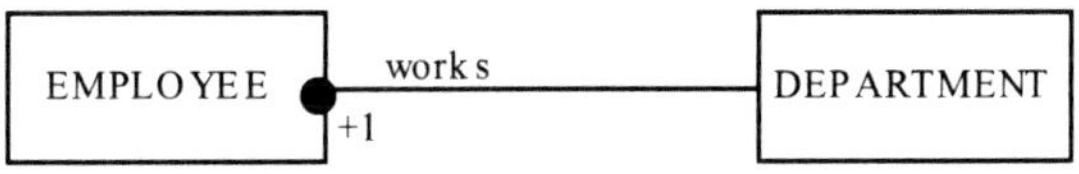

Figure 3. Cardinality Constraints Using MERISE

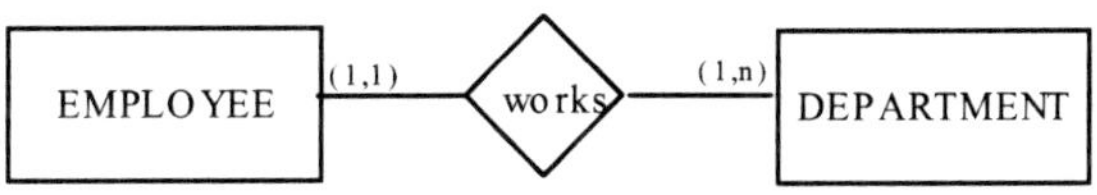

Figure 4. Cardinality Constraints Using ER Model

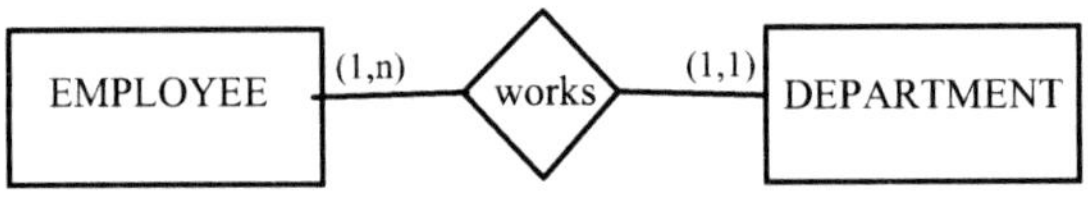

Figure 5. Cardinality Constraints Using Teorey Model

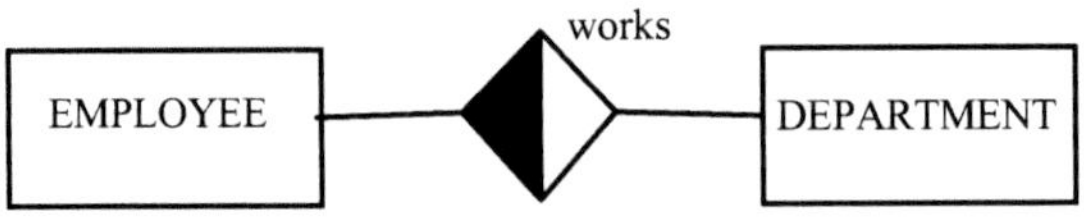

Notice that both examples represent the same semantics although expressed in different ways. Figure 4 shows Chen's notation of *Works* relationship. Comparing to MERISE notation, cardinality tags are exchanged (in MERISE notation cardinality tag is situated near the constrained entity, and in Chen notation the cardinality tag is located in the opposite ending). This difference reflects the distinct perspective adopted by these methodologies: MERISE methodology constraints the *participation of an entity* in the relationship and Chen methodology limits the *participation of a combination of the other entity(ies)* with an entity in the relationship. Thus sometimes a conceptual schema could be misunderstood if it had been created using another methodology. Figure 5 shows the same constraint expressed in the Teorey notation (Teorey, Yang & Fry, 1986); the shaded area represents a maximum cardinality of *n*. With this graphical notation only maximum cardinalities of 1 or *n* and minimum cardinalities of 0 or 1 are allowed.

Table 2 gives a summary of aforementioned concepts for binary relationships (A and B are entities participating in the relationship).

Table 2. Cardinality Constraints Summary for Binary Relationships

	Minimum Cardinality	Maximum Cardinality
0	*Optional*	*Inapplicable:* There are no occurrences in the relationship
1	*Mandatory:* It is mandatory that all occurrences of entity *A* participate in the relationship (there are at least an occurrence of entity B related to each occurrence of entity *A*).	*Determination*[1] *or Uniqueness:* There are at most an occurrence of entity *B* related to each occurrence of entity *B*.
k (>1)	*k-Mandatory:* It is mandatory that each occurrence of entity A participates at least *k* times in the relationship (there are at least *k* occurrences of entity *B* related to each occurrence of entity *A*).	*k-Limit:* There are at most *k* occurrences of entity *B* related to each occurrence of entity *A*.
N	*Without limit of minimum participation.*	*Without limit of maximum participation.*

Figure 6. Ternary Relationships versus Binary Relationships (First Solution)

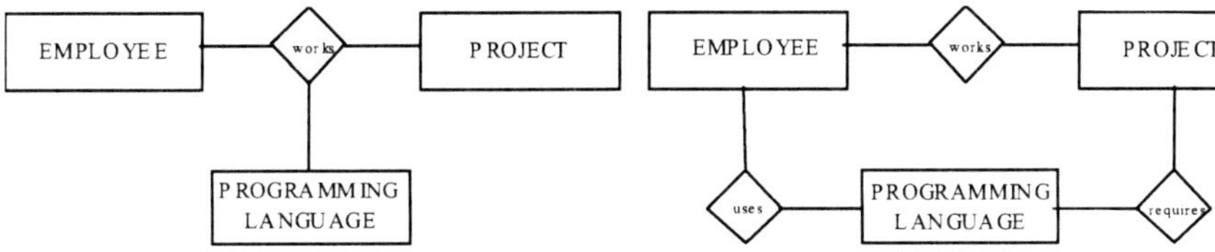

Higher-Order Relationships

In database conceptual modeling binary relationships are the most frequently used, in fact there are several data models that only allow this kind of relationship—see NIAM (Nijssen & Halpin, 1989). That is why most methodologies—see MERISE (Tardieu, 1989), OMT, (Rumbaugh, Blaha & Premerlani, 1991), UML, (OMG, 2000) and Teorey (1999)—do not put the emphasis on n-ary relationships (n>2). Although higher relationships are not so common, sometimes it is not possible to completely represent the UD using binary relationships; for instance, to represent the database requirement, "*it is required to know the programming languages used by the employees in the projects they are working,*" a ternary relationship would reflect this requirement,[4] while three binary relationships would not be able to represent the whole semantics (Figure 6); the combination of binary relationships *Works*, *Uses* and *Requires* would neither allow one to know the programming languages that a specific employee uses in a specific project nor the projects in which a specific employee is working with a specific programming language.

The suggested solution provided by the data models that exclusively consider binary relationships is to transform the higher-order relationship into one or more entities and to add binary relationships with the remaining entities (Ullman & Widom, 1997; Boman et al., 1997). Figure 7 shows this solution where an entity *Task* is introduced; three binary relationships connect entity *Task* with *Employee* and *Project* with *Programming Language* entities. The principal advantage of this approach is that it is nearer to relational model and thus, closer to implementation . However, this approach implies inclusion of entities that are not explicitly exposed in the UD and addition of complex constraints to keep the correct semantics. With these models, designer perspective is conditioned and the conceptual schema obtained could result in an artificial schema.

Keeping in mind that higher-order relationships are necessary in database conceptual modeling, several methodologies have generalized the cardinality constraint defi-

Figure 7. Ternary Relationships versus Binary Relationships (Second Solution)

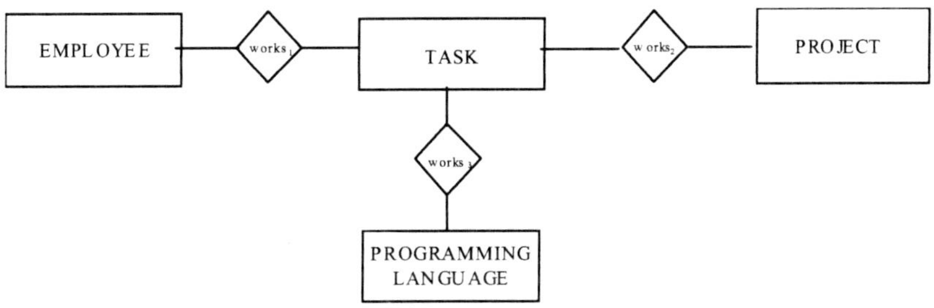

nition of binary relationships (in the two approaches previously commented), raising some difficulties that are explained below.

First, there is an inconsistency problem, depending on the adopted approach, because higher-order relationships do not represent the same semantics as binary relationships. Figures 8 and 9 represent Chen and MERISE cardinality constraints, respectively, for the semantic constraint: "an employee works in several projects and (s)he could use a programming language in each of them."

In the Chen approach the cardinality constraint of an entity depends on the remaining entities that participate in the relationship; thus, there are several problems in order to scale up his definition from binary to higher-order relationships, since the remaining entities could be combined in different ways. However, the most frequent generalization determines that a combination of all remaining entities is used in specifying the cardinality constraints of only one entity. Therefore, using the ER model notation in order to obtain the cardinality constraint of *Programming Language* entity (Figure 8), it is firstly to fix two occurrences of *Employee* and *Project* entities that are related by *Works* relationship and then to count the number of times (minimum and maximum) that occurrences of *Programming Language* entity could appear related to. Next, the same procedure is applied to *Project* entity (with pairs of *Programming Language* and *Employee* occurrences) and to *Employee* entity (with pairs of *Project* and *Programming Language* occurrences).

Figure 8 illustrates that minimum cardinality of Programming Language entity is 0, that is, there are occurrences of *Works* relationship that associate occurrences of *Employee* and *Project* entities, but with no occurrence of *Programming Language.*[5] This circumstance causes problems in identifying the relationship occurrences. The relationship is capable of representing occurrences with unknown information (the case of *Programming Language* in the example).

Figure 8. ER Cardinality Constraints Using Chen's Style

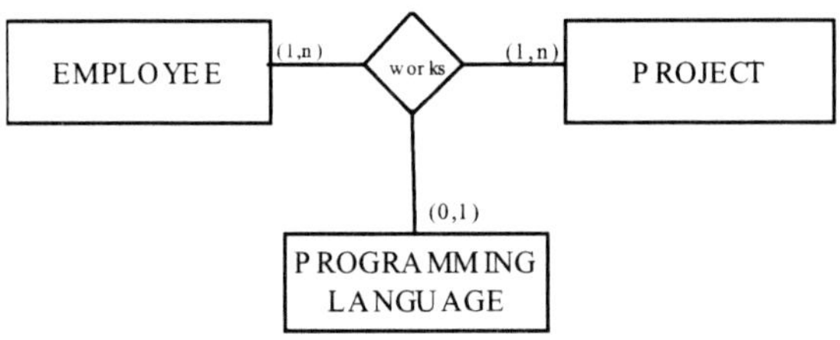

Figure 9. ER Cardinality Constraints Using MERISE Approach

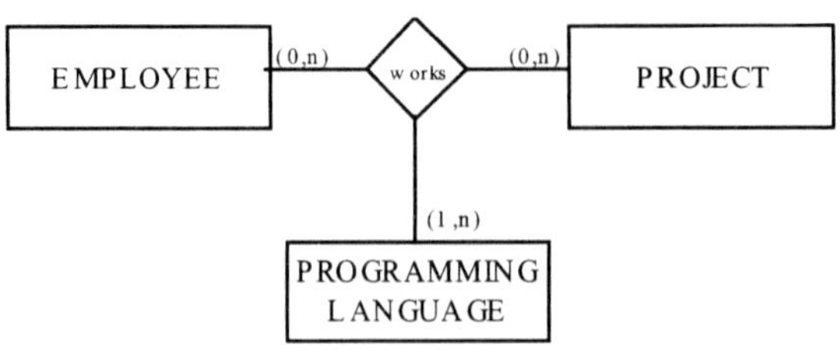

Figure 10. An Example of Functional Integrity Constraint in MERISE

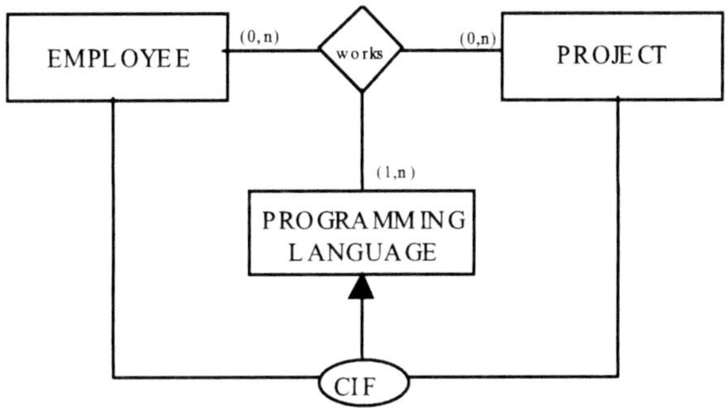

In summary, opposed to MERISE methodology, Chen's style presents three main problems: generalization, difficulty of the treatment of unknown information in relationships and the lack of information about the participation of each occurrence of associated entities. In contrast, generalization of cardinality constraint definition in MERISE methodology does not pose any problem because the semantics of cardinality constraints is the same in binary and higher-order relationships. Figure 9 illustrates an example of the *Works* ternary relationship; the cardinality constraint of *Programming Language* is obtained by counting the number of appearances of a specific *Programming Language* occurrence in the *Works* relationship. The cardinality constraints of *Employee* and *Project* entities are obtained in the same way.

Additionally, MERISE methodology includes a new construct called Functional Integrity Constraint (CIF[6]) which represents that one of the participating entities is completely determined by a combination of a subset of the other entities (an example is shown in Figure 10). Moreover, these CIF constraints have many implications in decomposing higher-order relationships as well as in transforming them into the relational model.

Therefore, the MERISE approach has two constructs to represent cardinality constraints, while the Chen approach only uses one. On the other hand, CIF constraints do not satisfactorily resolve the treatment of unknown information. Finally, minimum cardinality constraint in MERISE approach represents optional/mandatory participation[7] and, thus, maximum cardinality constraint typically will be *n*.

Table 3 (Soutou, 1998) shows the differences between the two approaches for cardinality constraints when higher-order relationships are transformed into the relational model.

Adopting a Cardinality Constraint Definition

The decision about adopting a cardinality constraint definition has several theoretical and practical consequences. Let the ternary relationship represent the requirement, "*There are writers that write books that may be concerning different topics.*" Figure 11 shows the conceptual schema solution using MERISE definition with the next interpretation: there may be occurrences of all entities that do not participate in the occurrences of *Writes* relationship. In this way, less semantics is represented by the cardinality constraints because it is not known how the participation of any of the *Author*,

Table 3. Summary of the Differences Among Cardinality Constraints

Cardinality	Models based on the ER model (MER)	Models based on Participation Constraint (MPC)
Min 0	Presence of NULL values	No constraint
Min 1	No constraint	An occurrence of the entity relation cannot exist in the n-ary relationship without being implicated in one occurrence
Min (n)	For each (n-1) record there are at least more than one occurrences for the other single in the n-ary relationship	An occurrence of the entity relation cannot exist in the n-ary relationship without being implicated in many occurrences
Max 1	For each (n-1) record there is a unique occurrence for the other single column in the n-ary relationship	Unique value for the column (No duplicates)
Max (n)	For each (n-1) record there is more than one occurrence for the other single column in the n-ary relationship	No constraint

Book or *Topic* entities in the relationship affects the participation of the remaining entities. Moreover, it is impossible to represent that there can be anonymous books, *Books concerning one or more Topics without Author.*

From Chen's perspective, the example could be modeled in two semantically equivalent ways (Figures 12 and 13), both of them considering anonymous books. The first solution is more compact although more complex: a unique ternary relationship collects the association semantics. The second solution is more intuitive because the ternary relationship reflects the books whose authors are known and the binary relationship that represents the anonymous books. The choice of a final solution depends on the designer perspective about the UD.

Both solutions imply that it is necessary to check that a specific book does not simultaneously appear as an anonymous book and a book with known author. In the first solution, this constraint could be modeled as a disjoint constraint among the occurrences of the ternary relationship while, in the second solution, it could be modeled as an exclusive-or constraint between the two relationships,[8] that is the pair *Book-Topic* that appears in the ternary relationship occurrences does not appear in any binary relationship occurrence in the case that the model includes this kind of constraint.

If the first solution is adopted, a review of the relationship definition is required due to the fact that occurrences of a relationship are a subset of the Cartesian product of the

Figure 11. Ternary Relationship Using MERISE Cardinality Constraints

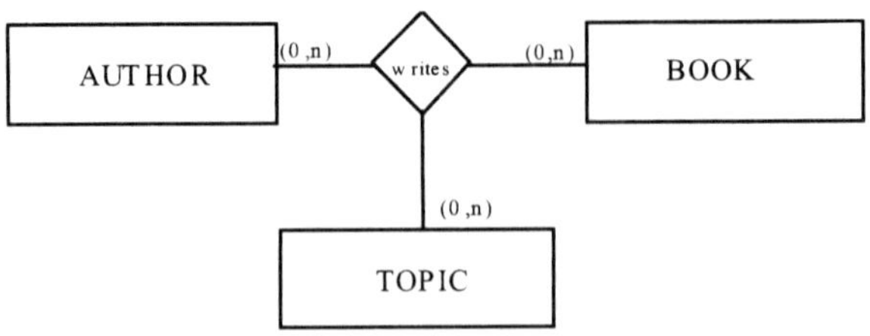

Figure 12. Ternary Relationship Using Chen's Style (First Solution)

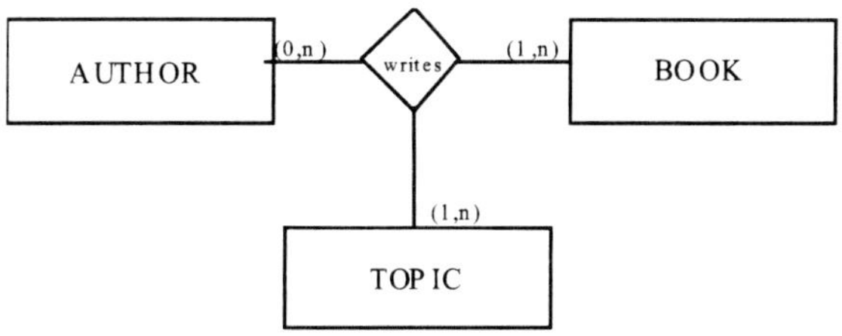

Figure 13. Ternary Relationship Using Chen's Style (Second Solution)

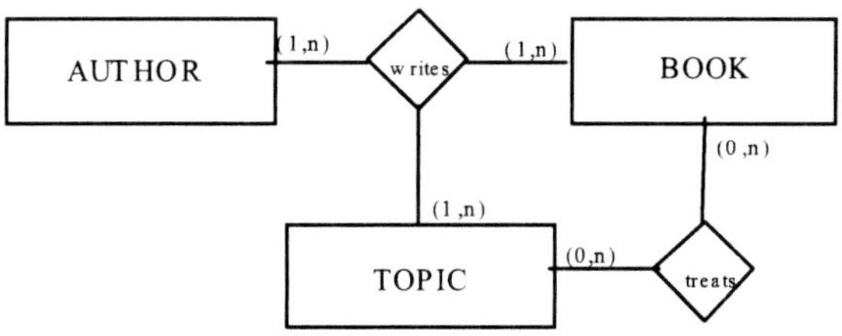

participant entity occurrences. If we admit a 0 minimum cardinality, it is supposed that the corresponding *Author* entity could have null values inside the relationship *Writes*.

If one of the main objectives of a conceptual model consists of an easy interpretation of the provided constructs as well as an easy application, then this first solution is not adequate. If we think of the second solution, this fits the relationship definition but does not support the associated semantics because the relationship *Treats* has a main feature that is formed by occurrences that do not take part of *Writes* occurrences, although they are semantically related. In summary, *Treats* is not any binary relationship whatsoever between *Book* and *Topic;* it is a semantically related relationship to *Writes* association.

Once the different interpretations and problems of cardinality constraints in binary and higher-order relationships have been exposed, our effort has to be focused on the next items:

1) The representation of Chen and MERISE cardinalities, due to each one specifying different properties of a Universe of Discourse.
2) To include a construct to represent semantically related relationships that cope with incomplete, unknown or not applicable information in a ternary relationship.

Figure 14 shows both Chen and MERISE cardinalities applied to the previous example concerning the relationship *Writes*. It can be observed that MERISE constraints are displayed as a tag in the line that links the entity to the relationship, near the diamond that represents the relationship. Chen constraints associated to an entity are located near the entity.

To solve the problem of incomplete, unknown or not applicable information, we propose to include a new construct called Complementary-Relationship (R^C) as is shown in Figure 15.

Figure 14. Ternary Relationship Using MERISE and Chen Cardinality Constraints

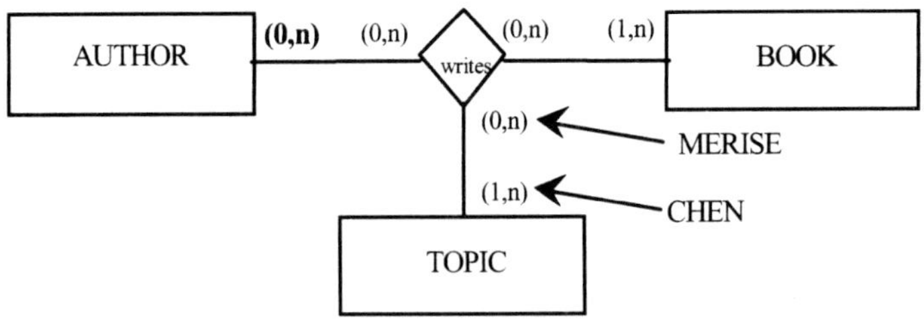

It can be noticed that Chen cardinality has been simplified because by including this new construct, the default minimum cardinality value is 1. If this cardinality is higher that 1, then this cardinality will be represented in the schema using a range (for instance, 2..*). The complementary-relationship *Writes*^{C} has the following properties:

a) It is a binary relationship.
b) The default cardinality is (0,n) although other cardinalities could also be considered.
c) pop(*Writes*)∩pop(*Writes*^{C}) = {}, where pop represent the relationship instances.

The cardinalities associated with this relationship are (0,n); this result can be fully studied in the work presented in Jones and Song (1998). In McAllister (1998) consistency rules for cardinality constraints in n-ary relationships are described. We have to lean on those rules to validate the EER schemata.

Some Reflections

After reviewing ER constructs, it seems necessary to deepen the definition, foundations, constructs and notation of the ER model, in order to achieve a conceptual tool able to reflect the situations that frequently appear in data modeling scenarios. Hence, redefinition of the ER model, taking into account previous aspects as well as the development of a wider notation, are tasks to be dealt with.

The detection and specification of abstractions in a UD that lead to correct and complete schemata are critical problems that combine psychological and methodological aspects. There are many other aspects associated with the specification of constraints. Their identification and validation require more formal treatments. Identification can be

Figure 15. Ternary Relationship Using Complementary Relations (Writes^C*)*

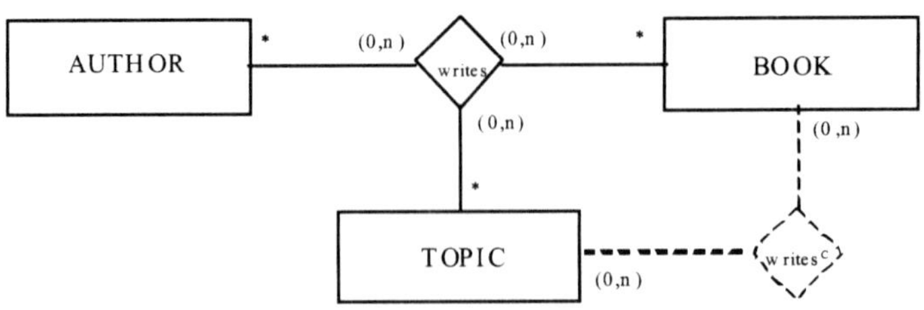

faced to a lexical analysis of a problem description. Syntactic and semantic validation of relationships is a critical aspect of internal coherence with the UD. All these topics are not analyzed in this chapter.

In this section a set of problems related to cardinality constraints and its influence on the other ER constructs have been analyzed, and important inconsistencies concerning this kind of constraint have been highlighted.

In order to solve these ambiguities, we propose to introduce a new notation and a new construct type for ternary relationships. The objective is to unify both types of cardinality constraints, Chen and MERISE approaches, in a coherent way with the definition of a relationship. This implies a greater simplicity in understanding these important constraints. Although the representation is a little more complex, especially if we study the generalization of the proposal, it is more complete due to the information required to represent any n-ary relationship that appears in the EER schema.

It is necessary to remark that if one of the Chen or MERISE cardinality constraints is adopted, then this cardinality allows us to specify only part of the semantics associated to a relationship (Génova, Llorens & Martínez, 2001).

The validation of cardinalities could be achieved by using the rules presented in McAllister (1998), both for cardinalities associated to a ternary relationship and the complementary relationship. In a first approach, the results explained in Jones and Song (1998) are used. These complementary relationships are called IBCs (Implicit Binary Constraints) and their cardinalities are (0, n) if they do not have any additional constraints.

The next section explains some topics involved in how to transform relationships into the relational model, trying to preserve the original EER semantics.

TRANSFORMATION OF EER SCHEMATA INTO RELATIONAL SCHEMATA

The major difficulty when transforming an EER schema into a schema relational is information preservation, generally to achieve a complete mapping between both models and to keep their inherent and semantic restrictions from an EER model to a relational model; the latter is quite complicated. Usually, restrictions that cannot be applied in the relational model must be reflected in the application programs in some different way, i.e., outside the DBMS. In this way, there are several extensions to the relational model proposed by Codd (1970, 1979), Date (1995) and Teorey (1999) that provide a more semantic model.

The principal transformation rules are described in most database textbooks (Elmasri & Navathe, 2000; Date, 1995; Ramakrishnan, 1997). In this section, we will show the transformation of relationships into a relational model.

A correct transformation of schemata and constraints expressed in them is necessary in order to preserve their intended meaning. Although initially the standard relational model (Codd, 1970) was insufficient to reflect all the semantics that could be present in a conceptual schema, it has been enhanced with specific elements that are used to preserve the original semantics. In this chapter, transformation of EER schemata into relational schemata is performed using an extended relational model with active capabilities (triggers).

There are other approaches, for example in Balaban and Shoval (2002), an extension of the EER model is made by including methods to control the semantics associated to Chen's cardinalities. This approach adds a dynamic component to the model, but any Database Management System supports it. Therefore, we are looking for solutions to control the semantic into the relational model.

Camps (2001) makes a complete analysis of the transformation of maximum cardinality constraints into the relational model, considering Chen and MERISE cardinalities for ternary relationships. He uses equivalencies between cardinality constraints and functional dependencies, but this work does not concern the transformation of the minimum cardinalities problem.

In this section, we are going to study the transformation of binary relationship in which concepts of Chen and MERISE cardinalities are similar. Then, we will explain the implications that this transformation has in the ternary relationship issue.

To carry out the transformation of cardinalities of the EER schemata into relational model without semantic losses, the relational model provides mechanisms to express semantic constraints. These mechanisms are: the use of primary key; the use of foreign keys and delete and update options; and the use of alternative keys (UNIQUE), NOT NULL and verification (CHECKS and ASSERTIONS) constraints and triggers.

The syntax provided for triggers is similar to the SQL3 proposal (Melton & Simon, 2002), excepting that procedure calls are allowed in order to interact with the user to capture the required data avoiding semantic losses.

The triggers will have the following structure:

```
CREATE TRIGGER trigger_name
BEFORE/AFTER/INSTEAD OF INSERT/DELETE/UPDATE

ON table_reference [FOR EACH ROW]

BEGIN

trigger_body

END;
```

For data input the following procedure will be used:

ASK_PK (table, primary_key), this procedure obtains the primary key of the "table."

Binary Relationships

In this section, we present two significant examples about the transformation of binary relationships.[9] For each case, a solution is provided using relational model constraints and triggers.

Transformation of N:M Binary Relationships

The N:M relationship *To_Have* (Figure 16) becomes a relation *To_Have*, that has as primary key attributes the set of attributes of the primary keys of the entities that it

Figure 16. AN:M Relationships

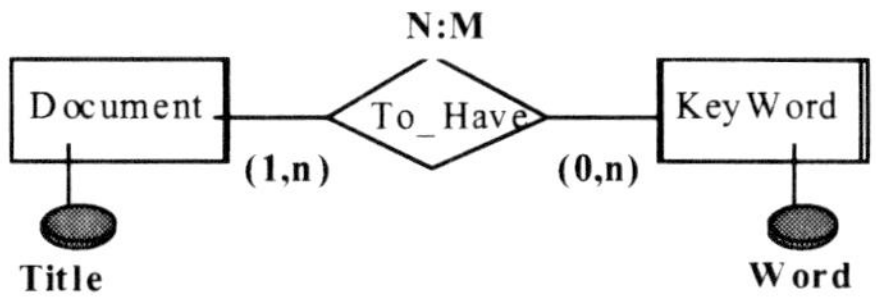

Figure 17. Relational Model Transformation of Figure 16

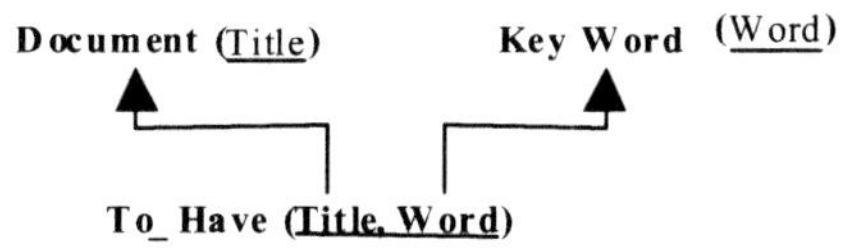

associates. Figure 17 shows the standard transformation as is described in the concerning literature (Date, 1995).

Let us study, according to minimum cardinalities, how the connection relation (*To_Have*) is defined, as well as the delete and update options of the foreign key, and if it is necessary to create some trigger to control these cardinalities when insertions, deletions and updates are performed in each one of the resulting relations.

The *Document* cardinality constraint is (0, n). Figure 16 shows the EER schema, and its standard transformation is displayed in Figure 17. The analysis of the possible semantic losses when an updating is made in *Document, KeyWord* and *To_Have* relations is shown in Table 4.

Notice reader that when the minimum cardinality is 0, the participation of *Document* in *To_Have* is optional; this implies that no restriction has to be added to the standard transformation since no semantic loss exists. Considering that the foreign key *Title* is part of the primary key, the delete and update options in the relation *To_Have* cannot be either SET NULL or SET DEFAULT.

On the order side, the *KeyWord* cardinality constraint is (1, n). In this case the minimum cardinality constraint is stronger than the *Document* minimum cardinality constraint; it is required that all occurrences of *KeyWord* have to be inevitably related to one or more occurrences of *Document*. As in the previous case, in the creation of the

Table 4. Semantic Loss in Cardinality (0, n) Updating Transactions

Relations	Updating	
Document	Insert/Delete/ Update	It is possible to insert/delete/update tuples into *Document* without connecting to *KeyWord*
KeyWord	Insert	It is not a case of study
	Delete/Update	It is possible to delete/update tuples from *KeyWord* without connecting to *Document*
To_Have	Insert	It is possible to insert tuples with no restriction
	Delete/Update	It is possible to delete/update from *To_Have* and to have some tuples of *Document* not connected

Table 5. Semantic Loss in Cardinality (1,n) Updating Transactions

Relations	Updating	
KeyWord	Insert	It is not possible to insert tuples into *KeyWord* without connecting to *Document*
	Delete/Update	It is checked by the FK delete/update option in *To_Have*
Document	Insert/Update	It is not a case of study
	Delete	It is not possible to delete tuples from *Document* and to have some tuples of *KeyWord* not connected
To_Have	Insert	It is possible to insert tuples with no restriction
	Delete/Update	It is not possible to delete/update from *To_Have* and to have some tuples of *KeyWord* not connected

relation *To_Have,* the delete and update options of the foreign key *Word* (similar to *Title*) cannot be either SET NULL or SET DEFAULT.

However, foreign key options are not enough to control the minimum cardinality constraint; it is necessary to assure that all occurrences of *KeyWord* are related to at least one occurrence of *Document* and, therefore, we must take care that the DB is not in an inconsistent state every time a new tuple is inserted into *KeyWord* or a tuple is deleted from *To_Have* (Table 5).

In order to preserve the semantics cardinality constraints, four triggers are required.

First, a trigger will be needed to create a tuple in *To_Have* when inserting into *KeyWord.* The two possibilities contemplated in the trigger are:

- The new occurrence of *KeyWord* is related to an occurrence of *Document* that is already in the relation *Document.*
- The new occurrence of *KeyWord* is related to a new occurrence of *Document.*

```
CREATE TRIGGER INSERTION_NM_(1,N)_KeyWord
BEFORE INSERT ON KeyWord
FOR EACH ROW
DECLARE
VK DOCUMENT.TITLE%TYPE;
BEGIN
ASK_PK (Document,:VK);
IF NOT EXISTS(SELECT * FROM Document WHERE Title=:VK) THEN
     BEGIN
     INSERT INTO Document (Title)
          VALUES (:VK)
     END;
INSERT INTO To_Have (Title, Word)
     VALUES (:New.Title, :VK)
END;
```

To control the deletion of tuples from the relations *To_Have* and *Document* and the update in *To_Have,* the following triggers are required to avoid that an occurrence of *KeyWord* is not related to any occurrence of *Document*:

```
CREATE TRIGGER DELETION_NM_(1,N)_Document
BEFORE DELETE ON Document
FOR EACH ROW
BEGIN
IF :Old.Title IN (SELECT Title FROM To_Have WHERE IN
   (SELECT Word FROM To_Have GROUP BY Word HAVING COUNT(*)=1))
THEN ROLLBACK (*we undo the transaction*)
END;

CREATE TRIGGER DELETION_NM_(1,N)_To_Have
BEFORE DELETE ON To_Have
FOR EACH ROW
BEGIN
IF :Old.Title IN (SELECT Title FROM To_Have WHERE Word IN
   (SELECT Word FROM To_Have GROUP BY Word HAVING COUNT(*)=1))
THEN ROLLBACK
END;

CREATE TRIGGER UPDATE_NM_(1,N)_To_Have
BEFORE UPDATE ON To_Have
FOR EACH ROW
BEGIN
IF :Old.Word<>:New.Word AND :Old.Title IN
   (SELECT Title FROM To_Have WHERE Word IN
   (SELECT Word FROM To_Have GROUP BY Word HAVING COUNT(*)=1))
THEN ROLLBACK
END;
```

Transformation of Binary 1:N

For binary 1:N relationships (Figure 18), there are two solutions when transforming them into the relational model:

(a) Propagating the identifier of the entity that has maximum cardinality 1 to the one that has maximum cardinality N, removing the name of the relationship (this implies semantic losses, see Figure 19). If there are attributes in the relationship, these will belong to the relation that possesses the foreign key (Date, 1995).

(b) Creating a new relation for the relationship as in the case of the binary N:M relationships (Fahrner & Vossen, 1995).

We will study case (a) using the example of Figures 18 and 19.

The *FootNote* cardinality indicates that each *FootNote* occurrence has to be related to at least one *Page* occurrence (see Figure 18), and thus insertion of new *FootNote* occurrences should be controlled. Moreover, if an occurrence of *Page* is deleted, it is necessary to control that no element of *FootNote* remains without being related to an element of *Page* (see Table 6).

To represent this cardinality the following triggers must be created:

Figure 18. A 1:N Relationship

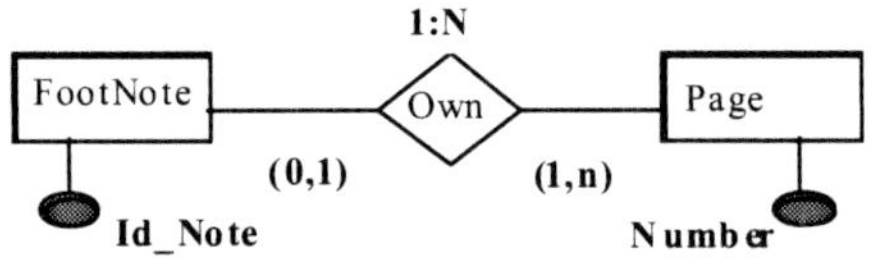

Figure 19. Relational Model Standard Transformation of Figure 18

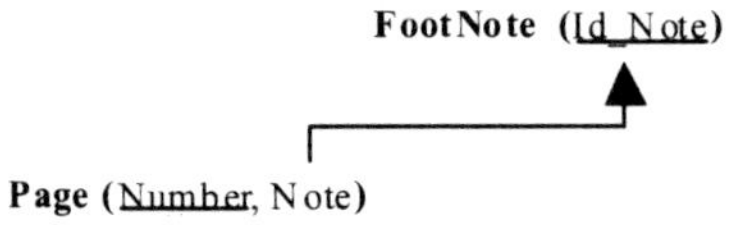


```
CREATE TRIGGER INSERTION_1N_(1,N)_ FootNote
BEFORE INSERT ON FootNote
FOR EACH ROW
DECLARE
VK DOCUMENT.TITLE%TYPE;
BEGIN
ASK_PK (Page,:VK);
IF NOT EXISTS(SELECT * FROM Page WHERE Number=:VK)
   THEN
      (*create a new tuple in Page that is related to the new occurrence of
      FootNote *)
      INSERT INTO Page(Number,Note)
      VALUES (:VK,:New.Note);
   ELSE
      UPDATE Page
      SET Note=:New.Note
      WHERE Number=:VK;
END;
```

Table 6. Semantic Loss in Cardinality (1, n) Updating Transactions

Relations	**Updating**	
FootNote	Insert	It is not possible to insert tuples of *FootNote* without connecting to *Page*
	Delete/Update	It is checked by the FK delete/update option in *Page*
Page	Insert	It is not a case of study
	Delete/Update	It is not possible to delete/update tuples from *Page* and to have some tuples of *FootNote* not connected

For the deletions and updates of tuples in the relation *Page*, the following triggers have been implemented:

```
CREATE TRIGGER DELETION_1N_(1,N)_Page
BEFORE DELETE ON Page
FOR EACH ROW
BEGIN
IF :Old.Number IN (SELECT Number FROM Page WHERE Note IN
   (SELECT Note FROM Page GROUP BY Note HAVING COUNT(*)=1))
   THEN ROLLBACK
END;
CREATE TRIGGER UPDATE_1N_(1,N)_Page
BEFORE UPDATE ON Page
FOR EACH ROW
BEGIN
IF :Old.Note<>:New.Note AND :Old.Number IN
   (SELECT Number FROM Page WHERE Note IN
   (SELECT Note FROM Page GROUP BY Note HAVING COUNT(*)=1))
   THEN ROLLBACK
END;
```

In order to control that the minimum cardinality is 0 (see Table 7), the foreign key *Note* (see Figure 19) has to admit null values. The delete and update options, besides RESTRICT or CASCADE, can be SET NULL; it will depend on the semantics in the UD. The update option will be CASCADE. In this case, it is not necessary to use triggers.

Since the Triggering Graph obtained for the previous triggers contains execution cycles, it is not a complex issue to control the possibility of non-termination. This would be carried out by eliminating the existing cycles from the Activation Graph if triggers are refined and they control the number of entity occurrences that remain unsettled in accomplishing the relationship cardinality constraints. Currently, an Oracle[10] prototype that perfectly reproduces this binary relationship behavior is available (Al-Jumaily, Cuadra & Martínez, 2002). The extension of this approach to contemplate several binary relationships naturally implies a larger interaction among the triggers being more problematic to guarantee the termination of the obtained set of triggers.

Ternary Relationships

In the previous section we presented the transformation of binary relationships to the relational model in order to guarantee the semantics specified by the cardinalities by

Table 7. Semantic Loss in Cardinality (0,1) Updating Transactions

Relations	Updating	
FootNote	Insert	It is not a case of study
	Delete/Update	It is checked by the FK delete/update option in *Page*
Page	Insert/Delete/ Update	It is possible to insert/delete/update tuples into *Page* without connecting to *FootNote*

means of an active rules-based technique (triggers). In this section we study the transformation of higher-order relationships: first, some problems concerning the use of ternary relationships are outlined; next, a semantics preserving transformation is defined for ternary relationships. In Dey, Storey and Barrow (1999), a similar analysis of transformation is performed, but considers a semantics of participation in cardinality constraints.

Several authors have attempted to reduce the complexity of transforming ternary relationships into the relational model, looking for solutions at the conceptual level and proposing that all ternary relationships become several binary relationships through an intermediate entity type (Ullman & Widom, 1997). This solution can be seen as a special case of the so-called *standard of the transformation* (Figure 21). However, we believe that to carry out this transformation at the conceptual level is hasty and may imply certain semantic loss (Silberschatz, Korth & Sudarshan, 2001).

On the other hand, Elmasri and Navathe (2000), Hansen and Hansen (1995) and others treat in different ways a ternary relationship in a conceptual model and its transformation into a relational model. They propose as a unique solution the transformation to the general case, although they recognize that combining the ternary relationship with one or more binary relationships could be of interest, even if cardinality constraints are not taken into account. In our opinion, cardinality constraints contribute so much to validating and transforming ternary relationships.

The transformation to the general case (Figure 20) translates each entity into a relation and the relationship into a new relation; the foreign key delete and update options would be defined in the cascade mode, as shown in Figure 21. The general case does not consider the relationship cardinalities.

If the Chen cardinality constraint is 1 for all entities, the standard transformation (Figure 21) can be applied by adding as primary key of *I* the three attributes that come

Figure 20. A Ternary Relationship

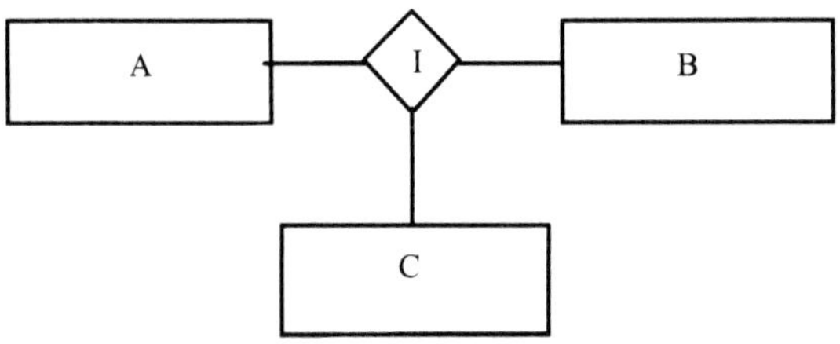

Figure 21. Standard Transformation of a Ternary Relationship

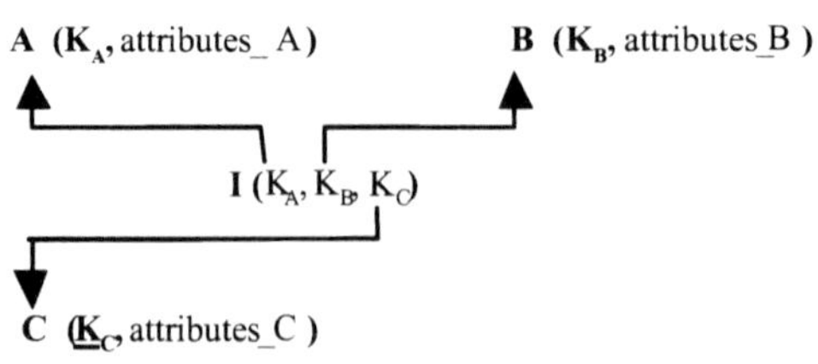

from the propagation of the primary keys of the entities associated by the relationship. Referential integrity in the relationship *I* would assure the semantics of the ternary relationship.

Although aforementioned authors propose to carry out the transformation in the conceptual schema by means of the use of binary relationships, the same problem remains due to the fact that transformation into the relational model of the *connecting entity* has as primary key the set of the primary keys of the participant entities *A, B* and C. By imposing the use of binary relationships, we believe that a limitation of the relational model is moved to the conceptual model, although it is an easier solution nearer to implementation aspects; for example most of the commercial CASE tools only support binary relationships in their models. Since we propose a conceptual model that is completely independent of any logical model, we must concentrate our efforts on the transformation process in order to allow the designer to model at the maximum abstraction level.

In the case that one complementary relationship exists, we must apply the transformation of binary relationship exposed in the previous section, but we will add semantic implications associated to this new relationship type.

In order to clarify the transformation, we present one example that reflects that a document is described by a set of *KeyWords* and *Topics* (Figure 22). The relationship *Describes* means that it is possible that there exist *KeyWords* belonging to *Topics* that do not appear in a *Document,* as well as that *Document* could incorporate a subset of keywords of a specific topic and it is relevant to collect this association (keywords of a topic included in a document).

If we apply the transformation rules for the EER schema shown in Figure 22, the reader may observe that it is necessary to add some constraints to the relational schema of Figure 23.

Figure 22. A Ternary Relationship with Complementary Describes C

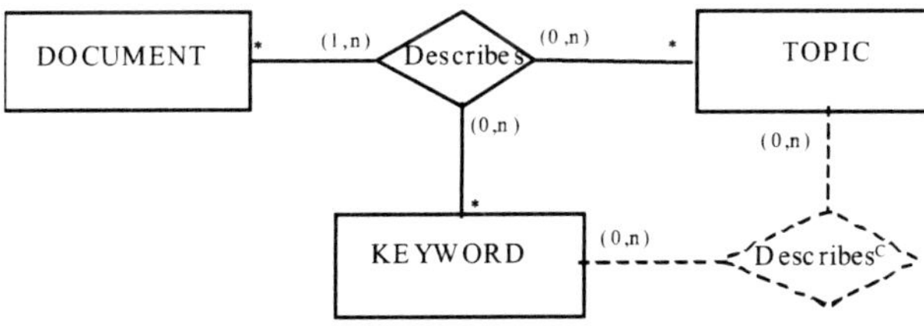

Figure 23. Relational Model Transformation of Figure 22

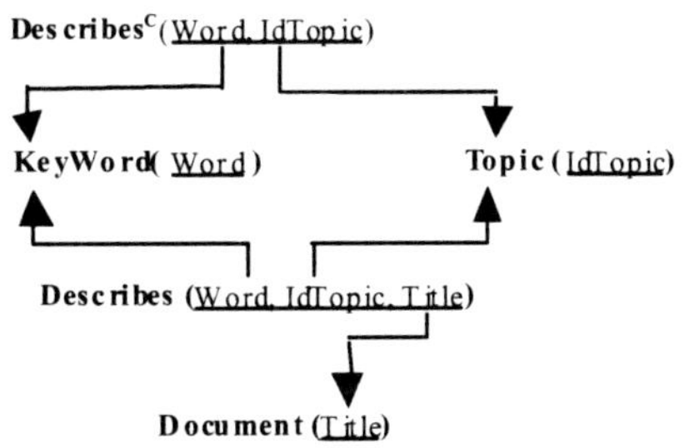

- Relations *Describes* and *Describes*^{C} are semantically related, so we should check the disjoint between both relationship instances.

```
CREATE ASSERTION Disjoint
CHECK (NOT EXITS        (SELECT Word, IdTopic
                        FROM Describes
                        WHERE Word, IdTopic IN (SELECT
                        Word, IDTopic FROM Describes^C)))
```

If the implementation is made in a commercial DBMS, it would be necessary to implement the disjoint through triggers.

For checking the mandatory cardinality of the *Document* entity in relation *Describes*, three triggers must be created: one for the insertion of tuples in *Document*, and others for the delete and update actions in *Describes* for preventing the existence of tuples in *Document* without relation.

To summarize, we may conclude that the inclusion of MERISE cardinality forces the creation of triggers to check the participation in the ternary relationship for those entities whose cardinality will be (1, n). Second, one assertion is enough for collecting the semantic associated to the complementary relationship. Furthermore, the transformation into a relational schema of a ternary relationship — that includes the Chen and MERISE cardinality and the new constructor "complementary relationship" — adds to the standard transformation of Figure 21 the following restrictions (Table 8):

Also, if there exists any complementary relationship, one assertion must be added to check the disjoint of tuples for each one.

PRACTICAL IMPLICATIONS

The main problem for most of the database designers is that, when using a conceptual model, in spite of its power in semantics collection, it is very complicated not to lose part of this semantics in the transformation into a logical model such as the relational model (Codd, 1979). Designers realize how to transform entities or classes, relationships or associations, but there exist other significant constraints, which are not

Table 8. Constraints Concerning to A and its Cardinalities Transformation

			Maximum Cardinality	
			N	1
Minimum Cardinality	Merise	0	Without Constraints	K_A Primary or Unique Key of **I**
		1	Insert Trigger into **A** and Update/ Delete Trigger into **I**	K_A Primary or Unique Key of **I +** Insert Trigger into **A** and Update/ Delete Trigger into **I**
	Chen	1	Without Constraints	K_B **and** K_C Primary Key or Unique of **I**

so easy to transform. This means that conceptual models are exclusively used as a validation tool and as a specification document of the user requirements. The database design will be carried out in a less abstract model and in a model which may be directly implemented in a DBMS.

In many situations, designers lean on CASE tools to carry out the transformation from conceptual to logical model. However, these tools merge conceptual with logical and even physical aspects, and apply simple rules that they know, so they only are useful to save time in design.[11]

In any case, constraint controls or business rules of an information system will be allocated by the different applications that access the database. In this way, developers will have the responsibility of controlling the database consistency. This distribution of the semantics has an associated potential problem of control, as well as Database inconsistencies.

At present, the proliferation of documents written in XML has had a deep impact on the database research area, due to the necessity to investigate new storage and query methods. Also, DTD's notion introduces the data model in XML's world. In that way, there are several studies that attempt to provide algorithms and techniques for mapping XML schemas to database schemata (Bernstein, Levy & Pottinger, 2000). In the field of conceptual models, methods for logical design and their associated transformations have been an object of analysis for some time (Batini, Ceri & Navathe, 1992; Dos Santos & Heuser, 2001), but due to the differences between the Entity Relationship Model (ERM) and XML, these skills cannot be directly reused. Mapping between XML and ERM has been widely studied by database researches. Some authors propose algorithms based on data mining or on natural language recognition techniques (Deutch, Fernandez & Suciu, 1998; Bourret, 2002; Florescu & Kossmann, 1999); on the other hand, algorithms exist that use regular grammars to collect semantics in the transformations (Lee & Chu, 2001; Lee, Murali & Wesley, 2002), and in this sense our proposal may help to include more restrictions in the mapping.

Due to the restrictions imposed by XML, other proposals are emerging, for instance XML Schema or RDF Model. These models provide richer schemata since they allow not only hierarchical associations between objects, but also other relationships types such as n-ary relationships (Lassila & Swick, 1999). For such schemata the mapping between them and conceptual schemata must be long investigated, and the cardinality constraints control exposed in this work may be useful.

We have attempted to present a methodology for achieving the transformation of a significant constraint into conceptual models, as cardinality or multiplicity constraint, with the objective of keeping their semantic in the database. Such attempt may be useful in the schemata conversions, besides those that stem from Web models, such as DTDs or XML schemas, in which the semantics of the cardinality constraints is very important for the well understanding of the data represented.

Due to the fact that relational model does not support full control for cardinality constraints, the methodology leans on ECA rules, built into several DBMSs, fitting them for activity. It has been impossible to collect all the semantics into the relational model. Additional elements not belonging to the model have been needed. In this way, in the triggers built, elements out of standard proposals, such as SQL3 (Melton & Simon, 2002), have been used. Next, the main characteristics needed are shown:

- User interaction
- Procedural capabilities
- Transactional capabilities
- External semantic control

User interaction is needed to solve the information management required in the trigger execution. In the internal constraints case, this interaction may be ruled by the DBMS from the schema information in the database (metadata). In the implemented triggers, user interaction is performed through invocation to procedures. The invocation to procedures as action of ECA rules is considered appropriate (ACT-NET Consortium, 1996) to allow the DBMS to control the information system. For example, this approach could be used for the problem of maintaining updated forms that are visualized by the user or as we have realized for the problem of conduct data entry. Commercial DBMSs give insufficient support for interacting with the user through a call to a procedure for data entrance, although it is possible to maintain several updates in a data structure and only make them effective if it is proven that they don't violate the cardinality constraint. That test will be carried out with triggers.

In some cases, in the case of user interaction, a potential problem is that the life of a transaction is dependent on the user's action. For example, if this user was absent from the work, the resources used by the transaction would be locked. A possible solution would be to establish a timer to force its end.

Many commercial RDBMSs have extended the SQL92 standard with procedural capabilities. The SQL3 standard (Melton & Simon, 2002) has a part (SQL/PSM) based in these capabilities. In addition to user interaction, at least the possibility of minimal control flow capabilities (a conditional statement), comparison and set membership is required.

The event of the triggers is always an update operation on the DB, thus they are activated in the scope of a transaction and the trigger execution must be integrated with transaction execution. Interaction with transaction is an active research field of Active DBMS. Moreover, they would solve the synchronization problems and the non-termination possibility that can take place in the interaction between rules and the usual operation of the DBMS. These problems would require the establishment of a concrete execution model, which is not the objective of this study (Ceri & Faternalli, 1997; Paton & Díaz, 1999). In particular, in the trigger body, a rollback of the whole transaction is needed. A nested transaction model (Orfali, Harkey & Edwards, 1999; Gray & Reuter, 1993) could be useful, such that it would allow re-entrance in the case that a procedure begins a transaction.

When using external procedures to control the semantics, the DBMS does not know what actions the procedures perform, so they may violate the integrity. A possible solution to this problem, chosen in this chapter, is to establish a contract or a commitment between the DBMS and the external procedure. In this way, the semantics control is only carried out by the DBMS, while the application procedures are only limited to data entry. To assure the execution of this contract, a concrete system could demand the application registration and certification procedures.

To ensure that the semantic is shared by all applications independently, access to the database is necessary to transfer the semantic control to the DBMS. This is especially significant with the tools that permit users to access the database contents. To maintain the semantics together with the database schemata is an open research and a way to fit to the schemas of the executability property (Hartmann et al., 1994; Sernadas, Gouveia & Sernadas, 1992; Pastor et al., 1997; Ceri & Faternalli, 1997). The case study presented in this chapter tends to adjust to this possibility, because it allows that the static semantics in the EER schema may decide the dynamic behavior in the database, although the system dynamic behavior is not studied.

FUTURE RESEARCH

In this chapter we have tried to study in depth and clarify the meaning of the features of conceptual models. The disagreements between the main conceptual models, the confusion in the use of some of their constructs and some open problems in these models have been shown.

Another important question treated in this chapter is the conceptual schemata transformation process into logical schemata. Some solutions have been presented in order to preserve the cardinality constraint semantics in both binary and ternary relationships for their implementation in a DBMS with active capabilities.

There are two main causes of semantic loss in database design. First, semantics collected in conceptual schemata are not enough to reflect the overall Universe of Discourse due to the limitations of conceptual constructors. This requires adding explicitly to the conceptual schema some informal statements about constraints. A notation extension to achieve a complete development of the rules of consistency to validate schema EER for reflecting the MERISE participation and Chen cardinality definition in higher-order relationships should be proposed.

On the other hand, in any database development methodology, there is a process devoted to transform conceptual schemata into logical schemata. In such process, a loss of semantics could exist (logical constructs are not coincident with conceptual constructs, for example, entities and relationships in conceptual schemata become relations in logical design). So, some algorithms with active rules must be applied to allow the logical models to keep their semantics.

In the last decade, multiple attempts of giving a more systematic focus to the resolution of modeling problems have been developed. One such attempt has been the automation of the database design process by using CASE tools that neither have enough intelligent methodological guidance, nor (usually) adequately support the design tasks. Commercial CASE tools for database developments do not cover the database design phase with real EER models, that is, they only provide graphical diagrammatic facilities without refinement and validation tools that are independent of the other development phases. CASE environments usually manage hybrid models (merging aspects from EER and relational models) sometimes too close to physical aspects and they use a subset of EER graphical notation for representing relational schemata. Castro et al. (2002) introduces the PANDORA[12] (acronym of Platform for Database Development and Learning via Internet) tool that is being developed in a research project which tries to mitigate some of the deficiencies observed in several CASE tools, defining methods and techniques for database development which are useful for students and practitioners. This tool incorporates a complete conceptual model, such as the EER model, adding the semantics into the relationships in the way we propose in this chapter.

ENDNOTES

1 From now on, we will use the original names (entity and relationship).

2 A cluster of entities is a disjoint union of types that can be considered as categories.

3 This concept is translated into the relational model into a Functional Dependency that can be used in refining the relational schema.

4 We suppose that there are not additional semantic constraints between the entities participating in the ternary relationship of type: "an employee works exactly in one department," "an employee uses one programming language," etc.

5 Maximum cardinality of 1 in Programming Language expresses a functional dependency: employee, project→programming language.

6 In French, constrainte d'intégrité fonctionnel.

7 The Chen approach is not able to express optional/mandatory participation, but it represents functional dependencies.

8 This exclusive-or constraint is not directly established between the two relationships because one is a ternary relationship while the other is a binary one. It is established between the binary relationship and an algebraic projection of the ternary relationship.

9 A complete analysis of binary relationships cardinalities appears in Cuadra et al. (2002).

10 © Oracle Corporation.

11 Sometimes, even if the tool learning cost is high enough, it is not a time saving.

12 CASE Platform for Database development and learning via Internet. Spanish research CICYT project (TIC99-0215).

REFERENCES

ACT-NET Consortium. (1996). The active database management system manifesto: A rulebase of ADBMS features. *ACM SIGMOD Record*, 25(3), 40-49.

Al-Jumaily, H., Cuadra, D. & Martínez, P. (2002). An execution model for preserving cardinality constraints in the relational model. *Proceedings of the 4th International Conference on Enterprise Information Systems (ICEIS'2002),* Ciudad Real, Spain.

Balaban, M. & Shoval, P. (2002). MEER — An EER model enhanced with structure methods. *Information Systems*, 27, 245-275.

Batini, C., Ceri, S. & Navathe, S.B. (1992). *Conceptual Database Design: An Entity-Relationship Approach.* CA: Benjamin/Cummings.

Batra, D. & Antony, S.R. (1994). Novice errors in conceptual database design. *European Journal of Information Systems,* 3(1), 57-69.

Batra, D. & Zanakis , H. (1994). A conceptual database design approach based on rules and heuristics. *European Journal of Information Systems,* 3(3), 228-239.

Bernstein, A., Levy, A. & Pottinger, R. (2000). *A Vision for Management of Complex*

Models. Technical Report, 2000-53. Available online at: http://www.research.microsoft.com/scripts/pubs/.

Boman, M. et al. (1997). *Conceptual Modeling*. Prentice Hall Series in Computer Science.Prentice Hall.

Bourret, R. (2002). *XML and Databases*. Available online at: http://www.rpbourret.com/xml/XMLAndDatabases.htm.

Buneman, P. et al. (1991). Using power domains to generalize relational databases. *Theoretical Computer Science*, 91, 23-55.

Camps, R. (2002). From ternary relationship to relational tables: A case against common beliefs. *ACM SIGMOD Record*, 31(2), 46-49.

Castro, et al. (2002). *Integrating Intelligent Methodological and Tutoring Assistance in A CASE Platform: The PANDORA Experience*. Cork, Ireland: Informing Science + IT Education Congress.

Ceri, S. & Fraternalli, P. (1997). *Designing Database Applications with Objects and Rules: The IDEA Methodology*. Addison-Wesley.

Chen, P.P. (1976). The Entity-Relationship Model: Toward a unified view of data. *ACM Transactions on Database Systems*, 1(1), 9-36.

Codd, E.F. (1970). A relational model of data for large shared data banks. *CACM*, 13(6).

Codd, E.F. (1979). Extending the Database Relational Model to capture more meaning. *ACM Transactions on Database Systems*, 4(4), 397-434.

Cuadra, et al. (2002). Preserving relationship cardinality constraints in relational schemata. *Database Integrity: Challenges and Solutions*. Hershey, PA: Idea Group Publishing.

Date, C.J. (1986). *An Introduction to Database Systems*. Reading, MA: Addison-Wesley.

Date, C.J. (1990). *An Introduction to Database Systems (Fifth Edition)*. Reading, MA: Addison-Wesley.

Date, C.J. (1995). *An Introduction to Database Systems (Sixth Edition)*. Reading, MA: Addison-Wesley.

Deutch, A., Fernandez, M.F. & Suciu, D. (1998). Storing semi-structured data with STORED. *ACM SIGMOD*.

Dey, D., Storey, V.C. & Barron, T.M. (1999). Improving database design through the analysis of relationships. *TODS*, 24(4), 453-486.

Dos Santos, R. & Heuser, C.A., (2001). A rule-based conversion of a DTD to a conceptual schema. *Lecture Notes in Computer Science*, 2224, 133-149.

Elmasri, R. & Navathe, S.B. (2000). *Fundamentals of Database Systems (Third Edition)*. Reading, MA: Addison-Wesley.

Fahrner, C. & Vossen, G. (1995). A survey of database design transformations based on the Entity-Relationship Model. *Data & Knowledge Engineering*, 15, 213-250.

Florescu, D. & Kossmann, D., (1999). Storing and querying XML data using an RDMBS. *IEEE Data Engineering Bulletin*, 22(3), 27-34.

Génova, Llorens, & Martínez. (2001). Semantics of the minimum multiplicity in ternary associations in UML. *Proceedings of the 4th International Conference on the Unified Modeling Language, Modeling Languages, Concepts, and Tools (UML 2001)*, Toronto, Canada, October 1-5. *Lecture Notes in Computer Science*, 2185, 329-341. Springer.

Gray, J. & Reuter, A. (1993). *Transactions Processing, Concepts and Techniques*. San Mateo, CA: Morgan Kaufmann.

Halpin, T. (2001). Information Modeling and Relational Database: From Conceptual Analysis to Logical Design. CA: Morgan Kaufmann.Hansen, G. & Hansen, J. (1995). *Database Management and Design.* City: Prentice-Hall.

Hartmann, T. et al. (1994). Revised version of the conceptual modeling and design language TROLL. *Proceedings of the ISCORE Workshop,* Amsterdam, 89-103.

Hull, R. & King, R. (1987). Semantic database modeling: Survey, application, and research issues. *ACM Computing Surveys*, 19(3), 201-260.

Jones, T.H. & Song, I.-Y. (1998). And analysis of the structural validity of ternary relationships in Entity-Relationship modeling. *Proceedings of the 7th International Conference on Information and Knowledge Management (CIKM'98)*, November, 331-339.

Lassila, O. & Swick, R. (1999). *Especificación del Modelo y la Sintaxis de RDF. W3C REC-rdf-syntax-19990222-es,* February. Available online at : http://www.w3.org/TR/1999/REC-rdf-syntax-19990222-es.

Lee, D. & Chu, W. (2001). CPI: Constraints-Preserving Inlining algorithm for mapping XML DTD to relational schema. *Data & Knowledge Engineering,* 39, 3-25.

Lee, D., Murali, M. & Wesley W. (2002). XML to relational conversion using theory of regular tree grammars. *Proceedings of the VLDB Workshop on Efficiency and Effectiveness of XML Tools, and Techniques (EEXTT)\/},* Hong Kong, China, August.

McAllister, A. (1998). Complete rules for n-ary relationship cardinality constraints. *Data & Knowledge Engineering,* 27, 255-288.

Melton, J. & Simon, A.R (2002). *SQL: 1999 Understanding Relational Language Components.* CA: Morgan Kaufmann.

Nijssen, G.M. & Halpin, T.A. (1989). *Conceptual Schema and Relational Database Design—A Fact-Oriented Approach.* New York: Prentice-Hall.

OMG. (2000). Unified Modeling Language Specification, Version 1-3. Object Management Group. *ACM Computing Surveys*, 31(1), 63-103.

Orfali, R., Harkey, D. & Edwards, J. (1999). *Essential Client/Server Survival Guide (Third Edition).* New York: John Wiley & Sons.

Pastor, O. et al. (1997). OO-METHOD: An OO software production environment for combining conventional and formal methods. In Olivé A. & Pastor J.A. (Eds.), *Proceedings of CAISE'97,* Barcelona, June. *Lecture Notes in Computer Science,* 1250, 145-158.

Paton, N.W. & Díaz, O. (1999). Active database systems. *ACM Computing Surveys,* 31(1), 63-103.

Peckham, J. & Maryanski, F. (1988). Semantic data models. *ACM Computing Surveys,* 20(3), 153-189.

Ramakrishnan, R. (1997). *Database Management Systems.* McGraw-Hill International.

Rumbaugh, J., Blaha, M. & Premerlani, W.J. (1991). *Object-Oriented Modeling and Design.* Englewood Cliffs, NJ: Prentice-Hall.

Sernadas, C., Gouveia, P. & Sernadas, A. (1992). *OBLOG: Object-Oriented, Logic-Based, Conceptual Modeling.* Research Report, Instituto Superior Técnico.

Silberschatz, A., Korth, F. & Sudarshan, S. (2001). *Database Design Concepts (Fourth Edition).* City: McGraw-Hill, July 2001.

Soutou, C. (1998). Relational database reverse engineering: Algorithms to extract cardinality constraints. *Data & Knowledge Engineering,* 28, 161-207.

Tardieu, H., Rochfeld, A. & Coletti, R. (1983). La Méthode MERISE. *Tome 1: Principles et Outils Les Editions d'Organisation,* Paris, France.

Teorey, T.J. (1999). *Database Modeling and Design: The Entity-Relationship Approach (Third Edition).* San Mateo, CA: Morgan Kaufmann.

Teorey, T.J., Yang, D. & Fry, J.P. (1986). A logical design methodology for relational databases using the extended Entity-Relationship Model. *ACM Computing Survey,* 18(2).

Thalheim, B. (2000). *Entity-Relationship Modeling. Foundations of Database Technology.* Berlin Springer-Verlag.

Ullman, J.D. & Widom, J. (1997). *A First Course in Database Systems.* Prentice-Hall International.

Chapter XVIII

Repairing and Querying Inconsistent Databases

Gianluigi Greco
Università della Calabria, Italy

Sergio Greco
Università della Calabria, Italy

Ester Zumpano
Università della Calabria, Italy

ABSTRACT

The integration of knowledge from multiple sources is an important aspect in several areas such as data warehousing, database integration, automated reasoning systems, active reactive databases and others. Thus a central topic in databases is the construction of integration systems, designed for retrieving and querying uniform data stored in multiple information sources. This chapter illustrates recent techniques for computing repairs as well as consistent answers over inconsistent databases. Often databases may be inconsistent with respect to a set of integrity constraints, that is, one or more integrity constraints are not satisfied. Most of the techniques for computing repairs and queries over inconsistent databases work for restricted cases and only recently there have been proposals to consider more general constraints. In this chapter we give an informal description of the main techniques proposed in the literature.

INTRODUCTION

The problem of integrating heterogeneous sources has been deeply investigated in the fields of multidatabase systems (Breitbart, 1990), federated databases (Wiederhold, 1992) and, more recently, mediated systems (Ullman, 2000; Wiederhold, 1992). A large variety of approaches has been proposed in the literature for performing data source integration. Many of them are embedded in more complex systems managing the interoperability and the cooperation of data sources characterized by heterogeneous representation formats.

The aim of data integration is to provide uniform integrated access to multiple heterogeneous information sources, which were designed independently for autonomous applications and whose contents are strictly related.

Integrating data from different sources consists of two main steps: first, the various relations are merged together, and second, some tuples are *removed* (or *inserted*) from the resulting database in order to satisfy integrity constraints.

In particular, there are several ways to integrate databases or possibly distributed information sources, but whatever integration architecture we choose, the heterogeneity of the sources to be integrated, often designed independently for autonomous applications, causes subtle problems. In particular, the database obtained from the integration process may be inconsistent with respect to integrity constraints, that is, one or more integrity constraints are not satisfied. Integrity constraints represent an important source of information about the real world. They are usually used to define constraints on data (functional dependencies, inclusion dependencies, etc.) and have, nowadays, a wide applicability in several contexts such as semantic query optimization, cooperative query answering, database integration and view update.

Since, the satisfaction of integrity constraints cannot generally be guaranteed, if the database is obtained from the integration of different information sources, in the evaluation of queries, we must compute answers which are consistent with the integrity constraints.

The following example shows a case of inconsistency.

Example 1. Consider the following database schema consisting of the single binary relation *Teaches (Course, Professor)* where the attribute *Course* is a key for the relation. Assume there are two different instances for the relations *Teaches*, D1={(c1,p1),(c2,p2)} and D2={(c1,p1),(c2,p3)}.

The two instances satisfy the constraint that *Course* is a key, but from their union we derive a relation which does not satisfy the constraint since there are two distinct tuples with the same value for the attribute *Course*.

In the integration of two conflicting databases, simple solutions could be based on the definition of preference criteria such as a partial order on the source information or a majority criteria (Lin & Mendelzon, 1996). However, these solutions are not generally satisfactory and more useful solutions are those based on: 1) the computation of 'repairs' for the database; 2) the computation of consistent answers (Arenas et al., 1999).

The computation of repairs is based on the definition of minimal sets of insertion and deletion operations so that the resulting database satisfies all constraints. The computation of consistent answers is based on the identification of tuples satisfying integrity constraints and on the selection of tuples matching the goal.

For instance, for the integrated database of Example 1, we have two alternative repairs consisting of the deletion of one of the tuples *(c2, p2)* and *(c2, p3)*. The consistent answer to a query over the relation *Teaches* contains the unique tuple *(c1, p1)* so that we don't know which professor teaches course *c2*.

Therefore, it is very important, in the presence of inconsistent data, to compute the set of consistent answers, but also to know which facts are unknown and if there are possible repairs for the database. In our approach it is possible to compute the tuples which are consistent with the integrity constraints and answer queries by considering as true facts those contained in every repaired database, false facts those that are not contained in any repaired database and unknown the remaining facts.

Example 2. Consider the integrated relation of Example 1 containing the tuples *(c1, p1), (c2, p2)* and *(c2, p3)*. The database is inconsistent and there are two possible repairs which make it consistent: *R1=(∅, {Teaches(c2, p2)})* and *R2=(∅, {Teaches(c2, p3)})* which delete, respectively, the tuples *(c2, p2)* and *(c2, p3)*, from the relation *Teaches*. The set of consistent tuples in the relation Teaches consists of the singleton *(c1, p1)*.

This chapter illustrates recent techniques for computing consistent answers and repairs for possibly inconsistent databases.

Organization of the Chapter

We first present some preliminaries on relational databases, disjunctive deductive databases and integrity constraints, and then we introduce the formal definition of repair, consistent answer and the different techniques for querying and repairing inconsistent databases. In particular we present:

(1) an extension of relational algebra, called flexible relational algebra, for inconsistent relations;
(2) the integrated relational calculus which extends relations and algebra for querying inconsistent data;
(3) a technique for merging relations based on majority criteria;
(4) a technique for querying and repairing inconsistent data based on the concept of residual;
(5) a technique for querying inconsistent databases based on the definition of a logic program for defining possible repairs;
(6) a technique for integrating and querying databases in the presence of incomplete and inconsistent information sources with key constraints and foreign key constraints defined upon the global schema;
(7) a technique which investigates the problem of answering queries upon databases that may be incomplete;
(8) a technique for repairing databases that repairs an inconsistent database without deleting tuples (*tuple-based* approach), but using a finer repair primitive consisting of correcting faulty values within the tuples (*value-based* approach); and
(9) a technique based on the rewriting of integrity constraints into disjunctive Datalog rules.

BACKGROUND

We assume that readers are familiar with relational and deductive databases and only recall here definitions which will be used in this chapter.

Relational Databases

We assume there are finite sets of relation names **R**, attribute names **A** and attribute values (also called *database domain*) **V**. A relation schema of a relation $R \in \mathbf{R}$ is of the form $(A_1, ..., A_n)$ where $A_1, ..., A_n \in \mathbf{A}$. A relational database schema is a set of relation schemas. Each attribute A has associated a domain denoted by DOM(A). The null value $\perp$ is not contained in DOM(A) and $DOM_\perp(A) = DOM(A) \cup \{\perp\}$.

A tuple for a relation R is a mapping assigning to each attribute A of R an element in $DOM_\perp(A)$, i.e., a list of values $(v_1, ..., v_n)$ where v_i is the value of the attribute A_i, for each *i* in *[1....n]*. A relation (instance) is a set of tuples. In the following, a tuple $(v_1, ..., v_n)$ of a relation *R*, will also be denoted by $R(v_1, ..., v_n)$.

The set of keys of a relation *R* will be denoted by *keys(R)*, and the primary key is denoted by *pkey(R)*. We assume that the value of the attributes in the primary key is not null.

Disjunctive Deductive Databases

A (disjunctive Datalog) rule *r* is a clause of the form:

$$A_1 \vee ... \vee A_k \leftarrow B_1, ..., B_m, \text{not } B_{m+1}, ..., \text{not } B_n, \qquad k+m+n>0$$

where $A_1, ..., A_k, B_1, ..., B_n$ are atoms of the form $p(t_1, ..., t_h)$, *p* is a predicate symbol of arity *h* and the terms $t_1, ..., t_h$ are constants or variables (Eiter, Gottlob & Mannila, 1998). The disjunction $A_1 \vee ... \vee A_k$ is the *head* of *r*, while the conjunction $B_1, ..., B_m, \textit{not } B_{m+1}, ..., \textit{not } B_n$ is the body of *r*. We also assume the existence of the binary built-in predicate symbols (comparison operators) which can only be used in the body of rules.

The *Herbrand Universe* U_P of a program P is the set of all constants appearing in *P*, and its *Herbrand Base* B_P is the set of all ground atoms constructed from the predicates appearing in *P* and the constants from U_P. A term (resp. an atom, a literal, a rule or a program) is *ground* if no variables occur in it. A rule *r'* is a *ground instance* of a rule *r*, if *r'* is obtained from *r* by replacing every variable in *r* with some constant in U_P. We denote by *ground(P)* the set of all ground instances of the rules in *P*.

An interpretation of *P* is any subset of B_P. The value of a ground atom *L* w.r.t. an interpretation *I*, $value_I(L)$, is true if $L \in I$ and *false* otherwise. The value of a ground negated literal *not L* is *not* $value_I(L)$. The truth value of a conjunction of ground literals $C = L_1, ..., L_n$ is the minimum over the values of the L_i, i.e., $value_I(C) = \min(\{value_I(L_i) \mid 1 \leq i \leq n\})$, while the value $value_I(D)$ of a disjunction $D = L_1 \vee ... \vee L_n$ is their maximum, i.e., $value_I(D) = \max(\{value_I(D)\ (L_i) \mid 1 \leq i \leq n\})$; if n=0, then $value_I(C) = true$ and $value_I(D) = false$.

A ground rule *r* is *satisfied* by *I* if $value_I(Head(r)) \geq value_I(Body(r))$. Thus, a rule *r* with empty body is satisfied by *I* if $value_I(Head(r)) = true$. In the following we also assume the existence of rules with empty head which define denials (under total semantics), i.e., rules which are satisfied only if the body is false ($value_I(Body(r)) = false$). An interpretation *M* for *P* is a model of *P* if *M* satisfies each rule in *ground(P)*. The (model-theoretic) semantics for a positive program, say *P*, assigns to *P* the set of its *minimal models MM(P)*, where a model *M* for *P* is minimal, if no proper subset of *M* is a model for P (Minker, 1982). The more general *disjunctive stable model semantics* also applies to programs with (unstratified) negation (Gelfond & Lifschitz, 1991). For any interpretation I, denote with P^I the ground positive program derived from *ground(P)*: 1) by removing all rules that contain a negative literal *not a* in the body and $a \in I$, and 2) by removing all negative literals from the remaining rules. An interpretation M is a (disjunctive) stable model of P if and only if $M \in MM(P^M)$.

For general P, the stable model semantics assigns to P the set $SM(P)$ of its *stable models*. It is well known that stable models are minimal models *(i.e.,* $SM(P) \subset MM(P)$*)* and that for negation-free programs, minimal and stable model semantics coincide *(i.e.,* $SM(P) = MM(P)$*)*. Observe that stable models are minimal models which are "supported," i.e., their atoms can be derived from the program. An alternative semantics which overcomes some problems of stable model semantics has been recently proposed in Greco (1999).

Extended Disjunctive Databases

An extended atom is either an atom, say A or its negation $\neg$A. An extended Datalog program is a set of rules of the form:

$$A_1 \vee \ldots \vee A_k \leftarrow B_1, \ldots, B_m, \text{not } B_{m+1}, \ldots, \text{not } B_n \qquad k+n>0$$

where $A_1, \ldots, A_k, B_1, \ldots, B_n$ are extended atoms.

A (2-valued) interpretation I for an extended program P is a pair $<T,F>$ where T and F define a partition of $B_P \cup \neg B_P$ and $\neg B_P = \{ \neg A \mid A \in B_P \}$. The semantics of an extended program P is defined by considering each negated predicate symbol, say $\neg$p, as a new symbol syntactically different from p and by adding to the program, for each predicate symbol p with arity n the constraint $\leftarrow p(X_1,\ldots,X_n), \neg p(X_1,\ldots,X_n)$ (Gelfond & Lifschitz, 1991; Greco & Sacca, 1990; Kowalski & Sadri, 1991). The existence of a (2-valued) model for an extended program is not guaranteed, also in the case of negation-(as-failure)-free programs. In the following, for the sake of simplicity, we shall also use rules whose bodies may contain disjunctions. Such rules, called generalized disjunctive rules, are used as shorthand for multiple standard disjunctive rules.

Disjunctive Queries

Predicate symbols are partitioned into two distinct sets: *base predicates* (also called EDB predicates) and *derived predicates* (also called IDB predicates). Base predicates correspond to database relations defined over a given domain and they do not appear in the head of any rule, whereas derived predicates are defined by means of rules.

Given a database D, a predicate symbol r and a program P, $D(r)$ denotes the set of *r-tuples* in D whereas P_D denotes the program derived from the union of P with the tuples in D, i.e., $P_D = P \cap \{r(t) \leftarrow \mid t \in D(r)\}$. In the following a tuple t of a relation r will also be denoted as a fact $r(t)$. The semantics of P_D is given by the set of its stable models by considering either their union (*possible semantics* or *brave reasoning*) or their intersection (*certain semantics* or *cautious reasoning*). A *query* Q is a pair (g,P) where g is a predicate symbol, called the *query goal*, and P is a program. The answer to a query $Q=(g,P)$ over a database D, under the possible (resp. certain) semantics is given by D'(g) where $D' = \bigcup_{M \in SM(PD)} M$ (resp. $D' = \bigcap_{M \in SM(PD)} M$).

DATABASES WITH CONSTRAINTS

Databases contain, other than data, intentional knowledge expressed by means of integrity constraints. Database schemata contain the knowledge on the structure of data, i.e., they give constraints on the form the data must have. The relationships among data are usually defined by constraints such as functional dependencies, inclusion dependencies and others. They are introduced to provide information on the relationships among data and to restrict the state a database can take.

Integrity Constraints

Integrity constraints express information that is not directly derivable from the database data. They are introduced to model the relationships among data and to prevent the insertion or deletion of data which could produce incorrect states. A database *D* has associated a schema $DS = (R_S, IC)$ which defines the intentional properties of *D*: R_S denotes the set of relation schemas whereas IC contains the set of integrity constraints.

Integrity constraints express semantic information over data, i.e., relationships that must hold among data in the theory. Generally, integrity constraints represent the interaction among data and define properties which are supposed to be explicitly satisfied by all instances over a given database schema. Therefore, they are mainly used to validate database transactions.

Definition 1. An integrity constraint (or embedded dependency) is a formula of the first-order predicate calculus of the form:

$$(\forall x_1 \ldots \forall x_n)\,[\Phi(x_1,\ldots,x_n) \supset (\exists z_1 \ldots \exists z_k)\,\Psi(y_1,\ldots,y_m)]$$

where $\Phi(x_1,\ldots,x_n)$ and $\Psi(y_1,\ldots,y_m)$ are two conjunctions of literals such that $x_1,\ldots,x_n$ and $y_1,\ldots,y_m$ are the distinct variables appearing in Φ and Ψ respectively, and $\{z_1,\ldots,z_k\} = \{y_1,\ldots,y_m\} - \{x_1,\ldots,x_n\}$ is the set of variables existentially quantified.

In the definition above, conjunction Φ is called the *body* and conjunction Ψ the *head* of the integrity constraint. Moreover, an integrity constraint is said to be *positive* if no negated literals occur in it (classical definitions of integrity constraints only consider positive nondisjunctive constraints, called *embedded dependencies* (Kanellakis, 1991)).

Six common restrictions on embedded dependencies that give us six classes of dependencies have been defined in the literature (Kanellakis, 1991):

- The *full* (or *universal*) are those not containing existential quantified variables.
- The *unirelational* are those with one relation symbol only; dependencies with more than one relation symbol are called *multirelational*.
- The *single-head* are those with a single atom in the head; dependencies with more than one atom in the head are called *multi-head*.
- The *tuple-generating* are those without the equality symbol.
- The *equality-generating* are full, single-head, with an equality atom in the head.

- The *typed* are those whose variables are assigned to fixed positions of base atoms and every equality atom involves a pair of variables assigned to the same position of the same base atom; dependencies which are not typed will be called *untyped*.

Most of the dependencies developed in database theory are restricted cases of some of the above classes. For instance, functional dependencies are positive, full, single-head, unirelational, equality-generating constraints.

In the rest of this section, we concentrate on *full* (or *universal*) disjunctive constraints, where Ψ is a possibly empty disjunction of literals and a literal can be either a base literal or a conjunction of built-in literals (i.e., literals using as predicate symbols comparison operators).

Therefore, an integrity constraint is a formula of the form:

$$(\forall X)\,[\,B_1 \wedge \ldots \wedge B_n \wedge \varphi \supset A_1 \vee \ldots \vee A_m \wedge \psi_1 \wedge \ldots \wedge \psi_k\,]$$

where $A_1,\ldots,A_m, B_1,\ldots,B_n$ are base positive literals, $\varphi, \psi_1,\ldots,\psi_k$ are built-in literals, X denotes the list of all variables appearing in $B_1,\ldots,B_n$ and it is supposed that variables appearing in $A_1,\ldots,A_m, \varphi, \psi_1,\ldots,\psi_k$ also appear in $B_1,\ldots,B_n$.

Often we shall write our constraints in a different format by moving literals from the head to the body and vice versa. For instance, the above constraint could be rewritten as:

$$(\forall X)\,[\,B_1 \wedge \ldots \wedge B_n \wedge \varphi' \supset A_1 \vee \ldots \vee A_m]$$

where $\varphi' = \varphi \wedge \text{not } \psi_1 \wedge \ldots \wedge \text{not } \psi_k$ is a conjunction of built-in atoms or in the form of rule with empty head, called *denial*:

$$(\forall X)\,[\,B_1 \wedge \ldots \wedge B_n \wedge \text{not } A_1 \wedge \ldots \wedge \text{not } A_m \wedge \varphi' \supset\,]$$

which is satisfied only if the body is false.

Example 3. The integrity constraint:

$$(\forall X)\,[\,p(X) \supset q(X) \vee r(X)\,]$$

called *inclusion dependency* states that the relation *p* must be contained in the union of the relations *q* and *r*. It could be rewritten as:

$$(\forall X)\,[\,p(X) \wedge \text{not } q(X) \wedge \text{not } r(X) \supset\,]$$

REPAIRS AND CONSISTENT ANSWERS

We now introduce some basic notions including what we understand as a consistent database, a consistent set of integrity constraints, a database repair and a consistent answer.

Definition 2. Given a database schema DS = (Rs,IC), we say that IC is consistent if there exists a database instance D over DS such that D |= IC. Moreover, we say that a database instance D over DS is consistent if D |=IC, i.e., if all integrity constraints in IC are satisfied by D, otherwise it is inconsistent.

Example 4. The set of integrity constraints:

$$(\forall x \forall y)[\, p(x,y) \wedge p(x,z) \supset x > y \,]$$
$$(\forall x \forall y)[\, p(x,y) \wedge p(x,z) \supset x < y \,]$$

is not consistent since there is no instance of relation p satisfying both constraints.

Intuitively, a *repair* for a (possibly inconsistent) database *D* is a minimal consistent set of insert and delete operations which makes *D* consistent, whereas a consistent answer for a query consists of two sets containing, respectively, the maximal set of true and undefined atoms which match the query goal; atoms which are neither true nor undefined can be assumed to be false.

More formally:

Definition 3. Given a database schema DS = <Rs,IC> and a database D over DS, a repair for D is a pair of sets of atoms (R^+,R^-) such that 1) $R^+ \cap R^- = \emptyset$, 2) $D \cup R^+ - R^- \models IC$ and 3) there is no pair $(S^+, S^-) \neq (R^+, R^-)$ such that $R^+ \subset S^+$, $R^- \subset S^-$ and $D \cup S^+ - S^- \models IC$. The database $D \cup R^+ - R^-$ will be called the repaired database.

Thus, repaired databases are consistent databases which are derived from the source database by means of a minimal (under total semantics) set of insertion and deletion of tuples. Given a repair R for D, R^+ denotes the set of tuples which will be added to the database, whereas R^- denotes the set of tuples of D which will be canceled. In the following, for a given repair R and a database D, $R(D) = D \cup R^+ - R^-$ denotes the application of R to D.

Example 5. Assume we have a database D = {p(a),p(b),q(a),q(c)} with the inclusion dependency $(\forall X)$ [$p(X) \supset q(X)$]. The database D is inconsistent since the constraint $p(X) \supset q(X)$ is not satisfied. The repairs for D are R1 = ({ q(b) },∅) and R2 = (∅, { p(b) }) producing, respectively, the repaired databases R1(D)={p(a), p(b), q(a), q(c), q(b) } and R2(D) = {p(a), q(a), q(c)}.

A (relational) query over a database defines a function from the database to a relation. It can be expressed by means of alternative equivalent languages such as relational algebra, 'safe' relational calculus or 'safe' non-recursive Datalog (Abiteboul et al., 1995; Ullman, 1988). In the following we shall use Datalog. Thus, a query is a pair *(g,P)* where *P* is a safe non-recursive Datalog program and *g* is a predicate symbol specifying the output (derived) relation. Observe that relational queries define a restricted case of disjunctive queries. The reason for considering relational and disjunctive queries is that, as we shall show in the next section, relational queries over databases with constraints can be rewritten into extended disjunctive queries over databases without constraints.

Definition 4. The set of repairs for a database D with respect to IC will be denoted by Repair(D,IC). A tuple t over DS is consistent with respect to D if t belongs to all repaired databases, i.e., $t \in \bigcap_{D' \in Repairs(D,IC)} D'$.

Definition 5. Given a database schema DS = (Rs,IC) and a database D over DS, an atom A is true (resp. false) with respect to (D,IC) if A belongs to all repaired databases (resp. there is no repaired database containing A). The set of atoms which are neither true nor false are undefined.

Thus, true atoms appear in all repaired databases, whereas undefined atoms appear in a proper subset of repaired databases. Given a database D and a set of integrity constraints IC, the application of IC to D, denoted by IC(D), defines three distinct sets of atoms: the set of true atoms $IC(D)^+$, the set of undefined atoms $IC(D)^u$ and the set of false atoms $IC(D)^-$.

Definition 6. Given a database schema DS = <Rs,IC>, a database D over DS and a query Q = (g,P), the consistent answer to the query Q on the database D, denoted as Q(D,IC), gives three sets, denoted as $Q(D,IC)^+$, $Q(D,IC)^-$ and $Q(D,IC)^u$. These contain, respectively, the sets of g-tuples which are true (i.e., belonging to Q(D') for all repaired databases D'), false (i.e., not belonging to Q(D') for all repaired databases D') and undefined (i.e., the set of tuples which are neither true nor false).

TECHNIQUES FOR QUERYING AND REPAIRING DATABASES

Recently, there have been several proposals considering the integration of databases as well as the computation of queries over inconsistent databases (Agarwal, 1992; Agarwal, Keller, Wiederhold & Saraswat, 1995; Arenas, Bertossi & Chomicki, 1999; Bry, 1997; Dung, 1996; Greco & Zumpano, 2000a, 2000b; Greco, Greco & Zumpano, 2001; Lin, 1996a, 1996b; Lin & Mendelzon, 1996, 1999; Lembo, Lenzerini & Rosati, 2002; Lenzerini 2002; Levy, 1996; Wijsen, 2003). Techniques for the integration of knowledge bases, expressed by means of first-order formulas, have been proposed as well (Baral, Kraus & Minker, 1991a, 1991b; Subrahmanian, 1994; Grant & Subrahmanian, 1995). Most of the techniques for computing queries over inconsistent databases work for restricted cases and only recently have there been proposals to consider more general constraints. In this chapter we give an informal description of the main techniques proposed in the literature.

Flexible Algebra

The flexible algebra extends relational algebra through the introduction of *flexible relations,* i.e., non-1NF relations that contain sets of non-key attributes, to provide semantics for database operations in the presence of potentially inconsistent data (Agarwal et al., 1995).

A flexible relation is obtained by applying the flexify (~) operator to a relation R with schema (K,Z), where K denotes the set of attributes in the primary key and Z is the set of remaining attributes. The schema of ~(R) is (K,Z,Cons,Sel,Src), where *Cons* is the *consistent status* attribute, *Sel* is the *selection status* attribute and *Src* is the *source attribute*. Thus, a flexible relation is derived from a classical relation by extending its schema with the *ancillary* attributes and assigning values for these attributes for each of the tuples. Obviously a classical relation is consistent by definition. Inconsistencies may arise if the integration of a set of consistent and autonomous databases is performed. In order to represent inconsistent data in a flexible relation, the method introduces the notion of *ctuple*.

A *ctuple* is defined as a cluster of tuples having the same values for the key attributes. A flexible relation is a set of ctuples. Two tuples t_1 and t_2 in the same ctuple are conflicting if there is some non-key attribute A such that $\perp \neq t_1[A] \neq t_2[A] \neq \perp$, where the interpretation given to the null value consists of *no information* (Zaniolo, 1984). A *ctuple* is consistent if it contains non-conflicting pairs of tuples. Note that a *ctuple* containing exactly a tuple is consistent by definition.

Example 6. Consider the following three relations R1, R2 and R3 coming, respectively, from the sources s1, s2 and s3.

R1			
Key	**Z1**	**Z2**	**Z3**
10	x	⊥	z
20	y	⊥	z

R2			
Key	**Z1**	**Z2**	**Z3**
10	x	y	z
20	y	⊥	⊥

R3			
Key	**Z1**	**Z2**	**Z3**
10	x	w	z

The integrated relation R consists of two ctuples (c1 and c2)

	R			
	Key	**Z1**	**Z2**	**Z3**
	10	x	⊥	z
c1	10	x	y	z
	10	x	w	z
c2	20	y	⊥	z
	20	y	⊥	⊥

where the ctuple c2 is consistent, whereas the ctuple c1 is not consistent.

As previously stated, in addition to the original attributes, the flexible operator extends the schema of the flexible relation with three ancillary attributes: *Cons, Sel* and *Src*. These attributes are instantiated by the application of the *flexify* operator. Each tuple of a flexible relation has a value for each ancillary attribute and the managing of these attributes is performed by the system.

- The *Cons* attribute defines the consistency status of the ctuple; its domain is *{true, false}* and all tuples in the same ctuple have the same value.
- The *Sel* attribute denotes the selection status of the ctuples. It contains information about possible restrictions on the selection of tuples in ctuples and its domain is *{true, false, maybe}*; all tuples in the same ctuple have the same value. For flexible

relations derived from source relations through the application of the *flexify* operator, its value is true, whereas for relations derived from other flexible relations, its value can also be *false* or *maybe*.

- The *Src* attribute refers to the source relation from which a particular tuple has been derived. Thus if we define a primary key for each ctuple, it would be *(Key,Src)*.

Example 7. The flexible relation derived from the relation of Example 6 is as follows:

	~R						
	Key	**Z1**	**Z2**	**Z3**	**Cons**	**Sel**	**Src**
c1	10	x	⊥	z	false	true	s1
	10	x	y	z	false	true	s2
	10	x	w	z	false	true	s3
c2	20	y	⊥	z	true	true	s1
	20	y	⊥	⊥	true	true	s2

In the above relation ~R, the value of the attribute *Sel* equal to *true* means that if the selection operator is applied to the tuples of the same ctuple, the resulting set is 'correct.'

Take for instance the relation *R* with attributes *(A,B,C)* with key attribute *A* and three tuples *t1=(a1,b,10)*, *t2 = (a1,c,10)* and *t3 = (a2,b,20)* where *t1* and *t2* are conflicting (they belong to the same ctuple with key "*a1*"). The selection $\sigma_{B='b'}(R)$ gives a (consistent) relation consisting of the tuples *t1* and *t3*. Moreover this result is not correct since the tuple *t1* is conflicting with *t2* in the source relation, whereas in the resulting relation, it is not conflicting with any tuple. This means that the attribute *Sel* for the ctuple with key value *a1* must be false (these tuples cannot be selected).

Flexible Relational Algebra

The Flexible Algebra defines a set of operations on the Flexible Relations. These operations are defined in order to perform meaningful operation in the presence of conflicting data. The full algebra for flexible relation is defined in Agarwal (1992). In this section we briefly describe some of the operation in this algebra. The set of ctuple operation includes *merging, equivalence, selection, union, Cartesian product* and *projection*.

The merge operator merges the tuples in a ctuple in order to obtain a single nested tuple referred to as *merged ctuple*. An attribute, say A, of the *merged ctuple* will be *null* if and only if this is the unique value the attribute A assumes in the ctuple.

Example 8. The merged relation derived from the relation of Example 7 is:

	Key	**Z1**	**Z2**	**Z3**	**Cons**	**Sel**	**Src**
c1	10	x	{y,w}	z	false	true	{s1,s2,s3}
c2	20	y	⊥	z	true	true	{s1,s2}

Two merged ctuples X(c1) and X(c2) associated with the schema *(K,Z,Cons,Sel,Src)* are equivalent (X(c1) ≅ X(c2)) if they do not conflict in any attribute but the Src attribute. More formally, X(c1) ≅ X(c2) if X(c1)[K] = X(c2)[K] and for each A in Z is: i) X(c1)[Cons] = X(c2)[Cons], ii) X(c1)[Sel] = X(c2)[Sel] and iii) either X(c1)[A] = X(c2)[A] or ⊥∈ *{ X(c1)[A], X(c2)[A] }*.

Two ctuples c1 and c2 are considered equivalent if the corresponding merged ctuples are equivalent.

Selection Operator

The *Sel* attribute will be modified after the application of selection operations. In particular, for a given ctuple *c* and a given selection condition θ, the attribute *Sel* will be: (i) true if θ is satisfied by all tuples in c, (ii) *false* if there is no tuple in *c* satisfying θ and (iii) *maybe* otherwise.

In classical relational algebra the select operator determines the selection status of a tuple for a given selection condition, thus the selection status over a tuple can be either *true* or *false*. In order to apply the selection predicate to a ctuple *c*, the selection predicate is applied to a nested ctuple *X(c)*. The semantics of the selection operator, in the flexible relational algebra, has to be extended to operate over non-1NF tuples; in fact the attributes of a ctuple may be associated with more than one value due to data conflicts.

Given a flexible relational schema *(K, Z, Cons, Sel, Src)*, a *simple partial predicate* is of the form *(A op λ)* or *(A op B)*, where A,B ∈ K ∪ Z, op ∈ {=,≠, >,≥, <, ≤} and λ is a single value, i.e., λ ∈ DOM(A) ∪ ⊥.

The predicate (*A op B)* evaluates to true, false or maybe as follows:

- true, if ∀ αi ∈ A, ∀ βj ∈ B | (αi *op* βj) is true.
- false, if ∀ αi ∈ A, ∀ βj ∈ B | (αi *op* βj) is false.
- maybe, otherwise.

The predicate (A *op λ)* is equivalent to (A op {λ}).

Obviously since the semantics given to null is that of no information, any comparisons with null values evaluate to false. Hence predicate *(a op λ)* evaluates to false if *a* or λ is null, and predicate *(A1 op A2)* evaluates to false if *A1* or *A2* is null.

Union Operator

The union operator combines the tuples of two source ctuples in order to obtain a new ctuple. Note that this operation is meaningful if and only if the two ctuples represent data of the same concept, and so their schema coincide and the value of the selection attribute is *true*. The union operation has to be applied before any selection operation, because the selection operation can lead to a loss of information.

A union of two ctuples *c1* and *c2* associated with schema *(K,Z,Cons,Sel,Src)* where *c1[K]= c2[K]*, denoted by *c= c1 ∪ c2*, is such that for each tuple t ∈ c, either *t ∈ c1* or *t ∈ c2*.

Integrated Relational Calculus

An extension of flexible algebra for other key functional dependencies, called *Integrated Relational Calculus*, was proposed by Dung (1996). The integrated relational calculus is based on the definition of *maximal consistent subsets* for a possible inconsistent database. Dung proposed extending relations by also considering null values denoting the absence of information with the restriction that tuples cannot have null values for the key attributes.

The integrated relational calculus overcomes some drawbacks of the flexible relational algebra:

- flexible relational algebra is not able to integrate possibly inconsistent relations if the associated relation schema has more than one key;
- the flexible relational model provides a rather weak query language.

The following two examples show two cases where the flexible algebra fails.

Example 9. Consider the database containing the single binary relation R whose schema is (employee,wife) with two keys {employee} (primary key) and {wife} (secondary key). Assume there are two different instances for R, R1 = {(Terry,Lisa)} and R2 = { (Peter,Lisa) }. Integrating R1 and R2 using the flexible model, we obtain the relation D = { (Terry,Lisa), (Peter,Lisa) }. Now asking "Whose wife is Lisa?" the flexible algebra will return the incorrect answer {Terry, Peter}. In this example it is evident that flexible algebra fails in detecting the inconsistency in the data in R1 and R2, due to the fact that wife is a key. A correct answer would have been that it is undetermined who is the husband of Lisa.

Example 10. Consider the database schema consisting of the single binary relation R with two attributes {employee, department} and {employee} being the primary key. Assume there are two different instances of R, R1= {(Terry, CS)} and R2={(Terry, Math) }. By integrating R1 and R2 using the flexible model, we obtain the relation D = { (Terry, {CS, Math}) }. Now asking the question "Who is employed in CS or Math?" the expected answer is { Terry }, but flexible model will give $\emptyset$, that is, it does not know who is working in CS or Math. Thus the flexible relational algebra is not able to express the selection formula (department = CS $\vee$ department = Math); moreover there is not even a way to ask a query like "Who is possibly employed in Math?"

The model proposed by Dung generalizes the model of flexible relational algebra. He argues that the semantics of integrating possibly inconsistent data is naturally captured by the maximal consistent subsets of the set of all information contained in the collection data.

The assumption in the Integrated Relational Calculus is that the values of the attributes in the primary key are correct.

Let R be a relation with schema (K,Z), where K is the set of attributes in the primary key and Z the set of remaining attributes. Given two tuples t and t' over R, we say:

- t and t' are *related* if $t[K] = t'[K]$, i.e., they agree on the key attributes;
- t and t' are *conflicting* if there exists a key K' of R such that i) for each $B \in K'$, $t[B] = t'[B] \neq \bot$ and ii) there is an attribute $A \in K \cup Z$ such that $\bot \neq t[A] \neq t'[A] \neq \bot$.
- t is *less informative* than t', denoted by $t \sqsubseteq t'$ if and only if for each attribute $A \in K \cup Z$ is $t[A] = \bot$ or $t[A] = t'[A]$.

A set of tuples *T* over *R* is said to be *joinable* if there exists a tuple *t'* such that for each $t \in T$, *t* is less informative than *t'*.

The notion of less informative can be extended to relations. Given two relation instances R1 and R2 over R, we say that R2 is less informative than R1 (and write R2 $\subseteq$ R1) if for each tuple t2 $\in$ R2 there exists a related tuple t1 $\in$ R1 (t1[K] = t2[K]) which is more informative than t2 (t2 $\subseteq$ t1).

The Integrated Relational Model

The *Integrated Relational Model* integrates data contained in autonomous information sources by a collecting step consisting of the union of the relations.

Let R1, R2 be two relations over a relation R with schema (K,Z). If the information collected from R1 and R2, represented by R = R1 $\cup$ R2, is consistent, R represents the integration of information in R1 and R2. Moreover, if R = R1 $\cup$ R2 is inconsistent, a maximal consistent subset of the information contained in R would be one possible admissible collection of information a user could extract from the integration.

Given a relation instance R, and two tuples t1, t2 in R with t1[K] = t2[K], the extension of t1 w.r.t. t2, denoted by ext(t1,t2), is the tuple derived from t1 by replacing every null value t1[a] with t2[a].

The extension of a relation R, denoted Ext(R), is the relation derived from R by first adding to R all possible extensions of tuples in R made with other tuples of R and next deleting tuples which are subsumed by other tuples. More formally,

Ext(R) = R' – { t in R' | $\exists$ t1 $\in$ R' s.t. t $\neq$ t1 and t $\subseteq$ t1}
where:
R' = R $\cup$ { ext(t1,t2) | $\exists$ t1, t2 $\in$ R }

Example 11. Consider the inconsistent relation R below. The relation R' is obtained from R by adding a tuple obtained by extending the tuple containing a null value. The relation Ext(R) is obtained from R' by deleting the tuple with a null value.

R		
emp	**tel**	**salary**
Terry	5709	35
Terry	⊥	20

R'		
emp	**tel**	**salary**
Terry	5709	35
Terry	⊥	20
Terry	5709	20

Ext(R)		
emp	**tel**	**salary**
Terry	5709	35
Terry	5709	20

Let $R_1,...,R_n$ be n relation instances over the same relational schema (K,Z).

- A possible integration of $R_1,...,R_n$ is defined as the relational representation of a maximal consistent subset of $Ext(R_1 \cup ... \cup R_n)$.
- The collection of all possible integrations of $R_1,...,R_n$ is defined as the semantics of integrating $R_1,...,R_n$ denoted by $Integ(R_1,...,R_n)$ (i.e., the set of maximal subsets of $Ext(R_1 \cup ... \cup R_n)$).

Example 12. The maximal consistent subsets of relation Ext(R) in the above examples are:

Ext(R)		
emp	**tel**	**salary**
Terry	5709	35

Ext(R)		
emp	**tel**	**salary**
Terry	5709	20

Querying Integrated Relations

Queries over integrated data are formulated by means of a language derived by relational calculus, called *integrated relational calculus*, through the insertion of quantifiers which refer to the possible integrations.

Example 13. Consider the inconsistent relation D = {(Frank, Ann), (Carl, Ann)} over the schema (employee, wife) with the two alternative keys {employee} and {wife}. Integ(D) consists of two possible integrations: {(Frank,Ann)} and {(Carl,Ann)}. The query "Whose wife is Ann?" can be formulated in the Integrated Relational Calculus by:

- $Q1 = \exists employee.R(employee,wife) \wedge wife = Ann$ which can be stated as *"Whose wife is Ann in a possible scenario?"*
- $Q2 = K(\exists\ employee.R(employee,wife) \wedge wife = Ann)$ which can be stated as *"Whose wife is Ann in every scenario?"* (here the modal quantifier *K* refers to all possible integrations).

In the first case the answer to the query Q1 is given by taking the union of the tuples matching the goal in all possible scenarios (brave reasoning), that is Ans(Q1) = {Frank, Carl}. The answer to the Query Q2 is obtained by considering the intersection of the tuples matching the goal in each possible scenario (cautious reasoning), thus Ans(Q2) = ∅.

Knowledge Base Merging by Majority

In the integration of different databases, an alternative approach, taking the disjunction of the maximal consistent subsets of the union of the databases, has been proposed in Baral et al. (1991a). A refinement of this technique was presented by Lin and Mendelzon (1996), who proposed taking into account the majority view of the knowledge bases in order to obtain a new relation which is consistent with the integrity constraint. The technique proposes a formal semantics to merge first-order theories under a set of constraints.

Semantics of Theory Merging

The basic idea is that, given a set of theories to merge $T_1,\ldots,T_n$ and a set of constraints *IC*, the models of the resulting theory, $Merge(\{T_1,\ldots,T_n\},IC)$, have to be those worlds 'closest' to the original theories, that is the worlds that have a minimal distance from $\{T_1,\ldots,T_n\}$. The distance between two worlds w and w', denoted by *dist(w,w')* is the cardinality of the symmetric difference of w and w', that is:

$dist(w,w') = |w \oplus w'| = (w-w') \cup (w'-w)$.

Then the distance between a possible world *w* and $\{T1,...,T_n\}$ is

$$dist(w,\{T_1,...,T_n\}) = \sum_{i=1}^{n} dist(w,T_i)$$

$$Merge(\{T_1,...,T_n\}, IC) = \{ w \mid w \text{ is a model of IC and } dist(w,\{T_1,...,T_n\}) \text{ is minimum}\}$$

Example 14. Consider the following three relation instances which collect information regarding author, title and year of publication of papers.

Bib1		
Author	**Title**	**Year**
John	T1	1980
Mary	T2	1990

Bib2		
Author	**Title**	**Year**
John	T1	1981
Mary	T2	1990

Bib3		
Author	**Title**	**Year**
John	T1	1980
Frank	T3	1990

From the integration of the three databases Bib1, Bib2 and Bib3, we obtain the database Bib.

Bib		
Author	**Title**	**Year**
John	T1	1980
Mary	T2	1990
Frank	T3	1980

The value of *Merge(Bib, {Bib1,Bib2,Bib3})* is equal to *Merge(Bib, Bib1) + Merge(Bib, Bib2) + Merge(Bib, Bib3) = 1 + 3 + 1 = 5* which is the minimum distance (among the relations satisfying IC) from the relations *Bib1,Bib2,Bib3*.

Thus, the technique proposed by Lin and Mendelson removes the conflict about the year of publication of the paper T1 written by the author John, observing that two of the three source databases that have to be integrated store the value 1980; thus the information that is maintained is the one which is present in the majority of the knowledge bases.

However, the 'merging by majority' technique does not resolve conflicts in all cases since information is not always present in the majority of the databases and, therefore, it is not always possible to choose between alternative values. In this case the integrated database contains disjunctive information. This is obtained by considering generalized tuples, i.e., tuples where each attribute value can be either a simple value or a set.

Example 15. Suppose now that in relation R3 the first tuple (John, T1, 1980) is replaced by the tuple (John, T1, 1982). The merged database contains now disjunctive information since it is not possible to decide the year of the book written by John.

Author	Title	Year
John	T1	{1980,1981,1982}
Mary	T2	1990
Frank	T3	1980

Here the first tuple states that the year of publication of the book written by John with title T1 can be one of the values belonging to the set {1980, 1981, 1982}.

In the absence of integrity constraints, the merge operation reduces to the union of the databases, i.e., $Merge(\{T_1,...,T_n\}, \{\}) = T_1 \cup ... \cup T_n$, whereas if *IC* is a set of functional dependencies, $Merge(\{T_1,...,T_n\}, IC) = T_1 \cup ... \cup T_n \cup IC$.

Computing Repairs

An interesting technique has recently been proposed in Arenas et al. (1999). The technique introduces a logical characterization of the notion of consistent answer in a possibly inconsistent database. Queries are assumed to be given in prefix disjunctive normal form.

A query *Q(X)* is a prenex disjunctive first-order formula of the form:

$$K\,[\vee_{i=1}^{s}\,(\wedge_{j=1}^{m_i}\,P_{i,j}\,(u_{i,j}) \wedge \bigwedge_{j=1}^{n_i} \neg\,R_{i,j}\,(v_{i,j}) \wedge \Psi_i\,)\,]$$

where K is a sequence of quantifiers, Ψ_i contains only built-in predicates and *X* denotes the list of variables in the formula.

Given a query *Q(X)* and a set of integrity constraints *IC,* a tuple *t* is a *consistent answer* to the query *Q(X)* over a database instance D, written $(Q,D) \models_c t$, if t is a substitution for the variables in X such that for each repair D' of D, $(Q,D') \models t$.

Example 16. Consider the relation Student with schema (Code, Name, Faculty) with the attribute Code as key. The functional dependencies Code → Name and Code → Address can be expressed by the following two constraints:

$$\forall (x,y,z,u,v)\,[\,Student(x,y,z) \wedge Student(x,u,v) \supset y=u\,]$$
$$\forall (x,y,z,u,v)\,[\,Student(x,y,z) \wedge Student(x,u,v) \supset z=v\,]$$

Assume there is an inconsistent instance of Student as reported in the figure below:

	Student	
Code	**Name**	**Faculty**
s1	Mary	Engineering
s2	John	Science
s2	Frank	Engineering

The inconsistent database has two repairs, Repair1 and Repair2.

Repair1		
Code	**Name**	**Faculty**
s1	Mary	Engineering
s2	John	Science

Repair2		
Code	**Name**	**Faculty**
s1	Mary	Engineering
s2	Frank	Engineering

The consistent answer to the query $\exists z\ Student(s1,y,z)$ is "Engineering," while there is no consistent answer to the query $\exists z\ (Student(s2,y,z)$.

General Approach

The technique is based on the computation of an equivalent query $T_\omega(Q)$ derived from the source query Q. The definition of $T_\omega(Q)$ is based on the notion of residue developed in the context of semantic query optimization.

More specifically, for each literal B, appearing in some integrity constraint, a residue $Res(B)$ is computed. Intuitively, $Res(B)$ is a universal quantified first-order formula which must be true, because of the constraints, if B is true. Universal constraints can be rewritten as denials, i.e., logic rules with empty heads of the form $\leftarrow B_1 \wedge ... \wedge B_n$.

Let A be a literal, r a denial of the form $\leftarrow B_1 \wedge ... \wedge B_n$, B_i (for some $1 \le i \le n$), a literal unifying with A, and θ the most general unifier for A and B_i such that variables in A are used to substitute for variables in B_i, but they are not substituted by other variables. Then, the residue of A with respect to r and B_i is:

$$\begin{aligned} Res(A,r,Bi) &= not((B_1 \wedge ... \wedge B_{i-1} \wedge B_{i+1} \wedge ... \wedge B_n)\ \theta\ ) \\ &= not\ B_1\theta \vee ... \vee not\ B_{i-1}\theta\ \vee not\ B_{i+1}\theta\ \vee ... \vee not\ B_n\theta\ . \end{aligned}$$

The residue of A with respect to r is $Res(A,r) = \wedge_{Bi|A=Bi\theta}\ Res(A,r,B_i)$ consisting of the conjunction of all the possible residues of A in r, whereas the residue of A with respect to a set of integrity constraints IC is $Res(A) = \wedge_{r\in IC}\ Res(A,r)$.

Thus, the residue of a literal A is a first-order formula which must be true if A is true.

The operator $T_\omega(Q)$ is defined as follows:

- $T_0(Q) = Q$;
- $T_i(Q) = T_{i-1}(Q) \wedge R$ where R is a residue of some literal in T_{i-1}.

The operator T_ω represents the fixpoint of T.

It has been shown that the operator T has a fixpoint for universal quantified queries and universal binary integrity constraints, i.e., constraints, which written in disjunctive format, are of the form: $\forall X\ (B_1 \vee B_2 \vee \theta)$ where B_1, B_2 are literals and θ is a conjunctive formula with built-in operators. Moreover, it has also been shown that the technique is complete for universal binary integrity constraints and universal quantified queries.

Example 17. Consider a database D consisting of the following two relations:

Supplier	Department	Item
c1	d1	i1
c2	d2	i2

Supply

Item	Type
i1	t
i2	t

Class

with the integrity constraint, defined by the following first-order formula:

$\forall(X, Y, Z)$ [Supply(X,Y,Z) $\wedge$ Class(Z,t) $\supset$ X=c1]

stating that only supplier *c1* can supply items of type *t*.

The database *D = { Supply(c1, d1, i1), Supply(c2, d2, i2), Class(i1, t), Class(i2, t) }* is inconsistent because the integrity constraint is not satisfied (an item of type *t* is also supplied by supplier *c2*).

This constraint can be rewritten as $\leftarrow$ *Supply(X,Y,Z)* $\wedge$ *Class(Z,t)* $\wedge$ X $\neq$ c1, where all variables are (implicitly) universally quantified. The residue of the literals appearing in the constraint are:

Res(Supply(X,Y,Z)) = not Class(Z,t) $\vee$ X = c1
Res(Class(Z,t)) = not Supply(X,Y,Z) $\vee$ X = c1

The iteration of the operator *T* to the query goal Class(Z,t) gives:

- T_0(Class(Z,t)) = Class(Z,t),
- T_1(Class(Z,t)) = Class(Z,t) $\wedge$ (not Supply(X,Y,Z) $\vee$ X = c1),
- T_2(Class(Z,t)) = Class(Z,t) $\wedge$ (not Supply(X,Y,Z) $\vee$ X = c1).

At Step 2 a fixpoint is reached since the literal *Class(Z,t)* has been 'expanded' and the literal *not Supply(X,Y,Z)* does not have a residue associated to it. Thus, to answer the query *Q = Class(Z,t)* with the above integrity constraint, the query $T_\omega(Q)$=*Class(Z,t)* $\wedge$ *(not Supply(X,Y,Z)* $\vee$ *X = c1)* is evaluated. The computation of $T_\omega(Q)$ over the above database gives the result *Z=i1*.

The following example shows a case where the technique proposed is not complete.

Example 18. Consider the integrity constraint $\forall$(X,Y,Z) [p(X,Y) $\wedge$ p(X,Z) $\supset$ Y=Z], the database D = { p(a,b), p(a,c) } and the query Q = $\exists$U p(a,U) (we are using the formalism used in Arenas et al., 1999). The technique proposed generates the new query T_ω(Q) = $\exists$U [p(a,U) $\wedge$ $\forall$Z($\neg$p(a,Z) $\vee$ Z=U)] which is not satisfied contradicting the expected answer which is true.

This technique is complete for universal binary integrity constraints and universal quantified queries. Moreover the detection of fixpoint conditions is, generally, not easy.

Querying Database Using Logic Programs with Exceptions

The new approach proposed by Arenas-Bertossi-Chomicki in Arenas, Bertossi and Chomicki (2000) consists of the use of a Logic Program with Exceptions (LPe) for obtaining consistent query answers. An LPe is a program with the syntax of an extended logic program (ELP), that is, in it we may find both logical (or strong) negation ($\neg$) and procedural negation (not). In this program, rules with a positive literal in the head represent a sort of general default, whereas rules with a logically negated head represent exceptions. The semantic of an LPe is obtained from the semantics for ELPs, by adding extra conditions that assign higher priority to exceptions. The method, given a set of integrity constraints ICs and an inconsistent database instance, consists of the direct specification of database repairs in a logic programming formalism. The resulting program will have both negative and positive exceptions, strong and procedural negations, and disjunctions of literals in the head of some of the clauses; that is, it will be a disjunctive extended logic program with exceptions. As in Arenas et al. (1999), the method considers a set of integrity constraints, IC, written in the standard format $\vee_{i=1}^{n} P_i(x_i) \vee \vee_{i=1}^{m}(\neg Q_i(y_i) \vee \varphi$ where φ is a formula containing only built-in predicates, and there is an implicit universal quantification in front. This method specifies the repairs of the database D that violate IC, by means of a logical program with exceptions Π^D. In Π^D for each predicate *P* a new predicate P' is introduced and each occurrence of *P* is replaced by *P'*. More specifically, Π^D is obtained by introducing:

1) **Persistence Defaults.** For each base predicate *P*, the method introduces the persistence defaults:

   $$P'(x) \leftarrow P(x),$$
   $$\neg P'(x) \leftarrow not\ P(x).$$

   The predicate *P'* is the repaired version of the predicate *P*, so it contains the tuples corresponding to *P* in a repair of the original database.

2) **Stabilizing Exceptions.** From each *IC* and for each negative literal *not* Q_{i0} in *IC*, the negative exception clause is introduced:

   $$\neg Q'_{i0}(y_{i0}) \leftarrow \wedge_{i=1..n} \neg P'_i(x_i), \wedge_{i \neq i0} Q'_i(y_i), \varphi'$$

   where φ' is a formula that is logically equivalent to the logical negation of φ. Similarly, for each positive literal P_{i1} in the constraint, the positive exception clause

   $$P'_{i1}(x_{i1}) \leftarrow \wedge_{i \neq i1} \neg P'_i(x_i), \wedge_{i=1..m} Q'_i(y_i), \varphi$$

   is generated. The meaning of the Stabilizing Exceptions is to make the ICs be satisfied by the new predicates. These exceptions are necessary but not sufficient to ensure that the changes the original subject should be subject to, in order to restore consistency, are propagated to the new predicates.

3) **Triggering Exceptions.** From the IC in standard form, the disjunctive exception clause

   $$\vee_{i=1..n} P'_i(x_i) \vee \vee_{i=1..m} Q'_i(y_i) \leftarrow \wedge_{i=1..n} not\ P_i(x_i), \wedge_{i=1..m} Q_i(y_i), \varphi'$$

   is produced.

The program Π^D constructed as shown above is a "disjunctive extended repair logic program with exceptions for the database instance D." In Π^D positive defaults are blocked by negative conclusions, and negative defaults, by positive conclusions.

Example 19. Consider the database D = {p(a), q(b)} with the inclusion dependency ID:

$$p(X) \supset q(X)$$

In order to specify the database repairs, the new predicates *p'* and *q'* are introduced. The resulting repair program has four default rules expressing that *p'* and *q'* contain exactly what *p* and q contain, resp.:

$p'(x) \leftarrow p(x);$
$q'(x) \leftarrow q(x);$
$\neg p'(x) \leftarrow not\ p(x)$ and
$\neg q'(x) \leftarrow not\ q(x);$

two stabilizing exceptions :

$q'(x) \leftarrow p'(x);$
$\neg p'(x) \leftarrow \neg q'(x);$

and the triggering exception:

$$\neg p'(x) \vee q'(x) \leftarrow p(x), not\ q(x).$$

The e-answer sets are *{ p(a), q(b), p'(a), q'(b), ¬p'(a) }* and *{ p(a), q(b), p'(a),q'(b), q'(b) }* that correspond to the two expected database repairs.

The method can be applied to a set of domain-independent binary integrity constraints *IC*, that is the constraint can be checked w.r.t. satisfaction by looking to the active domain, and in each *IC* appear at most two literals.

Query Answering in the Presence of Constraints

In Lembo et al. (2002), Calì, DeGiacomo and Lenzerini (2001a, 2001b) and Lenzerini (2002), a framework for data integration is proposed that allows us to specify a general form of integrity constraints over the global schema, and a semantics for data integration in the presence of incomplete and inconsistent information sources is defined.

Moreover, a method is defined for query processing under the above semantics when key constraints and foreign key constraints are defined upon the global schema.

Formally, a data integration system *I* is a triple $<G, S, M_{G,S}>$ where *G* is the global schema, *S* is the source schema and $M_{G,S}$ is the mapping between *G* and *S*.

More specifically, the *global schema* is expressed in the relational model with both key and foreign key constraints, the *source schema* is expressed in the relational model without integrity constraints, and the *mapping* is defined between the global and the source schema, i.e., each relation in *G* is associated with a view, i.e., a query over the sources.

Example 20. An example of a data integration system, reported in Calì et al. (2001b), is

I= $<G, S, M_{G,S}>$ where *G* is constituted by the following relation symbols:

student(Scode, Sname, Scity)
university(Ucode, Uname)
enrolled(Scode, Ucode)

and the constraints:

key(student) = {Scode}
key(university) = {Ucode}
key(enrolled) = {Scode, Ucode}
enrolled[Scode] $\subseteq$ student[Scode]
enrolled[Ucode] $\subseteq$ university[Ucode]

In the above, *S* consists of three sources: s_1, of arity 4, containing information about students with their code, name, city and date of birth; s_2, of arity 2, containing codes and names of universities; and s_3, of arity 2, containing information about enrollment of students in universities.

The mapping $M_{G,S}$ is defined by:

ρ(student) = student(X,Y,Z) $\leftarrow$ s_1(X,Y,Z,W)
ρ(university) = university(X,Y) $\leftarrow$ s_2(X,Y)
ρ(enrolled) = enrolled(X,Y) $\leftarrow$ s_3(X,Y)

The semantics of a data integration system is given by considering a source database *D* for *I*, i.e., a database for the source schema *S* containing a relation r^D for each source *r* in *S*.

Any database *G* is a *global database* for *I*, and it is said to be *legal* w.r.t. *D* if :

- It satisfies the integrity constraints defined in *G*.
- It satisfies the mapping w.r.t. *D*, i.e., for each relation *r* in *G*, the set of tuples r^B that *B* assigns to *r* contains the set of tuples $\rho(r)^D$ computed by the associated query $\rho(r)$ over *D*: $\rho(r)^D \subseteq r^B$

Note that each view is only considered *sound*, i.e., the data provided by the sources are not necessarily complete.

It is possible to formulate another assumption on views, in particular a view may be *complete*, i.e., for each view in *G*, it is $\rho(r)^D \supseteq r^B$ or *exact*, i.e., for each view in *G*, it is $\rho(r)^D = r^B$.

In this framework, the semantics of *I* w.r.t. a source database D, denoted $sem^D(I,D)$, is given in terms of a set of databases. In particular $sem^D(I, D) = \{ B \mid B \text{ is a legal global database for } I, \text{ w.r.t. } D\}$. If $sem^D(I, D) \neq \emptyset$, then I is said to be consistent w.r.t. D.

Answering Query

In this setting a query *q* posed to a data integration system *I* is a conjunctive query over the global schema, whose atoms have symbols in *G* as predicates.

A tuple $(c_1,\ldots,c_n)$ is considered an answer to the query only if it is a *certain* answer, i.e., if it satisfies the query in every database that belongs to the semantics of the data integration system.

More formally, a *certain answer* of a query q with arity n w.r.t. I and D is the set:

$$q^{I,D} = \{(c_1, .., c_n) \mid \text{for each DB} \in \text{sem}(I, D), (c_1, .., c_n) \in q^{DB}\}$$

where q^{DB} denotes the result of evaluating q in the database DB.

The *retrieved global database*, denoted by *ret(I, D)*, is obtained by computing each relation r of the global schema r^D by evaluating the query $\rho(r)$ over the source database D.

Note that the *retrieved global database* satisfies all the key constraints in G, as it is assumed that $\rho(r)$ does not violate the key constraints, thus if *ret(I,D)* also satisfies the foreign key constraints, then the answer to a query q can be done by simply evaluating it over *ret(I,D)*.

If it is the case that *ret(I,D)* violates the foreign key constraints, then tuples have to be added to the relations of the global schema in order to satisfy them.

Obviously in general there are an infinite number of legal databases that are coherent with the retrieved global database, even if it is shown that there exists one, the *canonical database*, denoted *can(I,D)*, that represents all the legal databases that are coherent with the retrieved global database.

Thus formally the answer to a query q can be given by evaluating *can(I, D)*. Anyhow the computation of the canonical database is impractical as generally the database can be infinite, thus in Calì et al. (2001b), an algorithm is defined that computes the certain answers of a conjunctive query q without actually building *can(I, D)*.

The algorithm transforms the original query q into a new query, called the *expansion of q w.r.t. G*, $exp_G(q)$ over the global schema, such that the answer $exp_G(q)$ over the (virtual) retrieved global database is equal to the answer to q over the canonical database, i.e., $exp_G(q)$ is independent of the source database D. Roughly the algorithm is based on the idea of expressing foreign key constraints in terms of rules of a logic program P_G with functional symbols (used as Skolem functions).

In order to build the program P_G:

- A new relation r', called *primed relation*, is added for each relation r in G.

$$r'(X_1,\ldots,X_n) \leftarrow (X_1,\ldots,X_n)$$

- For each foreign key $r_1[A] \subseteq r_2[B]$ in G where A and B are sets of attributes and B is a foreign key for r_2, this rule is added:

$$r'_2(X_1,\ldots,X_h, f_{h+1}(X_1,\ldots,X_h),\ldots,f_{h+1}(X_1,\ldots,X_h)) \leftarrow (r'_1(X_1,\ldots,X_h,\ldots,X_n))$$

  where f_i are Skolem functions and it is assumed, for simplicity, that the first h attributes are involved in the foreign key.

The program P_G is then used to generate the query $exp_G(q)$ associated to q. In particular P_G is used to generate the *partial evaluation tree* of the query q, whose non-empty leaves constitute the reformulation $exp_G(q)$ of the query q.

Example 21. Suppose the global schema G of a data integration system consists of the following three relations:

person(Pcode, Age, CityofBirth)
student(Scode, University)
city(Name, Major)

with the constraints:

key(person) = {Pcode}
key(student) = {Scode}
key(city) = {Name}
person[CityofBirth] $\subseteq$ city[Name]
city[Major] $\subseteq$ person[Pcode]
student[SCode] $\subseteq$ person[Pcode]

The logic program P_G uses the predicate *person'*, of arity 3, *student'*, with arity 1 and city with arity 2 and constitutes the following program:

$$\text{person}'(X,Y,Z) \leftarrow \text{person}(X,Y,Z)$$
$$\text{student}'(X,Y) \leftarrow \text{student}(X,Y)$$
$$\text{city}'(X,Y) \leftarrow \text{city}(X,Y)$$
$$\text{city}'(X,f_1(X)) \leftarrow \text{person}'(Y,Z,X)$$
$$\text{person}'(Y, f_2(Y), f_3(Y)) \leftarrow \text{city}'(X,Y)$$
$$\text{person}'(Y, f_4(X), f_5(X)) \leftarrow \text{student}'(X,Y)$$

Suppose the query q:

$$q(X) \leftarrow \text{person}(X,Y,Z)$$

The non-empty leaves of the partial evaluation tree of q provide the following expansion $q' = exp_G(q)$ of the query:

$$q'(X) \leftarrow \text{person}(X,Y,Z)$$
$$q'(X) \leftarrow \text{student}(X,W_1)$$
$$q'(W_2) \leftarrow \text{city}(Z,W_2)$$

Thus the expanded query searches for codes of persons not only in the relation *person*, but also in *student* and *city*, where, due to the integrity constraints, the codes of the persons are known to be stored.

The above approach is further extended by Lembo et al. (2002), who investigate the query answer problem in the same setting, but under a loosely sound semantics of the mapping.

The difference with respect to the previous case can be seen in a situation in which there is no global database that both is coherent with G and satisfies the mapping w.r.t. D. In this case $ret(I, D)$ violates the constraints in G, i.e., there exists $r \in G$ and t_1, $t_2 \in$

ret(I, D) such that key(r) = X, t_1 [X] = t_2 [X], and $t_1 \neq t_2$. Under the strictly sound semantics, this means that there is a legal database for *I* w.r.t. *D*.

In order to avoid this problem, a loosely sound semantics is defined that allows the user to always have a coherent database by restricting the set of tuples to those satisfying the constraints.

The semantics allows elimination of tuples from *ret(I, D)*, in particular it implies that the legal databases are the ones that are "as sound as possible"; thus it considers only databases coherent with the constraints that "minimize" the elimination of tuples from $t_1, t_2 \in ret(I, D)$.

The method for computing a certain answer identifies the databases legal w.r.t. to *I'*, which is obtained from *I* by eliminating all the foreign key constraints in *G*. Obviously each such database *B* is contained in *ret(I, D)*. Then the query reformulation technique for the strictly sound semantics previously illustrated is used.

Complete Answers from Incomplete Databases

Levy (1996) considered the problem of answering queries from databases that may be incomplete. A database is *incomplete* or *partial* if tuples in each relation are only a subset of the tuples that *should* be in the relation, and generally only a part of each relation is known to be complete. Formally this situation can be modeled as having two sets of relations, the *virtual* and the *available* relations.

The virtual relations are $\mathfrak{R} = R_1,\ldots,R_n$ while the available relations are $\mathfrak{R}' = R'_1,\ldots,R'_n$, and for every $i \in \{1..n\}$, the extension of the available relation R'_i contains a *subset* of the tuples in the extension of the virtual relation R_i.

The important question stressed in this chapter, and originally investigated by Motro (1989) and Etzioni, Golden and Weld (1994), is the *answer completeness* problem, i.e., deciding whether an answer to a given query is guaranteed to be complete even if the database is incomplete or, in other words, the answer contains all the tuples we would have obtained by evaluating the query over the virtual relations.

Clearly if it is known that $R'_i \subseteq R_i$ for each $i \in \{1..n\}$, then the answer to the query may be incomplete; however, it is often the case that an available relation, say R'_i, has the property of being *partially complete*, i.e., some parts of R'_i are identical to R_i.

The local completeness property guarantees that if the answer to the query just depends on the complete portion, it is guaranteed to be complete. Local completeness for a relation R' is specified by a constraint on the tuples of R that are *guaranteed* to be in R'.

More formally: given a relation *R* of arity *n*, where and $X_1,\ldots,X_n$ are variables standing for its attributes, a constraint *C* on the relation *R* is a conjunction of atoms that includes constants, variables from $X_1,\ldots,X_n$ and other variables. The relations used in *C* can be either database relations or comparison predicates, but not *R* itself. A tuple $a_1,\ldots,a_n$ satisfies *C* w.r.t. a database instance if the conjunction resulting from substituting a_i for X_i in *C* is satisfied in *D*. The complement of *C* is denoted by $\neg C$.

Moreover given a constraint *C* on the relation *R*, a database instance *D* that includes the relations *R* and *R'* is said to satisfy the local-completeness statement *LC(R',R,C)* if *r'* contains all the tuples of R that satisfy C, i.e., if the results of the following two queries are identical over D:

$q_1(X_1,\ldots,X_n) \leftarrow R(X_1,\ldots,X_n), C$
$q_2(X_1,\ldots,X_n) \leftarrow R'(X_1,\ldots,X_n), C$

The solution to the answer-completeness problem is given by showing that this problem is equivalent to the one of detecting the independence of a query from an insertion update, i.e., the problem of determining whether the answer to a query changes as a result of an insertion to the database.

In particular the connection is formalized as following:

Definition 7. Let Q be a union of conjunctive queries over the virtual relations $\mathfrak{R}$ and comparison predicates, and let Γ be a set of local completeness statements of the form $LC(R'_j, R_j, C_j)$, where $R'_j \in \mathfrak{R}$ and $R_j \in \mathfrak{R}$. The query Q is answer-complete w.r.t. Γ if and only if $In^+(Q,(R_j, \neg C_j))$ holds for every statement in Γ.

In the above definition $In^+(Q,(R_j, \neg C_j))$ states that the query Q is independent from the insertion update $(R_j, \neg C_j)$, i.e., for any database instance D and any database instance D' that results from D by adding to R some tuples that satisfy $\neg C_j$, Q(D)= Q(D').

Thus the problem of detecting independence can be solved by using one of the algorithms studied in the literature. In particular the algorithm for detecting answer completeness of a query proposed in the chapter adopts the method based on the equivalence of queries proposed in Levy and Sagiv (1993).

The equivalence problem is undecidable for recursive queries (Shmueli, 1993), while the answer-completeness problem is decidable in the following cases:

- if each of the C_js contains only arguments of R_j or constants; or
- if the head of Q contains all the variables of the body of Q, and neither the C_js or Q use the comparison predicates.

In the general case the problem of deciding answer-completeness is Π_2^p. The best-known algorithm for the independence problem and therefore for the answer-completeness problem is exponential, even if it is shown that if updates are described using a conjunction of comparison predicates, the independence problem can be decided in polynomial time.

Condensed Representation of Database Repairs for Consistent Query Answering

Wijsen (2003) proposed a general framework for repairing databases. In particular the author stressed that an inconsistent database can be repaired without deleting tuples (*tuple-based* approach), but using a finer repair primitive consisting of correcting faulty values within the tuples, without actually deleting them (*value-based* approach).

Example 22. Suppose the following set of tuples reporting the dioxin levels in food samples:

Sample	Sample Date	Food	Analysis Date	Lab	DioxinLevel
110	17 Jan 2002	poultry	18 Jan 2002	ICI	normal
220	17 Jan 2002	poultry	16 Jan 2002	ICB	alarming
330	18 Jan 2002	beef	18 Jan 2002	ICB	normal

and the constraints:

$$\forall\, s, d_1, f, d_2, l, d(\text{Dioxin}(s, d_1, f, d_2, l, d) \rightarrow d_1 \leq d_2)$$

that impose the date of analyzing a given sample cannot precede the date the sample was taken.

The first tuple in the Dioxin Database says that the sample 110 was taken on 17 Jan 2002 and analyzed the day after at the ICI lab, and that the dioxin level of this sample was normal. While the sample 110 respects the constraint, the sample 220 violates it. An inconsistency is present in the database and the author claims to "clean" it in a way that avoids deleting the entire tuple, i.e., acting at the attribute level and not at the tuple level.

Given an inconsistent database a consistent answer can be obtained by letting the database in its inconsistent state, and by propagating in the answer the consistent portion of the database, i.e., the set of tuples matching the query and satisfying the constraints. Because the repair work is deferred until query time, this approach is called *late-repairing*.

In this framework an alternative technique is proposed consisting of a *database transformation*. Given a satisfiable set of constraints Σ, i.e., a set of finite constraints, and a relation I, apply a database transformation h_Σ: I $\rightarrow$ I such that for every query Q, $Q(h_\Sigma(I))$ yields exactly the consistent answer to Q on input I and Σ. Observe that $h_S(I)$ is not necessarily a repair for I and Σ; it can be thought of as a "*condensed representation*" of all possible repairs for I and Σ that are sufficient for consistent query answering. The practical intuition is that an inconsistent database I is first transformed through h_Σ in such a way that the subsequent queries on the transformed database retrieve exactly the consistent answer; since databases are modified prior to query execution, this approach is called *early-repeating*.

Clearly for a given set of satisfiable constraints Σ, early and late repairing should yield the same set of consistent answers, hence $f_\Sigma(Q)(I)=Q(h_\Sigma(I))$, for every query and every relation.

General Repairing Framework

Before formally introducing the framework, let's give some preliminaries.

The framework focuses on unirelational database, and the set of constraints, denoted Σ, are expressed in a first-order (FO) language using a simple n-ary predicate symbol. A tableau is a relation that can contain variables. A tableau T is said to *θ-subsume* a tableau S, here denoted $T \rhd S$, if there exists a substitution θ such that $\theta(S) \subseteq T$. The *θ-subsumption*, commonly used between clauses, is here used between tableaux representing the negation of a clause: the tableau $\{t_1,\ldots,t_m\}$, can be treated as $\exists^*(t_1 \wedge \ldots \wedge t_m)$, i.e., as the negation of the clause $\forall^*(\neg t_1 \wedge \ldots \wedge \neg t_m)$. Clearly, T $\supseteq$ S implies T $\triangleright$ S; hence θ-subsumption weakens the order $\supseteq$.

If G is a tableau, then grd(T) denotes the smallest relation that contains every ground tuple of T. A valuation is a mapping from variables to constants, extended to be the identity on constants; a substitution is a mapping from variables to symbols, extended to be the identity on constants. Valuation and substitution are extended to tuples and tableaux in a natural way. We write *id* for the identity function on symbol, and $id_{p=q}$, where p and q are not two distinct constants, for a substitution that identifies p and q and that is the identity otherwise. That is, if p is a variable and q a constant, then $id_{p=q}$ = {p/q} If p and q are variables, then $id_{p=q}$ can be either {p/q} or {q/p}.

Given two tableaux T and S, of the same given arity, we write S $\triangleright$ T if there exists a substitution q such that $\theta(T) \subseteq S$. We write S ~ T if S $\triangleright$ T and T $\triangleright$ S; we write S $\succ$ T if S $\triangleright$ T and it does not hold S ~ T. A relation *F* (a tableau in this context) *subsatisfies* Σ if there exists a relation $J \geq F$ such that $J \models \Sigma$.

Fixing (or repairing) a relation *I* with respect to a set Σ of integrity constraints means modifying *I* in order to bring it in accordance with Σ, by ensuring the "*minimal change*" principle, i.e., the result of fixing has to be as close as possible to the initial relation.

In particular fixing a relation is an operation consisting of *downfixing* followed by *upfixing*. Downfixing means that we pass from I to F, called *fix*, such that $I \geq F$ and F subsatisfies Σ. Upfixing means that we subsequently pass from F to a relation $M \geq F$ such that $M \models \Sigma$, where M is called *mend*. In fixing a relation it is required that the result of fixing is as close as possible to the initial relation.

In this framework the minimal change principle is settled by using the *Maximal content preservation* criterion: downfixing retains as much as possible from the original relation, and upfixing consists of a minimal completion: F should be such that there exists no *F'* that also subsatisfies Σ and such that $I \geq F' \geq F$, i.e., *F'* is closer to *I* than *F*. Next, for a given *F*, *M* should be such that there exists no *M'* such that $M \geq M' \geq F$ and $M' \models \Sigma$. This criteria only relies on the order ≥.

For the order ≥, the $\supseteq$ or the θ-subsumption could be chosen. Anyhow the author points out that both results are inadequate. In particular $\supseteq$ is too *strong* for repairing, as it does not allow differentiation between tuples that agree on most attributes and tuples that disagree on all attributes: the tuples are simply treated as unequal in both cases, thus the repairing is tuple-based. On the other side $\triangleright$ is too *weak* for downfixing, as it can produce mends with spurious tuples. Therefore the author claims downfixing has to be based on a relation, denoted $\sqsubseteq$, in between $\supseteq$ and $\triangleright$.

More formally, given two tableaux T and S, of the same given arity, S $\sqsubseteq$ T if there exists a substitution θ such that $\theta(T) \subseteq S$ and $|\theta(T)| \subseteq |T|$. The latter condition ensures that θ does not identify distinct tuples of T.

Related to the chosen order, $\sqsubseteq$, fix and mend are defined as follows.

Given a relation I, of arity n, and a set of constraints Σ:

- A *fix* for I and Σ is a tableau F such that I $\sqsubseteq$ F, F subsatisfies Σ, and for every tableau F' if I $\sqsubseteq$ F' $\succ$ F, then F' does not subsatisfy Σ.
- A *mend* for I and *Σ* is a relation M with $M \models \Sigma$ such that there exists a fix F for I and Σ satisfying: (i) M $\triangleright$ F and (ii) for every relation M', if M $\succ$ M' $\triangleright$ F, then M' does not satisfy Σ.

Note that the requirement I $\sqsubseteq$ F in the above definition implies the existence of a substitution θ such that θ(F) ⊆ I and |θ(F)| ⊆ |F|, thus for a given tuple t∈ I, there can be at most one repairing tuple t' ∈ F such that θ(t') = t.

Trustable Query Answers

Obviously for a given relation and a given set of constraints, the number of mends is generally infinite. Thus the author investigates the problem of querying these mends in order to obtain a consistent answer, here called *trustable* answer, i.e., an answer satisfying the set of constraints.

More formally, given a unirelational database consisting of a relation I, of arity *n*, a set of constraints Σ and a query q, the ground tuple t is a *trustable answer* to q on input Σ if t ∈ q(M) for every mend M for I and Σ.

Example 23. Continuing Example 22, let us consider the query:

Answer(s) ← Dioxin(s, d_1, f, d_2 ,l, "alarming")

asking for samples with an alarming dioxin level.

The identification "220" is a trustable answer, but it is not a trustable answer for the query asking for a sample date of 17 Jan 2002. In fact many mends show a different sample date for the sample "220."

A class **Q** of queries is *early-repairable* w.r.t. a class of constraints **C**, if for every satisfiable set of constraints Σ in **C** and for every relation I, there exists a computable relation I' such that for every query q ∈ **Q**, q(I') is exactly the set of trustable answers to q on input I and Σ.

After formally defining the trustable answer, the author focuses on the classes of queries and constraints for which trustable answers can be effectively computed, examining conjunctive queries and full dependencies.

Tableau Queries and Full Dependencies

A *tableau query* is a pair (B,h) where B is a tableau and h is a tuple (called *summary*) such that every variable in h also occurs in B; b and h need not have the same arity. Let τ =(B,h) be a tableau query, and tT a tableau of the same arity as B. A tuple t is an *answer* to τ on input T if there is a substitution θ for the variables in B such that θ(B) ⊆ T and θ(h) = t. The set of all answers to t on input T is denoted τ(T).

A *full dependency* is either a *full tuple-generating dependency* (ftgd) or a *full equality-generating dependency* (fegd). A ftgd takes the form of a conjunctive query (B,h) where B and h have the same arity. The ftgd τ =(B,h) is satisfied by a tableau T, denoted T |= τ, if T ∪ τ (T) ~T. A fegd is of the form (B, p =q) where B is a tableau and p and q are symbols such that every variable in {p,q} also occurs in B. The fegd ε = (B, p =q) is satisfied by a tableau T, denoted T| = ε , if for every substitution θ, if θ(B) ⊆ T then θ(p), θ(q) are not two distinct constants and T ~ $id_{\theta(p)=\theta(q)}$ (T).

Example 24. Consider a relation *Manifacture* with four attributes denoting date, product, color and quantity, respectively. For example a tuple (12 Jan 2002, lock, green, 1000) means that 1,000 green locks have been manufactured on 12 Jan 2002. The production line is subject to a number of constraints:

ε_1

1	2	3	4
x	y	z	u
x	y	z'	u'
	z = z'		

ε_2

1	2	3	4
x	y	z	u
x	y	z'	u'
	u = u'		

ε_3

1	2	3	4
8 Jan 2002	y	z	u
	0 = 1		

τ_1

1	2	3	4
x	lock	z	u
x	key	z	u

In particular the fegds ε_1 and ε_2 express that the date and the product uniquely identify tuples in *Manifacture*. ε_2 captures the fact that 8 Jan 2002 was a day of strike, on which no products were manufactured (0 and 1 can be replaced by any two distinct constants). Finally the ftgd τ_1 expresses that each production of a lock involves the simultaneous production of a key in the same color.

The author shows that given two tableaux T and S and a set of full dependencies Σ, if $T \sim S$ and $T \models \Sigma$, then $S \models \Sigma$.

Moreover it is known from Plotkin (1969) that every finite set S of tableaux has a greatest lower bound under $\rhd$. More formally, a tableau L is a *lower bound* of a finite set S of tableaux if for each $T \in S$, $T \rhd L$. A lower bound G of S is called the *greatest lower bound* (glb) of S if $G \rhd L$ for every lower bound L of S.

The construction of glb and tableau query commute up to $\sim$. In fact given two tableaux T and S, a tableau query $\tau = (B,h)$, a glb of $\{T,S\}$ and a glb of $\{\tau(T),\tau(S)\}$, then $\tau(G) \sim F$.

Chasing Fixes

The chase, originally introduced for deciding logical implication, is used for repairing databases. In particular some results are generalized to tableaux that can contain constants, need not to be typed and in which equality is replaced by $\sim$. An artificial top element, denoted $\square$, is introduced to the semi-order $<T, \rhd>$. Let $T \neq \square$ and S be tableaux and Σ a set of full dependencies. We write $T \vdash_\Sigma S$ if S can be obtained from T by a single application of one of the following *chase rules*:

- If $\tau = (B,h)$ is a ftgd on Σ, then $T \vdash_\Sigma T \cup \tau(T)$.
- Let $(B, p=q)$ be a fegd of Σ, and θ a substitution such that $\theta(B) \subseteq T$. If $\theta(p)$ and $\theta(q)$ are two distinct constants, then $T \vdash_\Sigma \square$; otherwise, $T \vdash_\Sigma id_{\theta(p)=\theta(q)}(T)$.

A *chase* of T by Σ is a maximal (w.r.t. length) sequence $T = T_0, T_1, \ldots, T_n$ of tableaux such that for every $i \in \{1,\ldots,n\}$, $T_{i-1} \vdash_\Sigma T_i$ and $T_i \neq T_{i-1}$. Requiring that chases be maximal tacitly assumes that chases are finite.

Given a tableau $F \neq \square$ and a set of full dependencies, then:

- If T is a tableau in a chase of F by Σ, then $T \rhd F$.
- Each chase of F by Σ is finite.
- If $T \neq \square$ is the last element of a chase of F by Σ, then $T \models \Sigma$.

- If T≠□ is the last element of a chase of F by Σ, and θ is a valuation mapping distinct variables to new distinct constants not occurring elsewhere, then θ(T) |= Σ.

The author shows that given a set of full dependencies Σ and a tableau F ≠ □, then F subsatisfies Σ if *chase(F, Σ) ≠* □. Thus a set of full dependencies Σ is satisfiable if *chase({}, Σ) ≠* □.

Example 25. Continuing Example 24, the following figure shows a Manifacture relation together with fixes and chase results. The integrity constraints are violated: no items can have been produced on 8 Jan 2002, and the production of 100 blue locks must entail 100 blue keys. Moreover red and blue keys cannot have been manufactured on the same day.

Manufacture

1	2	3	4
8 Jan 2002	lock	blue	110
8 Jan 2002	key	red	110

F_1

1	2	3	4
x	lock	blue	110
x	key	z	110

chase(F_1, Σ) ~

1	2	3	4
x	lock	blue	110
x	key	blue	110

F_2

1	2	3	4
x	lock	z	110
x	key	red	110

chase(F_2, Σ) ~

1	2	3	4
x	lock	red	110
x	key	red	110

F_3

1	2	3	4
x	lock	z	110
x	key	red	110

chase(F_3, Σ) ~

1	2	3	4
x	lock	blue	110
x	key	red	110
x	key	blue	110

F_4

1	2	3	4
x	lock	blue	110
x	y	red	110

chase(F_4, Σ) ~

1	2	3	4
x	lock	blue	110
x	y	red	110
x	key	blue	110

F_5

1	2	3	4
x	y	blue	110
x	key	red	110

chase(F_5, Σ) ~

F_1 and F_2 assume that the date of 8 Jan 2002 and either color (red or blue) were mistaken. F_4 and F_5 assume that the date of 8 Jan 2002 and either product (key or lock) were mistaken. Finally, F_3 assumes that the date of 8 Jan 2002 should be replaced by different dates in either tuple of *Manufacture*. It is easy to verify that any other fix is equivalent under ~ to one of the five fixes shown.

The formally definition of *trustable tableau* is as follows: let $\mathfrak{I}$ be a minimal set of tableaux (w.r.t. ⊆), such that for every fix F for I and Σ, there exists some tableau F' ∈ $\mathfrak{I}$ such that F' ~ F. Let Ω be a minimal (w.r.t. ⊆) set of tableaux such that for every F ∈ $\mathfrak{I}$, there exists some tableau T ∈ Ω such that T ∈ chase(F, Σ). Let G be a glb of Ω, then G is called a *trustable tableau* for I and Σ.

Computation of trustable tableaux is shown to be computable for unirelation database with a set of full dependencies. The computation is quite complex as it involves solving NP-complete problems, like deciding the q-subsumption for determining the fixing.

Rewriting into Disjunctive Queries

In Greco and Zumpano (2000) a general framework for computing repairs and consistent answers over inconsistent databases with universally quantified variables was proposed. The technique is based on the rewriting of constraints into extended disjunctive rules with two different forms of negation (negation as failure and classical negation). The disjunctive program can be used for two different purposes: compute 'repairs' for the database, and produce consistent answers, i.e., a maximal set of atoms which do not violate the constraints. The technique is sound and complete (each stable model defines a repair and each repair is derived from a stable model) and more general than techniques previously proposed.

More specifically, the technique is based on the generation of an extended disjunctive program *LP* derived from the set of integrity constraints. The repairs for the database can be generated from the stable models of *LP*, whereas the computation of the consistent answers of a query *(g,P)* can be derived by considering the stable models of the program $P \cup LP$ over the database *D*.

Let *c* be a universally quantified constraint of the form:

$$\forall X\, [\, B_1 \wedge \ldots \wedge B_k \wedge \text{not } B_{k+1} \wedge \ldots \wedge \text{not } B_n \wedge \phi \supset B_0\,]$$

then *dj(c)* denotes the extended disjunctive rule

$$\neg B'_1 \vee .. \vee \neg B'_k \wedge B'_{k+1} \vee \ldots \vee B'_n \vee B'_0 \leftarrow (B_1 \vee B'_1), \ldots, (B_k \vee B'_k), \\ (\text{not } B_{k+1} \vee \neg B'_{k+1}), \ldots, (\text{not } B_n \vee \neg B'_n), \phi, \\ (\text{not } B_0 \vee \neg B'_0),$$

where B'_i denotes the atom derived from B_i, by replacing the predicate symbol *p* with the new symbol p_d if B_i is a base atom otherwise is equal to false. Let *IC* be a set of universally quantified integrity constraints, then $DP(IC) = \{ dj(c) \mid c \in IC \}$ whereas *LP(IC)* is the set of standard disjunctive rules derived from *DP(IC)* by rewriting the body disjunctions.

Clearly, given a database *D* and a set of constraints *IC*, $LP(IC)_D$ denotes the program derived from the union of the rules *LP(IC)* with the facts in *D*, whereas $SM(LP(IC)_D)$ denotes the set of stable models of $LP(IC)_D$ and every stable model is consistent since it cannot contain two atoms of the form *A* and $\neg A$. The following example shows how constraints are rewritten.

Example 20. Consider the following integrity constraints:

- $\forall X\, [\, p(X) \wedge \text{not } s(X) \supset q(X)\,]$
- $\forall X\, [\, q(X) \supset r(X)\,]$

and the database D containing the facts p(a), p(b), s(a) and q(a).

The derived generalized extended disjunctive program is defined as follows:

$$\neg p_d(X) \vee s_d(X) \vee q_d(X) \leftarrow (p(X) \vee p_d(X)), (\text{not } s(X) \vee \neg s_d(X)),$$
$$(\text{not } q(X) \vee \neg q_d(X)).$$
$$\neg q_d(X) \vee r_d(X) \leftarrow (q(X) \vee q_d(X)) \wedge (\text{not } r(X) \vee \neg r_d(X)).$$

The above rules can now be rewritten in standard form. Let P be the corresponding extended disjunctive Datalog program. The computation of the program P_D gives the following stable models:

$$M_1 = D \cup \{ \neg p_d(b), \neg q_d(a) \}, \qquad M_2 = D \cup \{ \neg p_d(b), r_d(a) \},$$
$$M_3 = D \cup \{ \neg q_d(a), s_d(b) \}, \qquad M_4 = D \cup \{ r_d(a), s_d(b) \},$$
$$M_5 = D \cup \{ q_d(b), \neg q_d(a), r_d(b) \} \text{ and } M_6 = D \cup \{ q_d(b), r_d(a), r_d(b) \}.$$

A (generalized) extended disjunctive Datalog program can be simplified by eliminating from the body rules all literals whose predicate symbols are derived and do not appear in the head of any rule (these literals cannot be true). For instance, the generalized rules of the above example can be rewritten as:

$$\neg p_d(X) \vee s_d(X) \vee q_d(X) \leftarrow p(X), \text{not } s(X), (\text{not } q(X) \vee \neg q_d(X))$$
$$\neg q_d(X) \vee r_d(X) \leftarrow (q(X) \vee q_d(X)), \text{not } r(X)$$

because the predicate symbols p, $\neg s_d$ and $\neg r_d$ do not appear in the head of any rule. As mentioned before, the rewriting of constraints into disjunctive rules is useful for both i) making the database consistent through the insertion and deletion of tuples, and ii) computing consistent answers leaving the database inconsistent.

Computing Database Repairs

Every stable model can be used to define a possible repair for the database by interpreting new derived atoms (denoted by the subscript "d") as insertions and deletions of tuples. Thus, if a stable model M contains two atoms $\neg p_d(t)$ (derived atom) and $p(t)$ (base atom), we deduce that the atom $p(t)$ violates some constraints and, therefore, it must be deleted. Analogously, if M contains the derived atoms $p_d(t)$ and does not contain $p(t)$ (i.e., $p(t)$ is not in the database), we deduce that the atom $p(t)$ should be inserted in the database. We now formalize the definition of repaired database.

Given a database schema $DS = (R_s, IC)$ and a database D over DS, let M be a stable model of $LP(IC)_D$, then a repair for D is a pair:

$$R(M) = (\{p(t) \mid p_d(t) \in M \wedge p(t) \notin D\}, (p(t) \mid \neg p_d(t) \in M \wedge p_d(t) \in D\}).$$

Given a database schema $DS = (R_s, IC)$ and a database D over DS, a repair for D is a pair of sets of atoms (R^+, R^-) such that 1) $R^+ \cap R^- = \emptyset$, 2) $D \cup R^+ - R^- \models IC$ and 3) there is no pair $(S^+, S^-) \neq (R^+, R^-)$ such that $S^+ \supset R^+$, $S^- \supset R^-$ and $D \cup S^+ - S^- \models IC$. The database $D \cup R^+ - R^-$ will be called the repaired database.

Thus, repaired databases are consistent databases which are derived from the source database by means of a minimal set of insertion and deletion of tuples. Given a repair R for D, R^+ denotes the set of tuples which will be added to the database whereas R^- denotes the set of tuples of D which will be canceled. In the following, for a given repair R and a database D, $R(D) = D \cup R^+ - R^-$ denotes the application of R to D.

Example 21. Assume we are given a database D = { p(a), p(b), q(a), q(c)} with the inclusion dependency $(\forall X)[\, p(X) \supset q(X)\,]$. D is inconsistent since $p(X) \supset q(X)$ is not satisfied. The repairs for D are $R_1 = (\{ q(b) \}, \emptyset)$ and $R_2 = (\emptyset, \{ p(b) \})$ producing, respectively, the repaired databases $R_1(D) = \{p(a), p(b), q(a), q(c), q(b)\}$ and $R_2(D) = \{ p(a), q(a), q(c) \}$.

Example 22. Consider the integrity constraint IC = $\{ (\forall(X,Y,Z))\,[\, Teaches(X,Y), Teaches(X,Y) \supset Y=Z \,] \}$ over the database D of Example 1. The associated disjunctive program DP(IC) is:

$$\neg Teaches_d(X,Y) \vee \neg Teaches_d(X,Z) \leftarrow (Teaches_d(X,Y) \vee Teaches(X,Y)),\ (Teaches_d(X,Z) \vee Teaches(X,Z)),\ Y \neq Z$$

which can be simplified as follows:

$$\neg Teaches_d(X,Y) \vee \neg Teaches_d(X,Z) \leftarrow Teaches(X,Y), Teaches(X,Z), Y \neq Z$$

since the predicate symbol $Teaches_d$ does not appear in any positive head atom.

The program $LP(IC)_D$ has two stable models $M_1 = \{ \neg Teaches_d(c2,p2) \} \cup D$ and $M_2 = \{ \neg Teaches_d(c2,p3) \} \cup D$. The associated repairs are $R(M_1) = (\{\}, \{Teaches_d(c2,p2)\})$ and $R(M_2) = (\{\}, \{Teaches_d(c2,p3)\})$, denoting, respectively, the deletion of tuples $Teaches_d(c2,p2)$ and $Teaches_d(c2,p3)$.

The technique is sound and complete:

- Soundness—for every stable model M of $LP(IC)_D$, $R(M)$ is a repair for D.
- Completeness—for every database repair S for D, there exists a stable model M for $LP(IC)_D$ such that $S = R(M)$.

Example 23. Consider the database of Example 5. The rewriting of the integrity constraint $(\forall X)[\, p(X) \supset q(X)\,]$, produces the disjunctive rule:

$$\neg p_d(X) \vee q_d(X) \leftarrow (p(X) \vee p_d(X)),\ (\text{not } q(X) \vee \neg q_d(X))$$

which can be rewritten into the simpler rule r':

$$\neg p_d(X) \vee q_d(X) \leftarrow p(X) \text{ not } q(X)$$

The program P_D, where P is the program consisting of the disjunctive rule r', has two stable models $M_1 = D \cup \{ \neg p_d(b) \}$ and $M_2 = D \cup \{ q_d(b) \}$. The derived repairs are $R(M_1) = (\{\}, \{p(b)\})$ and $R(M_2) = (\{q(b)\}, \{\})$ corresponding, respectively, to the deletion of $p(b)$ and the insertion of $q(b)$.

Computing Consistent Answer

We now consider the problem of computing a consistent answer without modifying the (possibly inconsistent) database. We assume the truth value of tuples, contained in the database or implied by the constraints, may be either *true* or *false* or *undefined*.

Given a database schema $DS = (R_s, IC)$ and a database D over DS, an atom A is true (resp. false) with respect to (D,IC) if A belongs to all repaired databases (resp. there is no repaired database containing A). The set of atoms which are neither true nor false are undefined.

Thus, true atoms appear in all repaired databases whereas undefined atoms appear in a proper subset of repaired databases. Given a database D and a set of integrity constraints IC, the application of IC to D, denoted by $IC(D)$, defines the three distinct sets of atoms: $IC(D)^+$ (true atoms), $IC(D)^u$ (undefined atoms) and $IC(D)^-$ (false atoms).

- $IC(D)^+ = \{ p(t) \mid p(t) \in D \text{ and } \forall M \in SM(LP(IC)_D) \text{ is } \neg p_d(t) \notin M \} \cup$
  $\{ p(t) \mid p(t) \notin D \text{ and } \forall M \in SM(LP(IC)_D) \text{ is } p_d(t) \in M \}$
- $IC(D)^- = \{ p(t) \mid p(t) \in D \text{ and } \forall M \in SM(LP(IC)_D) \text{ is } \neg p_d(t) \in M \} \cup$
  $\{ p(t) \mid p(t) \notin D \text{ and } \forall M \in SM(LP(IC)_D) \text{ is } p_d(t) \notin M \}$
- $IC(D)^u = \{ p(t) \mid p(t) \in D \text{ and } \exists M_1, M_2 \in SM(LP(IC)_D)$
  $\text{s.t. } \neg p_d(t) \in M_1 \text{ and } \neg p_d(t) \notin M_2 \} \cup$
  $\{ p(t) \mid p(t) \notin D \text{ and } \exists M_1, M_2 \in SM(LP(IC)_D) \text{ s.t. } p_d(t) \in M_1 \text{ and } p_d(t) \notin M_2 \}$

The *consistent answer* of a query Q on the database D, denoted as $Q(D,IC)$, gives three sets, denoted as $Q(D,IC)^+$, $Q(D,IC)^-$ and $Q(D,IC)^u$. These contain, respectively, the sets of g-tuples which are *true* (i.e., belonging to Q(D') for all repaired databases D'), *false* (i.e., not belonging to Q(D') for all repaired databases D') and *undefined* (i.e., set of tuples which are neither true nor false) and are defined as follows:

- $Q(D,IC)^+ = \{ g(t) \mid g(t) \in D \text{ and } \forall M \in SM((P \cup LP(IC))_D) \text{ is } \neg g_d(t) \notin M \} \cup$
  $\{ g(t) \mid g(t) \notin D \text{ and } \forall M \in SM((P \cup LP(IC))_D) \text{ is } g_d(t) \in M \}$
- $Q(D,IC)^- = \{ g(t) \mid g(t) \in D \text{ and } \forall M \in SM((P \cup LP(IC))_D) \text{ is } \neg g_d(t) \in M \} \cup$
  $\{ g(t) \mid g(t) \notin D \text{ and } \forall M \in SM((P \cup LP(IC))_D) \text{ is } g_d(t) \notin M \}$
- $Q(D,IC)^u = \{ g(t) \mid g(t) \in D \text{ and } \exists M_1, M_2 \in SM((P \cup LP(IC))_D) \text{ s.t.}$
  $\neg g_d(t) \in M_1 \text{ and } \neg g_d(t) \notin M_2 \} \cup$
  $\{ g(t) \mid g(t) \notin D \text{ and } \exists M_1, M_2 \in SM((P \cup LP(IC))_D) \text{ s.t.}$
  $g_d(t) \in M_1 \text{ and } g_d(t) \notin M_2 \}$

For instance, in Example 21 the set of true tuples are those belonging to the intersection of the two models, that is *p(a), q(a)* and *q(c),* whereas the set of undefined tuples are those belonging to the union of the two models and not belonging to their intersection.

Example 24. Consider the database of Example 17. To answer a query it is necessary to define, first, the atoms which are true, undefined and false:

- $IC(D)^+ = \{ Supply(c1,d1,i1), Class(i1,t) \}$, the set of true atoms.
- $IC(D)^u = \{ Supply(c2,d2,i2), Class(i2,t) \}$, the set of undefined atoms.

The atoms not belonging to $IC(D)^+$ and $IC(D)^u$ are false.

The answer to the query (Class, {}) gives the tuple *(i1,t)*.

Observe that for every database D over a given schema $DS = (R_s, IC)$, for every query $Q = (g,P)$ and for every repaired database D':

- each atom $A \in Q(D,IC)^+$ belongs to the stable model of $P_{D'}$ (soundness);
- each atom $A \in Q(D,IC)^-$ does not belong to any stable model of $P_{D'}$ (completeness).

Example 25. Consider the integrated database D = {Teaches(c1,p1), Teaches(c2,p2), Teaches(c2,p3)} of Example 1 and the functional dependency defined by the key of relation Teaches which can be defined as:

$$\forall \ (X,Y)\,[\,Teaches(X,Y) \wedge Teaches(X,Z) \supset Y=Z\,]$$

The disjunctive program LP_D has two stable models: $M_1=D \cup \{\neg Teaches_d(c2,p2)\}$ and $M_2=D \cup \{\neg Teaches_d(c2,p3)\}$. Therefore, the set of facts which can be assumed to be true contains the single element *Teaches(c1,p1)*.

We conclude by mentioning that the technique above proposed has been further extended by considering constraints and priorities on the alternative repairs (Greco & Zumpano, 2000b; Greco et al., 2001).

Introducing Repair Constraints

In the integration of databases, the presence of inconsistent data may be resolved by repairing the integrated database. In this section we introduce repair constraints which allow us to restrict the number of repairs. These constraints can be defined during the integration phase to give preference to certain data with respect to others and to define which repairs are feasible.

A *repair constraint* is a denial rule of the form:

$$\leftarrow up_1(A_1),\ldots, up_k(A_k), L_1,\ldots, L_n$$

where $up_1,\ldots,up_k \in$ { insert, delete }, $A_1,\ldots,A_k$ are standard atoms and $L_1,\ldots,L_n$ are standard literals.

Informally, the semantics of a repair constraint is as follows: if the conjunction $L_1,\ldots,L_n$ is true in the repaired database, then at least one of the updates $up_i(A_i)$ must be false.

Given a database D a set of integrity constraints IC and a set of repair constraints RC, a repair R, for D satisfies RC if for each:

$$\leftarrow insert(A_1),\ldots,insert(A_k),delete(B_1),\ldots,delete(B_h), L_1,\ldots,L_n$$

in RC: i) there is some A_i false in R^+ or ii) there is some B_i true in R^- or iii) there is some L_i false in *R(D)*. The repair R is said to be *feasible* if it satisfies RC. In the following we shall say that a set of repair constraints is consistent if all its rules are satisfied for some database *D*.

Example 26. Consider the database D = { p(a),p(b), q(a), q(c)} and the inclusion dependency

$$\forall\,(X)[\,p(X) \subset q(X)\,]$$

The repair constraints

$\leftarrow$delete(q(X))
$\leftarrow$insert(q(X))

state that the relation q cannot be modified. There is only one repair which satisfies the above repair constraints, namely $R1 = (\emptyset, \{p(b)\})$ that deletes the tuple *p(b)* from *D;* the other repair $R2 = (\{q(b)\}, \emptyset)$ inserting the tuple *q(b)* is not feasible.

Example 26. Consider the database D = {e(Peter,30000), e(John,40000), e(John,50000)} containing information about names and salaries of employees, and the integrity constraint

$\forall (X,Y,Z)[\, e(X,Y), e(X,Z) \supset Y = Z]$

There are two repairs for such a database: R1 = ($\emptyset$, {e(John,40000)}) and R2 = ($\emptyset$, {e(John, 50000)}), producing, respectively, the repaired databases D1={e(Peter,30000), e(John,50000)} and D2 = {e(Peter,30000),e(John, 40000)}.

The repair constraint

$\leftarrow$delete(e(X,Y)), e(X,Z), Z > Y

states that if the same employee occurs with more than one salary, we cannot delete the tuple with the lowest salary. Thus, it makes R1 not feasible since R1 deletes the tuple e(John,40000), but the repaired database R1(D) contains the tuple e(John,50000).

A *repairing database schema* is a pair *RS* = <*DS, RC*> where *DS* = <R_s, *IC*> is a database schema and RC is a set of repair constraints. For the sake of simplicity, hereafter a repairing database schema <<*Rs, IC*>,*RC*> will also be denoted by <*Rs, IC , RC* >.

The formal semantics of databases with both integrity and repair constraints is given by rewriting the repair constraints into extended rules with empty heads (denials). In particular, the sets of integrity constraints *IC* and repair constraints *RC* are rewritten into an extended disjunctive program LP. Each stable model of *LP* over a database *D* can be used to generate a repair for the database, whereas each stable model of the program $P \cup LP$, over the database *D*, can be used to compute a consistent answer of a query *(g,P)*.

Each model defines a set of actions (update operations) over the inconsistent database to achieve a consistent state.

Let *r* be a repair constraint of the form

$$\leftarrow \text{insert}(A_1),\ldots,\text{insert}(A_k),\text{delete}(A_{k+1}),\ldots,\text{delete}(A_m), B_1,\ldots,B_l, \text{not } B_{l+1},\ldots, \text{not } B_n, \varphi$$

where $A_1,\ldots,A_m, B_1,\ldots,B_n$ are base atoms and φ is a conjunction of built-in atoms. Then, *dj(r)* denotes the denial rule

$$\leftarrow A'_1, \ldots, A'_k, \neg A'_{k+1}, \ldots \neg A'_m, ((B_1, \text{not} \neg B'_1) \vee B'_1), \ldots, ((B_l, \text{not} \neg B'_l) \vee B'_l), (\text{not } B_{l+1}, \text{not } B'_{l+1}) \vee \neg B'_{l+1}), \ldots, (\text{not } B_n, \text{not } B'_n) \vee \neg B'_n), \varphi$$

where C'_i is derived from C by replacing the predicate symbol, say p, with p_d.

Let RC be a set of repair constraints, then DP(RC) = { dj(r) | r ∈ RC }. DP(IC,RC) denotes the set DP(IC) ∪ DP(RC).

In order to satisfy the denial rule dj(r): i) some atom A'_i (i=1...k) must be false (i.e., A_i is not inserted in the database), or ii) some atom $\neg A'_j$ (j= k+1...m) must be false (i.e., A_j is not deleted from the database), or iii) some formula $((B_i, \text{not}\neg B'_i) \vee B'_i)$ (i=1...l) must be false (i.e., the atom B_i is false in the repaired database), or iv) some formula $((\text{not } B_i, \text{not } B'_i) \vee \neg B'_i)$ (j=l+1...n) must be false (i.e., the atom B_i is false in the repaired database), or v) the conjunction of built-in literals φ must be false.

Observe that the formula $(B_i, \text{not } B'_i) \vee B'_i$ states that either the atom B_i is true in the source database and is not deleted by the repair or it is inserted into the database by the repair. Analogously, the formula $(\text{not } B_i, \text{not } B'_i) \vee \neg B'_i$) states that either the atom B_i is false in the source database and is not inserted by the repair or it is deleted from the database by the repair. Thus given set of integrity constraint IC and a given set of repair constraint RC, the rewriting technique generates a generalized extended disjunctive program denoted by *DP(IC,RC)*.

The extended disjunctive program *LP(IC,RC)* (resp. *LP(RC)*) is derived from *DP(IC,RC)* (resp. *DP(RC)*) by rewriting body disjunctions.

Example 27. Consider the database D={ p(a), p(b), s(a), q(a) }, the set of integrity constraints IC:

$\forall (X)[\, p(X), \supset s(X), q(X)\,]$
$\forall (X)[\, q(X) \supset r(X)\,]$

and the following set of referential constraints RC:

←insert(p(X))
←delete(p(X))
←insert(q(X))

The generalized extended disjunctive program DP(IC,RC) is:

$$\neg p_d(X) \vee s_d(X) \vee q_d(X) \leftarrow (p(X) \vee p_d(X)), (\text{not } s(X) \vee \neg s_d(X)), (\text{not } q(X) \vee \neg q_d(X)).$$
$$\neg q_d(X) \vee r_d(X) \leftarrow (q(X) \vee q_d(X)), (\text{not } r(X) \vee \neg r_d(X)).$$
$$\leftarrow p_d(X).$$
$$\leftarrow \neg p_d(X).$$
$$\leftarrow q_d(X).$$

It is worth noting that in some cases the disjunctive program can be simplified. For instance, the literals $\neg p_d(X)$, $s_d(X)$ and $q_d(X)$ can be deleted from the bodies of rules since the predicate symbols p_d, $\neg q_d$ and r_d do not appear in the heads of rules.

Further simplifications can be made by analyzing the structure of repair constraints.

An *update constraint*, UC, is a repair constraint of the form:

$\leftarrow up(p(t_1,..,t_n))$

where up $\in$ {delete,insert} and $t_1,..,t_n$ are terms (constants or variables).

Update constraints define the type of update operations allowed on the database.

In the presence of repair constraints containing only update constraints, the program produced by applying the above technique can be further simplified. In the following UC will be used to denote any set of update constraints.

Let IC be a set of integrity constraints and UC a set of update constraints. Then, for each denial $\leftarrow p_d(t_1,...,t_n)$ (resp. $\leftarrow \neg p_d(t_1,...,t_n)$) in LP(RC), delete all atoms $p_d(u_1,...,u_n)$ (resp. $\neg p_d(u_1,...,u_n)$) appearing in the head of rules in LP(UC) which are instances of $p_d(t_1,...,t_n)$. An atom $p_d(u_1,...,u_n)$ is an instance of an atom $p_d(t_1,...,t_n)$ if there is a substitution θ such that $p_d(u_1,...,u_n) = p_d(t_1,...,t_n)\ \theta$.

Example 28. Consider the sets of integrity and repair constraints of the previous example. By deleting from the rules in DP(IC) all head atoms which are instances of some literal appearing in DP(UC) ($p_d(X)$, $\neg p_d(X)$ and $q_d(X)$), we get the set of rules:

$$s_d(X) \leftarrow \quad p(X), (\text{not } s(X) \vee \neg s_d(X)), (\text{not } q(X) \vee \neg q_d(X)).$$
$$\neg q_d(X) \vee r_d(X) \leftarrow q(X), (\text{not } r(X) \vee \neg r_d(X)).$$

Moreover, the above rules can be further simplified by eliminating from their bodies the atoms which cannot be inferred; the resulting program is as follows:

$$s_d(X) \leftarrow p(X), \text{not } s(X), (\text{not } q(X) \vee \neg q_d(X)).$$
$$\neg q_d(X) \vee r_d(X) \leftarrow q(X), \text{not } r(X).$$

CONCLUSION

In the integration of knowledge from multiple sources, two main steps are performed: the first in which the various relations are merged together and the second in which some tuples are removed (or inserted) from the resulting database in order to satisfy integrity constraints.

The database obtained from the merging of different sources could contain inconsistent data. In this chapter we investigated the problem of querying and repairing inconsistent databases. In particular, after introducing the formal definition of repair and consistent answer, we presented the different techniques for querying and repairing inconsistent databases.

The technique proposed in Agarwal et al. (1995) only considers constraints defining functional dependencies and it is sound only for the class of databases having dependencies determined by a primary key consisting of a single attribute. The technique proposed by Dung considers a larger class of functional dependencies where the left parts of the functional dependencies are keys. Both techniques consider restricted cases, but the computation of answers can be done efficiently (in polynomial time).

The technique proposed in Lin and Mendelzon (1996) generally stores disjunctive information. This makes the computation of answers more complex, although the computation becomes efficient if the "merging by majority" technique can be applied.

However, the use of the majority criteria involves discarding inconsistent data, and hence the loss of potentially useful information.

Regarding to the technique proposed in Arenas et al. (1999), it has been shown to be complete for universal binary integrity constraints and universal quantified queries. This technique is more general than the previous ones. However, the rewriting of queries is complex since the termination conditions are not easy to detect and the computation of answers generally is not guaranteed to be polynomial.

The technique proposed (Calì et al., 2001b) for integrating and querying databases in the presence of incomplete and inconsistent information sources considers key constraints and foreign key constraints defined upon the global schema.

Wijsen (2003) proposed a general framework for repairing databases. In particular the author stressed that an inconsistent database can be repaired without deleting tuples (*tuple-based* approach), but using a finer repair primitive consisting in correcting faulty values within the tuples (*value-based* approach). The proposed technique is quite general and flexible; however, "trustable answer," whose computation requires solving NP-complete problems, can be obtained only for conjunctive queries and full dependencies.

The technique proposed by Greco and Zumpano (2000a, 2000b) is based on the rewriting of integrity constraints into disjunctive rules with two different forms of negation (negation as failure and classical negation). The derived program can be used both to generate repairs for the database and to produce consistent answers. It is more general than techniques previously proposed, and is sound and complete as each stable model defines a repair and each repair is derived from a stable model, but the computation of answers is also more complex.

ENDNOTES

1 Work partially supported by MURST grants under the projects "D2I." The second author is also supported by ICAR-CNR.

REFERENCES

Abiteboul, S., Hull, R. & Vianu, V. (1995). *Foundations of Databases.* Addison-Wesley.

Agarwal, S., Keller, A.M., Wiederhold, G. & K. Saraswat. (1995). Flexible relation: An approach for integrating data from multiple, possibly inconsistent databases. *Proceedings of the IEEE International Conference on Data Engineering*, 495-504.

Agarwal, S.S. (1992). *Flexible Relation: A Model for Data in Distributed, Autonomous and Heterogeneous Databases.* PhD Thesis, Department of Electrical Engineering, Stanford University.

Arenas, M., Bertossi, L. & Chomicki, J. (1999). Consistent query answers in inconsistent databases. *Proceedings of the International Conference on Principles of Database Systems*, 68-79.

Arenas, M., Bertossi, L. & Chomicki, J. (2000). Specifying and querying database repairs using logic programs with exceptions. *Proceedings of the International Conference on Flexible Query Answering,* 27-41.

Baral, C., Kraus, S. & Minker, J. (1991a). Combining multiple knowledge bases. *IEEE-Transactions on Knowledge and Data Engineering*, 3(2), 208-220.

Baral, C., Kraus, S., Minker, J. & Subrahmanian, V.S. (1991b). Combining knowledge bases consisting of first-order theories. *Proceedings of the International Symposium on Methodologies for Intelligent Systems*, 92-101.

Breitbart, Y. (1990). Multidatabase interoperability. *SIGMOD Record*, 19(3), 53-60.

Bry, F. (1997). Query answering in information systems with integrity constraints. *IFIP WG 11.5 Working Conference on Integrity and Control in Information Systems.*

Calì, A., Calvanese, D., DeGiacomo, G. & Lenzerini, M. (2001b). Data integration under integrity constraints. *Proceedings of the International Conference on Advanced Information Systems Engineering (CAiSE02)*, 262-279.

Calì, A., DeGiacomo, G. & Lenzerini, M. (2001a). *Models for Information Integration: Turning Local-as-View into Global-as-View.*

Dung, P.M. (1996). Integrating data from possibly inconsistent databases. *Proceedings of the International Conference on Cooperative Information Systems*, 58-65.

Eiter, T., Gottlob, G. & Mannila, H. (1997). Disjunctive Datalog. *ACM Transactions on Database Systems*, 22(3), 364-418.

Etzioni, O., Golden, K. & Weld, D. (1994). Tractable closed-world reasoning with updates. *Principles of Knowledge Representation and Reasoning.* 178-189.

Gelfond, M. & Lifschitz, V. (1991). Classical negation in logic programs and disjunctive databases. *New Generation Computing*, 3(4), 365-386.

Grant, J. & Subrahmanian, V.S. (1995). Reasoning in inconsistent knowledge bases. *IEEE-Transactions on Knowledge and Data Engineering*, 7(1), 177-189.

Greco, S. (1999). Minimal founded semantics for disjunctive logic programming. *Proceedings of the International Conference on Logic Programming and Nonmonotonic Reasoning*, 221-235.

Greco, S. & Saccà, D. (1990). Negative logic programs. *Proceedings of the North American Conference on Logic Programming*, 480-497.

Greco, S. & Zumpano, E. (2000a). Querying inconsistent databases. *Proceedings of the International Conference on Logic Programming and Automated Reasoning*, 308-325.

Greco, S. & Zumpano, E. (2000b). Computing repairs for inconsistent databases. *Proceedings of the International Symposium on Cooperative Database Systems for Advanced Applications*, 33-40.

Greco, G., Greco, S. & Zumpano, E. (2001). A logic programming approach to the integration, repairing and querying of inconsistent databases. *Proceedings of the International Conference on Logic Programming*, 348-394.

Hull, R. (1997). Managing semantic heterogeneity in databases: A theoretical prospective. *Proceedings of the Symposium on Principles of Database Systems*, 51-61.

Kanellakis, P.C. (1991). Elements of relational database theory. In van Leewen, J. (Ed.), *Handbook of Theoretical Computer Science, Volume 2.* North-Holland.

Kowalski, R.A. & Sadri, F. (1991). Logic programs with exceptions. *New Generation Computing*, 9(3/4), 387-400.

Lembo, D., Lenzerini, M. & Rosati, R. (2002). Incompleteness and inconsistency in information integration. *Proceedings of the 9th International Workshop on Knowledge Representation Meets Databases (KRDB 2002),* Toulouse, France.

Lenzerini, M. (2002). Data integration: A theoretical perspective. *Proceedings of the Symposium on Principles of Database Systems*, 233-246.
Levy, A. (1996). Obtaining complete answers from incomplete databases. *Proceedings of the International Conference on Very Large Data Bases (VLDB'96),* 402-412.
Levy, A. & Sagiv, Y. (1993). Dynamic worlds: From the frame problem to knowledge management. *Proceedings of the 19th International Conference on Very Large Data Bases,* 171-181.
Lin, J. (1996a). Integration of weighted knowledge bases. *Artificial Intelligence*, 83(2), 363-378.
Lin, J. (1996b). A semantics for reasoning consistently in the presence of inconsistency. *Artificial Intelligence,* 86(1), 75-95.
Lin, J. & Mendelzon, A.O. (1996). Merging databases under constraints. *International Journal of Cooperative Information Systems*, 7(1), 55-76.
Lin, J. & Mendelzon, A.O. (1999). Knowledge base merging by majority. In Pareschi, R. & Fronhoefer, B. (Eds.), *Dynamic Worlds: From the Frame Problem to Knowledge Management.* Kluwer.
Minker, J. (1982). On indefinite data bases and the closed world assumption, *Proceedings of the 6th Conference on Automated Deduction*, 292-308.
Motro, A. (1989). Integrity = validity + completeness. *TODS,* 14(4), 480-502.
Plotkin, G.D. (1969). A note on inductive generalization. In Meltzer, B. & Michie, D. (Eds.), *Machine Intelligence,* 5, 153-163.
Shmueli, O. (1993). Equivalence of Datalog queries is undecidable. *Journal of Logic Programming,* 15(3), 231-241.
Subrahmanian, V.S. (1994). Amalgamating knowledge bases. *ACM Transactions on Database Systems,* 19(2), 291-331.
Ullman, J.K. (1988). *Principles of Database and Knowledge-Base Systems, Volume 1.* Rockville, MD: Computer Science Press.
Ullman, J.K. (2000). Information integration using logical views. 239(2), 189-210.
Wiederhold, G. (1992). Mediators in the architecture of future information systems. *IEEE Computer,* 25(3), 38-49.
Wijsen, J. (2003). Condensed representation of database repair for consistent query. To appear at the *9th International Conference on Database Theory.*
Zaniolo, C. (1984). Database relations with null values. *Journal of Computer and System Sciences*, 142-166.

About the Authors

Shirley A. Becker is a Professor of Computer Information Systems at Northern Arizona University, USA, and the recipient of the Mark Layton Award for Research Excellence. Formerly she was at the Florida Institute of Technology and American University in Washington, D.C. Dr. Becker has published more than 50 articles in the areas of Web usability, Web accessibility, database and Web technologies, software engineering and process management. Dr. Becker is an Associate and Section Editor for the *Journal of Database Management* and *Journal of Informing Science*, respectively, and she serves on several editorial review boards. She has received awards to fund research from Texas Instruments, IBM, NSF and NASA JPL.

* * *

Witold Abramowicz is currently the Chair of the Department of MIS at The Poznan University of Economics, Poland. His particular areas of interest are information filtering to MIS, information retrieval and applications of knowledge discovery in MIS. He received his MSc from the Technical University of Poznan, Poland, PhD from the Wroclaw Technical University, Poland, and habilitation from the Humboldt University Berlin, Germany. He worked for three universities in Switzerland and Germany for 12 years. He chaired seven scientific international conferences and was a member of the program committees of 71 other conferences. He is an Editor or Co-Author of 11 books and 69 articles in various journals and conference proceedings.

Juan M. Ale is a Professor in the Computer Science Department, Faculty of Engineering of Buenos Aires University, Argentina. He holds degrees in scientific computation, systems engineering and computer sciences from Buenos Aires University. His current research interests include data mining, data warehousing and temporal databases.

Abraham Alvarez is a PhD student at the National Institute of Applied Sciences of Lyon, France. His current research interests include active databases, Web-based technologies and XML language. He received a diploma in Information Systems from the Joseph Fourier University. He is a member of the Information Systems Engineering Laboratory — LISI, at the INSA de Lyon, France. His e-mail is: Abraham.Alvarez@lisi.insa-lyon.fr.

Y. Amghar is an Assistant Professor of Management Information Systems at the Scientific and Technical University of Lyon, France. He received a PhD in Computer Science from the same university in 1989. His field of teaching concerns project management, databases and development processes. He is an active member of the Laboratory of Information Systems of INSA de Lyon. His current research interests include semantic and consistency of data, interoperability of applications and legal documents. He is the author of several papers related to these research activities and managed some projects about decisions support. He is also responsible for a research team working on the domain of enterprise memory and knowledge management.

Pável Calado received a BSc in Computer Engineering from the Superior Technical Institute of the Technical University of Lisbon. He then received an MSc in Computer Science from the Federal University of Minas Gerais, Brazil, where he is now a PhD student. He was awarded the Best Student Paper award at the ACM SIGIR conference in 2000 regarding his work on link analysis. His research interests include information retrieval, digital libraries, natural language processing, intelligent agents, and Web technologies.

Coral Calero holds an MSc and a PhD in Computer Science. She is Associate Professor at the Escuela Superior de Informática of the Castilla-La Mancha University in Ciudad Real, Spain. She is a member of the Alarcos Research Group, at the same university, specialized in information systems, databases and software engineering. Her research interests are: advanced databases design, database/datawarehouse quality, Web quality and software metrics. She is author of articles and papers in national and international conferences on these subjects and she belongs to the ATI association and is a member of its Quality Group. Her e-mail is: Coral.Calero@uclm.es.

R. Chbeir is an Associate Professor of Computer Science at the French University in Dijon. His current research interests are in the areas of multimedia database management, indexing methods, bioinformatics, and the development and use of information systems. He is a member of IEEE and has published in international journals (*IEEE Transactions on SMC, Journal of Methods of Information in Medicine,* etc.), conferences (Visual, IEEE, FLAIRS, IRMA, etc.) and books.

Yangjun Chen received his BS degree in Information System Engineering from the Technical Institute of Changsha, China, in 1982, and his diploma and PhD degrees in Computer Science from the University of Kaiserslautern, Germany, in 1990 and 1995, respectively. From 1995 to 1997, he worked as a Research Assistant Professor at the Technical University of Chemnitz-Zwickau, Germany. After that, he worked as a Senior Engineer at the German National Research Center of Information Technology (GMD) for almost three years. After a short stay at Alberta University, he joined the Department of

Business Computing at the University of Winnipeg, Canada. His research interests include document and Web databases, deductive databases, federated databases, constraint satisfaction problem, graph theory and combinatorics. He has about 70 publications in these areas.

Altigran S. da Silva received a BSc in Data Processing from the Federal University of Amazonas (UFMA), Brazil, and an MSc and PhD in Computer Science from the Federal University of Minas Gerais (UFMG), Brazil. He is an Associate Professor at the Computer Science Department of UFAM and an Associate Researcher of the UFMG Database Group. He has been working in research projects financed by Brazilian government agencies in areas such as information retrieval, databases, digital libraries, and Web technologies. He has also served as a referee for a number of international conferences and scientific journals.

Mauricio Minuto Espil is an Independent Consultant in Informatics. He received a degree in Computer Science from Buenos Aires University, Argentina, and is currently a PhD candidate at the same university. His current research interests include data warehousing, OLAP tools, non-monotonic reasoning and XML databases.

Dolores Cuadra Fernández received her MSc in Mathematics from Universidad Complutense of Madrid (Spain) in 1995. Since 1997 she works as an Assistant Lecturer at the Advanced Databases Group in the Computer Science Department of Universidad Carlos III of Madrid. She is currently teaching Database Design and Relational Databases. Her research interests include database conceptual and logical modeling, and advanced database CASE environments.

Paloma Martínez Fernández earned a degree in Computer Science from Universidad Politécnica of Madrid (Spain) in 1992. Since then, she has been working with the Advanced Databases Group in the Computer Science Department at Universidad Carlos III of Madrid. In 1998 she earned her PhD in Computer Science from Universidad Politécnica of Madrid. She is currently teaching Database Design, Advanced Databases in the Computer Science Department at the Universidad Carlos III de Madrid. She has been working in several European and national research projects about natural language processing, advanced database technologies, knowledge-based systems and software engineering.

Elena Castro Galán received an MSc in Mathematics from Universidad Complutense of Madrid in 1995. Since 1998 she works as an Assistant Lecturer with the Advanced Databases Group in the Computer Science Department of Universidad Carlos III of Madrid, Spain. She is currently teaching Relational Databases. Her research interests include database conceptual and logical modeling and mapping between schemas, advanced database CASE environments and information engineering.

M.M. Roldán García is a PhD student, supported by a Research Grant, in the Department of Computer Sciences of the University of Malaga. She received an MS in Computer Sciences from the University of Malaga (Spain) in 2000 and is currently working towards a PhD at the university. One of her current research programs involves the study of amalgamation of databases and Web technologies. Her research interests include heterogeneous data sources semantic integration, ontologies and indexing techniques.

Gianluigi Greco received the Laurea degree in Computer Science Engineering from the University of Calabria, Italy, in 2000. Currently, he is a first-year PhD student at the Faculty of Engineering of the University of Calabria. His research interests include logic programming, deductive database, database integration, query languages for semi-structured data and Web search engines.

Sergio Greco received the Laurea degree in Electrical Engineering from the University of Calabria, Italy. Currently, he is a Full Professor at the Faculty of Engineering of the University of Calabria. Prior to this, he was a Researcher at CRAI, a research consortium of informatics. He was a Visiting Researcher at the research center of Microelectronics and Computer Center (MCC) of Austin, Texas, and at the Computer Science Department of University of California at Los Angeles. His primary research interests include database theory, logic programming, deductive database, database integration, intelligent information integration over the Web, Web search engines and query languages for semi-structured data. He is a member of the IEEE Computer Society.

Alberto H.F. Laender received a BSc in Electrical Engineering and an MSc in Computer Science from the Federal University of Minsa Gerais, Brazil, and a PhD in Computing from the Universityof East Anglia, UK. He joined the Computer Science Department of the Federal University of Minsa Gerais in 1975 whre he is currently a Full Professor and the Head of the Database Research Group. In 1997 he was a Visiting Scientist at the Hewlett-Packard Palo Alto Laboratories. He has served as a program committee member for several national and international conferences on databases and Web-related topics. He also served as a program committee co-chair for the 19th International Conference on Conceptual Modeling held in Salt Lake City, Utah, in October 2000, and as te program committee chair for the Ninth International Symposium on String Processing and Information Retrieval held in Lisbon, Portugal, in September 2002. His research interests include conceptual database modeling, database design methods, database user interfaces, semistructured data, Web data management, and digital libraries.

A.C. Gómez Lora is a Teaching Assistant in the Department of Computer Sciences of the University of Málaga, Spain. He received an MS in Computer Sciences from the University of Málaga in 1997 and is currently working towards a PhD at the university. His research interests include hybrid techniques for recursive query evaluation and optimization in distributed systems and optimization techniques at query evaluation time.

Virpi Lyytikäinen is a PhD student at the University of Jyväskylä, Department of Computer Science and Information Systems, in Finland. For seven years she has been active in research and development projects in public administration and industry, where methods for electronic document management have been developed. Her research interests include structured documents and methods for electronic document management.

Ido Millet is an Associate Professor of MIS at Penn State Erie, USA. He earned his PhD from the Wharton School of Business at the University of Pennsylvania. His current research focuses on multi-criteria decision making and online procurement auctions. His industrial experience includes systems analysis and project management for large-scale information systems, consulting and software development. His e-mail is: ixm7@psu.edu.

J.F. Aldana Montes received a PhD from the University of Málaga, Spain, in 1998. He presently holds the rank of Assistant Professor in the Computer Sciences Department of the University of Málaga. Dr. Aldana acted as Program Chair for several BD conferences and workshops from 1999-2002. His current research interest involves the study of the adaptation of database technologies for Web usage. His areas of interests include distributed evaluation and optimization of complex queries, (semantic) query optimization and (ontology-based) semantic integration of information on the Web.

Mara Nikolaidou received a degree and a doctorate degree, both in Computer Science, from the University of Athens, Greece, in 1990 and 1996, respectively. She is currently in charge of the Library Computer Center of the University of Athens. Her research interests include distributed systems, digital libraries, modelling and simulation, and workflow systems.

Mario Piattini holds an MSc and a PhD in Computer Science from the Politechnical University of Madrid, Spain. He is a Certified Information System Auditor by ISACA (Information System Audit and Control Association) and Full Professor at the Escuela Superior de Informática of the Castilla-La Mancha University. Dr. Piattini is the author of several books and papers on databases, software engineering and information systems. He leads the ALARCOS research group of the Department of Computer Science at the University of Castilla-La Mancha, in Ciudad Real, Spain. His research interests are: advanced database design, database quality, software metrics, object-oriented metrics and software maintenance. His e-mail is: Mario.Piattini@uclm.es.

Jakub Piskorski has worked since 1998 at the Language Technology Lab in the German Research Center for Artificial Intelligence (DFKI). His areas of interest are centered around shallow text processing, information extraction, text mining and finite-state technology. He received his MSc from the University of Saarbrücken, Germany, (1994) and PhD from the Polish Academy of Sciences in Warsaw (2002). Directly after his studies he worked for four years in the Computer Science Department of the University of Economics in Poznan, Poland. He is an author of 17 articles in various conference proceedings, journals and books.

Johanna Wenny Rahayu received a PhD in Computer Science from La Trobe University, Australia, in 2000. Her thesis was in the area of object-relational database design and transformation technology. This thesis was awarded the 2001 Computer Science Association Australia Best PhD Thesis Award. Dr. Rahayu is currently a Senior Lecturer at La Trobe University. She has published a book and numerous research articles.

Berthier A. Ribeiro-Neto received a BSc in Mathematics, a BSc in Electrical Engineering, and an MSc in Computer Science all from the Federal University of Minas Gerais in Brazil.

He also received a PhD in Computer Science from the University of California at Los Angeles in 1995. Since then, he has been with the Computer Science Department at the Federal University of Minas Gerais where he is an Associate Professor. His main interests are information retrieval systems, digital libraries, interfaces for the Web, and video on demand. He has been involved in a number of research projects financed through Brazilian national agencies such as the Ministry of Science and Technology (MCT) and the National Research Council (CNPq). From the projects currently under way, the main ones deal with wireless information systems, video on demand (joint project with UFRJ, UCLA and UMass), and digital libraries (joint project with Virginia Tech). Dr. Ribeiro-Neto has also been supported by the Brazilian National Research Council (CNPq) through an individual research grant for the last six years. He has been in the program committee of several international events and is a member os ASIS, ACM and IEEE.

Airi Salminen is Professor at the University of Jyväskylä, Department of Computer Science and Information Systems, in Finland. She received her PhD in Computer Science from the University of Tampere in 1989. She was responsible for planning a new Master's Program in Digital Media at the University of Jyväskylä and has headed the program from its beginning in 1995. She has worked as a Visiting Research Associate at the University of Western Ontario, and as a Visiting Professor at the University of Waterloo, both in Canada. She has been the leader of several projects where research has been tied to document management development efforts in major Finnish companies or public-sector organizations. Her current research interests include document management, structured documents, user interfaces and semantic Web.

Ulrich Schiel received a bachelors degree in Mathematics (1971), a master's degree in Computer Science at PUC-RJ Brazil (1977), and a PhD at the University of Stuttgart, Germany (1984). Since 1978, he has been a Professor at Universidade Federal de Campina Grande (Brazil). He was a Visiting Reseracher at GMD-Darmstadt from 1989 to 1990, and at the Universidade do Minho in 1990. His research interests include cross-lingual information retrieval, Web semantics, temporal databases, information systems modeling and design, and distance learning.

Robert A. Schultz is Professor and Chair of Computer Information Systems and Director of Academic Computing at Woodbury University, Burbank, California, USA. He received his PhD from Harvard in 1971, in philosophy with extensive work in logic. He taught and published philosophy for 10 years, and was then Data Processing Manager for six years for a Forbes 500 company in Beverly Hills, California. Dr. Schultz joined Woodbury in 1989. He has publications and presentations in the areas of database design, the uses of IT in education and the philosophy of technology. His other major professional interests include the managerial aspects of information systems.

Manuel Serrano received his MSc in Computer Science and his Technical Degree in Computer Science from the University of Castilla-La Mancha, Spain. Currently, he is developing his PhD at the UCLM, and is Assistant Professor at the Escuela Superior de Informática of the Castilla-La Mancha University in Ciudad Real. He is a member of the Alarcos Research Group, at the same university, specialized in information systems, databases and software engineering. He is the Secretary of the ATI (Computer Technicians Association) group in Castilla-La Mancha. His research interests are: data warehouses, quality and metrics, and software quality. His e-mail is: Manuel.Serrano@uclm.es.

Saliha Smadhi got her PhD at the University of Aix-Marseille III (France) in March 1997. After teaching in various high schools, she rejoins the Computer Science Department of the University of Pau, France. She is member of the Laboratoire d' Informatique de l'Université de Pau et des Pays de l'Adour (LIUPPA) in the Computer Science Research Department. Since September 2000, she has taught as a Temporary Professor of teaching and research.

Prakash Gaurav Srivastava is currently studying at La Trobe University in Melbourne, Australia, and is in his final year of a Master's of Computer Science degree. In 2001, he completed a fourth-year computer science thesis under the supervision of Dr. Wenny Rahayu. The topic of this was, "Comparative Analysis of Query Structures in Relational and Object Relational Databases." In 2002, he completed his master's thesis under the supervision of Drs. Taniar and Rahayu. The title of his thesis was, "Query Optimization Using Rewriting Technique for Object Relational Database."

David Taniar received his PhD in Computer Science from Victoria University, Australia, in 1997 under the supervision of Professor Clement H.C. Leung. He is currently a Senior Lecturer at the School of Business Systems, Monash University, Australia. His research interest is in the area of databases, with particular attention on high-performance databases and Internet databases. He has published three computing books and numerous research articles. He is also a Fellow of the Royal Society of Arts, Manufacturers and Commerce.

Pasi Tiitinen is a PhD student at the University of Jyväskylä, Department of Computer Science and Information Systems, in Finland. Since 1996 he has participated in research and development projects in both industry and public administration, where methods for electronic document management have been developed. His research interests include user needs analysis and usability engineering in document management projects, and structured documents.

Aphrodite Tsalgatidou is a Professor at the Department of Informatics and Telecommunications of the National and Kapodistrian University of Athens, Greece. She has previously worked in the Greek PTT and in private companies. She holds an MSc and PhD in Computation from UMIST, Manchester, UK. Her current work focuses on Web services, service-oriented development, peer to peer computing, electronic and mobile commerce and business process reengineering. More information may be found at http://www.di.uoa.gr/~afrodite.

N. Moreno Vergara is a PhD student in the Department of Computer Sciences of the University of Málaga, Spain. She received her MS in Computer Sciences from the University of Málaga in 2000, and she is currently working towards a PhD at the university. Her research interests focus on ontology-based semantic integration and theoretical models for the Semantic Web, especially, query languages and reasoning mechanism for that environment.

Rodrigo C. Vieira received a BSc and an MSc in Computer Science from the Federal University of Minas Gerais, Brazil. Currently, he works as a System Analyst in the SIDS project at UFMG and is a Lecturer at the Informatics Department of Cotemig College. His research interests include databases, semistructured data, information retrieval systems, and digital libraries.

Ester Zumpano received the Laurea degree in Computer Science Engineering from the University of Calabria, Italy, (1998) and the PhD in Computer Science from the University of Calabria (2003). Presently she is an Assistant Professor at the Faculty of Engineering of the University of Calabria. Her primary interests include database theory, logic programming, deductive database, database integration and intelligent information integration over the Web.

Index

D

E

F

G

H

I

S

T

U

V

W

X